Wising

Wising Up the Marks

The Amodern William Burroughs

Timothy S. Murphy

University of California Press
Berkeley Los Angeles London

University of California Press
Berkeley and Los Angeles, California

University of California Press, Ltd.
London, England

Library of Congress Cataloging-in-Publication Data

Murphy, Timothy S., 1964–
Wising up the marks : the amodern William Burroughs / Timothy S. Murphy.
p. cm.
Includes bibliographic references (p.) and index
ISBN 0–520–20950–8 (cloth : alk. paper).—
ISBN 0–520–20951–6 (pbk. : alk. paper)
1. Burroughs, William S., 1914—criticism and interpretation. I. Title.
PS3552.U75Z76 1998
813'54—dc 21r96–53094

Printed in the United States of America

9 8 7 6 5 4 3 2 1

The paper used in this publication meets the minimum requirements of American National Standards for Information Sciences—Permanence of Paper for Printed Library Materials, ANSI Z39.48–1984.

For my parents,
Thomas A. S. Murphy (1939–1993),
Joyce E. Briggs and Robert L. Briggs

Contents

List of Abbreviations ix

Acknowledgments xi

Introduction:
"Nothing is True, Everything is Permitted" 1

Chapter One
Invisibility and Amodernism 16

Chapter Two
No Final Glossary: Fugitive Words in *Junky* and *Queer* 46

Chapter Three
"All Agents defect and all Resisters sell out": The Negative Dialectics of *Naked Lunch* 67

Chapter Four
"I Hassan i Sabbah *rub out the word forever*": The Dialectic of Treason and the Abolition of the Law in the *Nova* Trilogy 103

Chapter Five
The Wild Boys: Desire, Fantasy, and the Book of the Dead 142

Chapter Six
Quién es? Reconstitution of the Revolutionary Subject in Burroughs's Late Trilogy 169

Conclusion:
Burroughs's Fin de siècle: Listen to My Last Words Everywhere 201

Notes 233

Works Cited 256

Index 267

Abbreviations

In this study, William S. Burroughs's novels are cited parenthetically using the following abbreviations and editions:

C	*Cities of the Red Night.* New York: Holt, Rinehart & Winston, 1981.
J	*Junky.* 1953. New York: Penguin, 1977.
NE	*Nova Express.* New York: Grove, 1964. Reprinted in Burroughs, *Three Novels.* New York: Grove, 1980.
NL	*Naked Lunch.* New York: Grove, 1959.
P	*The Place of Dead Roads.* New York: Holt, Rinehart & Winston, 1983.
Q	*Queer.* New York: Penguin, 1985.
SM	*The Soft Machine.* New York: Grove, 1961, 1966. Reprinted in Burroughs, *Three Novels.* New York: Grove Press, 1980.
TE	*The Ticket That Exploded.* 1962. New York: Grove Press, 1967.
WL	*The Western Lands.* New York: Viking, 1987.
WB	*The Wild Boys: A Book of the Dead.* New York: Grove, 1969. Reprinted in Burroughs, *Three Novels.* New York: Grove, 1980.

Acknowledgments

I owe my most profound intellectual debts to my committee chair, Vince Pecora, who never misses a trick, avoids a debate, or pulls a punch yet somehow manages to assure his students of the value of their achievements, and to Ken Reinhard, who is as profligate in his interests as he is in his generosity. Sam Weber and Peter Wollen also gave me crucial advice and encouragement during that long march to the doctorate. Toni Negri has no doubt forgotten the spontaneous remarks he made in reaction to my underdeveloped theses in the fall of 1991, but those remarks and the paper I wrote in response to them were the true seeds of this book. I would also like to affirm my gratitude to my original chair, the late Joe Riddel, whose goodwill and encouragement allowed me to get this project under way in the first place. Jeffrey Nealon and Steven Shaviro, referees for the University of California Press, offered helpful suggestions for clarification, for which I thank them. Don't blame them for the obscurities and errors that remain.

The contributions of my comrades in arms—those who passed through graduate school with me—to this book have in many cases spanned as many years as I've known them. They watched me back into the project, just as they are now watching me back out the other side of it. Among the many who heard evasions, rehearsals, and revisions of the arguments herein, Luke Carson, Roxanne Eberle, and Colleen Jaurretche have surely put up longest with my vacillations and have done so with admirable restraint and good humor. Don't blame them, either.

What Juliana has given me is not visible in any specific aspect of the contents of this book, but rather in its very existence. I do not know why there should be something rather than nothing, but I'm glad that there is.

Sections of chapters 1 and 3 appeared under the title "William S. Burroughs between Indifference and Revalorization: Notes toward a Political Reading" in *Angelaki* 1.1 (1993), and another section of chapter 3 appeared in *Angelaki* 1.3 (1994) under the title "Herculean Tasks, Dionysian Labor: Michael Hardt and Antonio Negri on the Contemporary State-Form." Those sections appear here, in dismembered and revised form, by permission of *Angelaki*. Lyrics from "Caught, Can We Get a Witness?" by Ridenhour, Shocklee, and Sadler are quoted by permission of Def American Songs/Def Jam Recordings.

"Nothing is True, Everything is Permitted"

This study attempts to articulate an alternative to the dialectic of modernism and postmodernism, or (post)modernism for short, that dominates many discussions of American literature in the contemporary period. Such an alternative has already emerged at many points in the development of that literature, only to be misrecognized and recuperated within the dominant mode of reflexive postmodern writing by critics who have apparently been too dazzled by the postmodern and poststructural "ruptures" to see clearly. An alternative to (post)modernism in fact emerges at precisely the same aesthetic moment that the dominant or reflexive form of postmodernism does, in one of its key texts: Ralph Ellison's *Invisible Man.* Like Ellison's narrator, this alternative has remained largely invisible, despite its very real difference from its dominant counterpart, for many of the same reasons the narrator could not be seen by members of the dominant white culture. Unlike Ellison's canonical book, however, the major texts of this alternative form have only intermittently been recognized for their contributions to the state of contemporary cultural production, and these texts have not yet given rise to an adequate theoretical alternative to (post)modernism. Questions of cultural identity and otherness, of representation and materiality raised by Ellison's novel will help us begin to recognize and theorize this alternative as it takes shape in the novels of William S. Burroughs.

The explicit theoretical elaboration of alternatives to (post)modernism has begun recently in disciplines other than literary criticism, such as the sociology of Bruno Latour (who calls it "nonmodernism")[1] and the political philosophy of Antonio Negri (who calls it "anti-modernity").[2] These particular elaborations derive from the philosophical work of Gilles Deleuze, whose original insights and analyses have produced a critical language that evades the endless squabbling over terminology that marks most discussions of (post)modernism; this evasion also accounts in part for Deleuze's own relative "invisibility" in Anglophone critical circles. To make my own project more visible, I have chosen to call my version of the phenomenon *amodernism* to highlight what seems to me to be its distance from and resistance to the dialectical structure that defines (post)modernism; perhaps it would help to think of it as a heterogeneous third term, like "amoral" in relation to "moral" and "immoral." Amodernism, like the reflexive postmodernism we already recognize, accepts the failure of modernist ends (for instance, the resolution of gender, class, and ethnic conflicts and the concomitant spiritual unification of society) and means (for instance, the regeneration of myth as a centering structure), without taking the additional step of homogenizing all remaining difference into some version of Ferdinand de Saussure's negatively defined linguistic paradigm.[3] In other words, from an amodern point of view the disavowal of mass politics endorsed by Jean-François Lyotard's or Jean Baudrillard's postmodernism is not adequate, since that disavowal remains complicit with capital because it offers no way out of the system of domination that constitutes the present social order. The failure of a specific set of critical and resistant strategies, even strategies as far-reaching and apparently unsurpassable as those deployed under modernism, does not necessarily imply the failure of all such strategies, nor does the "closure of Western metaphysics" require us to jettison every point of our irreducible cultural histories.

This failure and this closure are not inevitable, but rather had to be produced, just as alternatives to them have been and continue to be produced. The task of this study is to trace an alternative trajectory through the literature and history of the contemporary period, a trajectory that participates in the production of new cultural values to replace those that (post)modernism has bankrupted and in so doing gives leverage to the kinds of theoretical writing that Deleuze, Negri, and Latour undertake. This trajectory maps the career of the American writer and artist William S. Burroughs, whose commitment to social transformation in the face of the postmodern evacuation of the political sphere is emblematic, I would claim, of literary amodernism in general. Amodern writers are better known than amodern theorists, though as a result of this notoriety they suffer for their "failures" to meet the criteria defined by the reflexive, formalist strain of postmodernism. From the point of view of this reflexive postmodernism, amodern writers are either lax in their compositional methods or misguided in their political commitments; both of these criticisms have been leveled, by critics and by other novelists, at Burroughs. Amodern literature, if we accept for the moment the bald assertion that it exists, develops from Ellison's promise to emerge from the liminal space of literature with a "plan of living" rather than an endlessly deferred "participation in language games" or an empty "love for the world through language" à la John Barth.

Although this is not the best place to advocate particular revisions of the canon (except, as always, implicitly), a partial list of candidates for inclusion may be helpful, at least in defining the stakes raised by the very idea of amodernism. If we take Ralph Ellison as our point of departure, we can cut across accepted lines of literary descent, going by way of Joseph Heller's *Catch-22*, the best of Kurt Vonnegut's and Ishmael Reed's work and of Hunter S. Thompson's journalism and novels, all of Thomas Pynchon, Toni Morrison, and Robert Coover, to the recent texts of Joanna Russ, Kathy Acker, and Darius James. Clearly this is a heterogeneous group of writers, in terms both of their actual texts and of their critical reception, so it may be presumptuous to confine them all to a single "tradition." Heller and Vonnegut, for example, were highly regarded by the academy through the mid-seventies, at which point they began their rapid descent out of the canon, while Morrison has experienced a symmetrical rise through the ranks to her current internationally sanctioned position. So rapid has been Pynchon's acceptance into the academy that he has been the subject of a study in the academic politics of canonization.[4] Russ has kept a low profile recently, while Thompson, Coover, Acker, and James have varying numbers of defenders but no consensus (in the form of a mass of studies) to legitimate their claims to importance. This heterogeneity should simply make evident the fact that there can be no single model of contemporary American fiction, not even an amodernist one. It should also be stressed that amodernist literature does not come *after* reflexive postmodernism, but contests it throughout the contemporary period.

Out of this odd mélange of writers and texts, and in the wake of *Invisible Man,* the choice of William S. Burroughs for more extensive consideration may appear merely provocative. But as a member of the generation of writers who matured in the wake of Ellison's promise of a "plan of living," he creates his fiction out of an awareness of the necessity of its fulfillment,[5] though he understands that necessity very differently than reflexive postmodernists do. Burroughs, too, is "*el hombre invisible,*" not least because his acquaintances in Tangier gave him that name—in ignorance of both H. G. Wells and Ellison. His invisibility stems primarily from the same circumstances that render Ellison's narrator and Deleuze invisible as well: he does not fit into a tidy category that is already subordinated to the larger scheme of capitalism. This invisibility has, until now, restricted his American academic influence much as it has restricted Deleuze's, but it has also allowed both amodernists a certain amount of intellectual liberty to articulate "plans of living" that are hostile to the constituted socius. To explicate these intersecting plans I propose the following schematic narrative, which, although it imposes an artificial linearity that is alien to the spirit of Burroughs's body of writing, will nevertheless serve as a heuristic device, a coordinate system that will help us to map the vicissitudes of Burroughs's strategies of disruption and reorganization.

Burroughs's literary career is defined by the central challenge he sets himself: to find an escape route from the linked control systems of capital, subjectivity, and language. His early novels, from *Junky* (*J,* 1953) to *Naked Lunch* (*NL,* 1959), address the accelerating dialectic of capitalist control of American society, a form of control that functions by transforming the individual into the "addict agent" who is the mirror image of the controller. These novels also articulate a critique of the "administered life" that parallels Max Horkheimer and Theodor W. Adorno's *Dialectic of Enlightenment.* He examines the reversibility of hostile social relations and the symmetry of opposed political factions, and he articulates his theory that language, which is a virus that uses the human body as a host, constitutes the most powerful form of control. In these works Burroughs, like Horkheimer and Adorno, cannot yet imagine a form of revolutionary practice to counter these forms of control; society appears trapped between the horns of capitalism's constitutive dialectic, which liquidates the singularity of the individual as well as the connections of community in order to produce the false universality of profit. As Burroughs writes later, money "eats quality and shits out quantity" (Burroughs and Odier 74), a situation that the writer cannot change but can only reveal. These works constitute what we might call the modernist subset of his writing.

In the aleatory *Nova* trilogy (1961–67), however, Burroughs recognizes the sterile form of the *dialectic itself* as his primary enemy and attempts to escape it by destroying the linguistic control system of syntax and by simultaneously abolishing the dialectical form of the Law. All of his subsequent texts can be understood as increasingly systematic and sophisticated attempts to evade the dialectic, which continually returns in unexpected forms to reinscribe Burroughs's revolutionary enterprise within despotic capital and language; in this, Burroughs's development quite strongly resembles that of Deleuze.[6] In their formal and thematic focus on language, however, the novels of the trilogy abet the postmodern turn away from historical potential and toward structural foreclosure. The "cut-up" experiments eventually lead him out of the cynicism of the *Nova* trilogy's reflexive postmodernism, however, and toward a renewed commitment to social change; in *The Wild Boys* and his recent works, Burroughs seeks ways to organize resistance to the new forms of control in the construction of revolutionary fantasies that can produce new social groups. In *The Wild Boys* (*WB*, 1971), these countercultural fantasies are still conceived as dialectically destructive forces that negate the given social order but refuse to offer new forms of social organization; thus their failure, like the failure of the radical student movements that inspired them, follows from the persistence of the dialectic. The trilogy *Cities of the Red Night (C), The Place of Dead Roads (P),* and *The Western Lands* (*WL;* 1981–87) continues this destructive task, but it also offers affirmative ways to reorganize society in order to avoid the powerful dialectics of social and linguistic control.

Such reorganization, finally, necessitates a change of terrain for Burroughs's work. He concludes *The Western Lands* with the admission that "he had reached the end of words, the end of what can be done with words. And then?" (*WL* 258) The open question suggests that something more is still to be done once language is abandoned. Deleuze uses very similar terms to describe what he sees as the task of revolutionary literature: "This modern literature uncovers a 'strange language within language' and, through an unlimited number of superimposed grammatical constructions, tends towards an atypical form of expression that marks the *end of language as such* (here we may cite such examples as Mallarmé's book, . . . Artaud's breaths, the agrammaticality of Cummings, *Burroughs and his cut-ups and fold-ins,* as well as [Raymond] Roussel's proliferations . . . and so on)."[7] The labor of eliminating the dialectic, and with the dialectic its handmaidens—language, capital, and the human subject—must take us into different realms; accordingly, this study will conclude by tracing the extension of Burroughs's literary project into film and recording to suggest what can happen after "the end of words."

This entire project is contained, potentially, in Burroughs's proclamation that "Nothing is True, Everything is Permitted." This phrase is his famous battle-cry against social and personal control, a slogan explicitly cribbed from the legendary Ismâ'îlî holy man-cum-terrorist Hassan i Sabbah. The phrase is quoted in most of Burroughs's books from the *Nova* trilogy onward, and it serves to conclude the "Invocation" that opens his most recent trilogy (*C* xviii). In the 1989 text "Apocalypse" (written as the introduction to a Keith Haring exhibition catalog and read by Burroughs on his first compact disc, *Dead City Radio*), Burroughs offers his own gloss on the phrase:

> Consider an apocalyptic statement: "Nothing is true, everything is permitted"—Hassan i Sabbah, the Old Man of the Mountain. Not to be interpreted as an invitation to all manner of unrestrained and destructive behavior; that would be a minor episode, which would run its course. Everything is permitted *because* nothing is true. It is all make-believe, illusion, dream, art. When art leaves the frame, and the written word leaves the page, not merely the physical frame and page, but the frames and pages of assigned categories, a basic disruption of reality occurs. The literal realization of art. Success will write "apocalypse" across the sky.

It is a question of causality and condition: if something is true, then something else must be maligned and prohibited by the Law as false, but if nothing is true—which is to say if there is no such thing as essential truth—then there can be no prohibition, no Law, and everything is permitted. And it is permitted precisely in the form of creative art, whose only condition and referent is itself.

The "basic disruption of reality" which Burroughs demands is neither the modern disruption of traditional structures of value, nor the postmodern disruption of modernist mythologizing; rather, it is the "literal realization of art," a realization which simultaneously requires the destruction of art as a separate category, as a mirror to nature and life. "[A]rt leaves the frame, and the written word leaves the page" in order to change material reality, not by asserting some essential truth that they alone could preserve against the ideological falsity of reality, but by multiplying and disseminating the creative power of the false, the untrue, the forgery. Art is falsehood or lie because it does not find its proof outside itself, through a process of truthful representation, but within itself, as Friedrich Nietzsche and Oscar Wilde argued. In much the same spirit, Deleuze specifies that the apocalyptic project of art is "not simply to eliminate fiction but to free it from the model of truth which penetrates it, and on the contrary to rediscover the pure and simple *story-telling function [fonction de fabulation]* which is opposed to this model. What is opposed to fiction is not the real; it is not the truth which is always that of the masters or colonizers, it is the story-telling of the poor, in so far as it gives the false the power which makes it into a memory, a legend or a monster" (Deleuze, *Cinema-2* 150). Such a memory or monster acts as a catalyst that precipitates a fused, revolutionary force out of the atomized subjects of oppression. This powerful story-telling or fabulatory function is the goal to which Burroughs in his novels and Deleuze in his philosophy aspire.

Deleuze has always taken a particular interest in American fiction—especially in works from the early modern, high modern, and contemporary periods—and like Burroughs he has never accepted the arbitrary distinctions many critics make between "serious" literature or "art," on the one hand, and "popular" or "commodity" literature, on the other.[8] In *Difference and Repetition,* Deleuze insists that even a book of philosophy should be, not a treatise on the pursuit and judgment of truth, but rather both a detective novel and a book of science fiction.

> By detective novel we mean that concepts, with their zones of presence, should intervene to resolve local situations. They themselves change along with the problems. They have spheres of influence where . . . they operate in relation to "dramas" and by means of a certain "cruelty." . . . Following Samuel Butler, we discover *Erewhon,* signifying at once the originary "nowhere" and the displaced, disguised, modified and always-recreated "here-and-now." . . . We believe in a world in which individuations are impersonal, and singularities are pre-individual: the splendor of the pronoun "one"—whence the science-fiction aspect, which necessarily derives from this *Erewhon.* (Deleuze, *Difference and Repetition* xx–xxi)

This generic doubling is at work in Burroughs's texts as well. He, too, makes use of the detective novel and science fiction in order to displace dogmatic structures of thought and transcendent structures of power. Deleuze himself insists that the comparison of his work with that of Burroughs "can bear on three points (the idea of a body without organs; control as the future of societies; the confrontation of tribes or populations in abandoned [*désaffectés*] spaces)."[9] These points of comparison, articulated with others, will constitute the framework of the following study. Make no mistake: Burroughs's work, like Deleuze's, is utopian, but not in the same way that modernist works are. Burroughs and Deleuze rely, not on the permanent grounding of truth (and Law) in modernist myth, but on the fluid mechanisms of desire in fantasy for their amodernist utopian drive. Our task, then, is to see how such an amodern libidinal or *fantasmatic* politics *works* in the writings of Burroughs and Deleuze.[10]

•

Before we embark on our survey of Burroughs's amodernist career, however, we must acknowledge the other major circumstance that has contributed to his academic invisibility: the events of his life have been extraordinary (almost as extraordinary as the contents of his novels), and they have often preoccupied his critics and interfered with the reception of his writing. That is, most criticism of Burroughs to date, from both inside and outside the academy, has been *moral* criticism directed at his referents in "real life," rather than analytical criticism directed at his work as writing. His life and his work, reductively perceived as congruent, have been held up to explicit or implicit moral standards and judged wanting in virtually every instance. First of all, there was moral and legal censure from the state, which banned *Naked Lunch* as obscene because of its matter-of-fact scatology; this censure was seconded by many critics of the mainstream media, who predictably denounced Burroughs's work as pseudoliterary pornography. At the same time, his depiction of largely unpunished and entirely "unredeemed drug addicts" offended the sensibilities of those involved in or sympathetic to the first American "war on drugs" during the fifties and sixties.[11] They apparently considered him a propagandist for opiates, in spite of the decidedly unglamorous routines concerning addiction that make up the bulk of his early work. His support of the radical student movements of the late sixties did nothing to disarm these defenders of literary morality.

Even partisans of the literary avant-garde with no ties to the "Establishment" have tended to see Burroughs in moral or moralizing terms. This is equally true of his supporters, like Norman Mailer and Allen Ginsberg, and his detractors, like David Lodge and Leslie Fiedler.[12] Fiedler in particular brought the moral denunciation of Burroughs full circle by aligning his aggressive homosexuality with what Fiedler piously saw as the "feminization" of American writing in the sixties, a tendency Fiedler thought must be counterrevolutionary in its passivity (Fiedler 516). Burroughs managed to offend the moral sensibilities of the Right, the Center, and the Left in equal measure. Despite the trend toward increasingly sophisticated models of critical reading in the seventies and eighties, Burroughs is still treated as a pariah because of many critics' misguided persistence in reducing his work to the status of an unmediated expression of a lifestyle they find personally or politically abhorrent. Such moralizing reading is no more confined to a single critical approach now than it was thirty years ago; Marxists often complain of Burroughs's political confusion and self-contradiction, while psychoanalytic critics bemoan his infantile refusal to accede to the symbolic order.

Let us take as an example of the effects of this continuing moral criticism one well-known aspect of his reputation: he is "widely perceived as a misogynist" (Burroughs, *Adding Machine* 124). While Burroughs's reputation for misogyny is not undeserved, clear hostility toward women on the sole basis of their gender is rare in his novels, and indeed his most often cited statements of misogyny are drawn from a single book of interviews conducted by Daniel Odier, *The Job* (1969–74). The early autobiographical novels contain virtually no female characters and no reflections on women's roles or functions, while the women in *Naked Lunch* are objects of hostility and contempt in exactly the same measure and terms as the men are. In these works Burroughs is not so much a misogynist as a thoroughgoing misanthrope in the style of his model, Jonathan Swift, and if anything is more even-handed in his disgust for the human species than Swift is. Burroughs, echoing his friend Brion Gysin, might well say, "Don't go calling *me* a misogynist . . . a mere misogynist. I am a monumental misanthropist [sic]. Man is a bad animal, maybe the only bad animal" (Gysin and Wilson xiv).

In his works of the sixties, Burroughs develops a more specific dislike for women, as his analysis of control and oppression becomes more complex and far-reaching; he thinks then that women "were a basic mistake, and the whole dualistic universe evolved from this error" (Burroughs and Odier, 116). Beyond this devaluation, however, he shares with many poststructural critics the conviction that binary opposition or "dualism is the whole basis of this planet—good and evil, communism, fascism, man, woman, etc. As soon as you have a formula like that, of course you're going to have trouble. The planet is populated by various groups and their conditions of life are completely incompatible and they aren't going to get together. It isn't a question of their just getting together and loving each other; they can't, 'cause their interests are not the same. Just take men and women for example, they'll never get together, their interests are not the same"(Burroughs and Odier, 97). He goes on to denounce the "anti-sex orientation of our society" which "is basically manipulated by female interests" and "fostered by [children's] upbringing and training, which is basically controlled by women" (Burroughs and Odier, 118–19). The novels of the same period, the *Nova* trilogy and *The Wild Boys,* dramatize these convictions in quite graphic ways, though they most often focus on the repressive elements of language and of state and corporate institutions rather than on gender dualism.

Such inflammatory formulations clearly constitute obstacles to many women as potential readers and critics of Burroughs's works (though not to all: two of the three book-length studies of his novels in English are by women)[13] and to male readers sympathetic to feminism. However, the contested but persistent incorporation of feminism into the academy has necessitated the reassessment of many of the canonical and semicanonical works of male writers, especially those from the most recent historical periods, in terms of their representations and ideologies of gender relations. In general these feminist reassessments have been marked by a more rigorous and more empirical analysis of the works in question than was carried out in "patriarchal" criticism of the same texts, which is certainly appropriate for a body of critical methods dedicated to bringing to light one of the most powerful systems of oppression in our culture. But Burroughs's misogyny, along with the biographical problem indissociably bound to it—his accidental killing of his wife—seems to have authorized many feminist critics to discount his writings in their entirety and even to abandon the most basic protocols of critical analysis when dealing with his work. His uncertain position in relation to the academy undoubtedly abets this abandonment, which is only the most effective manifestation of the long-standing moral resistance to his work.

Few, if any, extended feminist accounts or analyses of Burroughs's writing are readily available, which is not surprising given the explicitly reformist priorities of most feminist criticism (i.e., identification of patterns of oppression in the work of canonical writers and parallel revalorization of marginalized women writers) and his liminal position with respect to the institution of literature. Even Jennie Skerl and Robin Lydenberg's anthology of Burroughs criticism spanning three decades, *William S. Burroughs at the Front,* contains no concentrated feminist work on Burroughs, though many of the authors represented in it pursue analyses implicitly marked by feminist concerns. The most serious and paradigmatic feminist confrontations with Burroughs's works tend to appear, paradoxically, as afterthoughts or side-issues within larger theoretical/historical projects. Such confrontations are not only brief and ancillary but are also often marked by a refusal actually to read Burroughs's writing. Alice A. Jardine's *Gynesis: Configurations of Woman and Modernity* is a case in point. Her analysis of Burroughs as an exemplary avatar of "male American fiction" and its "external" (i.e., nonsemiotic, nonpsychoanalytic, non-French) relation to signification occupies less than a page and contains no citations from his texts. On the contrary, her analysis centers on the abstract method of Burroughs's cut-up procedure, which she describes as a "rearrangement of the textual surface according to a logic that is purely one of semantic isolation" resulting from an antimaternal "fear of association" common to American male writers (Jardine 234). The claim that the logic of cut-ups produces only "semantic isolation" is superficially plausible though ultimately untenable, as I will show later, and it would require a close reading of a cut-up text to demonstrate the point convincingly. The text to which Jardine refers the reader for such a demonstration, unfortunately, is *Naked Lunch,* which is not actually a cut-up text; Burroughs did not "discover" and begin using the cut-up method until 1959–60, after *Naked Lunch* had been published.

A similar refusal to read Burroughs mars Sandra Gilbert and Susan Gubar's monumental three-volume rereading of modern Anglophone literature, *No Man's Land.* Though their references to Burroughs amount to only three sentences on two pages in a project of well over a thousand pages, these sentences are particularly telling as indices of feminist response to him. In their chapter on "male male impersonators" in volume 3, Gilbert and Gubar briefly gloss the Beat writers (including Burroughs) as progenitors of "alternative male personae," novel social roles played by men, who often "ridicul[ed] the phallocentrism they associated with the authoritarianism of society." Despite this general satiric bent, Gilbert and Gubar insist that "in much of his work, Burroughs labels love 'a fraud perpetuated by the female sex,' arguing that 'the women of this world were only made to bang' " (Gilbert and Gubar 3: 331). The source of both Burroughs citations is not a Burroughs text but rather John Tytell's early study of the Beats, *Naked Angels*. Unfortunately for Gilbert and Gubar, as for Jardine, the source does not support the critics' claim. While the first quotation is indeed from Burroughs's writing (specifically, *The Job* 118), the second is actually drawn from Jack Kerouac's novel *Doctor Sax,* as Tytell notes when he cites it (Tytell 203). It is difficult to decide which lapse is more disturbing, the obvious misquotation on which the interpretation depends or the blanket refusal to engage Burroughs's writing directly rather than through a secondary source.

To what should a reader attribute these violations of the norms of critical argument? Perhaps the other occasion on which Gilbert and Gubar cite Burroughs can help clarify their rationale. In the first volume of their study, they introduce the issues and figures that will be the objects of their analyses in a long preparatory chapter entitled "The Battle of the Sexes." Therein they anticipate the argument they will make about the Beats in volume three, that many of these writers "were as committed as Stanley Kowalski [of Tennessee Williams's *Streetcar Named Desire*]—or Henry Miller—to the worship of the 'granite cock' and the 'marvellously impersonal' receptive cunt.' " As an example, they cite Gary Snyder's poem to a woman "he confessed . . . he had once beaten up[:] 'visions of your body / Kept me high for weeks' and, in particular, visions of her with 'a little golden belt just above/your naked snatch.' " Their brief paragraph concludes immediately thereafter by connecting this image to Burroughs's life: "As if literalizing Snyder's story, moreover, the Beat hero William Burroughs actually did shoot and kill his wife in 1951 while aiming at a champagne glass on her head" (Gilbert and Gubar 1: 52).

How, exactly, does Burroughs's situation "literalize" Snyder's confession of abuse? Neither Snyder's confession nor the citation from his poem mentions shooting or death. Do they mean to imply that Burroughs's "actual" shooting of his wife was the culmination of a pattern of spousal abuse driven by ambivalent sexual desire, a pattern established by Snyder? If that is the case, they should document their allegations; in fact, there is no evidence provided either by them or by the two existing biographies of Burroughs to suggest that such a pattern existed in any of his relationships with women (or with men for that matter).[14] Indeed, the only pattern for which we are given evidence in this passage is the one by which Gilbert and Gubar slander and discredit Burroughs: they exaggerate his misogynistic statements without regard for their contexts or conceptual underpinnings, then use the accidental shooting as the basis for an ad hominem dismissal based on nothing but innuendo.

Gilbert and Gubar are not the only feminist critics who follow this pattern; performance artist Karen Finley does something quite similar in her assemblage *Moral History* when she responds to a copy of Burroughs's *Naked Lunch* by scrawling across its cover the statement "William Burroughs, you are no hero to me—you shot your wife and got away with it. Oh, the emotional temperament of the artist."[15] Note Finley's use of the appellation "hero," which, like Gilbert and Gubar's identical usage, draws attention away from the writing and toward the fetishized figure of the author. Again, innuendo replaces argument: Finley implies that Burroughs "got away with it" because of his status as a male artist, when in fact the shooting occurred two years before Burroughs published his first novel, which met with critical indifference and commercial failure. He actually "got away with it" because the Mexican judicial system convicted him only of *imprudencia criminal* or criminal negligence (Morgan 200–202), which allowed him the opportunity to flee to Colombia and then to Tangier before he was sentenced.

This is most emphatically not to say that the killing of his wife is irrelevant to Burroughs's work. After a period of active bisexuality that extended from the late thirties to the early fifties and actually included two heterosexual marriages—the first a marriage of convenience that allowed a German-Jewish woman to escape to the U.S. from Yugoslavia before the Nazis took over (Morgan 64–71)—Burroughs chose to identify himself exclusively as a homosexual following his accidental shooting of his second wife (and the mother of his son), Joan Vollmer, in September 1951. In the author's introduction to *Queer* (*Q*), Burroughs admits that these events are linked with his vocation as a writer: "I am forced to the appalling conclusion that I would never have become a writer but for Joan's death, and to a realization of the extent to which this event has motivated and formulated my writing. I live with the constant threat of possession, and a constant need to escape from possession, from Control. So the death of Joan brought me in contact with the invader, the Ugly Spirit, and maneuvered me into a lifelong struggle, in which I have had no choice except to write my way out" (*Q* xxii). The closest Burroughs comes to narrating Joan's death is in a passage near the beginning of *Naked Lunch*, in which Lee, the narrator, is smoking marijuana with a pimp whom Lee ridicules because, significantly, this pimp can only communicate with other men through female intermediaries.

> I take three drags, Jane looked at him and her flesh crystallized. I leaped up screaming "I got the fear!" and ran out of the house. Drank a beer in a little restaurant—mosaic bar and soccer scores and bullfight posters—and waited for the bus to town.
>
> A year later in Tangier I heard she was dead. (*NL* 20)

This oblique presentation acknowledges Burroughs's anxiety about the event as well as his reluctance to take full personal responsibility for it. Indeed, nearly a half century later he is still trying to banish the "Ugly Spirit" that took possession of his life in 1951 (*Q* xix).

Burroughs's ambivalence in this regard certainly warrants analysis, but it does not justify the misrepresentation of the facts that provides a foundation for Gilbert and Gubar's and Finley's dismissals of his writings. Nor does his misogyny, which is often treated as a static element in his outlook, justify these shameful lapses from critical accuracy and honesty, any more than Ezra Pound's support of fascism or Gertrude Stein's enthusiasm for the collaborationist Marshal Pétain would justify their erasure from the tradition of modern American poetry.[16] Indeed, Burroughs's views on women have changed significantly since his first major enunciation of them in *The Job,* as have at least some of his representations of women in his recent fiction, a situation that has received virtually no attention from feminist critics. He no longer holds women solely responsible for the restrictive dualism that characterizes modern culture, and instead recognizes that men constitute the necessary dialectical antithesis in that dualism: he insists now that "it is not women *per se,* but the dualism of the male-female equation that I consider a mistake" (Burroughs, Letter 45). His practical goal is no longer what Allen Ginsberg called "the occlusion of women,"[17] but rather an extreme social and biological separatism that recognizes the "incompatible conditions of existence" of men and women, a point of view that is well established among some radical feminists. Ultimately, Burroughs envisions "an evolutionary step [that] would involve changes that are literally inconceivable from our present point of view," perhaps even changes that would "involve the sexes fusing into an organism" reminiscent of the spherical ur-hermaphrodite in Plato's *Symposium* (Burroughs, *Adding Machine* 124, 126).[18]

The developmental path of Burroughs's misogyny thus diverges from those of other infamous misogynists, especially that of his friend Norman Mailer. Mailer's constantly embattled hyper-heterosexuality expresses itself in his writings as an increasingly violent drive to dominate women physically and socially as a way of asserting his superiority to and power over them, while Burroughs's homosexual misogyny seeks merely to separate itself from the other sex/gender. This difference is not inconsequential; it is the difference between patriarchal enslavement and potential postpatriarchal autonomy. Unlike Mailer, Burroughs submits the stereotypes of patriarchy—the soldier, businessman, and politician—to witheringly direct satire by revealing their subordination to the totalitarian system of modern capitalism and its tool, the state. In this he is ideologically (though not stylistically) closer to Jean Genet, who Kate Millett claims "demonstrated the utterly arbitrary and invidious nature of sex role" by "revealing its primarily status or power definition" (Millett 343). Millett also admits that Burroughs, like Henry Miller, has served a distasteful but important protofeminist function by bringing sexual hostility and violence into the open for analysis: "As one recalls both the euphemism and the idealism of descriptions of coitus in the Romantic poets . . . or the Victorian novelists . . . and contrasts it with Miller or William Burroughs, one has an idea of how contemporary literature has absorbed not only the truthful explicitness of pornography, but its antisocial character as well. Since this tendency to hurt or insult has been given free expression, it has become far easier to assess sexual antagonism in the male" (Millett 46).

Feminist criticism has not substantially reassessed Burroughs's work in the quarter-century since the publication of Millett's book. Other feminist writers appear to agree with this assessment, though in less ambivalent terms. For example, Kathy Acker has always acknowledged Burroughs's influence on her assaultive accounts of conflicts of gender and sexuality, and Angela Carter names Burroughs as the contemporary writer who bears the closest resemblance to the Marquis de Sade, who put "pornography in the service of women" by granting them the same ruthless will to power and the same focused aggression against traditional images of women that he gave to his male characters (Carter 34, 36–37).[19]

In short, Burroughs's attitudes toward and representations of women are not simple, fixed, or arbitrary, and analyses of them should not be, either. As of this writing, no work of scholarship has fully met these conditions; nor will this study attempt to do so. On the contrary, the purpose of this study is to take seriously the radical philosophical and political claims Burroughs's writing makes, not to investigate the moral inconsistencies and gaps that complicate his ideas and representations of gender, though these issues will demand our attention at particular points in the argument. To achieve this study's primary purpose we will have to move freely from the most abstract cosmological and metaphysical models to the most specific, concrete historical circumstances and back again. If successful, this study will constitute not so much an apology for Burroughs's moral lapses or ideological excesses as a sympathetic critical perspective on the complexities, impasses, and potentialities of his work. To that end, we must first establish a context, both historical and theoretical, for his creative activities.

Chapter One

Invisibility and Amodernism

If the following study were to be a purely descriptive account of the cultural matrix of (post)modernism, we would have to begin with modernism, as the temporal precession of prefixes would imply. It will not be simply descriptive, however, but analytical, in that it will be concerned with the relations between the terms rather than their historical succession. Let us begin, then, in medias res, with the postmodernism that surrounds us on every side. We can even claim a precedent for this in Jean-François Lyotard's argument that "A work can become modern only if it is first postmodern" (*Postmodern Explained* 13). Since this term has a variety of definitions, we should be clear about what is meant here by the word. Postmodernism is everything you ever wanted in modernism, and less. It takes over, almost completely intact, all of the formal markers of modernism: structural fragmentation; all the polyvalent forms of parody or pastiche; the apparently neutral juxtaposition of "high" and "low" culture; and elaborate and self-consciously artificial formal principles. What it leaves out, however, is the aspect that, for many critics, serves as the motor of modernism: its imperative to provide a replacement for the lost orders of the past—through myth, through pure form, or through both. As T. S. Eliot writes of James Joyce (though it applies also to himself) in "*Ulysses,* Order, and Myth," one of the classic manifestoes of literary modernism, "In using myth, in manipulating a continuous parallel between contemporaneity and antiquity, Mr. Joyce is pursuing a method which others must pursue after him. . . . It is simply a way of controlling, of ordering, of giving a shape and a significance to the immense panorama of futility and anarchy which is contemporary history. . . . Instead of narrative method, we may now use the mythical method" (Eliot, "*Ulysses*" 483). Indeed, this is the standard reading of Eliot's own practice, especially in early works like "The Waste Land": "These fragments I have shored against my ruins" by affiliating them with the myths of the Fisher King and Tiresias (Eliot, *Poems* 69). Theodor W. Adorno defines the mythic method of modernism somewhat differently, as the willing of the new that, through the act of will, binds the new more firmly to tradition. "This explains the link between modernism and myth. The new wills non-identity but, by willing, inevitably wills identity" (*Aesthetic Theory* 33). His defense of modernism, however, rests on a negative version of the same premise as Eliot's: "By cathecting the repressed, art internalizes the repressing principle, i.e. the unredeemed condition of the world, instead of merely airing futile protests against it. Art identifies and expresses that condition, thus anticipating its overcoming" (27–28). In other words, modernism is the mode in which art retains its critical force under the specific repressive conditions of late capitalism.

This force is what postmodernism and the theories that purport to account for it omit. There are, of course, various versions of this omission of imperative. For Lyotard, the postmodern era is marked by the breakdown of the "master narratives" that legitimated aesthetic and political activity through the modern period; these master narratives, whether individual (the free realization of human potential) or social (the emancipation of the oppressed), underlay all ideas of "progress" in human affairs, but modernism revealed their attempts to provide historical closure and teleology to be mythological impositions on the recalcitrant and irreducible singularities of history. Modernism tried therefore to replace the original narratives with self-consciously artificial myth-narratives, as Eliot once wanted, and in so doing retain the imperatives of progress, but postmodernism accepts the breakdown without nostalgia. Lyotard maintains that criteria and methods still exist for aesthetic and teleological judgment, in the form of "paralogism" and "participation in language games."[1] For Jean Baudrillard, on the other hand, no such criteria exist because the postmodern is not the failure of progressive historical legitimation but the triumph of abstract mediation or signs. Baudrillard posits a structural equivalence between the parts of the sign, signifier and signified, and the parts of the value-form, exchange and use, and from this equivalence he generalizes to build a model of the postmodern based on pure symbolic exchange without production (and thus without producers or products). Instead of production, Baudrillard posits an immanent force, seduction, which drives exchange through a kind of uncritical aesthetic affirmation of capital. In such a flattened universe, no political or aesthetic space exists beyond the manipulation of simulacra through electronic media, which now define space and time. Mediation is all that exists, and it is by definition the abolition of difference and the triumph of the Same.[2]

Lyotard and Baudrillard disagree on many issues, but on at least one they agree: the Western tradition as a directed and emancipatory project has played itself out, and now can only present its fragments, either (for Lyotard) in the jagged shards of Adorno's negative aesthetics or (for Baudrillard) in the smooth screens of Marshall McLuhan's global media village, for the morose delectation of the postphilosophical critic. Such ruins remain infinitely generative of novelty, it is true, but it is a sham novelty, deprived of efficacy, of leverage for the transformation of practices. Thought can no longer appeal to progress for its legitimacy, nor can it use its own creativity as a foundation, since it is produced immediately as commodity/sign in circulation. In a situation like this, the fragments of the Western tradition can be permuted interminably—as they are in advertising, popular film, and television—but they can no longer be shored, as Eliot had hoped, against our ruins. Lyotard's pathos, like Baudrillard's narcissistic self-indulgence, is Eliot's mythic faith turned sour, just as postmodernism, in this formulation, is modernism that has turned against its own constitutive premises without being able to find replacements for those premises. If we wish, we can even pinpoint the formal (though perhaps not the historical) moment at which this turn took place.

•

The singularity of the literary works that we might, somewhat ironically, call "prophetic" lies in their ability to define, prospectively, a field of literary production that was heretofore undefined, to chart or even create an undiscovered country. Ralph Ellison's *Invisible Man* is one such work, standing self-consciously at the end of the cultural moment that Henry Adams—standing just as self-consciously at the end of "virginal" nineteenth-century American literary, political, and scientific culture—had foreseen in *The Education of Henry Adams:* the tremendous surge of "dynamic" productivity that would emerge from the then-embryonic modernist impulse.[3] Ellison offers a less symbolic and programmatic vision of the terrain ahead—the terrain that would become the landscape we now call postmodernism—than Adams did for modernism, perhaps because the shift Ellison explicates is harder to objectify in metaphorical images than was Adam's. The shift from the cult of the Virgin to the cult of technology involves a fairly straightforward substitution of objects within a consistent structure of meaning, while the shift from modernism to postmodernism involves a far more thorough investigation of the very logic of substitution and structure.

In opening up the postmodern territory that has provided homesteads for so many writers and critics, Ellison has really opened up two territories, or a single one with two distinct topographies. The first territory we must map, however, is the frontier between modernism and postmodernism. But to speak of modernism as a mass movement, a cultural trend, a coherent critique, or even a brute thing is to risk falling into inconsequential abstraction; any term that can, in principle, embrace the conscious primitivism of Pablo Picasso's early paintings as well as the rococo overdetermination of James Joyce's last novel, or the monumental functionality of Mies van der Rohe's public buildings as well as the attenuated formalism of Anton Webern's string quartets, lacks the specificity that the critic requires in a definition that is to be used as an analytical lever. Thus we must extract a subset from the many conflicting determinations that are grouped under "modernism," a subset that will hopefully grant us the leverage we need to interrogate some of the cultural objects that fall under those determinations.

Recall the trajectory of Ellison's novel: a young African American man, driven away from the segregated college environment through which he sought to "shape the destiny of [his] people" (32), attempts to find other ways to shape that destiny, first through his own private labor, and then through public political activism.[4] His efforts throughout the novel constitute a virtual compendium of modernist literary and political strategies: the search for individual "authenticity" against the indifference of mass production, figured in his disgust with college president Bledsoe's hypocritically conformist role-playing and then with the enforced alienation of industrial labor at Liberty Paints; faith in the power and historical validity of the progressive vanguard, in this case the socialist Brotherhood, and, through it, in the efficacy of his own oratory; the possibility of identification with the ethnic nationalism of Ras the Exhorter; bohemianism; and so on. These modernist strategies initially seem inevitable or unsurpassable to the narrator, however, because of his uneasy and incomplete acceptance of the central myth of cultural modernism: the assumption that there is necessarily an asymmetry between modern and "primitive" cultures—that is, between a fragmented, specialist, or "disciplinary" culture like the capitalist U.S. and totalized, mythically integrated cultures like those studied by anthropologists. Bruno Latour describes this constitutive assumption, which he calls the "Great Divide," as follows:

> [E]ven the most rationalist ethnographer is perfectly capable of bringing together in a single monograph the myths, ethnosciences, genealogies, political forms, techniques, religions, epics and rites of the people she is studying. . . . In works produced by anthropologists abroad, you will not find a single trait that is not simultaneously real, social and narrated. . . . [But] it is impossible to do with our own culture . . . what can be done elsewhere, with others. Why? Because we are modern. Our fabric is no longer seamless. Analytic continuity has become impossible. (Latour 7)[5]

This asymmetry is both *between* primitive cultures and modern culture and *within* modern culture itself, between the incommensurable disciplines of science, politics, and language. Unlike primitive cultures, modern disciplinary culture cannot be treated as a *totality.* The other modernist strategies of *Invisible Man,* from bourgeois individualism to Leninism, are grounded in this double assumption, this myth of myths.

The cultural asymmetry underpinning the narrator's activism is figured in Jim Trueblood's narrative of incest with his daughter in chapter 2. Incest and its taboos are, of course, the central themes of modern anthropology and psychoanalysis in their analyses of tribal cultures, including the (re)constructed tribal culture that lies at the historical origin—and in the unconscious—of modern culture itself. Trueblood has formerly been tolerated by the African American college administrators as a vocalist who would "sing what the officials called 'their primitive spirituals'" (Ellison 46) for white patrons; he thus serves as an object lesson in the difference between African American culture, which the white officials and patrons view mythically as a whole that embraces both the "primitive" actions and superstitions of the uneducated farmers and the "progressive" aspirations of the college-educated class, and white American culture, which has lost this unity to become historically and technologically fragmentary or "disciplined." To this extent, modernism is white, and the efforts of nonwhites to make themselves modern are doomed to failure (as witness the Liberty Paints episode, 192–225). Trueblood's incest, therefore, does not appall the white patrons, but merely confirms and intensifies their feelings of asymmetrical difference or superiority, while "all of us at the college hated the black-belt people, the 'peasants'. . . . We were trying to lift them up and they, like Trueblood, did everything it seemed to pull us down" (47). Indeed, it is for revealing Trueblood to the white patron Norton that the narrator is expelled. The narrator tries throughout much of the novel to distance himself from the atavistic "primitivism" that Trueblood represents, just as the narrator's white adversaries try to distance themselves from him; both sides use the same modernist strategies to construct and enforce this asymmetry.

All his avenues of action are ultimately blocked by the shortsighted and implicitly racist power lust—in other words, the constructed cultural asymmetry—of his supposed benefactors. His attempts to change American public life are doomed to failure by virtue of his wavering but still powerful commitment to modernism's myths. Out of this failure—or, more specifically, out of the "successful" public life that is contrasted to the failure of the narrator's modernist strategies in the course of the novel—appears the first, most readily recognizable form of the terrain that will become, in the decades that follow, postmodernism. Chapter 23 of *Invisible Man* (468–501) invents, for American fiction, the form of the *floating signifier* that will provide the fundamental structure of the most influential kind of postmodern writing, which I have called *reflexive postmodernism* to emphasize its focus on linguistic self-reference. Ellison first presents this kind of writing as a topographical form of public life.

This chapter finds the narrator, disgusted with the blindness of his socialist brethren toward their African American comrades, wandering through Harlem at night trying to avoid the hostile attention of African nationalist Ras the Exhorter's thugs by adopting a very simple disguise: dark glasses and a wide-brimmed hat (Ellison 471–72). Because of this cover, he is repeatedly mistaken for a man named Rinehart, who is simultaneously a pimp (472, 482–83), a confidence man (477), a numbers runner (480), a briber of police (481), and, paradoxically, a storefront preacher (485–86). The multiplicity of Rinehart's incarnations—his ability to "be both rind and heart," both surface and at least the illusion of depth—leads the narrator to an epiphany that opens the postmodern frontier by breaking with one half of the double modern asymmetry, the Great Divide *within* modern culture between bounded specializations and disciplines (while leaving the other half, the asymmetry *between* modern and primitive cultures, completely intact):

> His world was possibility and he knew it. He was years ahead of me and I was a fool. I must have been crazy and blind. The world in which we lived was without boundaries. A vast seething, hot world of fluidity, and Rine the rascal was at home. Perhaps *only* Rine the rascal was at home in it. . . . I

> wanted to know Rinehart and yet, I thought, I'm upset because I know I don't have to know him, that simply becoming aware of his existence, being mistaken for him, is enough to convince me that Rinehart is real. (487)

Note the genitives: "His world" or the "world in which we lived," as opposed to another, less sophisticated or even "primitive" one that has emerged and retreated earlier in the novel. Rinehart's pure, fluid superficiality, his manipulation of signifying systems as disparate as gambling and gospel, reveals to the narrator the existence of a world alien to his own bounded and fragmentary world of clear historical meaning and straightforward humanitarian progress. This other world is not elsewhere, however; it is *between,* in the spaces that the narrator's modernist thought and politics have not infiltrated: the black market, underground society, the shifting economy of the street, anywhere that flows of money, signs, and desire generate fleeting new structures out of ephemeral values. This partial break with modernity is mediated, coterminous with the circulation of representations, but Rinehart's world of flux requires no referentiality, no use value, no depth of characterization or meaning; indeed, Rinehart does not actually appear as a character in the novel, only as an overdetermined signifier. Nevertheless, he is "real" in that his activity can be represented, surmised on the basis of the irreducibly contradictory determinations of his career.

Ellison's narrator, momentarily stunned by this revelation of an interstitial alternative world (and by the serene indifference of his supposed allies toward his situation and the situation of his people), tries to construct a plan that will take these developments into account. "There were no allies with whom we could join as equals; nor were there time or theorists available to work out an overall program of our own—although I felt that somewhere between Rinehart and invisibility there were great potentialities" (499). The narrator's "feeling" for these "potentialities" helps him to recognize the impasses into which his own modern commitments (to the universal brotherhood of man, to scientific rationality, to the party as vanguard representing the mass of authentic—i.e., laboring—individuals) and strategies have led him. To realize the "potentialities," he begins to act like Rinehart, like the "rascal" or traditional Trickster: he starts "yessing them" (502), manipulating appearances, signs, in order to confirm the Brotherhood's imaginary world in which the political avant-garde dictates the actions of the ignorant masses, a world that he knows bears no relation to the real situation of the inhabitants of Harlem. He works formally, ironically, as the Trickster does, but no one can gauge his irony because it has become coterminous with his world: "An illusion was creating a counter-illusion" (504). Those illusory potentialities have also been realized, at least partially, in American fiction after Ellison, which has exploited Rinehart's gift for artifice, the self-conscious play of slipping signification that we might call the "Rinehart Effect" (on the model of illusory "special effects" in film rather than that of the material Coriolis effects in meteorology, for example) far beyond anything explicitly presented in *Invisible Man.*

For example, Vladimir Nabokov's *Pale Fire,* surely one of the high-water marks of literary postmodernism, is a triumph of pure formal artifice in its wholesale importation of literary criticism into the genre of the novel. The world-historical pretensions of its protagonist, Kinbote, are necessarily though minimally constrained by the very different contours of John Shade's autobiographical poem; in a simultaneous reductio ad absurdam and apotheosis of subjective criticism, Kinbote reads Shade's poem as a hermetic allegory of his own, perhaps imaginary, pseudo-Romanov experience. For the apparently incommensurable human experiences of the Russian revolution and middle-class America, Nabokov finds a purely formal common ground in art—specifically, in language—but then seals it off from all referentiality, not only by undermining the protagonist-critic's claim to literary and even psychological competence, but also by folding the book into itself structurally. For example, if one looks up the central mystery of the book, the missing Zemlyan Crown Jewels, in the index, one is sent to the entry on "Hiding Place," and from there one is sent to the entry on "*potaynik,*" and then on to "*taynik*"*:* "Russ., secret place; see Crown Jewels" (Nabokov 206, 207, 211, 213). The referents for the words, like the referent for the novel itself, are missing; words refer to other words via the game of "word golf," an exhaustive demonstration of Saussure's linguistic insight. John Barth's texts further clarify and even magnify this tendency in American fiction; if in Nabokov's hands the Rinehart Effect becomes baroque, in Barth's it becomes rococo.[6]

Along with Rinehart's formal or reflexive postmodernism, another postmodernism emerges from *Invisible Man,* but in a less obvious way, as a second topography that has been almost completely reduced to the first, self-reflexive terrain mapped by writers like Nabokov and Barth. This is the terrain I propose to call *invisible postmodernism,* or *amodernism,* to mark its furtive, almost imperceptible emergence from the same conditions that opened the frontier of postmodernism. As such, amodernism does not succeed postmodernism, but contests it throughout the postwar period. After his encounter with the signifiers that add up to Rinehart, Ellison's narrator begins to make use of the Rinehart Effect, "yessing them" by telling his superiors (who have become his adversaries as well) what they want to hear. He marries the Brotherhood's emancipatory historical rhetoric to Rinehart's rhetoric of roles, allowing one to complete the other and thus produce a tidy linguistic totality that renounces all extratextual (i.e., material/political) effect. He can opt for this artificial Rinehart role only briefly, however, before the unarticulated and (to the Brotherhood) unintelligible demands of the people he thinks he represents erupt and destroy his symbolic world. The Harlem riot, through its victims, forces the narrator to recognize that "By pretending to agree I *had* indeed agreed, had made myself responsible for that huddled form lighted by flame and gunfire in the street, and all the others whom now the night was making ripe for death" (541). Rinehart is, after all, a confidence man who works with irony and lies, just as the Rinehart Effect, and the reflexive postmodernism based upon it, relies on this vertiginous, undecidable irony, this pretense of agreement that, in Greil Marcus's words, is "just one more way of not having to mean what you said."[7] The Rinehart Effect is not revolutionary, but just business as usual under capitalism: caveat emptor, or never give a sucker an even break.

Carried along, without subjective intention, by the crowd of events, Ellison's narrator *passes through* the crystalline cityscape of Rinehart's reflexive postmodernism—as he has passed through the lofty but inhospitable mountains of mythic modernism—without stopping. He arrives, finally, in the liminal position of internal exile, under the basements of Harlem, where he lives off the status quo without contributing to it directly. This exile does not necessarily signify resignation or defeat, though it has been read that way; the narrator insists that he has not given up his radical desires, but rather has deferred them into a future that will allow them to be actualized:

> In going underground, I whipped it all except the mind, the *mind*. And the mind that has conceived a plan of living must never lose sight of the chaos against which that pattern was conceived. That goes for societies as well as for individuals. Thus, having tried to give pattern to the chaos which lives within the pattern of your certainties, I must come out, I must emerge. . . . Even hibernations can be overdone, come to think of it. Perhaps that's my greatest social crime, I've overstayed my hibernation, since there's a possibility that even an invisible man has a socially responsible role to play. (Ellison 567–68)

The novel ends with this promise, which Nabokov, Barth, and other reflexive postmodernists can and will simulate interminably, but it is the task of an as-yet-invisible postmodernism, of an amodernist literature and criticism, to make good on it.

What would it mean to make good on a promise like this one for a "plan of living"? Leaving aside the possibility that the narrator may in this instance be "yessing" the reader the way he "yessed" the Brotherhood—in other words, expanding the Rinehart Effect to encompass the entire book—it seems to me that there are two ways to fulfill this promise. The first I would call regressive, in that it would entail a retreat, not only from the historiolinguistic vertigo of reflexive postmodernism (the Rinehart Effect), but also from the impasse of modernist asymmetry (the Great Divide) that laid down the coordinates of that postmodernism. Among those who pursue this course, I would include Jürgen Habermas, Niklas Luhmann, and others who struggle to "complete" the project of modernity according to a communicative or systemic theory that preserves intact both aspects of the modern asymmetry: they advocate a social order premised on a vast extension of technological sophistication balanced by a vast reduction in subjective sophistication (particularly aesthetic and linguistic sophistication) that will ultimately revive a dangerously "premodern" form of social stratification.[8] This way of making good would leave us in a situation no better than the status quo. The second way of fulfilling the promise of a "plan of living" I would call progressive, or amodern, in that it would require us to work through the impasses both of modernism and of postmodernism without accepting the finality of (post)modernist definitions.[9] This means we can accept neither the constitutive asymmetry of modernism nor the partial restoration of symmetry in reflexive postmodernism; we must be willing to restore both of the symmetries, and in order to do that, we must find a point from which to apply force. Ellison's narrator finds such a point, a perspective from which he can restore the primitive/modern symmetry, just as he later uses Rinehart's perspective to restore the internal, disciplinary symmetry that modernism has denied.

The narrator initially shares with his nemesis, Bledsoe, a horror of Trueblood, who threatens "to pull us down" into the morass of primitive, premodern life (Ellison 47). Trueblood threatens to resituate the "modern" African Americans of the college on the "primitive" side of the Great Divide, the modern asymmetry that the narrator accepts, for the most part uncritically. The narrator is only fitfully committed to this asymmetry, however; in at least one scene—the yam interlude on the streets of Harlem—he breaks decisively with modernism and in so doing reveals the affirmative potentiality of amodernism. This scene occurs just before the eviction scene, in which he discovers his hortatory vocation. In the yam he recognizes his own connection to the South—not to its racist, protomodern inequalities, but to the enduring agrarian culture of freed slaves that he had reductively identified with Trueblood's overdetermined incest. He admits that this "primitive" culture contains "something we liked," which could, nevertheless, "cause us the greatest humiliation" (258) if revealed in a modern social setting. He fantasizes about accusing Bledsoe of atavistic "*Field-Niggerism*" (259), parallel to Trueblood's, in order to destroy Bledsoe's sham-modernist career. Then, reflecting on his own "primitive" taste for such a culturally marked object, he proclaims that "I yam what I am!" (260): he acknowledges the connection, not shamefully but joyfully, and breaks with the other half of the constitutive asymmetry, the asymmetry between his premodern communal culture and the modernism he adopted later.

This break, however, is almost immediately buried under the renewed modernism of the Brotherhood, which the narrator joins shortly after the eviction riot. As a socialist group, the Brotherhood is committed to the elimination of the capitalist division of labor, the internal fragmentation that constitutes one half of the modern myth, but the Brotherhood's commitment is based on the inexorable law of Marxist historical development, the "necessity of the historical situation" (Ellison 285), which reinscribes the other half of the myth: modernism's self-proclaimed break with its past. For the bulk of the book, the Brotherhood's historical theses determine the narrator's actions, reinstalling him in an asymmetrical, white-dominated world. The fact remains, however, that the symmetry between premodern and modern culture was restored, if only for a moment, in the narrator's affirmation.

Such an affirmation of connection, but not identity, with the totalized "primitive," or premodern, world provides us with a subjective precondition for invisible postmodernism, or amodernism, which would not necessarily be a McLuhanesque "new primitivism." From the point of view of this precondition, the "Great Divide" of modernism's double asymmetry appears as a double bind that reflexive postmodernism cannot escape: either modernism really does represent an asymmetrical "advance" over all other cultural formations, in which case the couple modernism/postmodernism constitutes a totalization defined *negatively* by this very asymmetry and exclusion, or modernism's claim of asymmetry is a ruse that conceals a fundamental symmetry or continuity with the premodern, in which case that couple (modernism/postmodernism) constitutes a *positive* totalization, defined by its specific contingent features just as "primitive" cultures are. I use the term *totalization* here in something like its Marxist sense; neither the arrogant blindness of the Brotherhood nor the imprecise refutations of postmodern anti-Marxists have exhausted the force of materialist analysis. The first case, (post)modernism as a negative totalization, is, in fact, the object of Fredric Jameson's far-reaching investigations culminating in *Postmodernism, or, The Cultural Logic of Late Capitalism.*

In the conclusion to *Postmodernism,* Jameson distinguishes the categories of "totality" and "totalization" in order to insist on the continuing value of "totalization" as a critical operation: "if the word *totality* sometimes seems to suggest that some privileged bird's-eye view of the whole is available, which is also the Truth, then the project of totalization implies exactly the opposite and takes as its premise the impossibility for individual and biological human subjects to conceive of such a position, let alone to adopt or achieve it" (Jameson, *Postmodernism* 332).[10] Totalization, Jameson continues, is merely an attempt to sum up, "to envelope and find a least common denominator for the twin human activities of perception and action." This definition of "totalization," borrowed from Jean-Paul Sartre, provides the rationale for Jameson's critical project. Most theories of postmodernism (Lyotard's, for example) explicitly repudiate the category of totality (which Marx called the mode of production) and implicitly reject totalization as an attempt to derive or construct a totality from fragmentary language games. This rejection is a symptom of the disavowal of the very capitalist totality that drives (post)modernism. Jameson therefore attempts to totalize postmodernism, to forge a tendential totality out of the shards of contemporary culture in order to interrogate late capitalism, which underlies it.

Jameson's central project, the rehistoricization of a resolutely antihistorical moment, is laudable, and his rehabilitation of the prematurely abandoned categories of totality and totalization takes him a long way, but it also leads him (as it leads those antitotalizing theorists whom he interrogates) to reduce the multiplicity of postmodern aesthetic practices and to propose (explicitly and intentionally, where others work implicitly and unintentionally)[11] exclusive criteria for postmodernism. These criteria are surprisingly similar to the criteria suggested by others, even though the analyses given surpass in complexity and explanatory force almost all of the competing analyses. What are the criteria that define postmodernism in Jameson's work? First, pastiche or satire that lacks the stable ironic perspective necessary to provoke indignation; second, a rigorous refusal to refer to or thematize anything other than the simultaneous banality and impossibility of referring or thematizing; and third, collapse of the temporal into the spatial, and of the historical into the formal. In this way, Jameson enters the consensual academic discussion of postmodernism, even though he deploys these criteria to analyze the French New Novel, video art, and New Historicist literary criticism—no longer or not yet standard exempla of postmodern aesthetic production. Yet the criteria apply equally well to many more traditional, even canonical objects of literary study, like the writings of Nabokov and Barth. Both meet Jameson's criteria—as they fit the consensual criteria of most theories of postmodernism—rather well.

Despite the many specific disagreements that have marked the development of these theories of aesthetic and cultural postmodernism, their development has generally been contained within a horizon of consensus that has defined valid theories of postmodernism according to their deployment of methodological self-reflexivity, based (sometimes covertly) in the unconditional rejection of categories of totality or totalization—a rejection that acts as a negative totalization itself. A theory of postmodernism is deemed valid (i.e., acceptable into informed academic discussion) if it characterizes its object as a very particular kind of totality or process of totalization that is distinct from older forms—that is, as an antitotality. In positive terms, the dominant theories of postmodernism stress incommensurability and singularity against the notions of totality and totalization, which are equated with each other and with political totalitarianism. Paradoxically, this formal reflexivity requires an implicit totalization of the writing process itself, in that it requires the kind of circular foreclosure of reference we saw in Nabokov. It requires a totalization that admits of no thinkable or representable outside ("il n'y a pas de hors-texte"), and, despite its devotion to singularity and incommensurability, of no real difference inside. Difference is confined to the Saussurean manifold of negative definition, and its productivity is limited to the infinite proliferation of language. The dominant theories of postmodernism are *dialectical,* not in the transcendent Hegelian sense, nor in Jameson's asymptotic sense, but in the negative sense given the term by Adorno and Herbert Marcuse: postmodernism is a static contradiction (as opposed to Hegel's standing negation), a dialectic that cannot be rationally resolved, between whose antitheses all of society, including the critic of postmodernism, is (apparently) laid out.

Jameson's project is promising enough, however, to deserve broadening into areas of artistic and theoretical dissent. The most significant effect of the critical consensus on postmodernism, outside of particular close readings of cultural artifacts, has been the exclusion from discussion of artworks and theories which differ from the dominant model. These alternative works and theories take two general forms, the modern and what I have called the amodern. The modern hostility to postmodernism deplores the hypertrophy of modernist techniques that has led to the liquefaction of modernist forms of resistance (critical irony, resistance to commodification); this account denies the assertion that postmodernism corresponds to the real and total commodification of modernist cultural practices—to Marcuse's "one-dimensionality"—in order to preserve a privileged space for political commitment and artistic contestation. This perspective includes not only aesthetic and political reactionaries like Karl Popper, who refuse the project of totalization outright, but also progressives like Habermas, who accept a limited totalization of "communicative rationality,"[12] but insist that the resultant totality can be fine-tuned so that social justice prevails.

The amodernist alternative to (post)modernism, briefly, shares the modernist and postmodernist suspicion of representational art and politics, but rejects both the constitutive asymmetries of modernist mythmongering and the postmodern abandonment of critique in the face of the procession of simulacra. Amodernism, I would argue, constitutes the approach to contemporary culture that can most effectively deploy in a positive manner the project of totalization that Jameson employs from a negative perspective. We still need to discover, however, the objective conditions that would be necessary and sufficient to found a critique of this case, in which (post)modernism appears as a positive process of totalization subject to a materialist critique. The critique of (post)modernism as a positive totalization requires two tools: first, a critical perspective from which the totalization can be undertaken, and second, a logic of relation that can "envelop" the manifold of particulars and enact the process of totalization. This is where Antonio Negri's theoretical insights become important. He suggests a strategy that can explicate the material conditions of our totalized (post)modern culture: an analysis of the real subsumption of human labor under capital that productively historicizes (post)modernism, as I will now outline.

In volume one of *Capital,* Marx distinguishes two moments of capitalist subsumption, the formal and the real. In the formal subsumption of labor, which dates from the Industrial Revolution, "capital subsumes the labor process as it finds it, that is to say, it takes over an *existing labor process,* developed by different and more archaic modes of production" (Marx, *Capital* 1: 1021). Labor production is coterminous with human history and as such provides a point of perspective from which totalization can be undertaken, but capitalist structures of exploitation arise at a very specific point within that history. Existing labor processes, characteristic of "primitive," or premodern, cultures, are allowed to continue within the larger economic horizon of capital; they are merely encysted and rationalized, to the extent that their organization allows, by extending working hours or increasing production quotas to increase absolute surplus-value, the productive power of labor. In this way, a number of traditional processes survive the Industrial Revolution as vestiges of older orders, and with them survive the forms of subjectivity specific to those orders. According to Negri, the Romantics' "negation of the revolution of the Enlightenment and their affirmation of the new cultural identities that were to emerge during the course of the nineteenth century" register their recognition of "a period of crisis and of the subjection of society and work to capitalist domination" (Negri, *Politics* 201, 207). Anglo-European Romanticism elaborates its critique of formal subsumption through its hostility toward protomodern rationality and rationalization and toward the labor market's logic of the interchangeability of workers, as well as through its celebration of the productive power of the singular creator, the divine artist. From this point of view, modernism is merely the exhaustive elaboration of Romanticism's implicit credo.

Formal subsumption gives way to real subsumption; archaic labor processes are forced to conform to a "*specifically capitalist mode of production*" which "not only transforms the situations of the various agents of production, it also *revolutionizes* their actual mode of labor and the real nature of the labor process as a whole" (Marx, *Capital* 1: 1021). Through the rational division of labor and the application of technology—the practical embodiments of the internal "Great Divide" of modernism—the old labor processes are reconstructed in the image of capital for the extraction of relative surplus-value, the productive power of *capital* rather than labor. The worker no longer confronts her own alienated labor in the form of the commodity she has produced since she is no longer directly involved in the productive process, but stands to one side of it as an attentive guard. Labor time can no longer be the measure of value since it no longer correlates to value produced; productivity is dispersed instead throughout all the space and time of society. Exchange-value no longer measures use-value. Capital thus "presses to reduce labor time to a minimum, while it posits labor time, on the other side, as sole measure and source of wealth" (Marx, *Grundrisse* 706), and it is precisely this contradiction that drives the postmodern crisis. The more labor is devalued, the more ruthless capital's logic of interchangeability becomes, until it reaches the threshold of perfect homogeneity: all workers become identical from the point of view of capital. This is the inevitable corollary of the Rinehart Effect's mediated break with modern disciplinary separation: in postmodernism, all singularity has been rationalized out of production, leaving a blank totality, not of immanence or of potential but of indifference. As a superficially antagonistic accommodation with the exclusionary, de-singularizing tendencies of modernism, reflexive postmodernism resembles Romanticism in that it "registers in real terms . . . what the romantics had documented in formal terms": the crisis of capitalist domination (Negri, *Politics* 207).

This interminable reflexivity is not the only response open to literary and critical practice in the period of real subsumption, as the final promise of Ellison's narrator perhaps demonstrates. Reflexive postmodernism represents only the most impoverished use of contemporary cultural innovation, just as Rinehart's protean black-marketeering represents only the most opportunistic use of the liminal spaces and hybrid ideas of this century. It clings to the capitalist axiomatic that constantly limits the explosive movement of production to forms that can be exploited for profit (Deleuze and Guattari, *Anti-Oedipus* 244–53). The crisis in the law of value precipitates a crisis in the exchangist model of social valorization; since exchange-value can no longer measure use-value (if it ever could), new values must be found and a new model of production constructed. The segments of contemporary culture incapable of thinking outside the exchangist model react to this breakdown with reflexive postmodernism; they accept the crisis, but deny that a transformational critique can be carried on after it and that other values can (and will) be constructed. Lyotard, for example, repudiates the project of human emancipation, in part because of its relation to the bankrupt category of the social critic, of the intellectual as idealist:

> The promise of emancipation was rekindled, championed and expounded by the great intellectual, that category born of the Enlightenment, defender of ideals and the republic. Intellectuals of today who have chosen to perpetuate this task in ways other than a minimal resistance to every totalitarianism, who have been imprudent enough to nominate the just cause in conflicts between ideas or powers—the likes of Chomsky, Negri, Sartre, Foucault—have been tragically deceived. The signs of the ideal are hazy. A war of liberation does not indicate that humanity is continuing to emancipate itself. (Lyotard, *Postmodern Explained* 96)

Ignoring the profound differences that separate the intellectual ideals of Chomsky and Sartre, on the one hand, from Foucault and Negri, on the other, Lyotard asserts that the only resistance left to us is "a minimal resistance to every totalitarianism," by which he apparently means an atomized, private resistance that is often directed as much against potential allies as it is against any form of aggregate or institutionalized domination.

In any event, the line of critical "imprudence" which he associates with Negri, Sartre, and Foucault will be of more use to us in the analyses that follow. For this line—the amodern heirs of Negri, Sartre, and Foucault—the crisis in the law of value means something else entirely: instead of critical impotence and the interminable procession of mediated simulacra, the crisis brings opportunity in "an epoch-making leap beyond everything that humanity has hitherto experienced" (Negri, *Politics* 203). It dramatizes the failure of the principles and practices upon which capital has based its domination: instrumental reason, normative subjective interchangeability, and dialectical resolution. To put it bluntly, capital needs labor production, at least in the form of consumers who will keep the process of exploitation running, but production does not necessarily need capital. Amodernism reveals the unresolvable antagonism between subjectivities and capital that capital has turned to its advantage through the dialectic, and this antagonism is capable of generating a new socius that dissolves the abstraction of labor into the singular power of new, amodern collectivities. Beyond the dialectic, which still governs postmodernism as it governed modernism, committed critique is once again possible, from the space-time of these new collectivities and the singularities of which they are composed.

The *nonexistence* of such collectivities is one of the fundamental assumptions of reflexive postmodernism, epitomized in Baudrillard's celebration of the "implosion of the social in the media" and the concomitant disappearance of the "masses" that political organizations claim to represent.[13] This assumption ignores a great deal of evidence that confronts us, in a distorted and misrecognized form, in the media every day. The constriction of representational politics into the almost imperceptible space between the ideological positions of reactionary major parties (not only in the United States but throughout the industrialized world), one of the truisms of postmodern cynicism, is contested by new forms of social organization that emerge precisely at the geographical points where this constriction is most severe: the use of Western technology to strengthen anti-Western, fundamentalist revolutions in once "pro-Western" Islamic states like Iran and Algeria; the rise of drug cartels, organized like multinational corporations, in regions of South America rendered politically unstable through American intelligence activity directed against earlier mass social movements that were hostile to American economic projects; the manipulation of the mass media by the Zapatistas in order to embarrass the Mexican government on the day the North American Free Trade Agreement takes effect; and, closer to home, the constitution of ethnic gangs as defenders against police brutality and purveyors of drugs within the ghettoes and barrios that form an internal Third World within the United States.[14] If we look back to the seventies, we find the model of the Italian *Autonomia* movement—in which Negri was a leading participant—which provided a mass alternative to representational politics in the form of a systematic replacement of capitalist economic organization by worker self-management and the auto-reduction of market prices. Further back, we may consider as a shadowy precedent the Makhnovist anarchist movement that held the Ukraine for nearly three years against the bureaucratization of Soviet state capitalism.[15] Such novel assemblages are often difficult to assess accurately because of their avoidance (or, alternatively, conscious manipulation) of the media, but this difficulty should not blind us to the real potentialities for nonrepresentational social reorganization that these collectivities reveal.

To make good on Ellison's promise of an amodern "plan of living," we must emerge from the internal exile to which the postmodern impasse has consigned us and articulate these collectivities that defy representation, these new Harlems occupying the edges of our social perceptions and the gaps between our political categories, in both senses of the word *articulate:* analyze them, criticize them, *speak* them within the space of language; but also extend, enact, and *construct* them within the social and material spaces that are irreducible to that space. This double project is what Gilles Deleuze and William S. Burroughs, in similar ways, undertake. As Deleuze argues, "Those who act and struggle are no longer represented, either by a group or a union that appropriates the right to stand as their conscience. Who speaks and acts? It is always a multiplicity, even within the person who speaks and acts" (Deleuze and Foucault 206). Likewise, Burroughs insists that "despite disparate aims and personnel of its constituent members the underground is agreed on basic objectives. . . . We intend to destroy all dogmatic verbal systems. The family unit and its cancerous expansion into tribes, countries, nations we will eradicate at its vegetable roots. We don't want to hear any more family talk, mother talk, father talk, cop talk, priest talk, country talk *or* party talk. To put it country simple we have heard enough bullshit" (*WB* 139–40).

•

This emphasis on fragmentation implies a certain rigidity in modernist culture, a rigidity that defines each area as the province of one or another discipline and excludes the practitioners of other disciplines from it. Modernist culture operates by defining spaces, both in geographical and conceptual terms, and as such could be described as an *architectonic* form of culture. Michel Foucault gave the name "disciplinary society" to what we are calling modernist culture. This, too, would serve to distinguish modernism from premodern cultures, in which, Latour claims, "hybridization" (the invention of new composite objects and methods, whether technological, social, or aesthetic) is slowed because members of premodern cultures carefully think "through the close connections between the social and the natural order so that no dangerous hybrid will be introduced carelessly" (Latour 41). Modernism, on the other hand, conceals a vast proliferation of such hybrids under the cover of specialization and disciplinary fragmentation that obscures these "close connections between the social and the natural order" and abjures general discussion and oversight of the disavowed proliferation. In modernist culture, only specialists are qualified to pass judgment on the hybrids produced within their own particular discipline, which they must do while admitting their ignorance of the larger ramifications of those hybrids within other disciplines and in the culture at large. Hence dangerous hybrids proliferate, such as holes in the ozone layer, the result of unreflective reliance on technological "solutions" to "problems" of hygiene (aerosols used in deodorants and hair-sprays) and climate (Freon-based refrigeration and air conditioning), or the American health-care crisis, the result of high-tech medical progress combined with knee-jerk free-market ideology. The rigidity of disciplinary boundaries and the fragmentation that results have granted modernism an immense productive power that is undermined by an equally vast impotence, the loss of a perspective from which to consider the ramifications of its activities.[16] It is this lost perspective, this totalizing impulse, that amodernism seeks to replace.

It should follow from this schematic presentation that reflexive postmodernism represents the auto-critique of, though not necessarily an escape from, modernism. This means that postmodernism accepts the fundamental premises of modernism, but radicalizes them further, and in so doing undermines the mythological edifice of modernism itself. Postmodernism perpetuates the ideology of the fragmentation of modern culture and its distance from traditional or primitive cultures, but criticizes the myths by which modernism hoped to reconcile itself to its self-imposed lack of unity. Thus it maintains much of the rigidity of architectonic modernism—indeed, in the cases of Nabokov, Barth, and others actually *extends* that rigidity—while simultaneously abandoning the pursuit of unification or of a perspective that drove modernism to adopt "grand narratives" of progress.

No doubt it is this rigidity of modernism and postmodernism that accounts for Gilles Deleuze's indifference to both terms. For Deleuze, "a society is something that never stops slipping away. . . . Society is something that leaks, financially, ideologically—there are points of leakage everywhere. Indeed, the problem for society is how to stop itself from leaking away" (Deleuze, "Intellectual and Politics" 21). This fluid idea of society and culture, among other aspects of his thought, has frustrated scholars who have tried to find a model of literary criticism in Deleuze's writings similar to the models they have found in the works of Jacques Derrida and Michel Foucault. Both Derrida and Foucault, I would argue, take as objects of their analyses the rigid regularities of modern society. Derrida's work, if it may be described schematically and in general, is focused on the conceptual binarisms that constitute the tradition of European philosophy and, by extension, social organization; deconstruction as a critical activity operates through close attention to the points at which the rigidity of Western rationality reveals a paradoxical fragility, a susceptibility to reversal that is held in check not by impersonal and objective logic but by the capricious violence of domination. Not surprisingly, this work has given impetus to criticism that is concerned more with the discourses that grant structure and value to a conceptual field than to the material practices that are legitimated within such a field. Foucault, on the other hand, concentrates on the practices of domination that are imposed on material bodies in social spaces, practices which institute new conceptual arrangements that can erupt into discourse, and so the forms of criticism largely inspired by his work—the so-called New Historicism as well as Cultural Studies—have emphasized the collaboration between literary discourse and material practices of power.

Deleuze's work has not yet given rise to such a recognizable form of aesthetic criticism, and despite the influence he wields and the respect he has inspired in France, he remains a kind of "invisible man" in Anglophone critical circles. Though Deleuze positions himself nearer to Foucault than to Derrida, he maintains his distance nonetheless: "Michel [Foucault] was always amazed by the fact that, despite all the powers, their underhandedness and their hypocrisy, we can still manage to resist. On the contrary, I am amazed by the fact that everything is leaking and the government manages to plug the leaks. In a sense, Michel and I addressed the same problem from opposite ends. . . . [F]or me society is a fluid—or even worse, a gas. For Michel it was an architecture" (Deleuze, "Intellectual and Politics" 21). This emphasis on the fluidity of society and of its (social, scientific, and aesthetic) productions has an important effect: it makes the articulation of a general, repeatable *method* of analysis not merely problematic (as it is in Derrida's work and, to a lesser extent, in Foucault's) but virtually impossible. Criticism becomes an activity akin to the "Ideal Game" of which Deleuze writes in *The Logic of Sense:* not only does difference in the form of chance intervene at specific moments defined by the game's rules, but also chance alters those very rules with every turn (Deleuze, *Logic of Sense* 58–65).

Deleuze rarely addresses himself explicitly to the problematic of modernism and postmodernism, though Negri attributes the most fruitful formulation of that problematic to him and Félix Guattari.[17] Even so, there are moments scattered throughout Deleuze's body of work that, when brought together, constitute both a critique of modernism and an amodernist alternative to it. Let us begin our explication of this critical alternative by considering the following statement, from *Anti-Oedipus:*

> We no longer believe in the myth of the existence of fragments that, like pieces of an antique statue, are merely waiting for the last one to be turned up, so that they may all be glued back together to create a unity that is precisely the same as the original unity. We no longer believe in a primordial totality that once existed, or in a final totality that awaits us at some future date. . . . We believe only in totalities that are peripheral. And if we discover such a totality alongside various separate parts, it is a whole *of* these particular parts but does not totalize them; it is a unity *of* all of these particular parts but does not unify them; rather, it is added to them as a new part fabricated separately. (Deleuze and Guattari, *Anti-Oedipus* 42)

At first glance, this would appear to be a critique of the modernist "mythical method," of a piece with Lyotard's postmodern denunciation of "grand narratives of legitimation," a repudiation of the nostalgia for originary unity that led Eliot to cherish the "fragments I have shored against my ruins" in the hope of reassembling them.

This characterization of the quotation would be adequate if the quotation stopped after the second sentence, but it does not. For in the third sentence Deleuze and Guattari insist that they do in fact "believe . . . in totalities" of the sort that Lyotard dismisses, even and especially if those totalities are "peripheral." What does this mean? It means, as the passage indicates, that totalities do exist, but not at a higher hierarchical level than that of the parts they purport to unify; totalities are produced *immanently,* as parts alongside the heterogeneous parts or fragments that constitute the range of disciplines, objects, and other hybrids invented under modernism. To return to the Sartrean vocabulary adopted earlier, we could say that what appear to be integrated totalities are really necessarily incomplete *processes of totalization.* Deleuze and Guattari use the term "peripheral" to emphasize both the epiphenomenality and the fragility of the processes of totalization that ripple through contemporary society. Peripheral totalizations are real without being either stable or necessary; they function as strategic or heuristic tools for the constitution of new forms of collectivity, in much the same way that "strategic essentialism" acts as a tool in cultural studies.

For Deleuze and Guattari, who have adamantly "remained Marxists" (Deleuze, *Negotiations* 171) when so many others (including Lyotard and Baudrillard) have abandoned the philosophy of praxis, there are actually two different forms of this peripheral process of totalization, the paranoid and the schizophrenic, which can be distinguished by their methods and ends. The paranoid model of totalization corresponds roughly to the Marxist concept of the specifically capitalist mode of production: it is a process of totalization that seeks to maintain the exclusionary rigidity of modernist disciplinary culture as a way of extracting surplus value, a totalization of the fetishized capitalist marketplace that is peripheral in the sense that it is not localizable in space and time but determines the distribution of space and time within capitalist society. The market, which, in the form of a circulation of abstract representations, has expanded (according to Baudrillard) to envelope art and even criticism, is perhaps the most tenacious and pernicious myth of modernism, the myth of a permanent yet flexible totality that is everywhere and nowhere. This paranoid totalization operates according to an "axiomatic," or open-ended set of ad hoc rules for exploitation, which is never fundamentally altered or reorganized, but is simply extended by addition when the rigidity of modernist culture threatens to block profit, according to the tendency, identified by Marx, for the rate of profit to fall within saturated markets.[18] From this point of view, the successes of the

U.S. Civil Rights Movement in the sixties, for example, should be attributed not to a fundamental shift in social ethics, but rather to the need for relatively affluent new groups of consumers to prolong the postwar expansion of the American economy. This would explain why there have been real increases in African American income and educational/career access, which can be managed by the market, but little real decline in exclusionary or racist attitudes, which cannot be so managed.

The schizophrenic model of totalization is just as peripheral as the paranoid version, just as precariously situated, and likely to shift into the paranoid mode. It is a revolutionary mode of totalization, however, because it is conscious of itself as a process without end. It constantly seeks to liquefy the rigid boundaries between disciplines and specializations, to decode completely the overcoded flows of labor and profit that circulate in a restricted fashion throughout the capitalist socius. For example, to the binary, male-female model of human sexuality, which is an axiomatic that is simply extended and reinforced when homosexuality is added as a "lifestyle option," Deleuze and Guattari propose the model of "a thousand tiny sexes" whose very multiplicity and instability would make exploitation prohibitively difficult.[19] The schizophrenic model seeks, not to maximize profit by minimizing change, but to maximize change, to push the flows that capitalism tries to manage to the point at which they overflow and make the extraction of profit and the exercise of control impossible. In this, schizophrenic totalization shares many features with Georges Bataille's conception of a "general economy" of excess and expenditure, a "primitive" model that evades the profit-driven subsumption of capital.[20] Deleuzean schizophrenia pursues this process through the construction and dissemination of revolutionary mass fantasy, fantasy that provides points of accretion for novel kinds of social groups.

The theory of groups in *Anti-Oedipus* is based on Sartre's distinction between two kinds of human ensembles, the *series* and the *group* (or *fused group*). The series is passive and determined in its internal relations by an outside force; Sartre's example is that of a set of people lining up at a bus stop to buy tickets and board, whose seriality is "produced *in advance* as the structure of some unknown group by the ticket machine attached to the bus stop" (Sartre 265). This means that an individual member of the series "*actualises* his being-outside-himself as a reality shared by several people and *which already exists*, and *awaits him*, by means of an inert practice, denoted by instrumentality, whose meaning is that it integrates him into an ordered multiplicity by assigning him a place in a prefabricated seriality" (Sartre 265). In other words, he enters into an already constituted ensemble marked by simple, mechanical repetition ("inert practice" or "instrumentality") whose place in the social organization is wholly determined by the constraints of that organization's structure and requirements ("a place in a prefabricated seriality"). This "inert gathering," Sartre claims, is "the basic type of sociality" (Sartre 348). Deleuze and Guattari's version of the series is the *subjugated group,* which is determined by the preexistent structures that the social order provides; it is predisposed to invest with desire "all of an existing social field, including the latter's most repressive forms" (Deleuze and Guattari, *Anti-Oedipus* 30). In this sense, a group remains subjugated even when seizing power if "this power itself refers to a form of force that continues to enslave and crush desiring-production . . . : the subordination to a socius as a fixed support that attributes to itself the productive forces, extracting and absorbing the surplus value therefrom; the effusion of anti-production and death-carrying elements within the system, which feels and pretends to be all the more immortal; the phenomenon of group 'superegoization,' narcissism, and hierarchy—the mechanisms for the repression of desire" (Deleuze and Guattari, *Anti-Oedipus* 348). We could speak here of ideology as one of the complex forms of investment or fantasy produced by the social system, or "socius," for the purposes of its own reproduction (for the socius is itself an aggregate form of desire), but we could speak equally well of modernist myth, inasmuch as it is presented simultaneously as the permanent ("immortal") base of value and as the legislating superego for the subjugated members of the group.

The alternative to this seriality, in Sartre's terminology, is the *group in fusion* or *fused group.* Such groups are ensembles that are "constituted by the liquidation of an inert seriality under the pressure of definite material circumstances, in so far as particular practico-inert structures of the environment were synthetically united to designate it, that is to say, in so far as its practice was inscribed in things as an inert idea" (Sartre 361). A fused group forms when a series is dissolved by the force of its collision with threatening material circumstances—the products of other series—that create the group as their object. Like the subject in *Being and Nothingness,* the fused group is produced through the look of the Other, but as Jameson notes, the Other in this case is no longer simply the category of objective exteriority but is embodied in the other individual members of the group: "the group no longer has to depend on the look of the outsider or enemy; a structure has been evolved such that the group carries its source of being within itself" (Jameson, *Marxism and Form* 253). The external determination of the series, its unification around an inert and instrumental appendage of the constituted social order, is displaced inward and then reprojected outward toward some material locus that signifies both the danger the group faces and its opportunity to protect itself, as in the case of the storming of the Bastille by the people of Paris during the French Revolution (Sartre 351–63).

The position of Sartre's fused group is held in *Anti-Oedipus* by the *subject-group*, which is distinct from the subjugated group. When confronted by the repressive fantasies provided by the socius or by subjugated groups, the subject-group responds by "launch[ing] a counter-investment whereby revolutionary desire is plugged into the existing social field as a source of energy" (Deleuze and Guattari, *Anti-Oedipus* 30).[21] The existing field is not affirmed, as it is by subjugated groups, but used as a negative base to impel the invention of other structures. "[It] is a group whose libidinal investments are themselves revolutionary; it causes desire to penetrate into the social field, and subordinates the socius or the form of power to desiring-production; productive of desire and a desire that produces, the subject-group invents always mortal formations that exorcise the effusion in it of a death instinct; it opposes real coefficients of transversality to the symbolic determinations of subjugation, coefficients without hierarchy or a group superego" (Deleuze and Guattari, *Anti-Oedipus* 348–349).[22] In other words, the subject-group produces investments that are actively hostile to the rigid structures of the socius. These investments depend not on a reflective consciousness, as they do in Sartre's phenomenological formulation, but on the impersonal connections of desire. Some of these investments take the form of fantasies, but unlike modernist myths, subject-group fantasies are "always mortal," in constant flux, and are incapable of instituting a permanent and restrictive Law. Such fantasies embody what Deleuze will later, in *Cinema-2*, call "the powers of the false."

Deleuze and Guattari emphasize Sartre's key point, which is that the displacement/projection of group determination is not objective but fantasmatic: the Bastille was not simply an objective threat (of military retribution) and promise (of defensive self-armament) to Parisians, and the production of a subject-group through its focus on the Bastille was not a rational and conscious decision made by the heretofore serialized individuals who would make up the group. The Bastille served as a mirror in which the members of the series could see projected their own fears and desires, but it was a mirror that operated at the level of what Jacques Lacan would call the "imaginary," at the level of fantasy, and it is through fantasy that they were fused. The same thing is true of the bus passengers, but their relation is planned and preestablished, not by themselves, but by the structure of the institution into which they enter. Their seriality, in relation to the transit authority, is permanent and indifferent; they are merely generic "passengers." This is the point that Deleuze and Guattari import into *Anti-Oedipus* and their other works: the investment of desire through fantasy can remain enmeshed in institutionalized, serialized ideology, but it can also itself produce group formations that are hostile (though not necessarily opposed, in the strict dialectical sense) to the already given relations of production, class, and subjectivity without necessarily presenting themselves as permanent replacements for those relations. In other words, from this perspective we see that Lacan's psychoanalytic imaginary operates through a fundamental process of misrecognition, but this misrecognition is itself normative, ideological, and mediated by the linguistic and objective category of the Other that produces the subject as an aftereffect. Deleuze and Guattari theorize instead an unmediated desire, free of lack and indifferent to the signifier, that flows as much through institutions and social movements as through Oedipal conflict.

These group fantasies are a specific form of what Deleuze called "simulacra" in the early essay "Plato and the Simulacrum" (Deleuze, *Logic of Sense* 253–66). Deleuze's primary intention in this essay is to distinguish the Platonic doctrine of the well-founded copy from the sophistic simulacrum. According to Deleuze, Plato calls the image of the Idea of Beauty in the soul of the true lover a *copy* of the Idea, in that it constantly testifies to the primacy of its origin in that Idea: the true lover loves that image in the loved object that resembles the Idea of Beauty. The false lover has no such image in her/his soul, and therefore cannot really love; the false lover *simulates* love, in that s/he bears an image that appears to manifest the love of Beauty inspired by its Idea, but has no internal relation to it. In the true lover, the copy-image resembles and preserves the Idea, while in the false lover there is no resemblance whatsoever, but merely an aggression toward the Idea. The logic of the simulacrum does not invert the relation between original and copy, thus making the copy primary, as Derrida argues, but rather inverts or suspends the judgment between copy and simulacrum that validates the former and condemns the latter.[23] The temporary, peripheral totalizations of subject-group fantasy are just such simulacra, which make no appeal to a transcendent Idea but instead function within a plane of immanence. Totalization is an open-ended process rather than a static entity.

The importance of art and literature in such a process of fantasmatic or simulacral invention is decisive: an aesthetic object functions for Deleuze and Guattari not only as an heirloom that bears witness to the historic values of a cultural tradition—that is, as a "document of civilization which is . . . at the same time a document of barbarism" (Benjamin 256)—but also as an intensifier of the decoding process that constitutes schizophrenic totalization. In many cases this intensified decoding participates in the critical revelation of ideological artifice that embraces strategies as diverse as Viktor Shklovsky's analysis of defamiliarization, Bertolt Brecht's "epic theater" of alienation, and Derrida's destructuring of metaphysical oppositions. More powerful artworks, like those on which Deleuze often focuses, can actually provide fantasmatic alternatives to the constituted socius that can inspire revolutionary subject-groups capable of undertaking the transformation of material practices. The relation of artworks and subject-groups is akin to the relation of theory and practice, as Deleuze and Foucault have displaced it. "At one time, practice was considered an application of theory, a consequence," while at others "it was thought to inspire theory, to be indispensable for the creation of future theoretical forms." For Deleuze and Foucault, however, the relation is different:

> On one side, a theory is always local and related to a limited field, and it is applied in another sphere, more or less distant from it. The relationship which holds in the application of a theory is never one of resemblance. Moreover, from the moment a theory moves into its proper domain, it begins to encounter obstacles . . . which require its relay by another type of discourse. . . . Practice is a set of relays from one theoretical point to another, and theory is a relay from one practical point to another. No theory can develop without eventually encountering a wall, and practice is necessary for piercing this wall. (Deleuze and Foucault 205–6)

If the obstacle or wall, from the point of view of postmodernism, is the absence of legitimating narratives (according to Lyotard) or the disappearance of any group that could act as Marx's "subject of history" (according to Baudrillard), then Deleuze's (and Guattari's) solution lies in the potentiality of art, on an equal footing with philosophy and science, to produce new social subject-groups: "Art . . . must take part in this task: not that of addressing a people, which is presupposed already there, but of contributing to the invention of a people. The moment the master, or the colonizer, proclaims 'There have never been people here', the missing people are a becoming, they invent themselves, in shanty towns and camps, or in ghettos, in new conditions of struggle to which a necessarily political art must contribute" (Deleuze, *Cinema-2* 217). Art provides flexible, local micronarratives, rather than a master narrative, of the liberation of desire. The proclamation "There have never been people here," which catalyzes the invention of art and consequently of a people, comes not only from the master and colonizer, but also from the postmodern critic: Baudrillard's thesis of the "implosion of the social in the media" abets this consolidation of power even as it claims to analyze it.

Deleuze's theory of forms of art that "contribut[e] to the invention of a people" in cinematic, plastic, and literary terms is fundamentally a theory of fiction or fabulation.[24] In *Cinema-2: The Time-Image,* he elaborates on the "powers of the false" that he locates in the postwar cinema. Classical cinema, like classical literature, depends on organic narration: "Organic narration consists of the development of sensory-motor schemata as a result of which the characters react to situations or act in such a way as to disclose the situation. This is a truthful narration in the sense that it claims to be true, even in fiction. . . . Truthful narration is developed organically, according to legal connections in space and chronological connections in time. . . . [N]arration implies an inquiry or testimonies which connect it to the true . . . [and it] always refers to a *system of judgement*" (Deleuze, *Cinema-2* 127, 133). This system of judgment is fundamentally the same as Plato's judgment against simulacra: truthful narration links events deterministically, according to resemblance and exclusion. Time, in this form of narration, is represented indirectly, through the movement of subjects in action; thus it is inferred from the transformation of space.

In the "crystalline narration" of postwar literature and cinema, on the other hand, the sensory-motor schemata—the identifications of subjects with actions on the screen or in the text—collapse into representations of images not linked by subjective action and give way to nonlocal relations that present direct, subjectless images of time, from which the active movements themselves now derive. Narration no longer "claims to be true," but rather "becomes fundamentally falsifying": "Falsifying narration, by contrast, frees itself from this system [of judgment]; it shatters the system of judgements because the power of the false (not error or doubt) affects the investigator and witness as much as the person presumed guilty. . . . Narration is constantly being completely modified, in each of its episodes, not according to subjective variations, but as a consequence of disconnected places and de-chronologized moments" (Deleuze, *Cinema-2* 133). It is not simply a matter of the narrator's unreliability, which has always depended upon an implied norm of narrative reliability, but of the problematization of narration itself. Traditional truthful narration, whether fictional or historical, insists on what G. W. Leibniz called "compossibility," the creation of simple and consistent story lines through the exclusion of incompatible alternatives. As the sinologist in Jorge Luis Borges's "Garden of Forking Paths" says, "In all fiction, when a man is faced with alternatives he chooses one at the expense of the others" (Borges 98). For Deleuze, the "power of the false . . . replaces and supersedes the form of the true, because it poses the simultaneity of incompossible presents, or the co-existence of not-necessarily true pasts. Crystalline description was already reaching the indiscernibility of the real and the imaginary, but the falsifying narration which corresponds to it goes a step further and poses inexplicable differences to the present and alternatives which are undecidable between true and false to the past" (Deleuze, *Cinema-2* 131). His model of fiction demands a subject who does not exclude alternatives but rather "chooses—simultaneously—all of them. He thus *creates* various futures, various times which start others that will in their turn branch out and bifurcate in other times" (Borges 98). Narration is freed from the despotism of compossibility and multiplied, producing a fertile network of potential trajectories through time.

Fiction is freed from the rigidity of its determinants and becomes something akin to improvisational jazz. The improviser chooses not only the present note to play, but the imaginary structure out of which it would have come and into which it will flow: "If I play a C and have it in my mind as the tonic, that's what it will become. If I want it to be a minor third or a major seventh that had a tendency to resolve upward, then the quality of the note will change."[25] Neither the structure of the past nor the structure of the future is given in advance; either can be manipulated in the present to produce different states of affairs. This is the role that artworks can play in the present, the role of fantasmatic structures that alter the direction and speed of the present moment by altering the past trajectory on which the present would have to travel. This multiplication of narrative lines and suspension of the unifying horizons of subjective consciousness and formal closure cannot be reduced to the superficial fragmentation of modernist style. Even collage, whether visual or literary, constitutes a higher-order project of unity that Deleuze, like Adorno, recognizes in modernist techniques: "the folding of one text onto another, which constitutes multiple and even adventitious roots (like a cutting), implies a supplementary dimension to that of the texts under consideration. In this supplementary dimension of folding, unity continues its spiritual labor. That is why the most resolutely fragmented work can also be presented as the Total Work or Magnum Opus" (Deleuze and Guattari, *A Thousand Plateaus* 6). The goal, then, is not permanent escape from unity or from closure, but the construction of strategic false unity, fantasmatic totalization, that can provide a focus and a material form for investments of desire that, in pursuing their own ends, also transform the socius. The purpose of art, for Deleuze, is to enable us "To reach, not the point where one no longer says I, but the point where it is no longer of any importance whether one says I" (Deleuze and Guattari, *A Thousand Plateaus* 3). This is also the purpose of amodernism: to further the production of subject-groups that can extend the differences that already fissure the capitalist socius into irreparable cracks. Such cracks are already the objects of William S. Burroughs's analyses in his first novels, *Junky* and *Queer.*

Chapter Two

No Final Glossary

Fugitive Words in *Junky* and *Queer*

"I awoke from The Sickness at the age of forty-five, calm and sane, and in reasonably good health except for a weakened liver and the look of borrowed flesh common to all who survive The Sickness" (*NL* xxxvii).[1] So begins the introduction to *Naked Lunch,* the book that established William S. Burroughs's literary notoriety and that still dominates it almost half a century and twenty books later. For most readers, Burroughs's career begins (and ends) with *Naked Lunch,* and even those who are aware of the texts that preceded it have only rarely granted those texts serious study. This situation is doubly unfortunate in that these early autobiographical novels, written before Burroughs was forty, not only provide "raw material" for the later formally experimental novels (as the few studies existent have shown), but also lay out, in precise historical detail and with telegraphic clarity, the social stakes, perils, and gambits of a literature and a criticism in the process of becoming amodern. These social variables, presented literally (in a fashion Burroughs will later describe as "factual") in the early novels *Junky* and *Queer* (both completed in 1953), form an equation that feeds back and complicates itself, ultimately giving rise to Burroughs's famous definition of the "Algebra of Need" in *Naked Lunch.* "Junk," Burroughs writes in *Junky,* "is a cellular equation that teaches the user facts of general validity" (xvi).

To learn the equation, its variables, and thus the general facts to which it grants one access without actually becoming a user of junk, the reader must make a journey through the terrain in which the junky and the queer flourish, a landscape defined by modern architecture and law, in equal measure. Both *Junky* and *Queer* portray the underworlds of North America in the forties and fifties: black-market economies of the flesh and spirit that implicitly parody the rising American consumer society. Burroughs made these underworlds his home for nearly a decade, and he writes of them with a participant's familiarity. The reader must witness and learn to understand, at Burroughs's insistence, the operation of "a way of life, a vocabulary, references, a whole symbol system, as the sociologists say" (*J* xiii). Burroughs himself often adopts the stereotypically modern role of sociologist or anthropologist, describing and analyzing the signs and events of the junky's daily routine—as well as the medical and legal institutions that seek to interpret those signs and control those events—from an "objective" point of view that differs from the viewpoints of his subjects. To this end, Burroughs both writes in and comments on the "hip" or "jive" idiom of the urban junky, even going so far as to provide a glossary of hip expressions in an appendix. The glossary—and the novel—concludes with a caveat, however, that calls this analytical objectivity into question: "It should be understood that the meanings of these words are subject to rapid changes, and that a word that has one hip meaning one year may have another the next. The hip sensibility mutates. . . . Not only do the words change meanings but meanings vary locally at the same time. A final glossary, therefore, cannot be made of words whose intentions are fugitive" (*J* 158). The fact that words change in meaning through time would not pose a problem for Ferdinand de Saussure or his structuralist progeny; the modern science of linguistics, and the more general science of signs, is predicated on the distinction between synchronic and diachronic, and only the simultaneous, synchronic structure of a "langue" is a fit object of semiological study. But in Burroughs's hip world, synchrony has no place: "meanings vary locally at the same time." The junky's language is a minor language, in Deleuze and Guattari's terminology: one that turns a dominant language against itself by putting its rules into a state of flux.[2] No abstract structure of rules, no langue exists, so no "final glossary" or general semiology is possible—only a cartography or topography that can follow the discontinuous flights of "words whose intentions are fugitive."

Let us approach this fugitive cartography first through the urban spaces involved. This is the junky's terrain, the phantom New York of *Junky* that shares the physical grid of streets and addresses with the New York(s) of Fiorello LaGuardia, Jackson Pollock, and Lionel Trilling, but subsists less in the separate destinations than in the open spaces *between*, the adjacent or transitional spaces: street corners, subway stations, doctors' waiting rooms, Skid Row bars, and short-term slum apartments—the whole itinerary of the addict. Like Mexico City, the primary setting of *Queer,* Burroughs's New York is "a terminal of space-time travel, a waiting room where you grab a quick drink while you wait for your train. That is why I can stand to be in Mexico City or New York. You are not stuck there; by the fact of being there at all, you are traveling" (*Q* 131–32). These underdetermined, liminal features of urban topography are among the most significant unanticipated legacies of economic modernization—the methodical effort to produce a manageable urban space that could efficiently house, transport, and maintain the masses of people sufficient to drive an emergent industrial and, later, consumer economy.[3] In Burroughs's novels, these liminal spaces form the stage for a critical social drama: the recognition that it was precisely the *manageability* of modern urban space (an aspect of what Burroughs later calls "control") that had fallen into crisis by the middle decades of this century, as a result of the de facto segregation of ethnic groups and the chasm between classes, both of which conflicts had been obscured during the Depression and the ensuing war years. This crisis—or rather the means that managerial institutions adopted to avert the crisis—forms the efficient cause and immediate context of *Junky* and *Queer.*

The first drug deal "William Lee" (Burroughs's pseudonymous narrator, given Burroughs's mother's maiden name)[4] recounts begins in the "Angle Bar" (*J* 2), the very name of which confirms its position between other determined and determining spaces. Like the subway tunnel and tenement apartment where the deal continues, the bar (and the other more or less indistinguishable spaces in which the novel's action plays itself out) is *underdetermined* in that its social function—its place in the managed urban environment—is essentially ambiguous: the bar is a space of leisure, the subway a space of transport, and the tenement a space of general reproduction for the laboring public; but they are all also semiprivate spaces that can harbor, at least temporarily, activities and agents that undermine the productive economic order that encompasses and totalizes those separate spaces. Even a street corner is semiprivate in this sense. Consider the symmetrical dynamics of junky-doctor relations, enacted in the liminal space of the doctor's waiting room:

> Doctors are so exclusively nurtured on exaggerated ideas of their position that, generally speaking, a factual approach is the worst possible. Even though they do not believe your story, nevertheless they want to hear one. It is like some Oriental face-saving ritual. One man plays the high-minded doctor who wouldn't write an unethical script for a thousand dollars, the other does his best to act like a legitimate patient. If you say, "Look, Doc, I want an M.S.

> script and I'm willing to pay double price for it," the croaker blows his top and throws you out of the office. You need a good bedside manner with doctors or you will get nowhere. (*J* 21)[5]

Even in the somewhat more determined space of the doctor's office, where activities and roles are generally delineated in advance, a kind of negotiation takes place that, if successful, subtly undoes the official hierarchy and displaces the doctor from his controlling position in the totality. This negotiation, this immobile displacement, is the fundamental operation that the junky performs on the semiprivate spaces that constitute his world. Negotiation of this sort even spawns an institutional space of its own, in the form of the Lexington Narcotics Farm in Kentucky, where junkies can consign themselves to a government-run timed reduction cure for addiction: despite its intention to provide junkies with a way to quit, the Lexington facility is used by many junkies merely as a temporary vacation from junk, a way to keep their habits manageable (*J* 59–68). They are not averse to using the state's beds and the state's morphine, but they do not use them as the state would like.

Given the structure of the capitalist economy, it is possible and indeed necessary for previously determined spaces, public or private, to be taken over by antiproductive agents, though these spaces do not necessarily then become underdetermined. For example, Lee refers to an "Irish pusher who started out capping a 1/16 ounce envelope of H and two years later, when he took a fall and went away for three years, he had thirty thousand dollars and an apartment building in Brooklyn" (*J* 41). Lee himself operates as a pusher out of a transient hotel, where the clerk warns him to be careful of his clientele: "'I used to be in illegitimate business myself years ago. I just wanted to warn you to be careful. You know, all calls come through the office. I heard one this morning and it was pretty obvious'" (*J* 56). The transition from illegitimate to legitimate business, it seems, must pass through semiprivate liminal spaces. At the novel's end, in Mexico City, a nameless Mexican politician even asks Lee if he knows "anyone who might be interested to buy an ounce of heroin" (*J* 149). Lee does not register any surprise at this, and in fact reports during the deal that "People meanwhile were walking in and out of the [politician's] office. Nobody paid us any mind sitting there on the couch with our sleeves rolled up, probing for veins with the needle. Anything can happen in the office of a Mexican politician" (*J* 150). The spatial progression of the novel, from street corners and one-night cheap hotels through the middle-class waiting rooms of doctors to the corridors of political power, recapitulates the widening gyre of the crisis: the rationalized decomposition of social space into ghettoes for specialized (economic, ethnic, and/or gendered) human contents gives rise to discontinuous communities of antiproductive agents like the pusher and the junky, who can use the rationalization of the spatial structure against itself. At the limit, all of social space—even the space occupied by the institutional managers of space, such as the politician—can become antiproductive.

The liminal spaces cannot fully determine what goes on within them, which is why the police enter the picture: as agents of the productive totality, they attempt to stabilize the relations and functions required of the liminal spaces by that totality. They mediate between the institutions of control and the spaces to be controlled. The control, or discipline, imposed by the police in order to stabilize the liminal spaces is a fundamentally *temporal* control. What makes the liminal spaces available to antiproductive agents like the junky is not the spaces' interiority or their particular locations, but regular gaps in the temporal pattern of surveillance undertaken by the police (and their surrogates). As Burroughs writes in *The Soft Machine (SM),* "The police never mesh with present time, their investigation far removed from the city always before or after the fact erupt into any café and machine-gun the patrons" (*SM* 160).[6] The police move through the liminal spaces—especially the streets, bars, and subway tunnels—according to a relatively regular rhythm, a pulse or "beat" that the junky must anticipate and complement; the junky plays a syncopated rhythm, as in ragtime or jazz, against the regular beat of the police. Thus, junky social organization is necessarily discontinuous, improvisatory, and not rigidly structured or centered.

Correlatively, the same rationalization of space the police are responsible for preserving brings them into contradiction with themselves. Lee is arrested only twice in the course of *Junky* (once in New York and once in New Orleans), but he and his junky compatriots are constantly on the lookout for the police. In New York, Lee is charged with a violation of Public Health Law 334, for "giving a wrong name on a prescription" during one of his negotiations with a doctor (*J* 27), and he is held in the Tombs—scene of Bartleby's death—for several days, during which he begins to go through withdrawal before his wife bails him out. He receives a four-month suspended sentence (*J* 41) because lying on a prescription is "a misdemeanor in New York" (*J* 85), as he tells the policemen who arrest him in New Orleans. That second arrest is more serious than the first: Lee is charged with possession of marijuana and heroin, and with the use of a vehicle in the commission of a felony drug purchase (because he drove his car to the pusher's neighborhood, *J* 93–94). This second arrest also exemplifies the contradictions, both banal and significant, within law enforcement institutions: on the banal side, Lee's lawyer pays off some of the detectives involved in return for crucial false testimony in the case (*J* 96). More significantly, Lee makes a deal with the New Orleans police, promising to "show [them] where the stuff is" if they give their "word that the case will be tried in Federal [court]" (*J* 84); the state police give their word, but the federal attorney refuses to prosecute because "there's an illegal seizure involved" (*J* 94) and thereby undermines the state attorney's case. The different levels of the law enforcement institution come into conflict in a way that can work in the junky's favor: the gaps between their respective jurisdictions—the spaces over which they exercise legal management—can become antiproductive spaces as well.

Despite such useful contradictions in law enforcement, the junky's existence is precarious at best, with his living spaces threatened by the police outside as well as by informers—"pigeons" or "stoolies"—inside his group, who make the landscape radically unstable. The line between inside and outside, between clandestinity and authority, is in constant flux. Lee outlines the logic of the informer as one of the mediators between the hierarchical police milieu and the discontinuous junky topography:

> Narcotics agents operate largely with the aid of informers. The usual routine is to grab someone with junk on him, and let him stew in jail until he is good and sick. Then comes the spiel:
>
> "We can get you five years for possession. On the other hand, you can walk out of here right now. The decision is up to you. If you work with us, we can give you a good deal. For one thing, you'll have plenty of junk and pocket money. . . . "
>
> Some of them don't need to be pressured. . . . The new pigeon is given marked money and sent out to make a buy. When the pigeon makes a buy with this money, the agents close in right away to make the arrest. . . . If the case is important enough, the pigeon may be called upon to testify. Of course, once he appears in court and testifies, the pigeon is known to the trade and no one will serve him. Unless the agents want to send him to another town (some especially able pigeons go on tour), his informing career is finished. . . . When this happens, his usefulness to the agents is at an end, and they usually turn him in. (*J* 56–57)

The narcotics agents are in the contradictory position of having to support an addict for some time in order to capture others, and though the agents do resolve this particular contradiction in the end by jailing the informer, the temporal and logical space it opens up leads to greater contradictions.

The institution of the police necessarily raises the formal question of the law that it nominally enforces, the determinations it attempts to impose on liminal spaces. If the architectural dimensions of the crisis of control can be measured in the increasing stratification and rigidity of modern ghettoes (both ethnic and economic), its legal dimensions come into focus most clearly in the joint efforts of American legislative and law enforcement organizations to criminalize a number of activities that were previously of marginal interest to the legal community. The most infamous of these efforts was, of course, the drive to criminalize "un-American activities," which was to culminate in the House Un-American Activities Committee (HUAC) investigations of the fifties—which Burroughs followed carefully. More relevant to *Junky* is a different criminalization effort: the criminalization of addiction. The two projects of criminalization were often identified with each other, however. Much has been written on the metaphorical economy of addiction in Burroughs's writings through the early sixties, but very little has been said about his legal economy of addiction. This is surprising, since Burroughs provides the reader not only with narratives explicitly involving this legal aspect, but also with precise criticisms of the particular laws—primarily New York Public Health Law 334 and the Harrison Narcotics Act—that contributed to the creation of the liminal and discontinuous "junky ghetto" through which he moved for nearly a decade.

The use of drugs—both narcotics and stimulants—was widespread in Europe and the U.S. during the late nineteenth century. In fiction, Sherlock Holmes injected a seven percent solution of cocaine whenever his cases failed to hold his interest, and Freud's earliest fame came as a result of his psychological cure for cocaine dependency as well as his use of cocaine in the treatment of certain disorders. Both examples attest to the fact that drug use, like alcoholism, was a marginally acceptable (if alarming) social habit as long as it remained a monopoly of the aristocracy and middle class—that is, as long as it did not interfere directly with labor production. World War I saw the first widespread use of many chemical substances in mass medical practice, including the use of morphine as a painkiller; many early addicts to heroin ("junk"), called "old-time junkies" in Lee's circle, were working-class soldiers and sailors who had developed their habits as a result of morphine treatment for combat injuries. Before World War II, these old-time junkies already formed a sizable subculture, marked by transient living arrangements and petty theft to support heroin habits. Lee's very first experience with opiates came as a result of his employment as a fence for a naval shipyard thief: the thief brings Lee a tommy gun to sell, and also offers him "something else [he] picked up . . . a flat yellow box with five one-half grain syrettes of morphine tartrate" (*J* 2). Before becoming a heroin dealer himself, Lee gets money to support his habit by "working the hole" (that is, the subway) as a "lush worker," a thief who preys on unconscious drunks (*J* 33–40).

The problem from the legislative point of view, as Burroughs realized, was not drug use per se; this could be seen in the repeal of Prohibition and the refusal of legislatures to recriminalize alcoholism when further antidrug sentiment arose.

> In 1937, weed was placed under the Harrison Narcotics Act. Narcotics authorities claim it is a habit-forming drug, that its use is injurious to mind and body, and that it causes the people who use it to commit crimes. Here are the facts: Weed is positively not habit-forming. You can smoke weed for years and you will experience no discomfort if your supply is suddenly cut off. . . . Weed does not harm the general health. In fact, most users claim it gives you an appetite and acts as a tonic to the system. . . . Weed does not inspire anyone to commit crimes. I have never seen anyone get nasty under the influence of weed. . . . I cannot understand why the people who claim weed causes crimes do not follow through and demand the outlawing of alcohol. Every day, crimes are committed by drunks who would not have committed the crime sober. (*J* 18)

Instead of being criminalized strictly on the basis of the crimes committed under their influence, drugs were classified according to their medical effects on the human body, and the sedatives, or narcotics (minus alcohol), were singled out for particular legal attention. Thus the Harrison Narcotics Act of 1914, among other statutes, outlawed many narcotics and made others available only by prescription (hence New York Public Health Law 334).[7] The real problem these laws were intended to address was not the negative medical effects of drug use, however, but rather the "proletarianization" of drug use that followed the introduction of government-financed, mass-produced painkillers and the consequent subculture of transience, lost production, and theft that arose around the stigmatized narcotics.

This is not to suggest that alcoholism was only a middle-class problem and this is the reason it was not criminalized; indeed, there were and are plenty of working-class alcoholics. Alcoholism as a social problem of production cut across class lines, however, in a way that narcotic addiction did not (or so it was widely believed): narcotic addiction, a vice of the "lower" classes, could therefore be used as a marker of class stigma, particularly as the subculture of addiction based itself on theft rather than on productive labor. This class stigma was overdetermined by moral stigma as narcotic addicts were literally demonized: they were labeled "fiends" (*J* viii, 64) and imagined to inhabit an infernal urban underworld of indulgence and crime that, perversely, was thought to make them *politically* subversive.[8] In New Orleans, one of Lee's random acquaintances hyperbolically dramatizes this strange connection between addiction and radicalism when he asks if Lee knows "how narcotics ties right in with Communism" (*J* 70). Lee asks him to specify, and the man, who believes Lee himself to be a federal narcotics agent, replies that "the same people are in both narcotics and Communism. Right now they control most of America. I'm a seaman. I've been shipping out for twenty years. Who gets the jobs over there in the NMU Hall? American white men like you and me? No. Dagos and Spiks and Niggers. Why? Because the union controls shipping, and the Communists control the union" (*J* 71). The man's paranoid fantasy welds the rationalization of ghettoes to the criminalization both of "un-American activities" and of addiction in a vast conspiracy that would be an absurdity were it not that the institutions of control themselves seemed to accept the idea of such a conspiracy.

Thus, the criminalization of addiction functions as a key tactic of a new strategy for managing modern urban space, as Lee makes plain: "When I jumped bail and left the States, the heat on junk already looked like something new and special. Initial symptoms of nationwide hysteria were clear. Louisiana passed a law making it a crime to be a drug addict. Since no place or time is specified and the term "addict" is not clearly defined, no proof is necessary or even relevant under a law so formulated. No proof, and consequently, no trial. This is police-state legislation penalizing a state of being. Other states were emulating Louisiana" (*J* 142). Burroughs is by no means reluctant to admit the dangers of addiction; on one level, *Junky* is virtually a catalog of the negative medical and social effects of heroin addiction on the individual. But these effects are insufficient to account for the virulence of the "anti-junk feeling [that] mounted to a paranoid obsession, like anti-Semitism under the Nazis" (*J* 142). This simile is not made idly, in hyperbole or ignorance; Burroughs had some first-hand experience with Nazism. After graduating from Harvard, he visited Austria and Yugoslavia in 1936–37, shortly before the *Anschluss* that joined them to

Nazi Germany, and there married Ilse Klapper, a German Jew, so that she could get a visa to leave Europe for the U.S.; they never lived together but remained friends, and were amicably divorced after she returned to Europe in late 1945 (Morgan 64–71). Like Nazi anti-Semitism, anti-junk paranoia is both an end in itself—a judgment against junkies—and a means to another end: a method of reasserting unified control over all the fragmented space of society.

We should be leery of the idea, suggested by some of Burroughs's readers in the late sixties, that the junky represents a kind of revolutionary figure simply because of the enormous apparatus of institutional power that is mobilized to constrain him and modify his behavior. Burroughs is actually quite clear on this issue: the junky is not revolutionary because he is not so much subversive as *antiproductive*. The junky does not attempt, consciously and radically, either to alter the constituted social organization of space and labor or to offer an alternative organization; rather, he takes advantage of the gaps and lacunae in the spatial and institutional organization in order to survive without contributing directly to production. He turns on and drops out. The junky consumes without producing, in a symmetrical parody of the capitalist managerial class; this parasitism is at the heart of Burroughs's well-documented metaphorical economy of addiction. Thus the junky is as dependent on the structure of industrial (and consumer) capitalism as the traditional entrepreneur is; indeed, we saw above that there was no insurmountable barrier between legitimate enterprise and illegitimate enterprise because they both pass by way of liminal spaces, and they are both ultimately measured only in general equivalence: in money (about which, as Marx said of wheat, we cannot tell how it was raised on the basis of its mere presence). Anti-junk/anti-junky paranoia, then, reflects not the anxiety of capitalist society over the threat of its revolutionary negation or undoing, but its anxiety over its own symmetrical repetition, its own image in a glass, darkly.

Not only is capitalist society haunted by the junky, its phantom double, but also capitalist society haunts the junky. After he has jumped bail in New Orleans and fled to Mexico City, Lee experiences a psychotic episode during the bout of alcoholism that follows one of his attempts to "kick" his heroin habit. He gets into an argument with a middle-class Mexican man, who threatens to turn Lee in to the police as a junky. Enraged, Lee returns to his apartment for a large pistol, with which he threatens the man until a policeman intervenes.

> I shoved the gun in the cop's stomach.
> "Who asked you to put in your two cents?" I asked in English. I was not talking to a solid three-dimensional cop. I was talking to the recurrent cop of my dreams—an irritating, nondescript, darkish man who would rush in when I was about to take a shot or go to bed with a boy. (*J* 130)

Lee has internalized the police function, but not fully enough to become a good citizen, for whom the ideology of the police is a second nature that controls his first. The dream cop does not limit Lee's extralegal activities any more than the demonized drug fiend limits the avarice of capital; the phantoms merely color their victims' existences with accusation, hostility, and terror.

American society's desperate anti-junk paranoia, which justifies the criminalization of addiction as a state of being, simultaneously inverts its own logic and gives rise to the figure who resolves, in parodic fashion, the antagonism between the junky and the police, between clandestinity and authority, and in so doing reveals the junky's complicity with the constituted order. This is the figure who will take center stage in Burroughs's fiction through the early sixties: the addict-agent.

> Now that the Narcotics Bureau has taken it upon itself to incarcerate every addict in the U.S., they need more agents to do the work. Not only more agents, but a different type of agent. Like during prohibition, when bums and hoodlums flooded the Internal Revenue Department, now addict-agents join the department for free junk and immunity. It is difficult to fake addiction. An addict knows an addict. The addict-agents manage to conceal their addiction, or, perhaps, they are tolerated because they get results. An agent who has to connect or go sick will bring a special zeal to his work. (*J* 144)

The addict-agent "resolves" the fundamental antagonism between the junky and the cop by becoming both at once, or rather by alternating between them; this resolution is parodic, however, because it remains merely formal and does nothing to transcend or eliminate the conflict. In this sense it might be better to say that the addict-agent is *paradoxical,* in Deleuze's sense of the term: a *paradox* is the irreducible coexistence of contradictory attributes in the same object, and as such is distinct from Kant's *antinomy,* in which contradictory attributes bear on slightly different objects, and from Hegel's *dialectic,* in which contradictory attributes bearing on the same object are reduced to an abstract resolution. The addict-agent is not *übermenschlich,* or revolutionary, and does not represent the transcending of the contradictions of postwar American society; he is rather the internalization, the preservation, and the extension of a conflict which cannot be resolved dialectically: the conflict between an accelerating dialectic of control and exploitation and an immanent community of desire that has not *yet* become revolutionary.

•

If *Junky* aspires to be a modern sociological analysis of such an unresolvable dialectic, *Queer* is Burroughs's first abortive attempt to elaborate such an idea of community. It is abortive for three reasons: first, because the text, as it has been published, seems to be unfinished; second, because the community narrated never achieves consummation; and third, because the novel, originally intended as a companion piece to *Junky,* was refused by the publishers and did not appear in print until 1985. This historical displacement brought *Queer* to light at precisely the point in Burroughs's career when he had returned to the problem of community for the first time since abandoning it after *Queer*'s failure. At this juncture, however, our task is to follow Burroughs's "fugitive words" in their transformation from sociological description into fictional invention, and his personal transformation from confessed criminal into literary revolutionary.

As Burroughs notes in his introduction to the novel, the behavior of the protagonist, Lee, will appear psychotic if its context is forgotten: he is a junky trying to kick his habit, and "When the cover is removed, everything that has been held in check by junk spills out" (*Q* xiii). Withdrawal means loss of control over the self, the body, and the outside world, as passages from *Junky* show: "The envelope of personality was gone, dissolved by his junk-hungry cells. Viscera and cells, galvanized into a loathsome insect-like activity, seemed on the point of breaking through the surface. His face was blurred, unrecognizable, at the same time shrunken and tumescent. . . . He did not have the concentration of energy necessary to hold himself together and his organism was always on the point of disintegrating into its component parts" (*J* 58, 100). This period of transition generally passes, leaving the junky exhausted but functional, in both the medical and economic senses. His body reorganizes itself, going from an antiproductive to a potentially productive state. Burroughs also writes in *Junky* that "Junk short-circuits sex" (*J* 124), and so withdrawal results in the often abrupt reconnection of the sexual circuits. Often the recovering junky will experience spontaneous orgasm, as Lee does during enforced temporary withdrawal in jail: "Sparks exploded behind my eyes; my legs twitched—the orgasm of a hanged man when the neck snaps" (*J* 94). This returning desire, after its long absence, often seems quite alien to the junky: at one point, Lee describes his lust as "an amoeboid protoplasmic projection, straining with a blind worm hunger to enter the other's body, to breathe with his lungs, see with his eyes, learn the feel of his viscera and genitals" (*Q* 36). Even when withdrawal is well under way, Lee complains that "'I want myself the same way I want others. I'm disembodied. I can't use my own body for some reason'" (*Q* 99).

Thus, *Queer* opens with Lee's frank assessments of the various "boys" who inspire his renascent sexual desire, including Eugene Allerton, the young man who serves as the primary focus for this desire and for the narrative desires that accompany the sexual ones. For junk blocks more than just sexual desire: "The drive to non-sexual sociability comes from the same place sex comes from, so when I have an H or M shooting habit I am non-sociable. If someone wants to talk, O.K. But there is no drive to get acquainted. When I come off the junk, I often run through a period of uncontrolled sociability and talk to anyone who will listen" (*J* 124–25). This statement explains why junkies do not form a community, and why the issue of community could not really be raised in *Junky* but had to await its own separate elaboration in *Queer:* junk negates sociability. *Queer* is the sequel to *Junky,* then, because intense sexual desire is the necessary physical sequel to heroin addiction, but also because compulsive speaking is the necessary social sequel to junk-imposed silence.[9] The connection Lee seeks, his embryonic community, is essentially communicative, for as Deleuze notes, "homosexuality is not production of desire without being at the same time formation of utterances. It's the same thing, to produce desire and to form new utterances."[10] In blocking this formation of utterances, junk abets the societal repression of homosexual desire just as its economy mimics capitalist enterprise; the silence it produces, however, is only one of many silences shrouding that desire (Sedgwick 3–4).

Despite this logical and symptomatological continuity, there is an important formal difference between the narrative of *Junky* and that of *Queer:* the former is recounted in the first person, while the latter, with the exception of its epilogue, is recounted in a third-person voice that is almost always limited to Lee's perspective. This distinction already implies the critique of subjectivity that Burroughs will elaborate in his later works, according to which subjectivity itself is a form of addiction to language, to the "I" of self-consciousness and identity as an instrument of control, both of the phenomenal world by the "I" and of the "I" itself by the ideological structure of its socius. The junky's silent socio-pathology bears witness to the power of this instrument of control. Burroughs summarizes his critique by reporting that "While it was I who wrote *Junky,* I feel that I was being written in *Queer*" (*Q* xiv). Hence when addiction is overcome by subjective effort or by an outside force (such as incarceration), the subject is "disintegrated" (*Q* xii), and its activities can only be narrated from the outside, in third person. "As Lee stood aside to bow in his dignified old-world greeting, there emerged instead a leer of naked lust, wrenched in the pain and hate of his deprived body and, in simultaneous double exposure, a sweet child's smile of liking and trust, shockingly out of time and out of place, mutilated and hopeless" (*Q* 18). In the absence of a governing addiction, the self is always an other, if not many others.

Once we see the otherness inherent in the self as it is revealed by withdrawal, Lee's tactics in wooing Allerton immediately become clearer. Having fallen from the pure state of junk-induced control, he must regain a much more precarious kind of control over his personal relations, just as he has had to regain control of his subjectivity and his body by treating them as fundamentally alien *objects;* his social circuits need to be reconnected as much as his sexual circuits did. In his transitional state, however, such connections function only intermittently, and he cannot rely on them.[11] Lee must reestablish contact with the otherness of other people in the same way as he reestablishes contact with his own internal otherness: by dramatizing it. To this end he deploys obscene and satirical comic monologues called "routines." These "routines" allow him to make simple one-way contact with other people while shielding him from the demands of reciprocal interpersonal relations, for which his addiction has left him unprepared. Allerton suspects this asymmetry from the beginning of his relationship with Lee: "He was now forced to ask himself: 'What does he want from me?' . . . He decided finally that Lee valued him as an audience" (*Q* 27). Initially, Lee employs these routines merely to amuse Allerton and keep his attention, but soon Lee is using them do things that would otherwise be quite difficult, like revealing his "queerness" to Allerton.

> "The Lees have always been perverts. I shall never forget the unspeakable horror that froze the lymph in my glands—the lymph glands that is, of course—when the baneful word seared my reeling brain: I was a homosexual. I thought of the painted, simpering female impersonators I had seen in a Baltimore night club. Could it be possible that I was one of those subhuman things? I walked the streets in a daze, like a man with a light concussion—just a minute, Doctor Kildare, this isn't your script. . . . " (*Q* 39).

The final parenthetical reflection reveals its generic origin: the routine arises not from radio and television's Kildare but from another, equally well established script, the psychiatric "confession" of deviance. This routine is less a coming-out narrative than a simultaneous parody of a coming-out narrative and of a confession of homosexual psychopathology (of the sort that became relatively common in the supposedly "tolerant" United States of the fifties);[12] it demonstrates Burroughs's mocking sense of American social conformity as well as his long-standing hostility (only partially masked by irony) toward effeminate homosexuals.[13] Lee brings the routine to a sentimental climax by quoting his invented mentor, the late queen "Bobo," to the effect that "'No one is ever really alone. You are part of everything alive.'"[14] This dramatizes, in a relatively neutral way, his sense that his subjectivity is somehow split, somehow alien to him, but he concludes with a provocative question that is also a bald proposition: "The difficulty is to convince someone else he is really part of you, so what the hell? Us parts ought to work together. Reet?" (*Q* 40).

This striking passage may help us to understand why Burroughs, despite being one of the most consistently visible and vocal American queer writers of the last forty years, has been virtually ignored by critics involved in the recent explosion of "queer theory." The apparent reasons for this generalized avoidance (which are, admittedly, conjectural and have been extrapolated from other arguments and tropes) are all bound up in the form and substance of the routine, and of *this* routine in particular. First, most accounts of queer experience cited by queer theorists are fundamentally phenomenological, even when they claim to be epistemological; for example, Eve Sedgwick's sophisticated and useful "epistemology of the closet" is predicated on a paradoxical phenomenology of homosexual experience within the double binds of heterosexist culture. This phenomenology, in turn, depends on a narrative norm of such experience (just as Edmund Husserl's transcendental phenomenology does) that implicitly grants identity to even the most fragmented and nonlinear artifact of queer aesthetic production, the overdetermined dialectical matrix of the closet itself: staying "in" (personally and professionally defensive self-repression) versus "coming out" (restricted and potentially dangerous liberation).[15] This model clearly corresponds to the critical, theoretical, or social labor of many such aesthetic artifacts and is undoubtedly a key tool for their elucidation, but not for Burroughs's novels. In his writing, at least, Burroughs has always already been "out" and spends little time narrating how he got there, though in *Junky* he treats the few situations involving Lee's sexuality with studied ambiguity. Indeed, usually he parodies such phenomenological narration, as in the Kildare routine above. The dialectic of "in" and "out" is of little use to Burroughs the novelist, as is the narrative norm based upon it.

Even so, the forms of social repression experienced by homosexuals are consistent objects of Burroughs's hostility and criticism and are treated in all of his books. But they are treated in a discontinuous fashion, dependent on the form of the routine. This discontinuity radically undermines all gestures of narrative or phenomenological closure: the routine mutates constantly as other scenes erupt into the "original" one, leading the reader by metonymy or parataxis into other domains, populated by completely different characters. In Alfred Kazin's words, Burroughs "writes scenes as fluently as other people write adjectives, so that he is always inserting one scene into another, *turning* one scene into another" (Kazin 263). The routine is a form of micronarrative that operates by multiplication and juxtaposition, but no set of these proliferating routines can be combined to form a unified macronarrative similar to a traditional short story or novel. In *Queer,* these routines are held together by the force of the autobiographical frame narrative, which only "unifies" them negatively by grounding them in a subject, Lee, whom they traverse and exceed in all directions. The later works, as we shall see, cannot unify the routines in a continuous narrative even to this simple extent. Burroughs's narrative style constitutes a kind of disjunctive queer "surrealism," in contrast to the sociopsychological "realism" of phenomenological narration in Sedgwick's model.

The second (conjectural) objection that our imaginary extrapolation of queer theory might make to Burroughs's work bears on the thematics of homosexuality in his work. As the above routine (and other scenes in *Queer*) demonstrates, Burroughs is actively hostile to some segments of the male homosexual population. Some aspects of his hostility—his dislike of effeminacy in homosexual men, for example—remain rather nebulously defined throughout his writings (though this may be related to his antagonistic stance toward "femininity" in general), but other aspects are quite rigorously worked out. First position among these rigorous aspects should be given to his critique of the fundamental identity of many queer and straight control strategies—that is, strategies by which one person establishes (psychological, economic, etc.) control over another or others. The asymmetries of dominance and submission, of coercion and acquiescence, are not confined to heterosexual relationships. This identity extends to the structure of the queer and the straight subject defined by language addiction. To critics dedicated primarily to excavating the radical difference of queer discourse and action from their hegemonic straight counterparts, as are many in the growing community of activist queer theorists, a critique such as Burroughs's may appear counterrevolutionary. This apparently thematic critique also derives ultimately from the form of the routine, in which the rapid metamorphosis of the characters into those things in opposition to which they have defined themselves—be they other characters, animals, machines, or even abstractions (like Death or Fertility)—undermines or at least complicates the characters' radical claims.

Obviously these routines are performative utterances rather than constative or descriptive ones. They are aggressive, mocking, and often derisive set-pieces whose purpose is to amuse, to entrance, and ultimately to seduce, and as such their adequacy to any nondiscursive state of affairs is a poor measure of their value. Late in the novel, Allerton responds to a particularly pointed and critical routine by saying, "'That isn't fair at all,'" to which Lee replies, "'It isn't supposed to be fair. Just a routine for your amusement, containing a modicum of truth'" (*Q* 103). This "truth" is not "fair," not accurate or adequate, but it is still true, not because it corresponds directly to an objective reality, but because it comes from elsewhere, from a place outside Lee the subject. At a crisis point in his relationship with Allerton, Lee "kibitzes" over a chess game between Allerton and a female friend, performing an elaborate routine that begins with chess as its subject. The routine quickly modulates into a thinly veiled allegory of Lee's situation: he describes an invented chess master as "a great showman" who was, "like all showmen, not above charlatanism and at times downright trickery. Sometimes he used smoke screens to hide his maneuvers. . . . " Lee pauses in mid-joke, realizing that "The routine was coming to him like dictation. He did not know what he was going to say next, but he suspected the monologue was about to get dirty" (*Q* 66). Allerton and the woman depart, but Lee cannot stop the flow of words despite the loss of his audience; over the succeeding four pages (*Q* 67–70) he develops "Corn Hole Gus's Used-Slave Lot," a piece about sexual commerce and slavery that also parodies his difficulties with Allerton. Recall Burroughs's claim that "I feel that I was being written in *Queer*" (*Q* xiv); this scene exemplifies that feeling and also exemplifies Burroughs's insistence that "Writers don't write, they read and transcribe something already written" elsewhere (*WL* 74).

Several of the specific routines in *Queer,* like "Tetrazzini the Chess Master," appear almost verbatim in *Naked Lunch,* while others foreshadow those in his later works. Of course, there are somewhat similar instances of foreshadowing in *Junky.* For example, during Lee's attempt to kick drugs after his first arrest, he experiences a hallucination of "New York in ruins. Huge centipedes and scorpions crawled in and out of empty bars and cafeterias and drugstores on Forty-second Street" (*J* 28). A more severe bout of hallucination strikes him during his alcoholic binge in Mexico City: "When I closed my eyes I saw an Oriental face, the lips and nose eaten away by disease. The disease spread, melting the face into an amoeboid mass in which the eyes floated, dull crustacean eyes. Slowly, a new face formed around the eyes. A series of faces, hieroglyphs, distorted and leading to the final place where the human road ends, where the human form can no longer contain the crustacean horror that has grown inside it" (*J* 133). A later experiment with peyote inspires dreams of chlorophyll addiction and transformations of humans into plants, anticipating the "Flesh Garden" sequences scattered through later novels. These dreams recur in a routine in *Queer* (*Q* 90). These brief visions already contain the characteristic surrealist features of Burroughs's mature style, with one significant difference: the surrealist sections of *Junky,* whatever their specific symbolism, are consistently naturalized as the hallucinations of a heroin addict and are thus reduced to mere indices of the addict's mental state, "random events in a dying universe" (*J* 139), while the wild visions of the later works are freed from this reductive "realistic" determination and consequently are able to develop their full symbolic ramifications. In a word, the *hallucinations* of *Junky* become the *routines* of *Queer;* the "fugitive words" that Lee the mock sociologist sought to describe and analyze in *Junky* overtake and recompose him, transforming him from confessing addict into communicating writer.

Initially disturbed by the uncontrollable otherness of these routines that pass through him, Lee begins to adapt himself to it during the journey through South America that concludes the main text of *Queer.* He and Allerton undertake this journey, announced at the conclusion of *Junky* (*J* 152), in order to find Yage ("*Bannisteria caapi,*" a natural hallucinogen "related to LSD6"),[16] a drug that Lee believes will make the user telepathic: "'Think of it: thought control. Take anyone apart and rebuild to your taste. Anything about somebody bugs you, you say, "Yage! I want that routine took clear out of his mind"'" (*Q* 89). Lee's use of the term "routine" in this context indicates how much of his own anxiety about his unstable subjectivity is being projected into this metaroutine. It goes on:

> "In some cases of schizophrenia a phenomenon occurs known as automatic obedience. I say, 'Stick out your tongue,' and you can't keep yourself from obeying. Whatever I say, whatever anyone says, you must do. Get the picture? A pretty picture, isn't it, so long as you are the one giving the orders that are automatically obeyed. Automatic obedience, synthetic schizophrenia, mass-produced to order. That is the Russian dream, and America is not far behind. The bureaucrats of both countries want the same thing: Control. The super-ego, the controlling agency, gone cancerous and berserk. . . . " (*Q* 91)

In later works, Burroughs gives this form of "automatic obedience" the name "Latah." This all-too-realistic conspiracy theory, which anticipates the insights of Burroughs's friends R. D. Laing and David Cooper as well as Foucault, Deleuze, and Guattari, is merely an extension of the logic of anti-junk paranoia that Burroughs examined from a sociological perspective at the conclusion of *Junky,* the self-contradictory logic that produces on the one hand the addict-agent and on the other the criminalization of addiction as a state of being.

Soon after this metaroutine, however, Lee begins to appreciate the literary advantages, not of telepathically controlling others, but of receiving "transmissions" from other subjects. When he notices some pubescent boys playing in Guayaquil, his desire for them causes him to experience something akin to a transmigration of self:

> He could feel himself in the body of the boy. Fragmentary memories . . . the smell of cocoa beans drying in the sun, bamboo tenements. . . . He was with the other boys, sitting on the stone floor of a deserted house. . . . The boys were taking down their torn pants. Lee lifted his thin buttocks to slip down his pants. He could feel the stone floor. . . . A boy sat down by Lee and reached over between his legs. Lee felt the orgasm blackout in the hot sun. (*Q* 96–97)

Lest this passage be dismissed as a mere sexual fantasy, it is followed immediately by another scene, this time of heterosexual identification: "Now he was in a bamboo tenement. An oil lamp lit a woman's body. Lee could feel desire for the woman through the other's body. 'I'm not queer,' he thought. 'I'm disembodied'" (*Q* 97). The force of the "telepathic" identification clearly exceeds the individual bodily desires and subjective structures of the narrator through whom it manifests itself.

The main text of *Queer* ends abruptly shortly thereafter, with Lee and Allerton failing to convince the "white *Brujo* [medicine man]" Cotter either to give them some Yage or to introduce them to a native *Brujo* who will (*Q* 121). The epilogue that follows, entitled "Mexico City Return," shifts the narrative from third to first person in its condensed account of

Lee's trip back through Central America to Mexico City in search of Allerton; Lee never reveals how he became separated from Allerton, nor how much time has passed since their quest for Yage. This transition from third to first person follows logically, however, from the development of Lee's "telepathic" ability to transcribe and report routines composed elsewhere. In "Mexico City Return" he has grown accustomed to the radical otherness that erupts from inside him or passes through him, on its way from an unknown origin to an uncertain end. Why, then, does he return to the first person, to the "I" that he used in *Junky?* Deleuze and Guattari offer an answer:

> Why have we kept our own names? Out of habit, purely out of habit. To make ourselves unrecognizable in turn. To render imperceptible, not ourselves, but what makes us act, feel, and think. Also because it's nice to talk like everybody else, to say the sun rises, when everybody knows it's only a manner of speaking. To reach, not the point where one no longer says I, but the point where it is no longer of any importance whether one says I. We are no longer ourselves. Each will know his own. We have been aided, inspired, multiplied. (Deleuze and Guattari, *A Thousand Plateaus* 3)

By the end of *Queer* the same thing has happened to Lee, and to the extent that Lee is a version of his creator, the same thing has happened to Burroughs himself.[17]

Lee's quest to find Yage has failed, but he has nonetheless found the thing he sought in Yage: "telepathy," the ability to fragment or (what amounts to the same thing) multiply his subjectivity in order to experience other subjectivities and perspectives. He knows that his initial routine on telepathy as a tactic of control (*Q* 91) is ironic—telepathy cannot be limited to control because it "is not in itself a one-way setup, or a setup of sender and receiver at all" (*J* 152). Recall the etymology of the word "telepathy": "to suffer from afar." Lee receives the routines, "suffers" them, and relays them, sending them along to others far away. In a word, he has become a *writer,* a scribe or scriptwriter to the infernal powers that send him his routines. But this does not make him into an archetype of the artist, nor does it make his story a bildungsroman. Many years later Burroughs will describe his experience of telepathy as follows: "Norman Mailer kindly said of me that I may be 'possessed by genius.' Not that I am a genius, or that I possess genius, but that I may be at times, possessed by genius. I define 'genius' as the nagual, the unpredictable, spontaneous, alive, capricious and arbitrary. An artist is possessed by genius sometimes, when he is so lucky."[18] Lee's quest to connect with Allerton has also failed, but he has nonetheless found something akin to what he sought in Allerton: a connection to the social world, the world of other people, a community. The fact that this community erupts within Lee—in the form of the "telepathic" routines—rather than coalescing around him reveals *Queer* to be as much a modern allegory of redemption as it is a hard-boiled autobiography. The "telepathic community" will become a limitation for Burroughs later, but for now it suffices.

It suffices because in this telepathic community Lee has something he has never had before: a function. In answer to the oft-asked question of why he became a junky, Lee responds that "You become a narcotics addict because you do not have strong motivations in any other direction. Junk wins by default" (*J* xv). The routines, the writing from elsewhere, give him the strong motivations he has heretofore lacked. But just what are these motivations, this function? The answer to this question is dramatized in the sequence that concludes *Queer:* Lee dreams that he is "a finder of missing persons . . . the Skip Tracer" who has finally found the lost Allerton. Lee as the Skip Tracer calls upon Allerton to "'Pay up or else,'" not in money but in the personal connection and affection he has denied Lee during the entire course of the novel (*Q* 132–33). Like the addict-agent, the finder of missing persons is a figure that recurs throughout Burroughs's fiction, but unlike the addict-agent, who dramatizes the unresolvable contradictions that the original "war on drugs" revealed in American society, the finder of missing persons dramatizes the potential for real subversion and new community grounded in the proliferation of ghetto subcultures. He works at the edges, in the liminal and underdetermined spaces that can harbor, for a time, the opponents of control, trying to bring people of different spaces together. But the missing persons he finds are not simply people who are lost, have been abducted, or have gone underground; more importantly, they are people who have not yet come into existence. "Art . . . must take part in this task: not that of addressing a people, which is presupposed already there, but of contributing to the invention of a people. The moment the master, or the colonizer, proclaims 'There have never been people here', the missing people are a becoming, they invent themselves, in shanty towns and camps, or in ghettos, in new conditions of struggle to which a necessarily political art must contribute" (Deleuze, *Cinema-2* 217). Lee's telepathic "virtual" community is such a people, a community to come, and both the subject and the object of his open-ended concluding promise are this community, as figured in Allerton: "We'll come to *some* kind of agreement" (*Q* 134).

"All Agents defect and all Resisters sell out"

The Negative Dialectics of *Naked Lunch*

Despite his immense productivity in the interim, Burroughs's literary notoriety is still based almost exclusively on the underground reputation of his controversial 1959 novel, *Naked Lunch*. The book was initially banned in Los Angeles and Boston on charges of obscenity, and was subsequently cleared of those charges in trials that constituted, some historians claim, the final efforts undertaken by the government (specifically, the California and Massachusetts State Attorneys General) to censor literature in the United States.[1] This notoriety has not led to the academic canonization of Burroughs's novel, however, as it did in a case to which the *Naked Lunch* trial is often compared: that of Joyce's *Ulysses*, cleared of obscenity charges in 1933.[2] Indeed, despite the favorable verdict, Burroughs's novel has remained on the fringes of American literary culture—as a result not so much of its notorious scatology as of its fragmentary structure and the apparently contradictory results of its implicit critiques. This marginalization appears all the more paradoxical in the aftermath of the film of *Naked Lunch*, a linear, neutralized, star-studded "adaptation" of the novel that could still prompt Peter Chernin, the new chairman of Twentieth-Century Fox, the studio that produced the film, to rebuke his predecessors who were responsible for it and vow never to make that sort of film again.[3]

What sort of film is it that can inspire such antipathy? Like any cinematic adaptation of a literary work, David Cronenberg's film of *Naked Lunch*, released in the U.S. in December 1991, is an enterprise of selection and thus of reduction. In this instance the reduction takes a form that is indicative of critical tendencies that have been gaining influence in Anglo-American circles for a number of years, and that are also at the root of the abrupt and strained attempt by the Anglo-American critical academy to accept and assess Burroughs's work. These tendencies go by the collective name of postmodernism, and the convergence of both academic and pop culture standards under its banner (that is, both critical and consumer acceptance of it) has led some critics (such as Jean Baudrillard) to proclaim the end of critique and of the social. This "nihilist," or reflexive, postmodernism operates through a process of aestheticization whereby the unassimilable fragments of contemporary social life, having lost the mythic totality of history or religion that bound them together under modernism, become the objects of the only gesture left to the nihilist subject: an abstract and totalizing aesthetic affirmation. That is, having no real understanding of, let alone control over, the movement and representation of events, the subject can only treat the discontinuous series of moments that confront her/him as an aesthetic object whose ends are beyond her/him, and perhaps beyond capital itself. The only judgment left, in this context, is an anemic version of aesthetic judgment that Baudrillard calls "seduction"; pure and practical reason have no material left on which to operate, no adequate schemata or projections of purposiveness, so neither rationality nor ethics can be grounded. Let us call this process of seduction (or, more accurately, reduction) *postmodernization* since, like modernization or rationalization, it is a method of abstraction by which capital integrates antagonism into the process of production.

In Cronenberg's *Naked Lunch,* this postmodernization acts both thematically and formally; indeed, the theme determines the form. Faced with the impossibility of filming the novel literally, due (again) in part to its insistent scatology but mostly to its resistance to linear narrative, Cronenberg decided to move "back from the page itself to include the process of writing the book."[4] Thus the character William Lee, whose narratives begin and end Burroughs's novel but do not provide it with a unifying thread, becomes the central figure in a surrealist film allegory of the apprenticeship of the writer, scripted and directed by David Cronenberg alone.[5] Lee (played by Peter Weller) is presented as a Burroughs surrogate—complete with Allen Ginsberg and Jack Kerouac look-alike friends, an addict wife named Joan (played by Judy Davis), and a paralyzing case of writer's block—who must approach his literary task as if he were a secret agent working for unknown powers. Like Burroughs, Lee must kill his wife to become able to write; Cronenberg dramatizes this by suspending virtually the entire narrative between the shooting of Lee's wife, Joan—which sends him on the run to the exotic medina of Interzone, where he finds the unintelligible warring forces that will provide him with material—and the shooting of Joan Lee's double, Joan Frost (an expatriate writer distantly based on Burroughs's Tangier acquaintance Jane Bowles, also played by Judy Davis), whom Lee attempts to seduce in order to solve the riddle of the forces at work in Interzone and in his own literary life.

None of this narrative material appears in Burroughs's *Naked Lunch*, beyond the frame character William Lee; conversely, only short fragments of Burroughs's writing appear in the film, generally as direct citation, as when Lee recites the famous Talking Asshole sequence (*NL* 131–33)[6] in an attempt to seduce an important contact. Cronenberg's "move back" from the discontinuity of *Naked Lunch*, which might have established its connections with its politico-historical situation, instead reduces the text to a hermetically self-reflexive abstraction: the narrative discontinuities and politically charged "routines" are naturalized (according to the model Burroughs himself provides in *Junky*) as the hallucinatory experiences of a drug-addicted writer, at the same time as they are drained of whatever extratextual significance they might have. This is particularly true of Cronenberg's treatment of homosexuality, which is labeled "the best all-around cover story an agent could have" (a cover story for heterosexuality, apparently, since the film's central relationship is Lee's affair with the two Joans)[7] and thus denied the critical force with which Burroughs endows it. It is also true of Cronenberg's views on addiction and on the control of drugs by state institutions, which are rendered merely aesthetic through the omission of Burroughs's reflections on actual drugs (and the police-state suppression of them), which ground the metaphorical economy of imagined drugs like black centipede meat and "Mugwump jissom" in the novel. Cronenberg uses the theme of writing and the figure of the writer—which are clearly present though hardly determining in the novel—as expedients both to impose linear form on the recalcitrant text and to render all of Burroughs's political interventions aesthetic, by taking them for metaphors of the writing process as it is lived by the writer.

For example, near the end of the film the Clark-Nova (a typewriter that transforms itself into an insect and serves as Lee's contact with the unknown powers for which he writes—Cronenberg's invention rather than Burroughs's) gives Lee a warning which quotes a well-known passage from the novel's antepenultimate chapter: "all Agents defect and all

Resisters sell out" (*NL* 205). In the course of the novel the reader has been introduced to a number of organizations and institutions competing for power over various markets and subjects, including "Islam Inc.," a group of capitalists who work to destabilize developing nations, and the four "Parties of Interzone" that broadly symbolize the political spectrum: the Liquefactionists, who try to dissolve all differences into their own identity and eliminate dissent; the Divisionists, who flood the world with identical replicas of themselves to the same end as the Liquefactionists; the Senders, who seek to perfect ever-more-certain methods of control, ultimately including telepathic control of all subjects; and the Factualists, who resist the reductive operations of the others in favor of an uncontrolled, multiple society (*NL* 162–69). The machinations of these organizations and their agents, as well as others, throughout the text give sense to the famous warning: one can never be sure what cause or organization one is serving, since one's own subjectivity is only a relatively autonomous product of conflicts between them. There is a dialectic of (conscious or unconscious) treason that constantly threatens to reverse oppositional social relations, a dialectic that was being manipulated with great skill by the twin Josephs, the Soviet Stalin and the American McCarthy, even as Burroughs was serving his literary apprenticeship. In the film, conversely, the warning is detached from its admittedly symbolic political context and coupled with an assertion of the writer's importance that leaves the warning almost completely without content: "all Agents defect and all Resisters sell out. That's the sad truth, Bill. And a writer lives this sad truth just like everybody else. The only difference is . . . he files a report on it."[8] The film ignores the text's implicit desire for collectivity—which must remain ambiguous given Burroughs's refusal to resolve the social antagonisms he identifies—and offers instead an abstract homage to the mediation of the writer. For Burroughs, "this is a Manichean conflict . . . [whose] outcome is in doubt" (Burroughs, *Adding Machine* 83), but the film presents his warning as a truism, a "sad truth," a defeatist statement on the ultimate indifference of resistance, except as an aesthetic vehicle.

The result of this series of reductions and substitutions is the almost total aestheticization of Burroughs's novel, the postmodernization of it. The structure of Burroughs's *Naked Lunch* is discontinuous since it is based on the formal unit of the routine, and unlike those in *Junky* and *Queer,* these routines are not attributed to a single hallucinating consciousness which naturalizes them; one would have to exercise great caution in extracting any simple generic or genetic element from the book.

The structure of Cronenberg's *Naked Lunch,* on the other hand, is one of the simplest and most linear imaginable: the quest of an exceptional individual to become an artist, the bildungsroman. The fact that this structure is masked in surrealist imagery should fool no one: the film is a celebration of the artist as creator and the dangers he must face in order to create, and as such the film is closer to Goethe's *Faust,* Byron's *Manfred* or even Joyce's *Portrait of the Artist as a Young Man* than to Burroughs's novel. Indeed, Cronenberg's film is replete with Romantic references, from the imperative to "Exterminate all rational thought,"[9] a sentiment about which Burroughs is ambivalent, to the refiguration of the feminine Muse (Joan Lee/Frost), a figure that is totally alien to all of Burroughs's work. By framing the novel with the scene of its writing, fictionalized or not, Cronenberg has transformed Burroughs's relentlessly unromantic and resolutely fragmented text into a whole, a totality encompassed and unified by its author's experience and simultaneously sealed off from the rest of the world.

This transformation is confirmed by the almost total absence of scenes actually based on *Naked Lunch* texts: the object of the film is the novel as artifact or hermetic thing, not as readable matter that can enter into relations with readers or become a meaningful part of social situations. Cronenberg's procedure is particularly reductive given Burroughs's stated intention to "rub out the word" and his imperative to plagiarize: "steal freely. . . . Words, colors, light, sounds, stone, wood, bronze . . . belong to anyone who can use them" (Burroughs, *Adding Machine* 20–21). Cronenberg has "rubbed out the word" of *Naked Lunch* by reifying it; thus his film of the novel is a fulfillment of Deleuze and Guattari's warning, cited earlier, against uncritical reliance on the disruptive effect of fragmentation or the disappearance of the author-function: "Take William Burroughs's cut-up method: the folding of one text onto another, which constitutes multiple and even adventitious roots (like a cutting), implies a supplementary dimension to that of the texts under consideration. In this supplementary dimension of folding, unity continues its spiritual labor. That is why the most resolutely fragmented work can also be presented as the Total Work or Magnum Opus" (Deleuze and Guattari, *A Thousand Plateaus* 6). *Naked Lunch* is not a cut-up text, but its "mosaic" structure of routines anticipates many of the disjunctive effects of the cut-ups.[10] Cronenberg has constructed his film entirely within this dialectical "supplementary dimension" of the act of writing, and he has given it the name of Burroughs's novel, despite the fact that the novel lies almost entirely outside that dimension. In becoming the "Total Work" that provides the occasion for the pseudo-Romantic, postmodernized film but not (much of) the film's material, *Naked Lunch* is drained of its politics—that is, its *specific* form, content, and sociohistorical trajectory. It is also drained of a good deal of its intrinsic interest. Despite sacrificing the novel's disjunct "obscurity" in favor of linear metaphorical simplicity, the film neither evoked uniformly positive reviews nor found a wide popular audience; hence the hostile vows of Twentieth-Century Fox's new chairman, on the one hand, and on the other Burroughs's damnation of the film with the faintest of praise (in his introduction to a book on the making of the film).

The film, however, only repeats in a condensed fashion the aestheticized reading of Burroughs that has been the source of whatever academic visibility and critical acceptance he now seems to have. After having been banned in the fifties, crowned by the counterculture of the sixties, and denounced as redundant in the seventies, Burroughs was elected, in the eighties, to the American Academy and Institute of Arts and Letters, on the basis of his influence as a "writer's writer," totally obsessed with technique. During this same period, academic attention began to turn his way as well, largely because of the revival of formalist study that accompanied and displaced the Anglo-American reception of structuralism and its variants and sequels: special issues of magazines and a few book-length studies of his novels appeared, generally concerned with textual innovations like the cut-ups or Burroughs's relation to one or another tradition in Western literature.[11] Though these analyses represented a real advance over earlier criticism, which focused almost exclusively on the content of Burroughs's works and judged it in almost exclusively moral terms, the recent postmodernist trend in analyses of Burroughs's texts has only corrected one reductive reading by falling into another, symmetrically opposite one.

Robin Lydenberg's study *Word Cultures: Radical Theory and Practice in William S. Burroughs's Fiction* is a paradigmatic case. She provides detailed formal and conceptual explications of *Naked Lunch* and the *Nova* trilogy that Burroughs wrote after it, and in the final sections of her book she attempts to cut Burroughs's texts into those of a number of French critics and philosophers, including Roland Barthes, Jacques Derrida, Julia Kristeva, and Deleuze and Guattari (without making any attempt to clarify the enormous distances that separate these thinkers' projects), in order to demonstrate the force of Burroughs's critique of logocentrism and representation. Despite the immense local value of her explications, her enterprise remains stalled at the level of abstract textuality (the "practice" of her title) and can only equate avant-garde literature with political revolution according to the *Tel Quel* model of the seventies.[12] As such, her analysis of Burroughs accounts reasonably well for the dialectical undecidability of the earlier works, but not so well for the irreducibly distinct social issues Burroughs addresses or for the formal shift in his writing beginning in the late sixties. Despite its greater sensitivity, Lydenberg's version of Burroughs performs reductive gestures of postmodernization quite similar to those of Cronenberg's film.

In his introduction to *Everything is Permitted: The Making of "Naked Lunch,"* Burroughs cites the following anecdote at the conclusion of a carefully lukewarm endorsement: "Raymond Chandler was once asked, 'How do you feel about what Hollywood has done to your novels?' He reportedly answered, 'My novels? Why, Hollywood hasn't done anything to them. They're still right there, on the shelf.'"[13] Burroughs's books, too, are still on the shelf, and there they remain because postmodernism hasn't been able to do anything to them, either. This critique of postmodernization is not meant to suggest that Burroughs's work is strictly modernist, that its superficial fragmentation conceals a deeper formal unity of myth which it asserts as a negative critique of the disorientation and alienation of rationalized modern existence (as, for example, in Adorno's defense of modernism in *Aesthetic Theory*); despite his use of some modernist techniques, Burroughs is not Joyce or Picasso. To understand Cronenberg's and Lydenberg's abstractions of Burroughs, we do not need a dialectic of "critical" modernism (a formulation that would no longer be tenable in any case, given the reactionary nostalgia and arrogant asymmetry on which all modernist visions of mythical unity are founded) against "nihilist" postmodernism that would simply be sublated into contemporary marketing and canon-construction strategies, nor the seductive aesthetic dialectic that is at work within postmodernization. Both of these models foreclose the possibility of critique as they enclose antagonism within capitalist production and its handmaiden, abstract representation or textuality. We need, rather, a critical strategy beyond the mythic dialectic itself, beyond its ability to resolve the "most resolutely fragmented work" into a unity that can only be *contemplated* as an artwork and *consumed* as a commodity. We need, therefore, an amodernist strategy, a modernism shorn of myth, if we are going to get Burroughs's books off the shelf and back onto the streets.

•

Our amodernist thesis, implicit in the previous chapter, is deceptively simple: Burroughs's work, including *Naked Lunch,* constitutes an exacting critique both of the social organization of late capital and of the logic of representation or textuality that abets it. This is not to suggest that Burroughs is a Marxist; he sometimes talks like one ("Intellectual uniformity is more and more necessary as the contradictions and failures of the society become more and more apparent"), but at other times he flatly, if reductively, rejects materialism ("much worse than the false promise of Christianity is the denial of *any* spiritual potentials, as exemplified in the dreary doctrine of Communism").[14] Burroughs's critique does, however, consistently maintain a relationship to Marxism, one that is best summed up in Louis Althusser's description of the relation of art to knowledge: "This relationship is not one of identity but one of difference" (Althusser 222). Difference is not nonrelation, nor is it contradiction or binary opposition; the opposite of knowledge is ideology rather than art, while the (traditional) opposite of Marxism is fascism rather than Burroughs's libertarian-anarchist politics.

The polemical introduction to *Naked Lunch,* "Testimony Concerning a Sickness," proposes the medical metaphor that recurs throughout the book: Burroughs and his narrators often appear as biomedical researchers, a role that succeeds that of the sociologist, whose science provides the narrative perspective in *Junky.* A brief passage from this introduction dramatizes the nondialectical difference that relates Burroughs's work to Marxism. In a lengthy diatribe against "the Algebra of Need" (*NL* xxxix), the parasitic social economy of addiction in all its forms, Burroughs cites Occam's Razor and "Ludwig Wittgenstein *Tractatus Logico-Philosophicus:* 'If a proposition is NOT NECESSARY it is MEANINGLESS and approaching MEANING ZERO'" (*NL* xlvi).[15] Following a brief digression on junky self-righteousness, he returns to this logical condition at the conclusion of the introduction, but complicates it: "Paregoric Babies of the World Unite. We have nothing to lose but Our Pushers. And THEY are NOT NECESSARY" (*NL* xlviii). This allusion to and displacement of the similarly hortatory conclusion of Marx and Engels's *Manifesto of the Communist Party* (even down to the emphatic capitalization: "The proletarians have nothing to lose but their chains. They have a world to win. WORKING MEN OF ALL COUNTRIES, UNITE!" [Marx and Engels 65]) considerably broadens the social and political stakes involved in Burroughs's logical critique. These are the stakes that we must specify in the course of this analysis of *Naked Lunch*.

Such a critique implies a position from which it is articulated, a position which has been foreclosed in the dominant theories of postmodernism, but which Burroughs reopens tentatively in *Junky* and *Queer* and decisively in his later works: the position of the fugitive. We have seen that Burroughs's consciousness, in both its political and aesthetic aspects, was forged in the crucibles of drug addiction and oppressed (but not repressed) homosexuality, and that, thanks to the demonization of addiction, many Americans seriously believed that traffic in "narcotics ties right in with Communism. . . . Because the union controls shipping, and the Communists control the union" (*J* 70–71). As an addict, Burroughs was thus assumed to be a subversive, an assumption that was confirmed by his homosexual "deviance." The exclusionary logic of social control—specifically, the assumption of a general equivalence uniting all forms of deviance—transforms Burroughs into an imaginary Communist. The real double marginalization that Burroughs lived and chronicled within these overlapping subcultures radicalized him, however, without benefit of orthodoxy (at that time, the dogma of the declining American Communist Party or of the flourishing American labor unions); thus the disaffection that struck the orthodox, unionist Left as a result of its vanguard claims and coalitionist strategies in the seventies and eighties did not significantly undermine his critique.

The necessarily clandestine activity of the addict and of the contemporary homosexual lies at the base of Burroughs's controlling metaphors in this period—organized crime and the secret agent—which feed off each other dialectically. It is true that capital has managed to incorporate both the addict and the homosexual subcultures into production, the first by the expansion and reconquest of the bourgeois drug market through cocaine and its derivatives, which reestablished class divisions within the black-market drug economy as well as in the judicial system that policed it, and the second by the more recent invention of a specifically "gay" market sector and consumer identity to sublate the antagonism expressed by "queers" like Burroughs. In fact, he anticipates this axiomatic operation, the indifference that results from subsumption, in *Naked Lunch:* "Junk is the ideal product . . . the ultimate merchandise. No sales talk necessary. The client will crawl through a sewer and beg to buy. . . . The junk merchant does not sell his product to the consumer, he sells the consumer to his product. He does not improve and simplify his merchandise. He degrades and simplifies the client. He pays his staff in junk" (*NL* xxxix).[16] As Burroughs implicitly reasoned in *Junky,* just as the addict is not the negation of the capitalist but his half-parodic double, so commerce in junk, the "ultimate merchandise," is the purest form of the fetishized capitalist "free market." Similarly, Burroughs parodies the commodification of homosexuality in "Hassan's Rumpus Room" (*NL* 74–83), a routine concerning a night club where the patrons, "Mr. Rich-and-Vulgar" and the "Queen Bees[. . .]([. . .]old women who surround themselves with fairies[. . .])" (*NL* 79, 80), are entertained by the hangings and subsequent ejaculations of attractive young men.

To suggest that Burroughs was radicalized as a result of experiences that were not strictly class-based and that he maintains a "differential relationship" to Marxism begs the question of his *specific* relation to *specific* issues and developments in Marxist analysis and organization. The answer is by no means simple or static; Burroughs's relation to Marxism is itself a historical aspect of his literary practice. If Burroughs's political commitments in the late forties and early fifties amounted to a kind of extreme modernist liberalism or libertarianism—dramatized in his opposition, ultimately in exile, to police-state drug hysteria and the oppression of homosexuals like himself[17]—then by the time he assembled *Naked Lunch* (between 1953 and 1959), his position had begun to take a form that resembled in several important ways the generalized critique of Anglo-European culture undertaken by the similarly exiled members the Frankfurt School of Social Research. In brief, this critique sought to expose the novel constraints on and forms of exploitation of the productive populace that had arisen in both fascist dictatorships (like Nazi Germany) and mass republics (like the U.S.) as a result of their common reliance on the rationalist heritage of the Enlightenment. The central document of this Frankfurt School critique, at least as it concerns us here, is Max Horkheimer and Theodor W. Adorno's *Dialectic of Enlightenment (DE),* written in Los Angeles in 1944 during their American exile—while Burroughs, not yet a junky, was acting as a literary agent provocateur to Ginsberg and Kerouac in New York.

Exile is perhaps the most crucial contextual factor linking these two critiques, because both for Horkheimer and Adorno and for Burroughs, exile was not chosen as a means of avoiding the deadening effects of social and cultural stasis, of escaping the conservatism that drove Joyce from Ireland and the Lost Generation from the U.S. Like Salman Rushdie, both Burroughs and the Frankfurt School Marxists fled their native countries because their freedom and even their very lives were immediately, overtly, and materially threatened by the transformation of the state apparatus of domination. Horkheimer and Adorno, like Thomas Mann and Arnold Schönberg, moved to Los Angeles to escape the repressive forces mobilized in Germany by Hitler and the Nationalist Socialists, while Burroughs jumped bail in Texas to avoid the American "anti-junk feeling [that] mounted to a paranoid obsession, like anti-Semitism under the Nazis" and that resulted in "police-state legislation penalizing a state of being" (*J* 142). Their punishments would not have been the narrow-minded censure of their neighbors, nor even the civil lawsuits that threatened Joyce whenever he considered a return to Ireland, but imprisonment at the least and perhaps, for Horkheimer and Adorno, death. Their surveys from exile, then, manifest the urgency, the timeliness, and the focus that only a temporary stay of execution can grant to a condemned prisoner. Exile also helps to explain the shift in Burroughs's concerns from his early novels: the constantly shifting American social geography of *Junky* cannot easily be investigated from Middle Eastern exile, and if that ideological landscape is to be criticized and transformed, the schizophrenic authorial self-doubt of *Queer* must give way to a paradoxically fluid rigor in the dissection of the subjective structures formed by and in the mechanisms of control.

As we explicate this common critical program, we must constantly bear in mind the fact that Burroughs's relation to the Frankfurt School's Marxist project is differential in Althusser's sense. Burroughs does not refer to Horkheimer or Adorno, or even to figures like Herbert Marcuse, who would come closer to Burroughs's own position in the late sixties; nor do they refer to him. There is no evidence that Burroughs has ever read any of the writings of these Frankfurt School critics. How, then, can he have a relation of any kind to them? The differential relation consists, essentially, in this: in response to similar novel features of modern society, Burroughs articulates a critique that is structurally and thematically similar to the critique articulated by Horkheimer and Adorno. The novel features to which both critiques respond are the reversible symmetry of antagonistic social positions like those of the police and criminals; the serene coercive power of mass-produced artistic and political culture, embodied in the Culture Industry; the purgative logic of social purity, which finds its fullest expressions in institutionalized Nazi anti-Semitism and American racism; and the reductive strictures of capitalist control and instrumental reason that underpin the other features.

First and foremost, we must recognize that while trying to place *Naked Lunch* in the venerable literary tradition of political satire, Burroughs actually places it in the theoretical tradition of ideology critique:

> The title means exactly what the words say: NAKED Lunch—a frozen moment when everyone sees what is on the end of every fork[. . . .]Certain passages in the book that have been called pornographic were written as a tract against Capital Punishment in the manner of Jonathan Swift's *Modest Proposal.* These sections are intended to reveal capital punishment as the obscene, barbaric and disgusting anachronism that it is. As always the lunch is naked. If civilized countries want to return to Druid Hanging Rites in the Sacred Grove or to drink blood with the Aztecs and feed their Gods with blood of human sacrifice, let them see what they actually eat and drink. Let them see what is on the end of that long newspaper spoon. (*NL* xxxvii, xliv)

On the witness stand in the Superior Court of Boston, Allen Ginsberg offered the following interpretation of this passage: "It relates to nakedness of seeing, to being able to see clearly without any confusing disguises, to see through the disguise . . . a complete banquet of all this naked awareness" (*NL* xxii). Likewise, Horkheimer and Adorno insist that "When public opinion has reached a state in which thought inevitably becomes a commodity, and language the means of promoting that commodity, then the attempt to trace the course of such depravation [*sic*] has to deny any allegiance to current linguistic and conceptual conventions, lest their world-historical connections thwart it entirely" (*DE* xi–xii). To "trace the course of depravation" or to "reveal what is on the end of the long newspaper spoon" is to criticize the established order of production and to demystify the rapacious violence of consumption; this task necessitates, on the part of the critic, a fundamental estrangement from the language and forms constitutive of the object of criticism. That these parallel critiques of ideology also share a certain discontinuity of expression should surprise no one: this formal discontinuity, as a response to the seamless "world of the administered life" (*DE* ix), is the last desperate tactic of an increasingly commodified cultural modernism that must ultimately give way either to the complicit vertigo of reflexive postmodernism or to the mythless struggle of an amodernist critical practice.[18]

In both *Naked Lunch* and *Dialectic of Enlightenment,* this estrangement is conceived in essentially modern terms as the determinate negation of the logic by which the integrated apparatus of domination operates. For Burroughs, this apparatus is ultimately based in language, in "the Word," whose control, though dissimulated, is total and which therefore can be attacked only by totalizing it: "The Word is divided into units which be all in one piece and should be so taken, but the pieces can be had in any order being tied up back and forth, in and out fore and aft like an innaresting sex arrangement" (*NL* 229). This totality of the Word cannot be attacked directly, for that would be to play into its own nominalist logic. "The word cannot be expressed direct. . . . It can perhaps be indicated by mosaic of juxtaposition like articles abandoned in a hotel drawer, defined by negatives and absence . . . " (*NL* 116). This explains, in part, the discontinuous structure of *Naked Lunch*, which acquires its critical force primarily through its paratactic juxtaposition of scenes and routines. In the "Atrophied Preface" that, in a parody of Hegelian logic, actually concludes the book, the narrator claims that "you can cut into *Naked Lunch* at any intersection point. . . . I have written many prefaces. They atrophy and amputate spontaneous[. . . .]This book spill off the page in all directions, kaleidoscope of vistas, medley of tunes and street noises, farts and riot yipes and the slamming steel shutters of commerce, screams of pain and pathos and screams plain pathic" (*NL* 224, 229). The Hegelian and later Marxist distinction between the *Forschung* and the *Darstellung*, the untidy labor of criticism and its finished product presented for use, has been abandoned here as it has in *Dialectic of Enlightenment*, itself constructed of fragments, "sketches and drafts which belong in part to the area of thought of the foregoing essays without being precisely locatable there, and in part offer advance summaries of problems to be treated in forthcoming works" (*DE* xvii). The work of critique cannot be made tidy and linear, cannot be given either a precise conclusion or the point of departure that paradoxically follows the conclusion, without being unmade as critique in equal measure. "You were not there for *The Beginning*. You will not be there for *The End*" (*NL* 220). Critique of ideology works, in the shadow of integrated capitalism, by way of the middle, the *Forschung*, whose open-ended anti-form may always be distinguished even under the smooth contours of an ideological *Darstellung*. As Deleuze puts it, "In a multiplicity what counts are not the terms or the elements, but what there is 'between,' the between, a set of relations which are not separable from each other. Every multiplicity grows from the middle, like the blade of grass or the rhizome" (Deleuze and Parnet viii).

In this sense, the central strategy of ideology critique from Marx and Nietzsche to the present is organized around the excavation of the operant *Forschung*, the labor of specific practices of domination, from the *Darstellung*, the orderly façade of Nature, Reason, or Universality. Critique is reason's attack on Reason, which does not make it an abstract or Romantic negation of Reason in favor of affect, but a specific, detailed, and determinate activity, the negation of Reason as rationalization. Here rationalization must be understood in both its senses, economic as well as psychological: as the rational division of labor that grounds capitalist society, and as the alibi that society gives itself to excuse its own activity. In *Naked Lunch* and *Dialectic of Enlightenment,* both aspects are the objects of a critique that refuses to separate the form of logical or narrative closure from the content of exploitation and control.

Control is based on knowledge, on the accumulation and manipulation of knowledge *of a certain kind:* Horkheimer and Adorno call this "instrumental" knowledge, reason that is subordinated like a tool to whatever end it is expected to serve. This definition suggests that reason has not always been, nor need always be, so subordinated; the Renaissance marks the beginning of the emancipation of thought from its subordination to theology, a change that reaches its climax in the Enlightenment and then declines to the contemporary reconquest of thought by the irrationality of capitalist production. The body, on the other hand, has a much longer history of subordination (*DE* 231–34) that hardly reaches a climax in Burroughs's claim that "The addict regards his body impersonally as an instrument to absorb the medium in which he lives, evaluates his tissue with the cold hands of a horse trader" (*NL* 67). The body has been subjected to many forms of domestication and discipline in the interests of productivity for almost all of recorded history, and from the point of view of capital its current organization—into the socially exploitable polarity of oral and anal drives consecrated by psychoanalysis—could hardly be improved. The productive subject produces surplus value not only by laboring, but also by consuming, to appease the negative "desires" of which it is made.[19] The addict does not necessarily escape this: even though he does not work, he does consume, and when he stops taking his drug, his body goes through a painful and disorienting period of transformation from antiproductive absorption instrument back into the (potential) instrument of production it was before (unless the withdrawal fails, in which case the instrumental addict structure returns).[20]

Instrumental rationality represents simultaneously the apotheosis of thought and thought's abolition, in its reduction of the world to "raw material" for production and its reduction of the self to the slave of that process. Thus thought is disciplined and controlled just as the productive body is:

> What appears to be the triumph of subjective rationality, the subjection of all reality to logical formalism, is paid for by the obedient subjection of reason to what is directly given. What is abandoned is the whole claim and approach of knowledge: to comprehend the given as such; not merely to determine the

> abstract spatiotemporal relations of the facts which allow them just to be grasped, but on the contrary to conceive them as the superficies, as mediated conceptual moments which come to fulfillment only in the development of their social, historical and human significance. The task of cognition does not consist in mere apprehension, classification and calculation, but in the determinate negation of each im-mediacy. (*DE* 26–27)

Rather than being determined in its operation by the shifting totality of historical mediations binding it to and at the same time differentiating it from the world, thought is determined repetitively and automatically by the restrictive ends of exploitation and profit. Instead of working through the relations of its means and ends, thought labors as a means in the service of a preestablished end.

> The technical process [of production], into which the subject has objectified itself after being removed from the consciousness, is free of the ambiguity of mythic thought as of all meaning altogether, because reason itself has become the mere instrument of the all-inclusive economic apparatus. It serves as a general tool, useful for the manufacture of all other tools, firmly directed towards its end, as fateful as the precisely calculated movement of material production. . . . At last its old ambition, to be a pure organ of ends, has been realized. (*DE* 30)

Reason, which formerly claimed to pass judgment on means from the point of view of ends, prostitutes itself by giving up, not some illusory autonomy it never really possessed, but rather its multiplicity of other mediations in order to focus on exploitation and profit. Instrumental rationality is the philosophy of the assembly line, "mass" consciousness in the sense of identical mass production, rather than the mass consciousness of the self-emancipating proletariat à la Georg Lukács.[21]

Burroughs formulates his version of this critique of instrumentalism in parodic terms, through the recurrent figure of Doctor Benway, the "*pure* scientist" and surgeon (*NL* 33, 131) whose work is constantly focused on the technology, the means, of control without apparent regard for the ends his work serves. Medical doctors are important "points of intersection" in *Naked Lunch,* as they were in *Junky,* because they are in a paradoxical position: like the police, they are trained to treat the "Human Virus" of control, to eradicate its symptoms, but they also earn their living off it and thus have an interest in preserving the virus. Benway first appears in the novel's second routine, which bears his name and sets up the paradigm most of the succeeding routines will follow; this routine follows the semi-autobiographical frame story of Lee the addict's flight from the New York City police across the continent to Mexico and ultimately to Tangier. Benway is described as a "manipulator and coordinator of symbol systems, an expert on all phases of interrogation, brainwashing and control" (*NL* 21); he claims that "The study of thinking machines teaches us more about the brain than we can learn by introspective methods. Western man is externalizing himself in the form of gadgets" (*NL* 24). The operational logic of the thinking machine or computer, rudimentary as it was in the fifties, implies an entire metaphysics and epistemology that Horkheimer and Adorno summarize in terms quite similar to Burroughs's: "Thinking objectifies itself to become an automatic, self-activating process; an impersonation of the machine that it produces itself so that ultimately the machine can replace it" (*DE* 25). The digital method of the computer, originally designed to free human minds from exhausting and repetitive computation, folds back on its users and remakes them in the machine's image. This image is a fundamentally behaviorist one: to control the output of the producer, be it human or machine, one must control both the input and the programming.

Benway claims to "deplore brutality" because "It's not efficient" (*NL* 21). He prefers to use less ostentatious methods when "somebody wants homogeneity at this juncture. Can do, but it costs" (*NL* 32). What is the cost? Total behavior modification:

> prolonged mistreatment, short of physical violence, gives rise, when skillfully applied, to anxiety and a feeling of special guilt. A few rules or rather guiding principles are to be borne in mind. The subject must not realize that the mistreatment is a deliberate attack of an anti-human enemy on his personal identity. He must be made to feel that he deserves *any* treatment he receives because there is something (never specified) horribly wrong with him. The naked need of the control addicts must be decently covered by an arbitrary and intricate bureaucracy so that the subject cannot contact his enemy direct. (*NL* 21)

This "need of the control addicts," which Burroughs analyzes by means of "The Algebra of Need" (*NL* xxxix, 206–9), is what Horkheimer and Adorno call the "administered life," which "dissolves the old inequality—unmediated lordship and mastery—but at the same time perpetuates it in universal mediation" (*DE* 12) by market and exchange-value. The threatening face of the feudal despot gives way to the invisible hand of the labor market, and the misery of the slave is concealed in the affectless machine. This is why Benway, anticipating Foucault's distinction between feudal "punishment" and modern "discipline,"[22] avoids outright torture: "torture locates the opponent and mobilizes resistance"

(*NL* 23–24). Instead, behavior modification, under the guise of science—the ultimate ideology of Reason—enrolls the subjects in their own control program. As Benway says, "A *functioning* police state needs no police" (*NL* 36) because the citizens police themselves in advance; they internalize the police function as discipline and respect for public order (the internalization Lee fails to complete in *Junky*).

The machine model does not lead, in Burroughs's hands, to the colorless technocracy of Huxley's *Brave New World,* however, because the benevolent technocracy has been Burroughs's point of departure: Benway has been working in the Freeland Republic, a parody of Scandinavian socialism "given over to free love and continual bathing" (*NL* 21). Instead, the machines, in becoming the goal of human control strategies, also become symmetrically susceptible to human mental disorders. In the "Benway" routine, the working people, whose brains resemble thinking machines, are the inmates of a vast and decrepit asylum or "Reconditioning Center" where they undergo Benway's sadistic control experiments. Benway and the narrator are forced to depart quickly when they learn that the asylum's "electronic brain went berserk playing six-dimensional chess with the Technician and released every subject in the R.C." (*NL* 37). The freed patients run amok, forming a tableau of insanity reminiscent of Bosch's and Breughel's allegorical paintings: "Junkies have looted the drugstores and fix on every street corner. . . . Catatonics decorate the parks. . . . Agitated schizophrenics rush through the streets with mangled, inhuman cries[. . . .] A coprophage calls for a plate, shits on it and eats the shit." Little by little, however, the patients are revealed to be something other than simply the mentally ill; they are also foreigners, members of noncapitalist cultures that have been both colonized and studied, anthropologically, by the West: "Amoks trot along cutting off heads, faces sweet and remote with a dreamy half-smile[. . . .]Arab rioters yipe and howl[. . . .]Religious fanatics harangue the crowd from helicopters[. . . .]Kwakiutl Cannibal Society initiates bite off noses and ears" (*NL* 37–38). These figures spring in part from Burroughs's study of anthropology, but also no doubt from his impressions of the Arab world surrounding him in cosmopolitan Tangier.[23] The last patients described are merely bores and hypochondriacs, yet still "the ugliness of that spectacle buggers description" (*NL* 39). The spectacle represents not the failure of Benway's control techniques, but rather their complete success and reproduction: "the fully enlightened earth radiates disaster triumphant" (*DE* 3).

This success is not limited to cases of explicit behavior modification, propaganda, and totalitarianism. We have already cited Burroughs's claim that "Junk is the ideal product . . . the ultimate merchandise" (*NL* xxxix). This means that the logic of addiction is generalizable: "Because there are many forms of addiction I think that they all obey basic laws" (*NL* xliv). He also recognizes that the organization of the narcotics industry, which includes the police institutions charged with its eradication, stands as the model of all capitalist organization.

> The pyramid of junk, one level eating the level below (it is no accident that junk higher-ups are always fat and the addict in the street is always thin) right up to the top or tops since there are many junk pyramids feeding on peoples of the world and all built on basic principle of monopoly:
>
> 1—Never give anything away for nothing.
>
> 2—Never give more than you have to give (always catch the buyer hungry and always make him wait).
>
> 3—Always take everything back if you possibly can.
>
> The Pusher always gets it all back. The addict needs more and more junk to maintain a human form. (*NL* xxxviii)

Neither the pusher nor the police agent is immune to this pyramidal relation. The paradigmatic commercial relationship, of pusher to junky or, more generally, seller to buyer, is dialectically reversible: "'Selling is more of a habit than using,' Lupita says. Nonusing pushers have a contact habit, and that's one you can't kick. Agents get it too" (*NL* 15). This reversibility is dramatized in the narrator's routine concerning Bradley the Buyer, a narcotics agent who becomes addicted to physical contact with junkies, and is ultimately driven to "assimilate" them—and later his superiors in the Narcotics Bureau—into his own body (*NL* 15–18). The logic also surfaces in the brief routine concerning the U.S. president's "Oblique Habit" which "might precipitate an atomic shambles" and for which he has "sacrificed all control, and is dependent as an unborn child" (*NL* 67). As Burroughs will put it later, the people in control are controlled by their need to control, their addiction to control.

The instrumentalization or mechanization of thought is a useful control strategy, a way to subordinate independent thought to existing, predominantly economic ends determined by the repetitive logic of capital, just as the division of labor subordinates the body. Within such a rigidly limited horizon of "rational" behavior, crime becomes simply a form of irrationality reflecting and indeed duplicating the prevailing structure of Reason, as shown by Burroughs's criminals (in the manner of the Marquis de Sade's Juliette).[24] This duplication was already at work in the liminal spaces of *Junky,* which provided a stage for the transition from illegitimate commerce to legitimate business. Such irrationality can quite easily out-reason the rational bourgeoisie, since "The criminal has always been bourgeois—like the retribution which consists in robbing him of his freedom" (*DE* 225). The individual's measure of value under capitalism is "self-preservation, successful or unsuccessful approximation to the objectivity of his function [in the process of production] and the models established for it. Everything else, idea and crime, suffers the force of the collective [norm], which monitors it from the classroom to the trade union" (*DE* 28). In spite of Kant's strenuous attempts to provide one, this collective norm of rationality or self-preservation does not contain a consistent ethics or morality in the necessary form of a "reason for persisting in society when interest is absent" (*DE* 85). Sade reveals the complicity between Reason and domination: the necessity of enforcing, by means of formal law, an unequal division of labor on the workers in order for the bourgeoisie to profit. "Whereas the optimistic writers [like Kant] merely disavowed and denied in order to protect the indissoluble union of reason and crime, civil society and domination" (*DE* 118), Sade and Friedrich Nietzsche reveal this union to be constitutive of rational society. The same is true for Burroughs.

The narrator of *Naked Lunch* is a junky who, by the conclusion of the novel, becomes a cop killer as well. The blatant criminality of these actions—along with his writing activity—separates the narrator from the more liminal criminals who populate the book. Benway himself is a fraudulent medical practitioner who is occasionally reduced to "hustling pregnant women in the public streets" so he can perform "cut-rate abortions in subway toilets" (*NL* 31). Salvador Hassan O'Leary, the "After Birth Tycoon," is another of Burroughs's demonic capitalist criminals, a trafficker in unsafe foods and medicines who wears a "well-cut suit made entirely from immature high denomination bank notes[. . . .]His operations extend through the world in an inextricable, shifting web of subsidiaries, front companies and aliases" (*NL* 155–56). Despite the fact that "A squad of accountant investigators have made a life work" of investigating Hassan, "His dossier contains three pages of monikers indicating his proclivity for cooperating with the law, 'playing ball' the cops call it. Others call it something else" (*NL* 156–57). Hassan moves freely between the police and the criminal worlds, playing them against each other for his own profit. Like A. J., Clem, Jody, and the others members of Islam Inc., Hassan confirms the fact that "Today the boundary line between respectable and illegal rackets has become objectively blurred and in psychological terms the different forms [of criminal] merge" (*DE* 227). The modern corporate state itself often operates by means of these ambiguous and liminal characters, as *Junky* demonstrates.

Islam Inc. is the organization for which all the ambiguous characters in the novel work, but "The exact objectives of Islam Inc. are obscure. Needless to say everyone involved has a different angle, and they all intend to cross each other up somewhere along the line" (*NL* 160). At the outset of the "Benway" routine, the narrator is "assigned to engage the services of Doctor Benway for Islam Inc." (*NL* 21). The later routine "Islam Inc. and the Parties of Interzone" (*NL* 144–69) is concerned with its machinations, but offers no reliable account of the organization. Instead, we are introduced separately to several of its leading figures, including Hassan, A. J., Clem, and Jody. If Hassan is the capitalist criminal figure who embodies the instrumentalization of reason, then A. J. is one possible version of a critical subversive; the narrator (whose own reliability is open to question) believes that A. J. "is on the Factualist side (which I also represent)," or the libertarian-anarchist side, even though A. J.'s "English accent waned with the British Empire, and after World War II he became an American by Act of Congress" (*NL* 146). A. J. is nominally a pornographer who produces and screens blue movies at his "Annual Party"; his primary function in the novel, however, is that of a practical joker who unmasks and undermines the pretensions of bourgeois culture:

> It was A. J. who[. . . .]dosed the punch with a mixture of Yage, Hashish and Yohimbine during a Fourth of July reception at the U.S. Embassy, precipitating an orgy. Ten prominent citizens—American of course—subsequently died of shame[. . . .]A. J. once reserved a table a year in advance *Chez Robert* where a huge, icy gourmet broods over the greatest cuisine in the world[. . . . A. J.] throws back his head and lets out a hog call; and a hundred famished hogs he had stationed nearby rush into the restaurant, slopping the haute cuisine. Like a great tree Robert falls to the floor in a stroke where he is eaten by the hogs. (*NL* 146, 148–49)

A. J. starts a similar orgy at the Metropolitan Opera, spikes the drinks of the Anti-Fluoride Society with a drug that destroys the gums, promotes homosexual intercourse at a religious boys' school, and lays waste to a trendy night club. To complicate matters, A. J. also disrupts the homosexual torture party in "Hassan's Rumpus Room" by screening a film of "the copulating rhythm of the universe[. . .]a great blue tide of life" (*NL* 81).

"A. J. claims to be an 'independent', which is to say, 'Mind your own business.' There are no independents anymore. . . . The Zone swarms with every variety of dupe but there are no neutrals there. A neutral at A. J.'s level is of course unthinkable" (*NL* 155). Though A. J. may not be an independent, it is still difficult to determine his actual allegiance with any certainty. Other members of Islam Inc. seem to be easier to peg, though the narrator's doubts, like the reader's, remain. Hassan presents a relatively clear picture of the opportunist stoolie, and Clem and Jody are grotesque incarnations of the Ugly American, "dressed like The Capitalist in a communist mural" (*NL* 142), who claim to be "Russian agents whose sole function is to represent the U.S. in an unpopular light" (*NL* 158) by ridiculing the Islamic faith, baiting native nationalists, and selling contaminated food. Since Burroughs wrote these sections while living in colonial Tangier at the time of the Moroccan independence movement, they probably have some basis in his experience, yet these characters remain explicitly ambiguous. They are simultaneously opportunistic and committed, serious and ironic, critical and ideological. Islam Inc. reveals, in mercilessly grotesque but hardly exaggerated terms, the collaboration between business, organized crime, and the state upon which capitalist rationality is based. Burroughs's practice certainly agrees with Horkheimer and Adorno's insistence that "Inasmuch as the merciless doctrines proclaim the identity of domination and reason, they are more merciful than those of the moralistic lackeys of the bourgeoisie" (*DE* 119).

This collaboration between business, crime, and state, which is obvious enough in the case of individuals, is even more apparent in the establishment of the "Parties of Interzone." There are three oppressive or despotic parties, the Liquefactionists, the Divisionists, and the Senders; and there is one subversive or libertarian party, the Factualists, which offers some possibility of resistance. Hassan is a member of the Liquefaction Party, which is committed to the conquest of control by eliminating the opposition through "protein cleavage and reduction to a liquid which is absorbed into someone else's protoplasmic being" (*NL* 82). The narrator later points out that "It will be immediately clear that the Liquefaction Party is, except for one man, entirely composed of dupes, it not being clear until the final absorption who is whose dupe" (*NL* 162). In their desire to eliminate rather than enslave their opponents, the Liquefactionists resemble the Fascists, as Ginsberg notes (*NL* xxvi). The "moderate" Divisionists seek the same result using opposite means—cloning—and would seem to embody the imperialist ambitions of both American market capitalism and Soviet state capitalism during this period: "They cut off tiny bits of their flesh and grow exact replicas of themselves in embryo jelly. It seems probable, unless the process of division is halted, that eventually there will be only one replica of one sex on the planet: that is one person in the world with millions of separate bodies" (*NL* 164). Too perfect a reproduction reveals the Divisionists' work, so "To avoid extermination of their replicas, citizens dye, distort and alter them with face and body molds" (*NL* 164) so that the replicas may pass as separate, independent individuals. Because of this, each Divisionist is suspicious of everyone but his own recognized replicas, and should any stranger "express a liberal opinion, another citizen invariably snarls: 'What are you? Some stinking Nigger's bleached-out replica?'" (*NL* 166).

The Senders, on the other hand, want to preserve those who are not their members as slaves, to be controlled by the transmission of orders. Their techniques were initially primitive: "The logical extension of encephalographic research is bicontrol; that is control of physical movement, mental processes, emotional reactions and *apparent* sensory impressions by means of bioelectric signals injected into the nervous system of the subject[. . . .]Shortly after birth a surgeon could install connections in the brain. A miniature radio receiver could be plugged in and the subject controlled from State-controlled transmitters" (*NL* 162–163). This crude mechanical apparatus would later be replaced by telepathic control, but in any case "The bicontrol apparatus is prototype of one-way telepathic control" (*NL* 163) of the sort that Lee denounces in the last chapters of *Junky* and *Queer*. Despite this superficial difference—enslavement instead of obliteration of others—this form of control, like the forms represented by the other two parties, has the same ultimate goal: the reduction of individual differences to a single despotic identity. "A telepathic sender has to send all the time. He can never receive, because if he receives that means someone else has feelings of his own could louse up his continuity. The sender has to send all the time, but he can't ever recharge himself by contact. Sooner or later he's got no feelings to send. You can't have feelings alone. Not alone like the Sender is alone—and you dig there can only be one Sender at one place-time . . ." (*NL* 163). The Senders initially appear neutral, and their apparatus seems just another technology that can be used for good or ill. "Artists will confuse sending with creation[. . . .]Philosophers will bat around the ends and means hassle not knowing that *sending can never be a means to anything but more sending, Like Junk*" (*NL* 168). Sending is not creative art because such art is telepathy, and as Lee notes at the end of *Junky*, "telepathy is not in itself a one-way setup, or a setup of sender and receiver at all" (*J* 152). Sending is instrumental thought in its purest form, a means rigidly determined by its irrational end.

Sending considered as an artistic activity directs us to a key link in both Burroughs's and Horkheimer and Adorno's analyses of control: the centrally controlled mass media, or "Culture Industry," which claims to supply mass-produced commodities to meet the entertainment needs of its independent consumers.

> The need which might resist central control has already been suppressed by the control of the individual consciousness. The step from the telephone to the radio has clearly distinguished the roles. The former still allowed the subscriber to play the role of subject, and was liberal. The latter is democratic: it turns all participants into listeners and authoritatively subjects them to broadcast programs which are all exactly the same. . . . The attitude of the public, which ostensibly and actually favors the system of the culture industry, is a part of the system and not an excuse for it. (*DE* 121–22)

Though Burroughs's early novels show occasional awareness of the increasingly pervasive one-way media (recall, for example, the "Dr. Kildare" reference in *Queer*), nothing in the early texts prepares the reader for the barrage of mass-media control technology that fills many of the pages of *Naked Lunch* and the works that follow.

This barrage begins on page two of *Naked Lunch,* when the narrator, having escaped a narcotics agent with the inadvertent help of a "Young, good looking, crew cut, Ivy League, advertising exec type fruit," yells "So long flatfoot!" at the cop, thereby "giving the fruit his B production" (*NL* 2). Horkheimer and Adorno claim that "Marked differentiations such as those of A and B films . . . depend not so much on subject matter as on classifying, organizing and labeling consumers" (*DE* 123); likewise, Burroughs's narrator recognizes the "fruit" as a particular kind of consumer: "You know the type comes on with bartenders and cab drivers, talking about right hooks and the Dodgers, calls the counterman at Nedick's by his first name. A real asshole" (*NL* 1). Inasmuch as the "fruit" stands in the same relation to the narrator as the Wedding Guest does to Coleridge's Ancient Mariner,[25] and the reader by extension occupies the same position (that of addressee or audience), the narrator's assessment of the "fruit" applies also to the reader: she is defined, at least initially, by her logical and narrative expectations of the development of a recognizable and entertaining story. "No independent thinking must be expected from the audience: the product prescribes every reaction: not by its natural structure (which collapses under reflection), but by signals" that are at base clichés (*DE* 137). Thus *Naked Lunch* reveals itself to be a long and self-conscious manipulation of media-generated signals and expectations. Indeed, Benway dreams of studying primitive people in Bolivia who show no evidence of psychosis so that he can learn more about the basic functioning of the human mind "before it is loused up by literacy, advertising, TV and drive-ins" (*NL* 33–34).

As Horkheimer and Adorno point out, the function of the Culture Industry is to create "the false identity of the general and the particular" (*DE* 121). The discontinuous narrative of *Naked Lunch* attempts to fracture this identity, to show the multiplicity of particulars that are not subsumed under the dominant generality of the media. As he did in *Junky,* Burroughs tries to reveal the material reality of the addict's life that is concealed by the demonized images of addiction that fill the media. He cites an unattributed media description of a woman taking a shot of heroin with a pin and an eyedropper: "You know how this pin and dropper routine is put down: 'She seized a safety pin caked with blood and rust, gouged a great hole in her leg which seemed to hang open like an obscene, festering mouth waiting for unspeakable congress with the dropper which she now plunged out of sight into the gaping wound'" (*NL* 9). On the next page, he offers "The real scene you pinch up some leg flesh and make a quick stab hole with a pin. Then fit the dropper *over, not in,* the hole and feed the solution" (*NL* 10).

Much later, in the set of routines significantly titled "Ordinary Men and Women," the narrator offers a cinematic treatment of gay romance concerning a jeweler who caters to wealthy women but steals their gems to support his gambling habit. He is sent to prison, where he meets a Mob hustler with whom he falls in love. "As continuity would have it, they are sprung at the same time" (*NL* 129) and are soon approached by their former employers, whom they refuse to appease. The final scene finds the lovers, in a dead-on parody of Hollywood romance clichés, overcoming all odds to stand iconically "at the tenement window, their arms around each other, looking at the Brooklyn Bridge. A warm spring wind ruffles Jim's black curls and the fine hennaed hair of Brad" (*NL* 130). Such a story would have been inconceivable for Hollywood in the fifties, and remains almost so today, but it does conform to the established conventions of romantic cinema: "As soon as the film begins, it is quite clear how it will end, and who will be rewarded, punished or forgotten" (*DE* 125). It thereby reveals both the distance that separates those conventions from many parts of American life and the insidious effect those conventions have even on those who cannot possibly fit into them. A homosexual identifying with the protagonists of Hollywood romances is like an African American identifying with the cowboys rather than the Indians in westerns, yet such identifications happen all the time, despite the fact that "Whenever the culture industry still issues an invitation naïvely to identify, it is immediately withdrawn" (*DE* 145).[26]

This impossible yet inevitable identification means that "Real life is becoming indistinguishable from the movies" because "The more intensely and flawlessly [the producer's] techniques duplicate empirical objects, the easier it is today for the illusion to prevail that the outside world is the straightforward continuation of that presented on the screen" (*DE* 126). The routine "A. J.'s Annual Party" dramatizes the intense effort that this illusive duplication requires, and its far-reaching effects. A. J. introduces "the Great Slashtubitch" (a pornographic parody of Ernst Lubitsch; see *DE* 154), who berates an actor, "'Get out of my studio, you cheap four-flushing ham! Did you think to pass a counterfeit orgasm on me! THE GREAT SLASHTUBITCH! I could tell if you come by regard the beeg toe[. . . .]Go peddle thy ass and know that it takes sincerity and art, and devotion, to work for Slashtubitch. Not shoddy trickery, dubbed gasps, rubber turds and vials of milk concealed in the ear" (*NL* 89). For Burroughs, the pornographic film is the film par excellence, which reveals that as a whole "the culture industry is pornographic and prudish. . . . To offer and deprive [the audience] of something is one and the same." Horkheimer and Adorno note that in the romantic Hollywood films that audience members take as paradigms of their own lives, "Precisely because it must never take place, everything centers on copulation" (140–41); Burroughs, in contrast, brings that copulation out into the open and reveals it as a control process. The remainder of this routine (from the stage direction "*On Screen*" on page 89 to page 103) consists of blue movies (with a musical soundtrack of "metallic cocaine bebop" and Duke Ellington's "East St. Louis Toodleoo," which would have struck Adorno as entirely appropriate) directed by the Great Slashtubitch; these depict sequences of both heterosexual and homosexual intercourse, each of which concludes with hanging, cannibalism, or surreal bodily metamorphoses, and which reach a logical, narrative, and erotic "climax" in the degrading display of the genitals of a prisoner condemned to hang by the sheriff assigned to execute him. After the final "Fadeout," the actors "take a bow with the ropes around their necks. They are not as young as they appear in the Blue Movies. . . . They look tired and petulant" (*NL* 103), despite the Great Slashtubitch's best efforts at "realism."

The narrator of *Naked Lunch* reflects explicitly on this paradoxical situation of indulgence and denial following what is perhaps the most famous and most analyzed routine in the novel, the "Talking Asshole" sequence (131–33). This routine, about a carnival performer who teaches his "asshole to talk" as a novelty act, but whose body is then taken over by the intelligent asshole, is not strictly pornographic—not in any obvious sense of appealing to "a prurient interest in sex"[27]—yet this kind of perverse transformation is precisely "the sex that passes the censor, squeezes through between bureaus, because there's always a space *between,* in popular songs and Grade B movies, giving away the basic American rottenness, spurting out like breaking boils, throwing out globs of that un–D.T. [undifferentiated tissue] to fall anywhere and grow into some degenerate cancerous life-form, reproducing a hideous random image" (*NL* 133). The undifferentiated tissue that covers the carny performer's mouth and blocks his speech enacts not only the inversion of the Western subjection of body to mind and materiality to representation, as Robin Lydenberg suggests,[28] but also the sham identity of the general and the particular in mass culture. This space between institutions, commodities, and subjects—the third term or mediate dimension in which the *Forschung* of domination is articulated—reveals the "basic American rottenness," the *Darstellung* of total integration and enforced indifference that is both the cause and the effect of the Culture Industry.

This fully integrated social organization, founded on the subordination of flesh and spirit to exploitation for profit, managed by means of ever more pervasive technologies of surveillance and propaganda, and functioning equally well on either side of the arbitrary line of legality, still requires one final component to ensure its exact reproduction: it needs an Other, one that is defined not by the society's own sham legality but by the Other's ethnically marked difference from the society's norm, in order to posit itself, negatively, as a complete (meta)subject. The "them" is the penultimate step on the road to the "us." This is the function that National Socialism thrust on the Jewish people and others, and that American society forced on natives, Asians, and freed slaves and their descendants. After World War II, this group grew to include communists and homosexuals as well; the logic of "racism" has grown flexible enough to exclude non–ethnic others. At base, this "racism" that is constitutive of rational society conforms to the dialectical logic of the police-criminal opposition explored in *Junky,* but racism displaces that *internal* opposition *outside* of the imaginary bounds of society itself, into a limbo beyond the responsibilities of legality and even of humanity. The "hog-balled, black-assed Communist Jew Nigger" (*NL* 123) of the racists' paranoid control hallucinations bears the stigma of society's disavowal of its own determining characteristics. If, as Horkheimer and Adorno claim, the "Jews constituted the trauma of the knights of industry who had to pretend to be creative," and thus "their anti-Semitism is self-hatred, the bad conscience of the parasite" (*DE* 175–76), then natives, African Americans, and communists constituted the trauma of bourgeois Americans who had to pretend to deserve their property.

The hallucinatory travels undertaken by the characters in *Naked Lunch* to locales both fictional and exotic do not obscure the book's fundamental concern with the United States of America, as the frame tale of Lee's flight demonstrates:

> Into the Interior: a vast subdivision, antennae of television to the meaningless sky. In lifeproof houses they hover over the young, sop up a little of what they shut out. Only the young bring anything in, and they are not young very long[. . . .]Illinois and Missouri, miasma of mound-building peoples, groveling worship of the Food Source, cruel and ugly festivals[. . . .]
>
> America is not a young land: it is old and dirty and evil, before the settlers, before the Indians. The evil is there waiting. (*NL* 11)

The evil of America, the "U.S. drag[. . .]like no other drag in the world" (*NL* 12), is the idea of a place without inhabitants, or at least without inhabitants who are human: the idea of a place where the land and the labor are free for the taking, but only for the first white man on the scene. There are many routines parodying anti-Arab rhetoric (for example, Clem and Jody's antics, *NL* 111–12, 158–60), but Burroughs's Orientalism does not appear in mature form until the *Nova* trilogy; the primary forms of racism analyzed in *Naked Lunch* are American anti-Semitism and anti-black racism.

Anti-Semitism, Horkheimer and Adorno claim, is in part the displacement of a reasonable aggression of the exploited workers against their exploiters. Jews "are the scapegoats not only for individual maneuvers and machinations but in a broader sense, inasmuch as the economic injustice of the whole class [of exploiters] is attributed to them" (*DE* 174). Though they are rigorously excluded from power in almost every field, Jews are still accused of conspiracy and cabal, usually in league with international communism against the Christian, capitalist U.S. In a symmetrically opposite position, African Americans and native Americans represent the "subhuman" classes upon whose hyper-exploitation (the slavery and systematic discrimination that allowed American whites to amass more wealth in a shorter time than Europeans, with more limited systems, could match) and extermination (the genocide that opened up the frontiers and made available for exploitation land that had never been owned and thus did not need to be purchased) the present commercial order is based. The two groups—imaginary exploiters and real exploited—are united in the racist conception of them as inhuman. That which is not human is, by definition, animal or natural and thus at war with the human, so for capital, "Civilization is the victory of society over nature which changes everything into pure nature" (*DE* 186).

The central passage involving racism and anti-Semitism appears late in the novel, in the routine called "The County Clerk." The title character is, significantly, a bureaucrat in charge of supplying government records for use in civil lawsuits; he is so intentionally inept that the cases drag on "until the contestants die or abandon litigation[. . .]the only cases that actually go to trial in the Old Court House are those instigated by eccentrics and paranoids who 'want a public hearing'" (*NL* 169). Lee must get an affidavit of illness to avoid eviction from the house where he is squatting, and to do so he must appease the Clerk, who wastes his clients' time with relentlessly digressive racist anecdotes of his youth in the American South:

> "[. . .]the bog makes a bend, used to be nigger shack there. . . . They burned that ol' Nigger over in Cunt Lick. Nigger had the aftosa and it left him stone blind. . . . So this white girl down from Texarkana screeches out:
>
> "'Roy, that ol' nigger is looking at me so nasty. Land's sake I feel just dirty all over.'
>
> "'Now Sweet Thing, don't you fret yourself. Me an' the boys will burn him.'
>
> "'Do it slow, Honey Face. Do it slow. He's give me a sick headache.'
>
> "So they burned the nigger and that ol' boy took his wife and went back up to Texarkana without paying for the gasoline and old Whispering Lou runs the service station couldn't talk about nothing else all Fall: 'These city fellers come down here and burn a nigger and don't even settle up for the gasoline.'" (*NL* 175–76)

As befits an official of the judicial system, the Clerk's anecdote is concerned with justice, but it is "justice" for the white entrepreneur and not for the black victim, whose innocence is so obvious that the tale becomes absurd.

At the end of this anecdote, the Clerk announces that he is going into the "privy" where he "often spent weeks[. . .]living on scorpions and Montgomery Ward catalogues," so Lee must make a personal request that the Clerk will accept: using a stolen university alumni card, he appeals to the Clerk "as one Razor Back to another." The Clerk remains suspicious because Lee doesn't "look like a bone feed mast-fed Razor Back to me. . . . What you think about the Jeeeeews. . . . ?" The Razor

Back is a breed of hog, of course, and therefore a source of pork, which Jews, according to the rules of Kasruth but more importantly according to *stereotype,* are not allowed to eat. Lee answers by rote, as if to some perverse catechism, "you know yourself all a Jew wants to do is doodle a Christian girl. . . . One of these days we'll cut the rest of it off." This, of course, is the correct response: the Clerk admits that "you talk right sensible for a city feller. . . . Find out what he wants and take care of him. . . . He's a good ol' boy" (*NL* 177). The face of the state, or at least of the bureaucracy that is the state's most tangible avatar, is the face of appalling racist violence presented in the guise of folksy humor. The very language of this bureaucracy is a racist and anti-Semitic code, and only those with the right credentials (and, it goes without saying, appearance) can negotiate its convolutions.

With the successful positing of an Other to define, negatively, the limits of the social order, the labor of the production of control reaches its end, but this does not mean that the labor of control also ends. An amount of labor equivalent to that necessary for production must be expended regularly to reproduce control, and to improve the always already outmoded technology of control. Thus the "Atrophied Preface" at the end of *Naked Lunch* concludes with a resigned admission of this interminable process:

> A heaving sea of air hammers in the purple brown dusk tainted with rotten metal smell of sewer gas. . . . young worker faces vibrating out of focus in yellow halos of carbide lanterns. . . . broken pipes exposed. . . .
>
> "They are rebuilding the City."
>
> Lee nodded absently. . . . "Yes. . . . Always. . . . " (*NL* 235)

The City of capitalist control is always being rebuilt because it is always being torn down. Both tasks are undertaken simultaneously by its exploited classes, on behalf not of its revolutionary foes but of its most dedicated defenders.

•

The differential relationship between Burroughs's critique of the postwar world and that of Horkheimer and Adorno extends not only to these substantive analyses of new forms of domination, but also to the significant lacuna the two critiques share. This lacuna can best be understood in light of the development of Marxist thought in the twentieth century, a line of development from which Horkheimer and Adorno mark their own difference. Until recently, the history of Marxism followed a dialectical pattern of development, carried along on the antithetical horns of the method that was also its constitutive dilemma: investigation of the mechanisms of capitalist domination, on the one hand, and the constitution of a revolutionary subject position, on the other. This pattern found its model in Marx himself, in the formal and substantial antithesis of *Capital,* the objective treatise on capitalist domination, to the earlier *Grundrisse,* the subjective account of insurrectionary organization. This dialectic may be found also in Lenin's thought, where it has had the most far-reaching practical consequences, as well as in Lukács's *History and Class Consciousness* and in the writings of Rosa Luxemburg and Antonio Gramsci. In the work of the Frankfurt School and its descendants, however, one of the terms of this dialectic falls away: the constitution of the revolutionary subject all but disappears, leaving only the critique of mechanisms of domination. Revolutionary subjectivity is no longer possible in light of contemporary techniques of domination like the Culture Industry. This is the source both of Horkheimer and Adorno's pathos and of their "negative dialectic," which—like Herbert Marcuse's one-dimensionality—bear witness to the expansion of capitalist contradiction beyond the ability of the dialectic to resolve it. The influence of this monological version of Marxism has been tremendous, especially on those who seem to have taken it a step further, like Jean-François Lyotard and Jean Baudrillard (who seem to have learned a few tricks from *Dialectic of Enlightenment,* particularly with regard to the media).

Throughout *Dialectic of Enlightenment,* Horkheimer and Adorno allude to the prospect of revolution and the historical subject who would carry out that task, but these allusions are either devoid of specific content or are restricted to an almost Althusserian advocacy of "class struggle in theory" itself. Consider this point, which intervenes in the summing up of "The Concept of Enlightenment": "true revolutionary practice depends on the intransigence of theory in the face of the insensibility with which society allows thought to ossify" (41) and not on the working class because the "reduction [of the working masses] to mere objects of the administered life, which preforms every sector of modern existence including language and perception, represents objective necessity, against which they believe there is nothing they can do" (38). Since all the forms of Enlightenment, from formal education to film production, are actually successful forms of mass deception, the only revolutionary gesture that remains is the negation of Enlightenment, the determinate negation of sovereign instrumental Reason by critical reason. There seems to be no possibility of any radical action arising from those who are directly exploited, and all that can be expected is radical thought from the philosophers, for whom, as for the capitalist himself, "exemption from work—not only among the unemployed but even at the other end of the social scale—also means disablement" (*DE* 35).

Burroughs, too, in the wake of his failure to complete and publish *Queer*—the abortive groundwork of his own metaphysics of community—largely succumbs to pessimism in the face of the integrated totality of capitalist control. In *Naked Lunch,* his only statements on the possibility of revolution, while provocative, are made in parenthetical asides like the following passage from "Ordinary Men and Women":

> Democracy is cancerous, and bureaus are its cancer. A bureau takes root anywhere in the state, turns malignant like the Narcotics Bureau, and grows and grows, always reproducing more of its own kind, until it chokes the host if not controlled or excised. Bureaus cannot live without a host, being true parasitic organisms. (A cooperative on the other hand *can* live without the state. That is the road to follow. The building up of independent units to meet the needs of the people who participate in the functioning of the unit. A bureau operates on the opposite principle of *inventing needs* to justify its existence.) (*NL* 134)

The novel contains no clear-cut examples of what such a cooperative would look like under the conditions of late capitalism, however, to counter the demonic cartels, corporations, and bureaus that surround the narrator and reader.

Some of the most disturbing and apparently pessimistic passages in *Naked Lunch* may actually offer points of departure for radical social change. We have seen how the disciplined body, like thought, is domesticated and subordinated to the process of production as an instrument—how the body's very organization abets capitalist control. This does not mean that other forms of bodily organization are not conceivable, some of which could effectively resist capitalist exploitation. In *Anti-Oedipus* and elsewhere, Gilles Deleuze and Félix Guattari define the "body without organs" as "the unproductive, the sterile, the unengendered, the unconsumable," the "imageless, organless body" that stands as the degree zero of desire and subjective organization and as a result cannot be inserted into a process of production without being transformed into an organism wholly defined by its productive functions (Deleuze and Guattari, *Anti-Oedipus* 8). The body without organs—which is not an object or a state but a "becoming" or *process*—is revealed with particular clarity in the surreal hallucinations of narcotic withdrawal in *Junky;* freed from that naturalized narrative context, in *Naked Lunch* these visions serve as object lessons in the construction of the body without organs.

Consider this early passage, which describes the transformation of a kicking junky: "no organ is constant as regards either function or position . . . sex organs sprout anywhere . . . rectums open, defecate and close . . . the entire organism changes color and consistency in split-second adjustments" (*NL* 9). Later in the novel, Drs. Benway and Schafer discuss the (mis)organization of the human body immediately before the "Talking Asshole" routine: "Instead of a mouth and an anus to get out of order why not have one all-purpose hole to eat *and* eliminate? We could seal up nose and mouth, fill in the stomach, make an air hole direct into the lungs where it should have been in the first place . . . " (*NL* 131). Deleuze cites these passages from *Naked Lunch* later when he insists that "In fact, the body without organs does not lack organs, it simply lacks the organism, that is, this particular organization of organs" upon which exploitation is based.[29] It is this "lack" (from the point of view of capitalist control, of course) that makes the body without organs potentially revolutionary: it frees the body, at least temporarily, from its subjection to an exploitable oral-genital organization and opens it up to other forms of subjective organization and thus to the other forms of social organization implied by different subject-structures.

In Burroughs's investigation of the body without organs that results from drug addiction, Deleuze and Guattari recognize an important precursor of their own search for an alternative to capitalist control, but they also see the abyss into which such a formulation can lead without vigilance and caution. The junky can overshoot the body without organs, can turn the process into a terminal state, the results of which we have already seen: the affectless, immobile body of the satisfied addict, which only rouses itself to search for more junk. If it does not succumb to this stasis of addiction, the body without organs of the withdrawing addict falls just as easily back into the structure of the disciplined, productive body of capitalism. It is only in the period between the two endpoints, during the process of becoming, that the body without organs can take on a revolutionary valence, though this is hardly inevitable (Deleuze and Guattari, *A Thousand Plateaus* 149–66). This becoming only appears intermittently in *Naked Lunch*, and never gives rise to subjective structures that can construct alternative social systems, but it comes to be a regular part of Burroughs's writing, both in content and in style, in the works that follow.

There are other alternatives, even more embryonic, that point toward the kinds of solutions to control that Burroughs develops in the eighties, when he returns to the idea of a utopian community as a response to life in the administered society. The most evocative of these, explicitly presented as a Yage-induced hallucination, is the opening of "The Market":

> The blood and substance of many races, Negro, Polynesian, Mountain Mongol, Desert Nomad, Polyglot Near-East, Indian—races as yet unconceived and unborn, combinations not yet realized pass through your body. Migrations, incredible journeys through deserts and jungles and mountains (stasis and death in closed mountain valleys where plants grow out of genitals, vast crustaceans hatch inside and break the shell of body) across the Pacific in an outrigger canoe to Easter Island. The Composite City where all human potentials are spread out in a vast silent market. (*NL* 106)

This routine, which goes on to delineate the organizational problems facing such an ontologically and biologically anarchistic vision of society, anticipates some of the insights into the revolutionary possibilities of the body without organs that Deleuze and Guattari will draw from the world-historical visions of schizophrenics in *Anti-Oedipus*. Yet despite this intriguing potentiality, Burroughs is unable to offer any real solutions to the problems of radical organization.

Still, there is at least one nominally radical or libertarian group in the novel, the Factualists, with whom Burroughs himself identifies, according to Ginsberg's testimony (*NL* xxvi). "The Factualists are Anti-Liquefactionist, Anti-Divisionist, and above all Anti-Sender," as their "Tentative Bulletins" attest. On the Divisionists: "We must reject the facile solution of flooding the planet with 'desirable replicas.' It is highly doubtful if there are any desirable replicas, such creatures constituting an attempt to circumvent process and change." On the Liquefactionists: "We must not reject or deny our protoplasmic core, striving at all time to maintain a maximum of flexibility without falling into the morass of liquefaction." And on the Senders:

> Emphatically we do not oppose telepathic research. In fact, telepathy properly used and understood could be the ultimate defense against any form of organized coercion or tyranny on the part of pressure groups or individual control addicts. We oppose, as we oppose atomic war, the use of such knowledge to control, coerce, debase, exploit or annihilate the individuality of another living creature. Telepathy is not, by its nature, a one-way process. To attempt to set up a one-way telepathic broadcast must be regarded as an unqualified evil. . . . (*NL* 167)

These position papers or party platform planks, which represent Burroughs's own consistently maintained political views, are unexceptionable but at the same time insufficient, in that they remain purely negative. They are defined solely by their opposition to the despotic parties and have no positive content.

This restricted radicality, limited as it is to strict opposition, reaches its zenith in the narrator's penultimate monologue. He identifies himself here as the "Exterminator" because "At one brief point of intersection I did exercise that function[. . . .]Sluiced fat bedbugs from rose wall paper[. . .]and poisoned the purposeful Rat, occasional eater of human babies. Wouldn't you?" (*NL* 205).[30] His new job is an extension of that old one: "Find the live ones and *exterminate.* Not the bodies but the molds you understand—but I forget that you cannot understand. We have all but a very few. But even one could upset our food tray. The danger, as always, comes from defecting agents: A. J.,[. . .]Lee and the Sailor and Benway. And I know some agent is out there is the darkness looking for me. . . . Because all Agents defect and all Resisters sell out . . . " (*NL* 205). This program of extermination, like Horkheimer and Adorno's practice of critique, is a form of determinate negation, the wielding of the double-edged sword of reason against its own commodified image. It is directed at "molds," at the production line of identical repetitions of Word or thought, rather than at individual "bodies," but this makes it no less destructive and, as the final caveat makes clear, no more certain of success than the control strategies it attacks.

The narrator's impasse reveals that the world of *Naked Lunch* has closed in on itself, has occupied all of the available logical space with its contradictory determinations. Its paradoxes, generated by reason, cannot be resolved or made productive, but can only be negated by reason. The dialectic of control, like the dialectic of Enlightenment, is, finally, a negative dialectic between whose opposing terms all of society is laid out as on a lunch plate or an assembly line. The only escape hatch, as Adorno would agree, is open to the artist who can negate the system, not in material reality, but in the structure of his work. The artist himself cannot resist or escape, but the work can. The final routine of *Naked Lunch,* "Hauser and O'Brien," dramatizes this precarious space of resistance. While preparing a shot of heroin, Lee is interrupted by Hauser and O'Brien, two narcotics agents who have been ordered to arrest Lee and to "Bring in all books, letters, manuscripts" in his possession (*NL* 209). Lee offers to help them set up a pusher so that they will allow him to finish his shot, after which he pulls out a pistol and kills them. He assumes that he will be hunted down for this act and prepares to flee the city: he packs his manuscripts, purchases a large quantity of heroin, and moves into a gay bathhouse for the night.

The next morning, he calls the Narcotics Bureau from a pay phone to inquire about the murder investigation he feels sure is under way. To his surprise, the operator insists that no officers named Hauser or O'Brien work there, and that there is certainly no investigation of their deaths under way. On his way out of the area in a taxi, Lee realizes what has happened:

> I had been occluded from space-time like an eel's ass occludes when he stops eating on the way to the Sargasso. . . . Locked out. . . . Never again would I have a Key, a Point of Intersection. . . . The Heat was off me from here on out . . . relegated with Hauser and O'Brien to a landlocked junk past where heroin is always twenty-eight dollars an ounce[. . . .]Far side of the world's mirror, moving into the past with Hauser and O'Brien . . . clawing at a not-yet of Telepathic Bureaucracies, Time Monopolies, Control Drugs, Heavy Fluid Addicts:
>
> "I thought of that three hundred years ago."
>
> "Your plan was unworkable then and useless now. . . . Like Da Vinci's flying machine plans. . . . " (*NL* 217)

Like *Naked Lunch* itself, Lee's writings (in which the Narcotics Bureau took such an interest) have negated the totality of capitalist control and thrown him outside its limits, but since those limits are coterminous with the limits of reason, he is outside time and space and outside history as well. Burroughs will explore this extrahistorical nonspace, this negative subject-position, in his works of the sixties and seventies before returning to an affirmative historical perspective in the eighties.

As at the end of *Queer,* in reaching this place outside history Lee has reached a point of stability from which to attack the machinery of control, but in the face of the threatening "not-yet," which is historically inevitable yet subject to change, he lacks a viable plan of attack. Like the police, he will not be able to mesh with present time until he finds an alternative to the negative dialectics that control capitalist society. These "Telepathic Bureaucracies" and "Time Monopolies" will form the substance of the *Nova* trilogy. Lee's stable point, though extrahistorical, is not static but rather metastable, the way the attractors of chaos theory are metastable: it partakes of a stability founded on rapid, apparently disorderly fluctuation that, at a higher level, contains its own order. The rapid montage of routines in *Naked Lunch,* like the even more disorienting cut-ups of the *Nova* trilogy, give fleeting form to this fluctuating perspective. In escaping the determinations of capitalist control, this extrahistorical metastability offers the promise of a critique that would not remain negative, but it also threatens to collapse into idealism, compromise, and collaboration with the dominant order of control in spite of its critical intentions. Capital, too, wants nothing more than an end to history and the forms of resistance to which history gives rise.

According to Burroughs's recurrent medical metaphor, control is a disease for which the "'Treatment is symptomatic'—which means in the trade there is none[. . .]except to make the patient as comfortable as possible" (*NL* 43, 189). This diagnosis is articulated by doctors—themselves figures of control—however, so we must remain skeptical about the exception, especially since Burroughs's own prescription seems to be to make the reader/patient as uncomfortable as possible, perhaps to suggest that in fact "Poverty, hatred, war, police-criminals, bureaucracy, insanity, all symptoms of the Human Virus[. . .]*can now be isolated and treated*" (*NL* 168), as the Factualists claim. We will have to wait for the countercultural break of the late sixties for these fragmentary insights to be articulated into a full-scale revolutionary program of treatment for the cancerous "metastasis" of control (*NL* 232). The immediate consequence of this uncertain diagnosis is Burroughs's demand for more tests, more analysis of the Human Virus, in the form of "a sequel to *Naked Lunch*" which will be "A mathematical extension of the Algebra of Need beyond the junk virus. Because there are many forms of addiction I think they all obey basic laws" (*NL* xliv). This "mathematical extension," complicated by Burroughs's discovery of the cut-up technique and his increasingly active collaboration with the painter Brion Gysin, ultimately produced three sequels, *The Soft Machine, The Ticket That Exploded,* and *Nova Express,* which together comprise the *Nova* trilogy, Burroughs's most formally radical work, to which we now turn our attention.

Chapter Four

"I Hassan i Sabbah *rub out the word forever*"

The Dialectic of Treason and the Abolition of the Law in the *Nova* Trilogy

After *Naked Lunch,* the *Nova* trilogy, composed of the novels *The Soft Machine* (*SM,* 1961, revised 1966), *The Ticket That Exploded* (*TE,* 1962, revised 1966 and 1967), and *Nova Express* (*NE,* 1964), is the most famous of Burroughs's literary projects. It is also the subset of his work that is most difficult to read, by virtue of its often aleatory syntax, and for that reason alone the trilogy has been both an obstacle to academic assessments of Burroughs and a perennial favorite among nonacademic, "bohemian" readers. For many critics, Burroughs's use of the cut-up technique in the trilogy was proof a priori that his writing could no longer be interrogated for objective meaning or structure (if it ever could have been), but had to be treated like Rorschach inkblot tests of the reader's associative patterns. That is, his use of cut-ups meant that Burroughs could no longer be treated as an author, that his writings were no longer *his* but belonged entirely to his readers. Other readers refused to grant cut-ups even that much merit, and claimed that the procedure eliminated the possibility of aesthetic value. Even Burroughs's friends sometimes came to this kind of hostile conclusion. In 1960, Burroughs, Gregory Corso, Sinclair Beiles, and Brion Gysin published a first slim volume of cut-up texts entitled *Minutes to Go.* On the last page of *Minutes to Go,* Gregory Corso repudiated the cut-up experiments on the preceding pages as "uninspired machine-poetry":

> I join this venture unwillingly *and* willingly. Unwillingly because the poetry I have written was from the soul and not from the dictionary; willingly because if it can be destroyed *or* bettered by the 'cut-up' method, then it is poetry I

> care not for, and should be cut up. Word poetry is for everyman, but soul poetry—alas, is not widely distributed. (63)

Corso's pious lament over having his "soul poetry" "destroyed," like his elitist claim to a poetic inspiration beyond the reach of "everyman," is paradigmatic of the many negative responses to Burroughs's experiments, but Corso's denunciation also reveals the stakes of Burroughs's enterprise.

Readers who call the cut-ups simply destructive are irresponsible, however, and their reactions often stem from misunderstanding of the technique, coupled with a refusal to learn how to read cut-up texts (and, often, a refusal to look at the texts at all). Once its fundamental strategies are understood, the *Nova* trilogy is no more difficult to read than Gertrude Stein's *Tender Buttons* or Joyce's *Finnegans Wake,* two "unreadable" works which have experienced popular and scholarly revivals of interest in recent years. Like the pun that serves as the basis of *Finnegans Wake,* the basic cut-up technique is very simple: one takes at least one printed text, physically cuts it up into fragments, and reassembles the fragments in random order. There are several variables which can be manipulated to produce cut-up texts of varying degrees of randomness. If one cuts out wide or long sections of text, more of the original syntax remains intact and disjunctions occur less frequently. The quadrant method of cutting up, in which one cuts a single sheet of paper into four equal parts and reorders the parts, preserves perhaps the most of the original sense. If one cuts the text into very small sections, the disjunctions will occur more often and the syntax will be commensurately less normal; indeed, one can even cut individual words apart and recombine them to form new words. One can also cut two or more texts together, which can produce jarring juxtapositions if the texts deal with disparate subjects. If what the reader seeks is artistry or poetry in the traditional sense—the subjective imposition of an order onto raw material—she will find it here, in the selection of original texts and in the choice and arrangement of the cut-ups that are generated.

Burroughs credits his awakening to the cut-up method to his friend Brion Gysin, an expatriate American painter and writer whom Burroughs met in Tangier and with whom he later lived in Paris and London. Gysin himself attributes the discovery of cut-ups to the Zurich dadaist Tristan Tzara, who composed instant poems by pulling words at random out of a hat.[1] Burroughs claims that "The cut-up method brings to writers the collage, which has been used by painters for fifty years. And used by the moving and still camera" in film montage and multiple exposure ("Cut-Up Method," 29). Even these comparisons are insufficient to explain the radicality of cut-ups, however. The cut-ups do not reproduce the artificially structured "stream of consciousness" of Joyce or Virginia Woolf, or even the carefully constructed textual "montage" of the "Camera Eye" sequences in John Dos Passos's *U.S.A.*, let alone the elaborate dialectical montages of Eisenstein; these techniques are methods of control whereby the artist imposes his or her will on resistant symbolic material. As Burroughs insists, "You cannot *will* spontaneity. But you can introduce the unpredictable spontaneous factor with a pair of scissors," in other words by cutting up the text ("Cut-Up Method," 29). The experimenter can use his or her own words, or any other words by any other writer: "Poets have no words 'of their very own.' Writers don't own their words. Since when do words belong to anybody. 'Your very own words,' indeed! And who are you?" ("Cut-Up Method," 34).

Burroughs claims for the cut-ups an almost mystical power of prophecy: "If you cut into the present, the future leaks out."[2] The words contain, in themselves, all the possible permutations into which they can enter, so the experimenter can discover the future by cutting up the syntax and recombining the words to reveal their possibilities.[3] Burroughs also insists that cutting up a text that is explicitly dedicated to a certain goal will reveal the hidden motives of the text and its author, a thesis that he tests repeatedly on mass media texts, which appear often in the trilogy. The validity of his claim of prophecy is beyond the scope of this study, but the claim that cutting up reveals motivations and intentions hidden in ideological texts has some basis. In the chapter of *Nova Express* entitled "Chinese Laundry," Burroughs cuts up an article opposing the "maintenance" of addicts (a British program whereby addicts were supplied with cheap heroin to prevent them from committing crimes to support their habits) by former Assistant U.S. Attorney General Malcolm Monroe, called "Fighting Drug Addiction: The 'Clinic Plan,'" published in the magazine *Western World* in October 1959.[4] The text that emerges from Burroughs's cut-up operations dramatizes the dilemma of the trilogy: the police forces that combat criminals depend on those same criminals for their own continued existence.

> Now you are asking me whether I want to perpetuate a narcotics problem and I say: "Protect the disease. Must be made criminal protecting society from the disease."
>
> The problem scheduled in the United States the use of jail, former narcotics plan, addiction and crime for many years—Broad front "Care" of welfare

> agencies—Narcotics which antedate the use of drugs—The fact is noteworthy—48 stages—prisoner was delayed—has been separated—was required—
>
> Addiction in some form is the basis—must be wholly addicts—Any voluntary capacity subversion of The Will Capital And Treasury Bank—Infection dedicated to traffic in exchange narcotics demonstrated a Typhoid Mary who will spread narcotics problem to the United Kingdom—Finally in view of the cure—cure of the social problem and as such dangerous to society—
>
> Maintaining addict cancers to our profit—pernicious personal contact—Market increase—Release the Prosecutor to try any holes—(*NE* 51)

This cut-up, which succinctly states the central conflict of the *Nova* trilogy, also reveals that the antidrug rhetoric of the fifties and sixties served merely to cover up the real intention of the government agencies assigned to tackle the problem: to "Protect the disease" of addiction that was the source or "basis" of their existence, to maintain the "addict cancers" from which they drew their "profit." Any real "cure of the social problem" would actually be "dangerous to society." This was the situation that Burroughs had already recognized in the addict-agents of *Junky* and *Naked Lunch:* the reversible symmetry of roles, cop and criminal, imposed by formal relations of legality that Foucault would analyze ten years later in *Discipline and Punish.* Perhaps this anticipation of Foucault's influential critical insight is evidence of the cut-ups' real power of prophecy.

In revealing the constitutive contradiction of the Law (the term is capitalized to remind us that it refers to a concept rather than a particular law), the cut-up method challenges the hegemony of that Law and offers a method for abolishing it. In a passage of *The Ticket That Exploded* that alludes back to the introduction to *Naked Lunch,* Burroughs again cites Wittgenstein, followed by Marx and Engels: "Wittgenstein said: 'No proposition can contain itself as an argument' = The only thing *not* prerecorded in a prerecorded universe is the prerecording itself which is to say *any* recording that contains a random factor" (*TE* 166). The constraints of Law constitute a virtual prerecording, a determining influence that the past has on the present, locking the future into dull repetition, but such a determinism can be circumvented by means of cut-ups. On the next page, another parody of the *Communist Manifesto* appears, advocating the revolutionary valence of affordable recording technology in the form of Phillips' portable Carry Corder: "Carry Corders of the world unite. You have nothing to lose but your prerecordings" (*TE* 167). This challenge that cut-ups make to the Law—not only to copyright law but to the abstract form of the Law that defines society and its component agents—constitutes the theoretical labor of Burroughs's trilogy, and it grants the reader access to the explicit level of narrative in the trilogy as well.

•

The *Nova* trilogy is largely a hybrid of two hoary popular genres, the science fiction novel and the detective story—a combination that became Burroughs's standard means of organizing his narrative material. As we have seen, Deleuze views philosophy also as a hybrid form combining the detective novel and science fiction.

> By detective novel we mean that concepts, with their zones of presence, should intervene to resolve local situations. They themselves change along with the problems. They have spheres of influence where . . . they operate in relation to "dramas" and by means of a certain "cruelty." . . . Following Samuel Butler, we discover *Erewhon,* signifying at once the originary "nowhere" and the displaced, disguised, modified and always-recreated "here-and-now." . . . We believe in a world in which individuations are impersonal, and singularities pre-individual: the splendor of the pronoun "one." Whence the science-fiction aspect, which necessarily derives from this *Erewhon.* (Deleuze, *Difference and Repetition* xx–xxi)

This passage accurately describes Burroughs's trilogy, in which the question "And who are you?" (asked earlier of anyone who claimed to have "Your very own words, indeed!") takes on a profoundly impersonal, antisubjectivist perspective. The "local situation" under scrutiny is the living environment of this planet, seen from the perspective of alien powers of exploitation and control as well as from the viewpoint of Law; the primary "concept" used to "resolve" this "local situation" will be that of the Law.

As we should expect from the compositional techniques used to construct it, the narrative constituted by the trilogy is discontinuous, both within each individual novel and from each novel to the next in the series. Passages of linear narrative last for several pages at most, either preceding or succeeding a passage that cuts up the contents of that particular linear narrative; such doubled passages are organized in a rather broad thematic pattern within the larger chapter-like units of each novel. Many passages, both of cut-ups and of linear narrative, are repeated throughout all three novels and act like refrains or choruses to unify, to some small extent, the fractured story. In light of these, and of Burroughs's own comments on the trilogy, it is possible to discern the broad outlines of an organization arising spontaneously from the material, without the conscious predetermination a modern artist would impose.

The first novel, *The Soft Machine,* is "concerned with just description of the factors involved and the scene [of the conflict], which corresponds somewhat with the planet Venus[. . . .]And also in *Soft Machine* there's[. . .]a good deal of narrative material that's concerned with reincarnation. This is the concept of the street of chance, not sure of what kind of reincarnation you're going to have" (Burroughs, "Interview with Allen Ginsberg"). This reincarnation material draws upon the hanged man's orgasm, from *Naked Lunch,* as a means of transmigration of identity and hence of immortality. The second volume, *The Ticket That Exploded,* continues the description of the "set" and provides an allusive, indirect, and cut-up account of the conflicts therein, while the third novel, *Nova Express,* "is more directly concerned with the struggle" in detail and with its theoretical foundations and material ramifications. Indeed, Burroughs suggests that "*Nova Express* would probably have the clearest [statement]" of thematic summation.[5] My strategy in approaching the trilogy will therefore be retrospective: after broadly sketching the development of the first two volumes of the trilogy, I will explicate the conflict and its possible solutions through a close examination of *Nova Express,* and then move backward to examine the specifics of the earlier novels.

As Jennie Skerl notes, *The Soft Machine* is concerned with exposing the "social control of mankind throughout human history by the manipulation of bodily needs" (Skerl 52). Indeed, the very title refers to "the human body under constant siege from a vast hungry host of parasites[. . . .]what Freud calls the 'id' is a parasitic invasion of the hypothalamus [and] What Freud calls the 'superego' is probably a parasitic occupation of the mid brain where the 'rightness' centres may be located."[6] The routines that make up *The Soft Machine* are set in widely disparate historical periods, though they all take place in a setting that Burroughs describes as the planet Venus (science fiction "writers have equated it with something like South America," an area Burroughs knows well).[7] There is no clear development from routine to routine, but rather a sort of random juxtaposition of chapters, as if the narrative had "come unstuck in time," as Kurt Vonnegut wrote in *Slaughterhouse-Five.* The first chapter/routine, "Dead on Arrival," apparently opens in the sordid present of *Naked Lunch* but progresses backward through American history, while the final routine, "Cross the Wounded Galaxies," acts as a negative "creation myth" in Skerl's words, describing the dawn of language as the result of a devastating plague: "In the pass the muttering sickness leaped into our throats, coughing and spitting in the silver morning[. . .]sick apes spitting blood laugh. sound bubbling in throats torn with the talk sickness[. . . .]We waded into the warm mud-water. hair and ape flesh off in screaming strips. stood naked human bodies covered with phosphorescent green jelly[. . . .]When we came out of the mud we had names" (*SM* 177–78). The "coughing and spitting" alludes to Burroughs's recurrent archetypal junky, who is always "coughing and spitting in the junk-sick morning" through *Naked Lunch* and the later works. This Paleolithic plague announces the coming of the "Explosive Bio-Advance Men out of space," revealed in *The Ticket That Exploded* to be the Nova Mob, who "cross the wounded galaxies" to find new "marks" (the con man's term for his victims, which also suggests the needle tracks or marks by which addicts are identified, as well as the marks on paper that constitute language) that they can subject to their linguistic and bodily control tactics (*SM* 182). The intervening chapters present paradigms of such control in corporate ("Trak Trak Trak"), cultural/religious ("The Mayan Caper"), and gender ("Gongs of Violence") terms.

The basic premise of Burroughs's trilogy does not receive explicit exposition until the second volume, *The Ticket That Exploded.* The routine entitled "the nova police" offers a discursive presentation of the antagonisms between the Nova Mob and its marks, and between the Mob and the Nova Police who pursue it, both of which antagonisms have heretofore appeared only in allusive cut-ups. The expositor, in this instance, is "Inspector J. Lee of the nova police" (*TE* 54), who addresses a press conference called to provide the public with an explanation of the situation. He begins: "i doubt if any of you on this copy planet have ever seen a nova criminal—(they take considerable pains to mask their operations) and i am sure that none of you have ever seen a nova police officer—When disorder on any planet reaches a certain point the regulating instance scans *police*—otherwise—Sput—Another planet bites the cosmic dust" (*TE* 54; also *NE* 49–50). Naturally the Inspector puts his intervention in the best possible light. He and his forces have arrived to save the Earth from disorder and destruction. And who are the instigators of this disorder? Nova criminals, like the Heavy Metal Kid and the Subliminal Kid, led by "Mr and Mrs D also known as 'Mr Bradly Mr Martin' also known as 'the Ugly Spirit'" (*TE* 55). "The basic nova technique is very simple: Always create as many insoluble conflicts as possible and always aggravate existing conflicts—This is done by dumping on the same planet life forms with incompatible conditions of existence[. . . .] Their conditions of life are basically incompatible in present time form and it is precisely the work of the nova mob to see that they remain in present time form, to create and aggravate the conflicts that lead to the explosion of a planet, that is to nova" (*TE* 54–55, also *NE* 52). Such conflicts, the Inspector claims in Nietzschean fashion, are not moral but biological: "There is of course nothing 'wrong' about any given life form since 'wrong' only has reference to conflicts with other life forms" (*TE* 55, also *NE* 52). Both kinds of conflict, however, are subject to the Law: the moral conflict to the reversible dialectic of legality, and the biological conflict to the normative formulae of physical science.

So what can the Nova Police do about these mobsters? "We intend to arrest these criminals and turn them over to the Biological Department for the indicated alterations" (*TE* 56, also *NE* 52–53). But arresting Nova criminals is a tricky business:

> nova criminals are not three-dimensional organisms—[. . .]but they need three-dimensional human agents to operate—The point at which the criminal controller intersects a three-dimensional human agent is known as 'a coordinate point'—And if there is one thing that carries over from one human host to another it is *habit:* idiosyncrasies, vices, food preferences—[. . .]a gesture, a special look, that is to say the *style* of the controller—A chain smoker will always operate through chain smokers, an addict through addicts—Now a single controller can operate through thousands of human agents, but he must have a line of coordinate points—[. . .]It is only when we can block the controller out of all coordinate points available to him and flush him out from host cover that we can make a definitive arrest—Otherwise the criminal escapes to other coordinate (*TE* 57–58, also *NE* 54)

These criminals are *viruses,* "defined as the three-dimensional coordinate point of a controller" (*NE* 68), which invade the human body and in the process produce language, like the plague that struck the apes at the end of *The Soft Machine.* Language is both the medium and the effect of their control.

Arrest is not the end; the "indicated alterations" must be ordered and a sentence meted out to the Nova mobsters. This task falls to the "Biological Courts," which administer the biological, and thus the physical, law. The double sense revealed in this use of the word "law"—for both regularities in nature (physical law) and constraints placed on social action (judicial law)—will remain central to Burroughs's critique of dogmatic authority. Lee admits that the Courts are in "a deplorable condition at this time": "No sooner set up than immediately corrupted so that they convene every day in a different location like floating dice games, constantly swept away by stampeding life forms all idiotically glorifying their stupid ways of life—most of them quite unworkable of course" (*TE*

56, also *NE* 53). The Earth case does not go to trial until near the end of *Nova Express,* where many of these points are reiterated; the trial will therefore be discussed below. In any event, once the trial is finished, the Nova Police intend to vacate the scene. Lee also admits that he is "quite well aware that no one on any planet likes to see a police officer so let me emphasize in passing that the nova police have no intention of remaining after their work is done—That is, when the danger of nova is removed from this planet we will move on to other assignments—We do our work and go—"(*TE* 54, also *NE* 50). Unlike other law-enforcement agencies, the Nova Police claim to disappear when they are no longer needed, rather than stay around and manufacture work for themselves, the way terrestrial law-enforcement agencies do—recall the cut-up antidrug article. As his name and intentions indicate and as he later admits openly, Inspector Lee is Burroughs's double: "The purpose of my writing is to expose and arrest Nova Criminals. In *Naked Lunch, Soft Machine* and *Nova Express* I show who they are and what they are doing and what they will do if they are not arrested. Minutes to go[. . . .]With your help we can occupy the Reality Studio and retake their universe of Fear Death and Monopoly—(Signed) INSPECTOR J. LEE, NOVA POLICE" (*NE* 14).

All this technical exposition, complete with answers to audience questions, obscures the most important point in Lee's presentation: who or what is the "regulating instance" that sends for the police in the first place? Lee insists that the Nova "blockade" has been "broken by partisan activity[. . .]that cut the control lines of word and image laid down by the nova mob" (*TE* 56), and he cites details of partisan recruitment to distract his audience from the crucial point, which is revealed in a parenthesis: the leader of the partisans is actually one of the Nova Mobsters, Willy the Rat, who has "informed on his associates" (*TE* 55). This betrayal has been announced much earlier, in the "Uranian Willy" chapter of *The Soft Machine,* when "Uranian Willy the Heavy Metal Kid, also known as Willy the Rat[. . .]wised up the marks" (*SM* 155).[8] Just before the beginning of the "nova police" routine, however, at the end of "operation rewrite," the unnamed narrator claims that the conflicts managed by the Nova Mob can be "written out" of the Reality Film script, and that "alternative solutions" to the problem can be found, to which his listeners, the subjugated marks, respond, "'*No hassan i sabbah—we want flesh—we want junk—we want power—*.'" The marks want to remain under control; the situation has clearly gotten out of hand. The narrator, finally given a name, concludes, "'That did it—Dial *police*'" (*TE* 54). Whether he is called Willy the Rat or Hassan i Sabbah, the traitor (like the Nova Policeman) is clearly the figure of the writer or Rewriter—of Burroughs himself, who "had to call in the nova police to keep all these jokers out of the Rewrite Room" (*TE* 54), as the contemporary recorded routine "Burroughs Called the Law" makes clear.[9] Willy's treachery is not actually narrated in detail until the "Chinese Laundry" chapter of *Nova Express* (56–58), but its effects reverberate throughout the trilogy.

The significance of this treachery for the further development of Burroughs's engagement with the "Telepathic Bureaucracies" and "Time Monopolies" of control (*NL* 217) cannot be overstated. We have seen Burroughs's incisive analysis and parody of the reversible logic of oppositional social relations, the "dialectic of treason," in both *Junky* and *Naked Lunch*. That is, the imperative that founds the police—"Apprehend lawbreakers"—leads them to negotiate "deals" with some lawbreakers in order to capture others and ultimately to manufacture new criminals to keep themselves in business, while the imperative that founds private enterprise—"Produce profit"—leads entrepreneurs to blur and even erase the line between legitimate and illegitimate business ("shady or legitimate the same fuck of a different color," *SM* 28) in order to maximize their returns. Without this reversibility, capitalist society would come apart. The police compromise themselves by protecting and even supporting criminals who testify, but without the testimony that this support encourages, the police would be unable to make cases against organized criminals and thereby justify their jobs. Criminals suborn cops with bribes in a symmetrical manner by appealing to the entrepreneur's imperative to profit, which underlies even the police imperative to order. And if entrepreneurs did not operate illegitimate businesses, or at least incorporate illegitimate aspects into their legitimate businesses, their profit margins would suffer and they would fail. Thus the environment in which these reversals operate is both necessarily clandestine and socially ubiquitous.

This secrecy is constitutive of the subjective forms that operate in this environment. Organized crime, by its very nature, is secretive and communal, bound together by family ties and blood oaths. As Jean-Paul Sartre argues, to swear such an oath is to promise to carry out certain positive tasks and, more importantly, "To swear is to say, as a common individual: you must kill me if I secede. And this demand has no other aim than to install Terror within myself as a free defence against the fear of the enemy" (Sartre 431). In other words, as Jameson notes, the oath "must include its own principle of enforcement, and implicitly each member pledges his own death should he in the future break the unity of the group and turn traitor to it. He therefore, in a sense, consents in advance to the Terror" such as the bloodshed that followed in the wake of the French Revolution (Jameson, *Marxism and Form* 254) and the similar reprisals that the Mob makes against informers. The fear of the enemy (the police) and the Terror of the vengeful Mob are symmetrical for both the undercover cop (who may be bribed) and the treacherous mobster. The investigators of organized crime must double the secrecy and violence of the Mob's oaths in order to infiltrate and expose it; informers and undercover agents must take the secret blood oaths of the Mob and then break them, in the name of a "higher" or prior oath which is, despite Sartre's denial, fundamentally the same as the social contract (Sartre 420).[10] Like the contract, the oath represents the group's bid for survival, for social permanence in the face of the radical flux of commodified individual desires. By taking an oath, the cop or mobster submits himself voluntarily to the jurisdiction of the Law that constitutes the group.

Likewise, entrepreneurs violate the particular laws constraining their behavior in the name of the most fundamental Law of capitalism, profit at any price. There is no irony in the fact that both mobsters and private entrepreneurs consider themselves simply adventurous businessmen; indeed, this fact is a tautology. The treason that both constitutes and ultimately destroys individual social subjects (who are quickly replaced within the opposed groups so that society can continue to function) is not limited to American market capitalism, however. In fact, the dialectic of treason finds one of its most extreme historical embodiments in the Soviet Union, in Joseph Stalin's show trials of 1936–38, during which apparently faithful Communist Party members were accused of conspiring to overthrow the Soviet government and return Russia to capitalism, were tortured into signing prefabricated confessions, and were executed. The most striking feature of this "Great Purge" is the fact that most of the accused, despite their apparent innocence, pleaded guilty to treason in order to avoid compromising Stalin's regime, in which they continued to believe despite the regime's treatment of them; their denial of historical "truth" in favor of ideological "truth" was not confirmed until 1956, during the international "thaw" of the Khrushchev era, when Burroughs was composing *Naked Lunch* in Tangier.[11]

The United States was quick to reproduce this Orwellian tragedy on its own terms; near the end of *The Soft Machine* Burroughs bids "Ta ta Stalin" (*SM* 164) shortly before announcing his "stand on the Fifth Amendment" to avoid "the question of the Senator from Wisconsin: 'Are you or have you ever been a member of the male sex?'" (*SM* 168). The "Senator from Wisconsin" is Joseph McCarthy, the most visible prosecutor of suspected communists during the Cold War, whose name has since become synonymous with paranoid opportunism. The question "Are you or have you ever been . . . ?" is Burroughs's parodic version of McCarthy's perennial question to accused communists, which actually ended with the words "a member of the Communist Party"; invoking the Fifth Amendment and refusing to answer this question was interpreted as an admission of guilt. Burroughs's version of the question links the apparently "natural" attribute of sex or gender with the apparently "cultural" choice of communist sympathy, and in so doing complicates this fundamental but rarely interrogated binary opposition. He also identifies, as he did in *Junky,* the metonymic chain that accounts for the equation of social and sexual "deviance" with political subversion in mainstream American ideology. The House Un-American Activities Committee hearings, dominated by McCarthy from 1950 to 1954, demonstrated how easy it was to circumvent the freedoms guaranteed by the U.S. Constitution and reproduce the hysterical atmosphere of the Moscow show trials. It has become commonplace to point out that many people accused of communist sympathies during those years were merely liberals and leftists who justified their activities on the basis of what they assumed to be the *difference* between the U.S. and the Soviet Union: constitutionally guaranteed freedom of thought and expression.[12] These issues must have had particular resonance for Burroughs at that time, since he was engaged in the legal defense of *Naked Lunch* against obscenity charges as he composed the early versions of the *Nova* trilogy.

These historical events demonstrate the extent of the problem that Burroughs identified in the terroristic dialectic of treason, but they provided him with only incidental material for the trilogy. The central symbolic structure of the trilogy is the conflict between organized crime and the police, both bound by oaths and operating everywhere in secret, mediated by the informer through whom all other roles communicate and to whom all those roles can ultimately be reduced.[13] The question the trilogy must address, then, is whether this dialectic can be evaded and the conflict neutralized without setting the stage for a return of the same old antagonistic positions and the same old conflict. Both the police and the Mob function on the basis of implicit or explicit loyalty oaths, with each side trying to out-commit the other and bring about the betrayal of the enemy by the enemy; since the informer is central to this situation, might it be possible for an informer to upset the dialectic, perhaps by performing an act of superbetrayal, an act of treason to end all future treason? Could a traitor destroy not only the group he betrays, but also the oath itself, the very condition of the group's existence? In 1957 something like this happened: Joseph Valachi, a highly placed New York Mafioso, testified against his former comrades in the Mob before a Senate committee hearing. The story was carried in all the American media. Mobsters had "ratted" before, but none with Valachi's connections or on his scale; he was not content merely to testify to individual crimes committed by his former colleagues, but went so far as to reveal in detail the very foundation of his former loyalty, the Cosa Nostra blood oath.[14]

In the face of this spectacular act of treason, some commentators at the time predicted the imminent demise of the Mafia, which to Burroughs would have implied the equally imminent demise of the Mafia's symmetrical reflection, the Federal Bureau of Investigation and the police. The logic of the situation would dictate that only a similarly highly placed figure in the Nova Mob could reveal both the general strategy underlying its organization and the specifics of its operation. If the primary means of control is language—the Word—then all writers are, in principle, implicated in the Nova Conspiracy, including Lee (Burroughs's early alter ego) and Burroughs himself. As a junky, Burroughs's physical body is one of the "coordinate points" for the Nova Mobster, who operates "through addicts" (*TE* 57). Therefore, Burroughs's consciousness is actually that of a Nova Mobster, "Uranian Willy the Heavy Metal Kid" (*SM* 155), or even Hassan i Sabbah, who is privy to all of the parasitic secrets concealed behind the Nova Mob's mask of benign linguistic symbiosis (*TE* 54). Thus he can call the Nova Police and "rat" to them with sufficient force, he hopes, to destroy the Mob altogether and put the Police out of business at the same time. He can, perhaps, eliminate the only thing that guarantees the permanence of these repressive social structures: the Law to which the oaths or social contracts submit individual subjects, the Law that allows the structures to reproduce themselves. If he can do this, he can put the flux of individual desires back into rigid social relations, just as the cut-up method puts flux into syntax. But such an act, a transgression to end all transgression, will also expose him to the wrath of the groups he has betrayed: the Nova Mob and, perhaps, the Nova Police as well. In the aftermath of this textual situation, it is perhaps not wholly coincidental that Burroughs was actually declared by L. Ron Hubbard's Church of Scientology to be in "Condition of Treason" following his abandonment of the church in

1968 and his subsequent composition of critical articles "ratting" on its techniques of psychological analysis and control.[15]

"Willy the Rat" is an obvious nickname for Burroughs, the addict writer who betrays his former criminal companions, but where does "Hassan i Sabbah" (*TE* 54) come from? The name does not appear at all in *The Soft Machine,* but from the second routine of *The Ticket That Exploded* to the end of *Nova Express,* Hassan i Sabbah is a regular point of reference, generally as a term of comparison that reveals the inauthenticity and Nova Mob–like intentions of various pretenders to leadership of the human marks. Well into *The Ticket That Exploded,* for example, the narrator denounces the "welchers[. . .]who can't cover their bets and never intended to cover—the 'Hassan i Sabbahs' from Cuntville USA backed by yellow assassins who couldn't strangle a hernia—Self-appointed controllers of 'the Rotting Kingdom' strictly from Grade B Hollywood" (*TE* 137). This sarcastic comparison implies that Hassan i Sabbah is a legitimate leader of the partisans, and that he commands real and deadly assassins. Beyond this and similar scenes that cut through the "media" of control, *The Ticket That Exploded* offers the reader no further insight into the significance of Hassan i Sabbah; to explore that significance, we must turn to *Nova Express.*

Nova Express opens, paradoxically, with a chapter written in the imperative entitled "Last Words." At first it is difficult to determine whose last words are being spoken: "Listen to my last words anywhere. Listen to my last words any world. Listen all you boards syndicates and governments of the earth. And you powers behind what filth deals consummated in what lavatory to take what is not yours. To sell the ground from unborn feet forever—" (*NE* 11). The "last words" themselves are straightforward: "Listen: I call you all. Show your cards all players. Pay it all pay it all pay it all *back.* Play it all pay it all play it *all* back. For all to see" (*NE* 11). The speaker wants the secret controllers to reveal themselves, to "play back" the tapes, to the people that they control—the marks—and to give those people back what the controllers have stolen. The repetition of the phrases "pay it all" and "play it all" gives the imperative a ritual or incantatory cast. The controllers ask for more time, to which the speaker, alluding to the first volume of cut-ups, replies, "I say to all these words are not premature. These words may be too late. Minutes to go" (*NE* 12). The controllers invoke secrecy by appealing to their executive privileges and the interests of national security,[16] which provokes the still unidentified speaker to rage:

> Are these the words of the all-powerful boards and syndicates of the earth? These are the words of liars cowards collaborators traitors. Liars who want time for more lies. Cowards who can not face your "dogs" your "gooks" your "errand boys" your "human animals" with the truth. Collaborators with Insect People with Vegetable People. With any people anywhere who offer you a body forever. To shit forever. For this you have sold out your sons. Sold the ground from unborn feet forever. Traitors to all souls everywhere. You want the name of Hassan i Sabbah on your filth deeds to sell out the unborn? (*NE* 12)

This passage lays out the real terms of the Nova Mob's parasitic takeover of human life, which it has covered up in various ways but which is revealed in the controllers' derogatory terms for their prey, as well as their attitudes toward these hosts. Thus the passage functions as a critique of the Mob's ideology of benign coexistence and mutual benefit.

Hassan i Sabbah's name, invoked as an ironic legitimation in the last sentence, has popped up at irregular intervals throughout the second novel of the trilogy, but is still not immediately recognizable to most readers. The name is repeated in the next paragraph of "Last Words," which reveals the speaker himself to be Hassan i Sabbah: "What scared you all into time? Into body? Into shit? I will tell you: '*the word*.' Alien word '*the*.' '*The*' *word* of Alien Enemy imprisons '*thee*' in Time. In Body. In Shit. Prisoner, come out. The great skies are open. I Hassan i Sabbah *rub out the word forever.* If you I cancel all your words forever. And the words of Hassan i Sabbah as also cancel. Cross all your skies see the silent writing of Brion Gysin Hassan i Sabbah" (*NE* 12). The first lines articulate one of the basic themes of the trilogy: humanity is subjugated not only by "Alien Enemies" but by its "own" language in every possible way. Language, "*the word*," imprisons people in material bodies, which are subject to decay and little better than excrement, when they could be flying through the "great skies," free from materiality. Language interpellates individuals into a social order that is organized to benefit the controllers, and gives those individuals generic "identities" that are no more individual than the definite article, the paradoxical term that grants specificity to common nouns even though "the" itself is no less generic than the nouns it modifies. "To speak is to lie" (*NE* 14). "Word and Image write the message that is you on colorless sheets determine all flesh" (*NE* 30) because in fact "Word *is* flesh" (*NE* 71) and image—specifically, film—is the master narrative of human life. The name of Hassan i Sabbah, who is here equated with Brion Gysin (as he is in *The Ticket That Exploded*) rather than with Burroughs himself, reappears in the explicit performative that "cancel[s] all your words forever," including the very "words of Hassan i Sabbah" that perform the "rubbing out" or cancellation. Throughout the rest of the novel, this operation recurs often.

The name "Hassan i Sabbah" is a central point of reference in the *Nova* trilogy, despite the fact that Hassan i Sabbah rarely appears in any of the books as a character. He functions rather as an author-surrogate, a godlike figure, subject of imperative curses and object of magical invocations, whose incarnations, or *avatars,* under different names, fill the novels; as such Hassan i Sabbah is unquestionably the central figure in Burroughs's later literary cosmology. Hassan i Sabbah does not appear at all in the early autobiographical novels or in *Naked Lunch;* Burroughs's first reference to him occurs in the epigraph to *Minutes To Go:* "'Not knowing what is and what is not knowing *I knew not.*' Hassan Sabbah's 'Razor'." The source of the epigraph is not given, but the term "Razor" alludes to the famous logical principle of the Scholastic philosopher William of Ockham (or Occam, as Burroughs prefers to spell the name), already mentioned in the introduction to *Naked Lunch* and equated there with Wittgenstein's claim that "If a proposition is NOT NECESSARY it is MEANINGLESS" (*NL* xlvi).[17] Ockham himself wrote it thus: "What can be explained by the assumption of fewer things is vainly explained by the assumption of more things" (Ockham xxi).[18] This principle is often paraphrased as the scientist's or detective's motto, that the simplest explanation which covers the known facts is probably the correct one. The statement attributed to Hassan i Sabbah in the epigraph is a much stricter version of Ockham's principle. Ockham's Razor presupposes that the relation between the thing to be explained and the things that must be assumed to produce an explanation is self-evident—in other words, that causality and its representation in conceptual language are simple, unproblematic operations not requiring further investigation. Hassan i Sabbah's Razor, on the other hand, does not take those operations for granted, but rather questions the grounds of their self-evidence. Since the speaker does not assume in advance the difference between knowledge and its negation—the difference that is the precondition of all knowing, including the knowledge of the conditions necessary for knowledge—he cannot know anything with assurance and certainty, and therefore cannot determine which explanation is simplest and thus true. Hassan i Sabbah's Razor is Burroughs's version of the hermeneutic circle.

The "Razor" of the epigraph also alludes to the contents of *Minutes To Go:* the very first published cut-up experiments, including those made by Brion Gysin on the day when he first "sliced through a pile of newspapers with my Stanley blade . . . picked up the raw words and began to piece together texts."[19] By extension it alludes to the cut-up contents of the *Nova* trilogy as well. No doubt it was Gysin, a longtime resident of Tangier and a dedicated student of Arabic and North African culture, who introduced Burroughs to the history of the Muslim holy man Hassan i Sabbah, the Old Man of the Mountain and Master of the Assassins, just as he introduced Burroughs to Moroccan music and philosophy.[20] In the interviews with Terry Wilson published as *Here to Go: Planet R-101*, for example, Gysin repeats an old (and apocryphal) story about Hassan i Sabbah's childhood friendship with the poet Omar Khayyam (of *Rubaiyyat* fame) and the statesman Nizâm al-Mulk. According to legend, the three friends vowed to assist one another should any of them achieve success; when Nizâm al-Mulk became vizier to the Sultan of the Saljûq Turks, he arranged a stipend for Omar and a court post for Hassan. Unfortunately, this put Nizâm and Hassan in conflict. Hassan was assigned to provide an account of the revenues of the realm, but "he found when he came to deliver his speech on the exchequer that his manuscripts had been cut in such a way that he didn't at first realize that they had been sliced right down the middle and repasted. . . . All of his material had been cut up by some unknown enemy and his speech from the Woolsack was greeted with howls of laughter and utter disgrace and he was thrown out of the administration. . . . So he was the victim of a cut-up" (Gysin and Wilson 98).[21] The threefold conjunction in Burroughs's literary practice—collaborations with Gysin, experiments with the cut-up method, and adoption of Hassan i Sabbah as a central symbolic figure—may be why Burroughs equates Gysin with Hassan i Sabbah in the opening section of *Nova Express* and elsewhere. But this conjunction is only part of the rationale behind Burroughs's figurative use of Hassan i Sabbah.

Hassan i Sabbah is quoted in almost all of Burroughs's major works after *Minutes To Go*. This first citation, "Hassan Sabbah's 'Razor,'" recurs occasionally in later works (for example, *NE* 114), but it is soon superseded by another quotation of similarly unspecified origin: "'*Nothing Is True—Everything Is Permitted—' Last Words Hassan I Sabbah*" (*NE* 131).[22] This same citation appears in *The Ticket That Exploded*, without the attribution, immediately before the "nova police" routine (*TE* 54). If the "Razor" is (anti-)epistemological and demonstrates the inaccessibility of true knowledge, the "Last Words" are simultaneously (anti-)ontological, in their denial of the existence of truth (which remained at least an abstract possibility in the "Razor"), and ethical, in their assertion that "Everything Is Permitted." Indeed, Burroughs understands this Dostoyevskian statement to mean that "Everything is permitted *because* nothing is true"; thus the (anti-)ontological antecedent renders the ethical consequent equally (anti-)ontological. These "Last Words" reveal Hassan i Sabbah's ultimate function in Burroughs's novels: he represents the abolition of traditional, formal ethical Law in the face of an unknowable, because unrepresentable, ontology of difference that generates its own ethics. We still do not know, however, what gives Hassan i Sabbah the power to "rub out the word" of the Law.

•

Though Burroughs's symbolic use of Hassan i Sabbah may appear wholly personal, in fact it generally remains quite close to the few historical facts that we have concerning the real Muslim leader. Hasan-i Sabbâh, or Hassan i Sabbah as Burroughs prefers to spell it,[23] was one of the leaders of a dissident Islamic sect called the *Ismâʿîlîs,* a particularly militant subset of the *Shîʿa,* or Shiites, who claim a special reverence for and descent from ʿAlî, the cousin and son-in-law of Mohammed; central to their strain of Muslim faith is the belief that members of this line of descent are the "only legitimate rulers . . . and moreover the only authoritative religious teachers, *imâms*" (Hodgson 8).[24] The Shîʿa were a minority in the relatively unified Islamic empire of the eighth and ninth centuries, and the Ismâʿîlîs were a minority of the Shîʿa; the dominant form of Islamic practice and government was Sunnism, a pragmatically liberal and consensual synthesis of the many competing interpretations of Islamic tradition. "Sunnism represented a conscious effort to cling to those community symbols which had widest support already, rejecting any conflicting minority emphasis in the name of community solidarity" (Hodgson 6). Among these symbols were the Koran; the *hadîth* (the record of the Prophet's worldly actions distinct from the divine revelation of the Koran); the *shahâda,* or statement of witness ("There is no god but Allâh, and Mohammed is His prophet"); and, most importantly for our account of Burroughs, the *sharîʿa,* or body of ritual canon law that prescribed and proscribed the daily actions of believers. Since there were many versions of this ritual law, "to improve community solidarity [the Sunnîs] admitted the possibility of a number of alternatively acceptable systems of sharîʿa, which the faithful might choose among within broad limits" (Hodgson 6).

Ismailism is an offshoot of Shiism that derives its name from Ismâʿîl, son of a Shîʿa *imâm* and reputed father of a line of *imâms* to whom the Ismâʿîlîs granted exceptional power.

> Among the early Shîʿa there seems to have been much speculation concerning . . . the nature of the afterlife, the possibility of divine inspiration, the meaning of ritual prescriptions. There was a tendency, labeled *ghuluww,* exaggeration by its opponents, to carry these speculations farther than most Muslims felt consistent with religious propriety, giving the imâm and even the ordinary believer too high a spiritual station. . . . The imâm had sometimes been made vaguely divine by the ghuluww teachers; the Ismâʿîlîs [later] tied him to philosophical tradition as the Microcosm par excellence, in whom the metaphysical soul of the universe was personified. He had access to metaphysical reason itself, personified in the inspired Prophet, and could so guarantee a rational interpretation of the Prophet's seemingly arbitrary directives. (Hodgson 9–10)

Thus Ismailism, which posited an incarnate source of absolute transcendent knowledge in the material world, found itself at odds with the liberal and consensual order of Sunnism, which relied on rational debate and communal agreement.

Since the Sunnîs were numerically superior and controlled most of the Islamic governments, the Ismâʿîlîs could only hope to impose their ideas through revolution. In a few places, such as Egypt, they were successful and established enduring dynasties; elsewhere (and after the collapse of the Ismâʿîlî state in Egypt) the reaction to their tactics forced them to dissimulate their beliefs: "the faithful must practice what was called among the Shîʿites *taqiyya,* concealing their true allegiance from the worldly authorities lest persecution wipe out the faith" (Hodgson 12). This dissimulation found a rationale in the Shiite doctrine of *zâhir* and *bâtin,* which corresponds in many ways to the Platonic distinction between appearance and essence. "The imâm was [the] ultimate source of the inward and universal sense underlying the outward, evident sense of Koran or hadîth. The outer formulas set forth in these scriptures were called the *zâhir;* the hidden meaning of them, which the imâm revealed, was called the *bâtin*" (Hodgson 10). For many Ismâʿîlîs, this doctrine implied at least the impermanence and at most the irrelevance of the laws of the *sharîʿa* which were seen as a form of *zâhir*—for the enlightened believer who had gained transcendental insight into the *bâtin* revealed by the *imâm.*[25]

Hassan i Sabbah enters the historical stage at this point, during the decline of the Egyptian Ismâʿîlî state. A convert to Ismailism, he studied in an Egypt in which governmental authority, while symbolically vested in an *imâm,* was actually held by a military dictator. Thereafter he established his headquarters at *Alamût,* or Alamout, a fortress built atop a virtually inaccessible mountain on the southern shore of the Caspian

Sea, in what is now the Gilan province of northern Iran; from this fortress he takes his honorific title "the Old Man of the Mountain."[26] There, according to history as well as legend, he acquired a second honorific, "Master of the Assassins," as the leader and trainer of a legion of killers, the *fidâ'îs,* whose infamy spread throughout the Islamic world and Christendom during the Crusades; it is primarily in the capacity of teacher of subversive assassins that Hassan i Sabbah enters Burroughs's later works. Indeed, the very word "assassin" comes from the Arabic *hashîshiyyûn,* meaning "user of hashish," which was popularly though probably erroneously applied to the followers of Hassan i Sabbah (Hodgson 134–37). Legends reported by Marco Polo have it that Hassan i Sabbah's castle at Alamout contained a beautiful garden; when young men visited him, he served them a drugged banquet and, while they slept, had them carried into this garden where they awakened to find themselves surrounded by pliant boys and women, fine wine, and food. After a short time in the garden, the men were again drugged and returned to Hassan i Sabbah's dining room, where they were told upon waking that they had been granted a foretaste of the afterlife that awaited them if they agreed to do the Old Man's bidding.

These aspects of the Alamout legend appear in many places in Burroughs's trilogy and later works. The castle of Alamout itself is mentioned in *The Ticket That Exploded* ("Great wind voices of Alamout it's you?"—*TE* 119), and it is described paradoxically in *Nova Express* as the "cold windy bodiless rock" of immortality and transcendence that Hassan i Sabbah offers instead of the dangerously seductive delights of the flesh and the word (*NE* 13). Those who accept Hassan i Sabbah's offer become his assassins after exhaustive training; many passages in the trilogy (as well as in the subsequent *Mayfair* "Academy" essay series and parts of *The Job*) describe the intellectual and physical education of partisan "cadet" assassins in the "color writing of Hassan i Sabbah" (*NE* 83–84, 136–42). The legendary garden appears in many guises in the trilogy, but most often as a version of the deadly "Garden of Delights" described in "winds of time," the second routine of *The Ticket That Exploded:* "a vast tingling numbness surrounded by ovens of white-hot metal lattice[. . . .]Outside the oven funnels is a ruined area of sex booths[. . .]orgasm addicts stacked in rubbish heaps like muttering burlap[. . . .]The Garden of Delights. . GOD" (*TE* 8). Burroughs has apparently placed these two aspects of the legend—the eager assassins and their promised reward—in opposition to one another, or perhaps he simply demands that "partisans" be willing to imagine a disembodied

Garden of Delights, offered by Hassan i Sabbah, to combat the carnal Garden of the Nova Mobsters. In any case, the "winds of time" routine parallels the "Last Words" routine that opens *Nova Express* in offering the partisans a choice between the terminal pleasures of the flesh and the bodiless immortality of Hassan i Sabbah.

Several important aspects of the trilogy that Burroughs associates with Hassan i Sabbah have no apparent grounding in this part of the historical record, however. In particular, there seems to be no historical rationale for Burroughs's attribution of the destruction of language or the oft-repeated quotation "Nothing is true, everything is permitted" to Hassan i Sabbah. This fact suggests that Burroughs's Master of Assassins may be a composite of several figures, especially since he is not the only figure in Ismâʿîlî history who has a direct bearing on Burroughs's work in the *Nova* trilogy and later works. It is possible, of course, that Burroughs merely extended, according to his own figurative intentions, the few historical facts he had learned about the Old Man from Gysin and elsewhere. But further historical study of Ismailism offers a very compelling rationale, not only for these apparently unfounded attributions to Hassan i Sabbah, but also for Burroughs's overall task in the *Nova* trilogy: the end of the reversible dialectic of treason and the abolition of the Law.

Though Hassan i Sabbah was the leader of the *fidâ'î* assassins and an important theologian in his own right, he never claimed to be the divine *imâm;* he was, rather, the *hujja,* or "witness," the still-hidden *imâm*'s interpreter and representative. Hassan i Sabbah, who had no male children, was succeeded by one of his lieutenants, whose grandson, Hasan II, was apparently named for the first Old Man.[27] Hasan II was therefore neither a direct descendant of ʻAli nor a grandson of the Old Man, a point that his father, the Old Man's successor, made clear: even though he was to lead the Ismâʿîlîs, Hasan II was not the *imâm.* Two and a half years after Hasan II claimed the Ismâʿîlî leadership upon the death of his father, however, he did proclaim himself Caliph, or divinely appointed ruler. This was not all: during the holy month of Ramadan in 1164—perhaps to the sound of the "flutes of Ramadan" that accompany many pivotal scenes in Burroughs's *Nova* trilogy (*SM* 13, *NE* 30, 32)—Hasan II also proclaimed the arrival of the *Qiyâma,* the "Great Resurrection" of the dead that corresponds in Islam to the Apocalypse in Christianity,[28] and simultaneously declared himself to be the *Qâ'im,* or Judge of the Resurrection.[29] What Hasan II proclaimed, in effect, was the end of historical time and of the material world.

The most important practical effect of this proclamation was the abolition of the *sharîʿa,* the ritual or canon law, as part of the now-superseded *taqiyya,* or dissimulation of the faith. The *sharîʿa* constrains the behavior of the believer constantly and in many ways; it consists of the rules of behavior, both private and social, outlined in the Koran itself,[30] as well as the aforementioned *hadîth,* or collection of the Prophet's mundane actions, and the authoritative interpretations of these rules and actions given by the historical *imâms.* For the liberal Sunnî majority, the *sharîʿa* acted as a crucial social glue to bind divergent versions of Islam into a more or less cohesive society, but for the extremist Ismâʿîlîs, the law was merely a temporary expedient, an external form, or *zâhir,* to be imposed while the believer's internal revelation, or *bâtin,* was lacking and to be abandoned once that revelation matured. When one achieved revelation, one could no longer transgress because all of one's actions would be divine by definition; therefore, the law ceased to apply, and in fact any action became the only measure of itself.

The abolition of the Law begins, for the Ismâʿîlîs, as a necessary transgression of it. In principle if not in practice, this abolition does not end there. When Hasan II declared the arrival of the Qiyâma, he declared that this arrival required that the Ismâʿîlîs consciously and willfully break the *sharîʿa* by breaking the ritual fast they undertook during Ramadan. Indeed, as *Qâʾim,* Hasan II insisted that those believers who *refused* to break the law be given the punishment formerly reserved for lawbreakers (Hodgson 158). This period seems to have been rather brief, however—"a minor episode, which would run its course," as Burroughs would later claim of his own interpretation of the *Qiyâma,* or Apocalypse.[31] Hasan II was soon assassinated, presumably by Ismâʿîlîs who refused to accept the radical transformation of daily life that the Qiyâma entailed. But his revolution was carried on by his son, Muhammad II, who extended the claims of Hasan II, declared his father to have been the *imâm* as well as the *Qâʾim,* and announced that he himself therefore was the *imâm* also. Muhammad II ruled for forty-four years, during which time the doctrine of Qiyâma formed the basis of everyday life for the Ismâʿîlîs of Alamout.

Fundamental to Hasan's idea of resurrection was the interpretive doctrine of *zâhir* and *bâtin,* as it was reinterpreted at Alamout. As Henry Corbin argues, Islam is similar to Judaism and Christianity in that each is "*ahl al-kitãb,* a people in possession of a sacred Book, a people whose religion is founded on a Book that 'came down from Heaven'" and which contains "the law of life within this world and [the] guide beyond it." Therefore, for Muslims as for Jews and Christians, "The first and last task is to understand the *true meaning* of this Book" (Corbin 1). These religions thus share a basically interpretive or hermeneutic orientation toward the world, which, in Christianity, has been superseded by a typological or historical (apocalyptic) orientation as a result of the hegemony of the institutionalized Church over interpretation. No such institution or hegemony exists in Islam, where each believer must interpret for him- or herself the inner meaning of the Koran (and of other sacred texts like the *hadîth*), which is hidden by the literal word. Because

> the conditions of mankind are always changing . . . the *sharî'at,* or the Divine law revealed to mankind, must change. Thus, if the prophet leaves to them a book, its language must be allegorical, and its teachings must be expressed in similes. Only these are intelligible to the primitive people; they cannot understand anything beyond the outward meaning of things, *zâhir,* because they are in their intellectual development similar to brutes. . . . But those who are capable of understanding the inner meaning (*bâtin*), and themselves seek for knowledge of the real (*haqiqat*), living not only by their lower instincts, but also by reason and thought,—these can perceive the meaning of those instructions and commandments. . . . Therefore the letter, *zâhir,* of the religious teaching (*sharî'at*), which is concerned with the world as it appears to us, must be continually changing, while the inner meaning of it, the *bâtin,* which is the revelation of the eternal laws (*haqâ'iq*), is concerned with the world of reality; and since the latter is the same as the world of Divinity, it is unchangeable.[32]

Each individual must rise through the hierarchy of appearance to essence, through the word to its meaning, without the dogmatic guidance of a priest. The Muslim has the *imâm,* of course, but the *imâm* is, according to Hasan II and Muhammad II, the divine reality itself and does not stoop personally to enlighten the masses.

This is where Burroughs's quest to "rub out the word" finds its most compelling formulation: Hasan II "proclaimed 'a day when one does not know by signs, and doctrines, and indications,' but 'he who particularizes the self of the Essence with his own self, particularizes all signs and indications'; and therefore 'deeds and words and indices come to an end'; for whoever would 'reach [Essence or truth] through names and through its distorted and twisted attributes is veiled [from the truth]" (Hodgson 155, citing the *Haft Bâb-i Abî Ishâq*). The *zâhir/bâtin* dualism seems to be identical to the signifier/signified dualism, so in declaring an end to the domination of the *zâhir,* or material world, Hasan II and his successor proclaimed the end of language's illusion.

The *imâms* appear to have fallen into the fallacy of essential meaning that has plagued the West since Plato and that has been so thoroughly criticized in recent years. They have rubbed out the signifier or word, yet they still conceive the "unchangeable" meaning itself in linguistic—that is, in negative and dualistic—terms as a signified. Despite his agreement with this preliminary action, Burroughs ultimately rejects the dualism (in the form of both linguistic dialectics and sexual difference) that remains determinant in the Alamout account. Indeed, for Burroughs the two forms of dualism mask a single antihuman conspiracy: the Nova Mob's bid to take over the Earth by intensifying binary conflicts. The leader of the Mob, Mr Bradly Mr Martin, is himself a doubled character and may also be an autoparasitic double star that consumes itself (*NE* 69). We have already discussed briefly the routine in *The Ticket That Exploded* entitled "operation rewrite," in which Hassan i Sabbah suggests that the Nova Mob can be written out of the script for the Reality Film; when his subordinates insists that they "*want flesh*[. . .]*junk*[. . . and] *power,*" he calls the Nova Police. At the beginning of that routine, however, the Nova problem is defined primarily in terms of language. "The 'Other Half' is the word. The 'Other Half' is an organism. Word is an organism. The presence of an 'Other Half' a separate organism attached to your nervous system on an air line of words can now be demonstrated experimentally[. . . .]Man has lost the option of silence. Try halting your sub-vocal speech. Try to achieve even ten seconds of inner silence. You will encounter a resisting organism that *forces you to talk*. That organism is the word."[33] The Word is the parasite that doubles the human host, that imprisons the subject in body, time, and shit. The parasitic Word presents itself as part of the organism, when in fact it preys on the organism vampirically. Worse, the Word has split the human host along sexual lines and given rise to the dualism of gender: "The human organism is literally consisting of two halves from the beginning word and all human sex is this unsanitary arrangement whereby two entities attempt to occupy the same three-dimensional coordinate points giving rise to the sordid latrine brawls which have characterized a planet based on 'the Word,' that is, on separate flesh engaged in endless sexual conflict—[. . . .]It will be readily understandable that a program of systematic frustration was necessary in order to sell this crock of sewage as Immortality, the Garden of Delights and *love*—" (*TE* 52). The dualism of the Word, unlike sexual dualism, is also the method Burroughs uses to overcome the Word itself; he is still a writer, and "rub out the word" is still a linguistic imperative. But this simple opposition must be complicated, as must the simple dualist model of the Qiyâma.

Some contemporary Islamic historians, such as Jorunn J. Buckley and Christian Jambet, dispute the dualist or dialectical interpretation of the Qiyâma in favor of a tripartite model of Ismâʿîlî ontology, which resembles Charles Sanders Peirce's semiotics more than Ferdinand de Saussure's binary semiology. These nondualist interpretations provide a rationale for the Alamout project that is more in line with Burroughs's own critique of dualism. The passage cited above from the *Kalâm-i Pir* actually contains three terms, of which we have discussed only two, *zâhir* and *bâtin*. Buckley claims that there is a third term, beyond the *zâhir*, the signifier, and the *bâtin*, the signified: *haqîqa*, or reality itself, of which the *bâtin* is merely the conceptual image or "revelation" (Buckley 146–47). To be fair, Hodgson himself supports this tripartite reading in his table of corresponding levels of reality, faith, and social status, even though he actually presents a dualist reading in his argument. People are divided into three categories in Ismailism (Hodgson 173):

ʿâmm (common people)
khâss (elite)
akhâss-i khâss (super-elite)

This division functions on the basis of three categories of relation to Divinity:

tadâdd (opponents)
tarattub (order)
wahda (union)

All non-Ismâʿîlîs, be they Sunnîs, Christians, or barbarians, are "opponents"; the relatively unenlightened common Ismâʿîlîs represent the "order" of Ismâʿîlî society, while the advanced students of Koranic and *imâm*-derived wisdom experience "union" with the *imâm*. Only the people of order and the people of union are resurrected. Each of these categories has its own distinct relation to the divine good:

sharîʿa (ritual law)
tarîqa (the way)
qiyâma (resurrection)

Ritual law serves the opponents, just as "the spiritual way" of Ismailism serves the common Ismâʿîlîs. The total abolition of the Law is reserved for the super-elite, the people of union. Each category exists on and has access to a different level of reality:

shakl (form)
maʿnî (meaning)
haqîqa (reality)

Opponents see and indeed are themselves only the outer form, while simple Ismâʿîlîs participate in the inner meaning, and the super-elite alone contemplate in themselves essential reality. These categories, according to Muhammad II, have always functioned implicitly in the Islamic world, but the Qiyâma institutes a new set:

ʿadm (nonexistence)
juzʾî (partial)
kullî (total) (Hodgson 173)

Thus, with the arrival of the Great Resurrection, the non-Ismâʿîlî opponents have ceased to exist and can be ignored, while the common Ismâʿîlîs have only a partial existence; only the super-elite exist fully in the Divine realm. For them, the dialectic of signification implicit in the *zâhir/bâtin* opposition has ceased to exist also (Hodgson 173).

Yet this tripartite scheme, so reminiscent of Plato's class-based hierarchy of ignorance, belief, and knowledge,[34] implies that class divisions continued to exist during the Qiyâma, which does not actually appear to have been the case. Most of the common Ismâʿîlîs supported both Hasan II and Muhammad II, and the earlier hierarchy of believers faded. Hodgson notes that "one gathers from the lack of any practical notice of the hierarchical rankings . . . that in the fortress society they were ceasing to be ordered in the old formal way, or else that such rankings were ceasing to play a great role." This is because "Under the new dispensation . . . with the whole population at least potentially on a common level in the presence of the imâm-qâʾim, there was no further room for such rankings at all" (Hodgson 158). Thus the tripartite ontology apparently tended to reduce class division and antagonism, rather than increase it as we might imagine.

The reason for this reduction may be that, by definition, only one member of Ismâʿîlî society is a member of the super-elite, like the philosopher-king in Plato's imaginary state: the *imâm* himself. But the *imâm* is unlike the philosopher-king because he is the Microcosm "in whom the metaphysical soul of the universe was personified" (Hodgson 10), while the philosopher-king can only contemplate the metaphysical plane of Being. Such personification was extended to its full implications in the Qiyâma, when, with the abolition of the material universe along with the external Law, the *imâm* became the sum total of existence, outside of whom there was nothing. Corbin specifies that "the return to the World beyond—the world of spiritual entities—is the transition to a state of existence in which everything takes the form of human reality, since it is the human being alone who possesses speech, the *logos*" (Corbin 98). The law only had meaning as the path toward the *imâm,* so now that he has come, "The whole sharî'a is [rendered] meaningless, not truly existent, except insofar as, in the spiritual resurrection, a changed perspective upon the things it speaks of shows them as foreshadowing the personal office of holy figures," of whom the most important is the *imâm* (Hodgson 169). It is as the personification of the universe that the *imâm* Muhammad II, like his father Hasan II, can claim the power to annihilate the material *zâhir* world, and in so doing eliminate the addictive subjectivities of his followers: "by focusing their attention on [the *imâm*], they could be made to forget themselves, and be led to the divine hidden within him" (Hodgson 165). The *imâm* is *reality itself,* prior to all allegorical signification (*zâhir/bâtin*), and, as the highest "form of human reality" in possession of the Logos, he is also master of that signification.[35] Since the *Qâ'im,* or divine Judge, is subordinate to the *imâm,* the *imâm* can abolish his own activity of judgment as well. This is precisely the paradoxical power that Burroughs attributes to Hassan i Sabbah, the power to "*rub out the word forever,*" to "cancel" even his own words (*NE* 12), to eliminate the dialectic of signification and its attendant binarisms (of gender, criminality, class) that pass from the traitorous Nova Mobster through his coordinate point, the junky writer.

Such power can, according to this model, eliminate the Law as well, or it can fall back into the dialectics it has exceeded; such was the case at Alamout, where the apocalyptic reforms of Hasan II and Muhammad II were reversed by the latter's successor, Hasan III. "The sharî'a was re-established in the Ismâ'îlî dominions after forty-seven years' abeyance, and the younger generation had to learn at least to seem able to fulfill the ritual duties of Sunnî Muslims" (Hodgson 217). No attempt was made to revive the Shiite *sharî'a* of the earlier Ismâ'îlîs; by now law was

Law, "an outward imposition in any case—taqiyya, in the sense in which Hasan II had eliminated it at the Qiyâma" (Hodgson 218). Without the paradox of vigilant forgetting of the Law, the community falls back into the dialectic of Law and the transgression of it that only strengthens that Law further. St. Paul recognized this logic when he insisted on the fundamental position of the Law: Law creates the possibility of sin, which in turn creates the opportunity for redemption and return to the province of the Law. Burroughs recognizes the danger of this logic as well and will dedicate the rest of his career to the analysis and testing of its limits, beginning with the residual effects of linguistic representation that survive the aleatory processes of the cut-up method. Yet this danger of the Law's return should not blind us—as it often blinds those of a more Hegelian bent—to the possibility of its elimination, a possibility whose realization Burroughs presents not as inevitable but as contingent upon the efforts of those who desire it. "This is a Manichean conflict. The outcome is in doubt" (Burroughs, *Adding Machine* 83). This contingent and paradoxical power to proclaim the end of words, scribble the end of writing, and sentence the Law to oblivion, is the power that Burroughs names, appropriately, "Hassan i Sabbah."

•

The power that allows "Willy the Rat" Burroughs, as coordinate point for the treasonous Mobster Hassan i Sabbah, to "wise up the marks" and reveal the machinations of the Mob is the same power that may put the Nova "heat" out of business. The Nova Police, Inspector Lee claims, is different from every other police force in human history, because it does not reproduce itself, does not remain in existence once its work is done: "we do our work and go," as Inspector Lee said in *The Ticket That Exploded.* It is not clear that it does so by the end of the trilogy, and Burroughs remarked in an interview published shortly after the completion of the trilogy that even after the partisans' "Break through in Grey Room," the Nova Police remain an ambivalent force: at the climax of the trilogy,

> the underground and also the nova police have made a break-through past the guards and gotten into the darkroom where the films are processed, where they're in a position to expose negatives and prevent events from occurring. They're like police anywhere. All right, you've got a bad situation here in which the nova mob is about to blow up the planet. So the Heavy Metal Kid calls in the nova police. Once you get them in there, by God, they begin acting like any police. They're always an ambivalent agency. . . . In other words,

> once you get them on the scene they really start nosing around. Once the law starts asking questions, there's no end to it.[36]

Yet the ideal of a police force that would be less ambivalent, that would really "do [its] work and go," remains important for Burroughs's work from this point forward, and it is theorized at many points in the trilogy.

If the Nova Police can really be put out of business along with their opponents—which is by no means certain—it is because they are not so much dialectically and linguistically constructed social subjects, which must constantly recreate the conditions of their own existence, as they are biochemical agents, which react to a limited set of conditions and disappear once those conditions vanish.

> The difference between this department and the parasitic excrescence that often travels under the name 'Police' can be expressed in metabolic terms: The distinction between morphine and apomorphine[. . . .]The Nova Police can be compared to apomorphine, a regulating instance that need not continue and has no intention of continuing after its work is done[. . . .]Now look at the parasitic police of morphine. First they create a narcotic problem then they say that a permanent narcotics police is now necessary to deal with the problem of addiction. (*NE* 50–51)

The police force itself is a kind of second-order addiction, or meta-addiction, that feeds on the simple, first-order addictions of junkies, homosexuals, dissidents, and criminals; if these criminals vanish, the police must create more in order to justify their own survival. They must insist upon the linguistic identities of their opponents in order to maintain their own identities; thus they are called the "Logos Police" (*NE* 146), who work for "Ideology Headquarters" (*NE* 81). Unlike the standard, specular police, who must prosecute "society's disapproval of the addict" (*TE* 216), "all concepts of revenge or moral indignation must be excised from a biologic police agent" (*NE* 80) like the Nova Police. They act like apomorphine, the nonaddictive cure for morphine addiction that Burroughs used and then promoted for many years. In the trilogy its value is even greater, because it eliminates the basis of addiction: the word and the image. "Apomorphine is no word no image—It is of course misleading to speak of a silence virus or an apomorphine virus since apomorphine is anti-virus" (*NE* 47). Nevertheless, the narrative later recounts the use of the "Silence Virus" to cause a "Silence Sickness," which destroys "citizens who had been composed entirely of word" (*NE* 77).

Before we can judge the veracity of Inspector Lee's claim about the Nova Police—if indeed we ever can—we must endure the trial of the

Nova Mob in the Biologic Courts. This trial constitutes one of the longest and most coherently focused passages in the entire trilogy; it begins near the end of the "Gave Proof Through the Night" routine (a version of "Twilight's Last Gleamings," an oft-repeated early piece composed with the help of Burroughs's childhood friend Kells Elvins) and continues to the end of "This Horrible Case" (written in collaboration with Ian Sommerville). Our traitor hero, the Heavy Metal Kid, has "brought suit against practically everybody in the Biologic Courts" (*NE* 111), so at the first hearing the judge, like the Ismâʿîlî *Qâʾim* "many light years away from possibility of corruption," orders "biologic mediation": "the mediating life forms must simultaneously lay aside all defenses and all weapons[. . .]and all connection with retrospective controllers under space conditions merge into a single being which may or may not be successful" (*NE* 112). Immediately the "Man at The Typewriter[. . .]presents the Writ: [. . .]I have canceled your permissos through Time-Money-Junk of the earth[. . . .]All your junk out in apomorphine—All your time and money out in word dust drifting smoke streets." The "Gods of Time-Money-Junk" attempt escape, shouting "You called the Fuzz—you lousy fink," but are caught by the partisans and brought to the Court (*NE* 114).

"This Horrible Case" narrates the actual progress of the Nova case, offering the reader an explanation of how the double "biologic law," of descriptive physical regularity and prescriptive social constraint, functions. The Court "enables any life form in need of legal advice to contact an accredited biologic counselor trained in the intricacies and apparent contradictions of biologic law." The precedent that will be invoked in the Nova Mob trial is the "Oxygen Impasse," a "classic case presented to first year students":

> Life Form A [which] arrives on alien planet[. . .]breathes "oxygen"—There is no 'oxygen' in the atmosphere of alien planet but by invading and occupying Life Form B native to alien planet they can convert the "oxygen" they need from the blood stream of Life Form B—The Occupying Life Form A directs all the behavior and energies of Life Form B into channels calculated to elicit the highest yield of oxygen—Health and interest of the host is disregarded[. . . .]For many years Life Form A remains invisible to Life Form B[. . . .]However an emergency[. . .]has arisen—Life Form B *sees* Life Form A[. . .]and brings action in the Biologic Court alleging unspeakable indignities,[. . .]demanding summary removal of alien parasite[.] (*NE* 117–18)

Life Form A responds to the accusation by claiming its "absolute need" of food, in the form of Life Form B. This general case corresponds adequately to the Nova Mob case, if we substitute "Nova Mob" for "Life Form A" and "human marks" for "Life Form B." The precedent is a "basic statement in the algebra of absolute need—'Oxygen' interchangeable factor representing primary biologic need of a given life form" (*NE* 118).

The precedent does not function in the Biologic Courts quite as it would in an earthly court. Instead of acting as a general concept, the range of which determines the decision to be reached in the case, the precedent case serves as material for cut-ups: "From this statement the students prepare briefs—sift cut and rearrange so they can view the case from varied angles and mediums" (*NE* 118). Instead of imposing a *general* similarity on the *singular* case at hand, the precedent allows the lawyers to reveal and extend differentiation by means of the cut-up method. This procedure allows the student defense counselor to "anticipate questions of the Biologic Prosecutor," the most important of which is the following: "Was not the purpose of [Life Form A's] expedition to find 'oxygen' and extract it at any price?" (*NE* 120). The counselors "must be writers" because "the function of a counselor is to *create* facts that will tend to open biologic potentials for his client. One of the great early counselors was Franz Kafka and his briefs are still standard" (*NE* 120). Therefore the counselor cuts passages from Kafka's *The Trial* into a brief on the specific case in order to generate a useful set of new facts and to introduce new potential relations that will allow the client to evade the biologic law. The resulting brief shows how difficult the case will be: its three pages offer only "one phrase[. . .]on which a defense can be constructed—'They sometimes mutate to breathe here'—That is if a successful mutation of Life Form A can be called in as witness" (*NE* 125). If Life Form A, the Nova Mob, can mutate into a nonparasitic form, the defense can avoid the suicidal argument of "absolute biologic need" (suicidal because all biologic need, as Inspector Lee implied, is merely relative to the life form involved [*TE* 55, *NE* 52]) and thus evade the constraints imposed by the biologic law.

The Nova Mob case never receives a definitive ruling at any point in the trilogy, however. In the final section of *Nova Express,* "Pay Color," one of the partisans (the "Subliminal Kid") demands that the "Boards Syndicates Governments of the earth *Pay*—Pay back the Color you stole—": the red of flags and Coca-Cola signs, stolen from penises, blood, and the sun; the blue of police uniforms stolen from sea, sky, and human eyes; and the green of money, stolen from flowers and rivers (*NE* 131). In the face of this challenge, and perhaps also in the face of the legal "biologic mediation" that may turn against them, the Mob decides to "pay off the marks" and avoid any penalties (*NE* 132). This out-of-court settlement may be why no clear ruling is ever handed down. A more provocative reason would be that no ruling can come down because the Law itself has been abolished in Uranian Willy the Heavy Metal Kid's treason, because the Mob has been undone and, with the same stroke, the Police have been put out of business, leaving nothing over which the Biologic Courts can claim jurisdiction. The reversible symmetry on which the Law was premised and which the Law has constantly reproduced has perhaps been eliminated. The absurd "moral" implications of physical or biologic "law," ridiculed by Nietzsche a century ago, can finally be laid to rest, too.[37] This conclusion, unfortunately, must remain a tantalizing hypothesis in the face of the ultimate indeterminacy of the trilogy.

The abolition of the Law has one further conceptually necessary consequence that is important for our understanding of Burroughs's efforts in the *Nova* trilogy, whether or not such an abolition actually takes place therein: the end of time. Ismâ'îlî gnostic thought is not as rigidly teleological as Christianity, with its single endpoint to history. The Shiite predecessors of Hasan II articulated instead a cyclic idea of temporality that Henry Corbin has named "hierohistory," or "metahistory," to signify the centrality of archetypal recurrences (similar to Biblical typology or Christology) in the revelation of its meaning (Corbin 61–68, 86–90). Hodgson describes the concept in these terms:

> The Sunnî position was based on a lively sense of the decisive importance of certain historical events—the revelation to Mohammed, and the triumph of Islâm; it emphasized the consensus of the community which derived from them by a continuing historical tie. The Ismâ'îlî philosophers required a sense of history and of human nature in direct contrast to this. To support the utter sovereignty of each imâm, historical continuity of development must be replaced by a sense of historical repetition. History became a matter of types: each generation reproduced the recurrent archetypes, so that each moment was complete within itself. (Hodgson 19)

History was seen not as a developmental process but as a rigidly determined succession of abstract and eternal structures; no future was conceivable that was not conditioned by this determinism.

This concept corresponds precisely to Burroughs's theory of historical time as flat repetition without the possibility of novelty, according to which "the image past molds your future imposing repetition as the past accumulates and all actions are prerecorded and doped out and there is no life left in the present sucked dry by a walking corpse muttering through empty courtyards under film skies of Marrakesh" (*TE* 189).[38] As he implies throughout the trilogy, "history is fiction" (*NE* 13), the two-dimensional film set that serves as a backdrop for the "old army game from here to eternity" narrated in countless routines throughout Burroughs's body of work. There is only one possible escape from this confining determinist vision of history: "It is time to forget. To forget time. Is it? I was it will be it is? No. It was and it will be if you stand still for it. The point where the past touches the future is right where you are sitting now on your dead time ass hatching virus negatives into present time into the picture reality of a picture planet. Get off your ass, boys" (*TE* 196). The tenses of the Word and the self-similarity of the Image lock human history into the tedious repetition of past time, because "time is getting dressed and undressed eating sleeping not the actions but the *words* . . What we *say* about what we do. Would there be any time if we didn't say anything?" (*TE* 114) Like Nietzsche, Burroughs insist that the only escape from repetitive time is the abolition, through forgetting rather than transgression, of the Word that binds us to time. This is what Hasan II and Muhammad II hoped to achieve in making the Qiyâma the situation of daily life at Alamout, and what Burroughs similarly hopes to achieve by invoking the power of "Hassan i Sabbah who wised up the marks to space" (*NE* 72) in order to "*rub out the word forever*" (*NE* 12). This abolition of historical time, which will accompany the abolition of the Law of the Word, will lead us "'All out of time and into space. Come out of the time-word "the" forever. Come out of the body-word "thee" forever. There is nothing to fear. There is no thing in space. There is no word to fear. There is no word in space'" (*SM* 162).

Nova Express ends with Burroughs's advice on how to achieve the silence that is necessary to end the dualistic conflict between parasitic Word and human host, between the dead past that holds the present and future in a vampiric death-grip and the possibility of a revolution that will eliminate all the rules: "When you answer the machine you provide it with more recordings to be played back to your 'enemies' keep the whole nova machine running—The Chinese character for 'enemy' means to be similar to or to answer—Don't answer the machine—Shut it off—" (*NE* 153). The machine cannot forget, since it has the repetition of memory inscribed in every one of its parts, but it can be "shut off" by sabotage. Specifically, one must give the machine scrambled, cut-up recordings of its own memory/control words and let it fall into a self-destructive feedback loop. The *Nova* trilogy itself is nothing but such a cut-up recording, a Trojan

Horse aimed at the control machine of language that is most effective, paradoxically, when it makes the least syntactic sense. Hence Burroughs's enigmatic farewell to the reader, the "last words" of the trilogy, can only allude, indirectly, to the task he has tried to execute: "Well that's about the closest way I know to tell you and papers rustling across city desks . . . fresh southerly winds a long time ago" (*NE* 155). To tell us any other way would be to give the machine fresh answers for it to play back, fresh energy for its dialectics, which, like the Crab Guards of the Biologic Courts, "can not be attacked directly since they are directly charged by attack" (*NE* 76).

Paradoxically, this expository conclusion to *Nova Express* does not actually represent the conclusion of the Nova conflict that drives the trilogy; that (anti-)narrative conclusion occurs instead, as Burroughs notes, at the end of the second volume, *The Ticket That Exploded,* in a routine called "silence to say goodbye" (*TE* 183–202), which "winds it up" through an enactment of "the action of the Nova or of the explosion itself[. . .]dissolving everything into a vibrating, soundless hum" (Burroughs, "Interview with Allen Ginsberg"). Therefore we will now have to move backward through the trilogy. The general conclusion, the success of the partisan uprising, is announced twenty pages before "silence to say goodbye": "Control machine is disconnected—Word fell out of here through the glass and metal streets—God of Panic pipes blue notes through dying peoples—The law is dust—The wired structure of reality went up in slow-motion flashes—" (*TE* 155). The "wired structure of reality" that has been destroyed is the structure of the Reality Film. In a contemporary interview Burroughs points out that "Implicit in *Nova Express* is a theory that what we call reality is actually a movie. It's a film—what I call a biologic film."[39] This concept of the Image that accompanies and assists the Word is central to all of Burroughs's other formulations of the problem of ideology and reality, history and the body. "To conceal the bankruptcy of the reality studio it is essential that no one should be in a position to set up another reality set. The reality film has now become an instrument and weapon of monopoly. The full weight of the film is directed against anyone who calls the film in question with particular attention to writers and artists" (*TE* 151). The linear determinism and subliminal constructedness of the Reality Film has infiltrated all aspects of human life "until there is no way to distinguish film from flesh and the flesh melts" (*TE* 69) away into the film. At certain points in the trilogy, however, it becomes clear that "The film bank is empty" (*TE* 151) and control has been broken, following the partisans' "Break through in Grey Room" (*TE* 104; *NE* 37, 62).

The routine "silence to say goodbye" opens lyrically as "our actors bid you a long last goodbye"; the routine consists of elegiac cut-ups of other routines from the trilogy interspersed with brief narratives of cut-ups being performed by writers, engineers, soldiers, and others. The marks that drew the Nova Mob, having been "wised up" by Willy the Rat, are nowhere to be seen: "'Marks?—What Marks?'—Identity fades in empty space—last intervention" (*TE* 183). Willy the Rat's treason echoes through the routine; so does the denunciation of static time: "It is time to forget. To forget time" (*TE* 196). The final uncut passage serves as another negative creation myth like the one that concluded *The Soft Machine,* but this time it is the creation myth for a new, Wordless world:

> In the beginning was the word and the word was bullshit. The beginning words came out on the con clawing for traction—Yes sir, boys, its hard to stop that old writing arm—more of a habit than using—Been writing these RXs five hundred thousand years and sure hate to pack you boys in with a burning down word habit—But I am of course guided by my medical ethics and the uh intervention of the Board of Health—no more—*no más*—My writing arm is paralyzed—ash blown from an empty sleeve—do our work and go—(*TE* 198)

The voice that speaks here is a composite of all the characters of the trilogy, from the apparently repentant Nova Mobster to the self-promoting Nova Police inspector to the Burroughs-surrogate writer; all, of course, are voices that pass necessarily through the telepathic writer on their way from the unknown place from whence they came to their unimaginable final destination.

The last pages of "silence to say goodbye" offer the farewells of each of the trilogy's major recurrent characters. Mr Bradly Mr Martin offers the penultimate farewell to conclude the "faded story of absent world just as silver film took it—" (*TE* 201). He laments: "sure you dream up Billy who bound word for it.. in the beginning there was no Iam..[. . .] no Iam there..no one..silences..[. . .] Iam the stale Billy..I lived your life a long time ago..sad shadow whistles cross a distant sky..*adiós* marks this long ago address..didn't exist you understand.." (*TE* 202). Mr Bradly Mr Martin is also Billy, an alternate version or variation of Burroughs himself, the writer "who bound word for" the trilogy; like him, all subjects are just minor variations on the repetitive structure of "Iam," the self-definition of God.[40] Indeed, the reader is told at the other "end" of the trilogy, "You are yourself 'Mr Bradly Mr Martin'" (*NE* 154). Billy is the "boy I was who never would be now..a speck of white that seemed to catch all the light left on a dying star..and suddenly I lost him..my film ends..I lost him long ago..dying there..light went out..my film ends" (*TE* 202). As Mr Bradly Mr Martin's film ends, so ends the Reality Film, at least until the next screening. Hassan i Sabbah, appropriately, has the last word here, as he does so often throughout the trilogy: "Last round over—Remember I was the ship gives no flesh identity—lips fading—silence to say goodbye." As he declares this, silence descends over the world, ending abruptly the continuous chatter of the inevitable swindlers and con men who try to convince themselves that "This Hassan I Sabbah really works for Naval Intelligence and . . Are you listening B. J.?" (*TE* 202). Hopefully, we have taken the multiplied narrator's advice to "disinterest yourself in my words[. . . .]Disinterest yourself in anybody's words" (*TE* 198), and so no one is listening. That silence, that disinterest, would signify victory for the partisans under Hassan i Sabbah. As proof of this victory, the last page of *The Ticket That Exploded* contains no print, but instead Gysin's calligraphic permutations of the routine's title, which quickly decompose into the free lines of some forever illegible script (*TE* 203).

This final passage is as melancholy and elegiac as the final passage of *Nova Express* is sober and descriptive (or at least as sober and descriptive as cut-ups get), but why would Burroughs want to conclude the trilogy in two distinct places? What purpose could thus be served? Burroughs has never offered an explanation for this paradox, but an account of sorts follows from the fundamental insights of the cut-up method. If the point of the cut-ups is to break the rigid and linear historio-logical determinism of syntax to allow the future to leak out, as Burroughs claims, then it would be inconsistent to reinscribe that linear logic at a higher level by subordinating the cut-ups' rupture to traditional narrative structure—in other words, to arrange the trilogy itself in linear order. The structure of the entire trilogy must be cut up in order to break the deterministic logic of repetitive time. Deleuze has offered a provocative explanation for this sort of operation, which he claims is constitutive of all eruptions of novelty into the static world of repetitive time. His explanation, presented (appropriately enough) shortly after Burroughs completed his revisions of the *Nova* trilogy, involves three distinct syntheses of time. The first synthesis of time is the passive synthesis of the living present, which contracts all of the past and the future and allows time to pass unidirectionally; the past and the future belong to this pregnant present, "the past in so far as the preceding instants are retained in the contraction[,] the future because its expectation is anticipated in this same contraction" (Deleuze, *Difference and Rep-*

etition 70–71). The past and future are merely dimensions or modalities of this pregnant present that is constantly divided against itself. The second synthesis is the active synthesis of the pure past in memory that represents the old past and the current representation of that past: "The present and former presents are not, therefore, like two successive instants on the line of time; rather, the present one necessarily contains an extra dimension in which it represents the former and also represents itself" (Deleuze, *Difference and Repetition* 80). In this synthesis, the pure past is the a priori, the general element that founds representation and that coexists with every current present as its constitutive and normative myth. In static, determined time, only the first two syntheses operate, and the future is locked into simple repetition of the past. The third and final synthesis, however, is the static synthesis of the pure and empty form of time, which displaces the relation between the others to create a differential repetition, the future (Deleuze, *Difference and Repetition* 88–89).[41] The third synthesis comes between the other two, breaking their fundamental symmetry and allowing the living present a chance to affirm a difference into the new future.

Deleuze's temporal logic may appear abstract, but we can translate it easily back into Burroughs's language of cut-ups: in affirming chance, which he calls the "spontaneity" which "You cannot *will*" (Burroughs, "Cut-Up Method," 29), Burroughs can "cut into the present" so that "the future leaks out."[42] The future, the escape from static repetition in history, always exists as a virtual or potential time within each static moment, a potential time that can be brought into reality by an act of subjectless affirmation, just as the cut-up permutation of words can reveal all the alternatives hidden by the linear arrangement of syntax. This is the most compelling measure of success of the *Nova* trilogy and of the cut-up method in general: they bring the future into the present and in so doing break—if only for a moment, in a certain place, and for a small group of readers—the habits, language, and history that bind its readers to a self-destructive past. This is the performative, rather than constative, effect the *Nova* trilogy had on its author and continues to have on its readers. As Burroughs will write many years later, "I have blown a hole in time with a firecracker. Let others step through" (C 332).

•

The success of the cut-up method can also be measured by its influence: in the course of the sixties, many writers and artists in many countries experimented with variations on it, and some discovered preferred versions of their own. *The Fall of America* (1965–71), perhaps Allen Ginsberg's most significant (though not his best-known) achievement as a poet, would not have taken the form it has, had he not followed Burroughs's lead in abandoning stream of consciousness in favor of the collage of multiple sources. Tom Phillips' "treated Victorian novel," *A Humument,* was born when he "read an interview with William Burroughs and, as a result, played with the 'cut-up' technique," and decided to "push these devices into more ambitious service."[43] Many less well known writers and artists adopted variants of the cut-up as well. By the late sixties, Burroughs reached a double impasse, however. At the formal level, the critical force of the cut-up method began to dissipate, as it was taken up and applied too rigidly by less talented writers, especially in Europe, who revealed its limits by discovering the formal and stylistic indifference to which the procedure often led. At the level of social critique, the progressive incorporation into the order of production of the antagonistic subject positions from which the critique was articulated led to abstraction and opened the door to the kind of postmodernization that dominates the few current critical discussions of Burroughs's work. Nevertheless, the *Nova* trilogy also marks the beginning of Burroughs's critique of the temporality of social control as the accelerating dialectic of capital, based initially on his analysis of the Mayan calendar and caste system.[44] This particular critique reaches its mature form several years later, after the countercultural break, in *Ah Pook Is Here* and "The Limits of Control": the acceleration of subjective time and the concomitant collapse of space forms "an exact parallel here with inflation, since money buys time." More explicitly, he insists that money is shit, not for psychoanalytic reasons, but because "It eats youth, spontaneity, life, beauty and above all it eats creativity. It eats quality and shits out quantity. . . . The more the machine eats the less remains. So your money buys always less. This process is now escalating geometrically" (Burroughs and Odier 73–74). Burroughs here approaches the crisis of the law of value—which Antonio Negri analyzed so astutely[45]—from the point of view of capitalist control, in order to demonstrate the self-destructive tendency of its dialectical motion (though he doesn't "mean to suggest that control automatically defeats itself, nor that protest is therefore unnecessary": Burroughs, *Adding Machine* 120). But in the *Nova* trilogy he examines it primarily from the positions of subjects and collectivities subjected to control; Deleuze has observed that "'Control' is the name proposed by Burroughs to characterize the new monster, and Foucault sees it fast approaching" (Deleuze, *Negotiations* 178).

Although the Beat Generation with which Burroughs was identified was being incorporated into academic and publishing institutions by the late sixties, it served not as an imitable model but as a "rhizomatic" relay (Deleuze and Guattari, *A Thousand Plateaus* 22) for the social movements that followed: the student-led antiwar and ecology movements grew into mass movements that cut across traditional national and class lines, as the new subjectivities—formed in resistance to capital's response to the labor unions, the civil rights movement, the Beats, and others—recognized their collective nature. Burroughs took to the streets to follow these developments, covering the riots surrounding the 1968 Democratic National Convention in Chicago for *Esquire* magazine[46] and calling for "more riots and more violence" from the students (Burroughs and Odier 81). The experience of mass activity, coupled with the nondualistic interpretation of writing he had conceived in the course of the *Nova* trilogy, led Burroughs out of the reflexive impasse of the cut-ups; *The Wild Boys: A Book of the Dead,* published in 1969, signaled his recognition of and commitment to the new forms of subjectivity revealed by the massification of the student movements, as well as his return to the narrative scene or routine as his basic compositional unit. This experience also led him to alter his basic metaphors, from organized crime and the secret agent, too easily trapped in the formal dialectic of treason, to the revolutionary group, committed to the transformation of society by means of the total elimination (rather than the dialectical maintenance) of its opponents.[47] In a sense, then, *The Wild Boys* represents the most important turning point in Burroughs's career, and we will now examine it.

Chapter Five

The Wild Boys

Desire, Fantasy, and the Book of the Dead

In *Bright Book of Life,* his survey of postwar American fiction, Alfred Kazin sums up Burroughs's work from *Naked Lunch* through *The Wild Boys* by presenting him as an obsessive auto-eroticist, engaged in "transcribing open sexual fantasy into literary energy"[1] and producing in the process an almost hermetic set of personal myths. Burroughs's texts have no real referent in, or even connection to, reality in Kazin's view: "Burroughs's fiction happenings are a wholly self-pleasing version of what D. H. Lawrence called the 'pure present.' Lawrence meant that the act of creation could renew the world. What Burroughs means by it is reverie, a world forever being reshuffled in the mind, a world that belongs to oneself like the contents of a dream" (Kazin 263). This reading is fundamentally the same as the postmodernization carried out by Cronenberg and Lydenberg, despite its distinct critical framework. What is striking about Kazin's reading of Burroughs is its explicit assumption that Burroughs's production of fantasy is in some way solipsistic or at least narcissistic, rather than world-historical and political; this appears especially difficult to understand in light of the overt political content we have found in Burroughs's major texts from *Junky* forward. Lydenberg at least attributed a political *intention,* textualist though it was, to Burroughs's formal experimentation. Moreover, many recent theories of ideological fantasy have demonstrated the very *practical* effect of fantasy in resolving, at the level of imaginary representations, contradictions inherent in the material relations of production.[2]

The Marxist critique of ideology is, of course, an example of the seriousness that critics other than Kazin have granted to the social problem of fantasy, particularly in its group form: ideology is the medium by which historically and socially determined relations of power are mystified, masked by the appearance of inevitability; it is the fantasmatic medium through which culture appears as nature. This is not to suggest that all fantasy necessarily serves as cover for already constituted systems of power; such a position would be tenable only if we could avoid the force of the various critiques of metalanguage that have been articulated in the last several decades. The assumption that fantasy is necessarily more complicit than a critical realism in masking the relations of power depends upon an image of unmasking or demystification as science, in the old Marxist sense of an objective account of the material relations of production. But the later works of Herbert Marcuse, Theodor Adorno, and others have demonstrated the impossibility of finding a definable position outside of those relations in which to ground a straightforward dialectical critique.[3] Burroughs recognizes this difficulty as well, as the extrahistorical perspective of the narrator at the conclusion of *Naked Lunch* shows. From another perspective, Jacques Derrida has demonstrated, with respect to Claude Lévi-Strauss's structural anthropology, that metalinguistic translation of myth simply produces another myth that cannot claim any greater "adequacy" to the supposed facts than the myth it purports to explain.[4] The dialectical critique of ideology itself produces ideology, and the structural study of myth itself produces myth.

The various critiques of demystification leave us, then, without access to a privileged level of reality that would allow us to determine the adequacy of any representation of the world to that world; truth can no longer be conceived as this adequacy, and therefore no traditional hermeneutic approach will be able to provide the grounds for the transformation of existing practices of exploitation and domination by simply unmasking the status quo.[5] This is most emphatically *not* to say that all ideologies are equivalent to one another, nor that all myths are the same. In fact, the burden of this chapter is to follow out Kazin's most interesting insight: the possibility that desire, in the form of fantasy, represents not a retreat from the world, nor an imaginary justification of its failings, but the creation and transformation of it. Deleuze describes this power of fantasy as its ability to produce "the indiscernibility of the real and the imaginary" through the abandonment of normative standards of truth as representational adequacy (Deleuze, *Cinema-2* 132). Kazin himself is willing to attribute this power of fantasy to Lawrence but not to Burroughs, insisting that for Burroughs, "Self and world become utterly opposed places," and therefore "the world becomes a nut place simply because it is the opposite of the private movie theater," not because the fantasy identifies real problems or material contradictions in the world (Kazin 267).

Kazin's narcissistic model of fantasy, however, is not adequate to Burroughs's literary practice; Burroughs's longtime friend and former lover Allen Ginsberg offers a better one. In the introduction to a collection of Burroughs's letters to him, Ginsberg points out that Burroughs composed many of the routines that would go into *Naked Lunch* and the *Nova* trilogy in letters he sent to Ginsberg in the mid-fifties, after their love affair had ended; these routines, some of them quite disturbing and scatological (like the famous "Talking Asshole" sequence, in the letter dated 7 February 1954), were apparently intended as means of seduction. Ginsberg describes Burroughs's textual courtship as "an exquisite black-humorous fantasy . . . and a parody of his feelings, lest his desire be considered offensive. . . . The reader will thus recognize many of the 'routines,' that later became *Naked Lunch,* as conscious projections of Burroughs's love fantasies—further explanations and parodies and models of our ideal love schlupp together."[6] Through these routines, Burroughs hoped to win the errant Ginsberg back. Burroughs's writing, then, has never been autoerotically hermetic, as Kazin implies, or hermeneutic; rather, it is performative. It does not attempt to describe something that exists outside of itself, but to intervene in a particular conjunction of necessarily libidinal (and political) circumstances. Clearly Burroughs's writing is not singular in this respect, since it is difficult to imagine any literary work that is not intelligible as such an intervention; what is important for my argument is not this abstract, generalized performativity, however, but the affirmative valence of seduction it takes on in Burroughs's apparently negative and even repulsive works. The issue here is not the *fact* that Burroughs's writing is effective, but *how* exactly it is effective—which is to say, how it can be politically transformative or affirmative despite (or even because of) its reliance on violence, alienation, and disgust. The fact that Burroughs's attempts both to win Ginsberg back and to change contemporary society have apparently not succeeded should not blind us to the profound seriousness and inventiveness with which he pursued those goals. Marshall McLuhan recognized this effective side of Burroughs's work early on: "It is amusing to read reviews of Burroughs that try to classify his books as nonbooks or as failed science fiction. It is a little like trying to criticize the sartorial and verbal manifestations of a man who is knocking on the door to explain that flames are leaping from the roof of our home."[7] The means Burroughs finds to get us out of the house may have no simple referential relation to the danger, but those means must be judged on the basis of their effects rather than their truth.

This perspective not only refutes Kazin's reductive assessment of Burroughs's writing as a "private movie theatre" in which "Self and world become utterly opposed places," but also argues for the political efficacy of Burroughs's texts, both virtual and actual. Given the contexts in which he wrote, from the now-lost early texts of the twenties through the "queer" perspectives on McCarthy-era hysteria and the violent activism of the late sixties to his recent revisionary history of the Enlightenment, it is possible to claim (or denounce) Burroughs's fantasmatic writing for pure narcissistic aestheticism only by ignoring the context of political engagement into which he sent his literary interventions, a context that he discovered among his peers and later reconstructed, not only for his own literary purposes, but also for the use of others with similar convictions. Such a context could be called an *audience,* a community of addressees, to anticipate the argument a little. This audience, itself a fantasy to the extent that it is the product of the investment of desire and simultaneously its object, will be as much a focus of our investigation as Burroughs's text will be.

Why is it necessary to bring up the issue of fantasy and its status at this point in the study of Burroughs's work? As we have seen, Burroughs's infamous early fiction, *Naked Lunch* (1956) and the *Nova* trilogy (1961–67), provides what we might provisionally call a negative, or high modernist, fantasy from the point of view of social transformation: that is, a fantasmatic allegorization of the contemporary social order that Burroughs himself admits functions as a "new mythology for the space age" (Burroughs and Mottram 4). This "negativity" of the early fiction—its refusal to offer viable alternatives to the problems it addresses—is largely consistent with Adorno's powerful account of modernism's critique of capitalism: "By cathecting the repressed, art internalizes the repressing principle, i.e. the unredeemed condition of the world, instead of merely airing futile protests against it. Art identifies and expresses that condition, thus anticipating its overcoming" (Adorno, *Aesthetic Theory* 27–28). All modernist works can do is negate, through their own hypertrophic form, the parallel organization of the social order, as Burroughs's early works attempt to do. The Nova Mob and its deeply covered agents, Mr Bradly Mr Martin, and the whole range of political parties in *Naked Lunch* are horrific figures that can be recognized as hyperbolically depraved versions of segments of the political infrastructure of the postwar United States, while even the Factualists and the Nova Police who oppose the Mob are implicated in their opponents' work. Robin Lydenberg has explicated the theoretical labor of these novels, though she has not fully appreciated their social implications.

What interests us here, however, is Burroughs's invention of a new set of fantasies during the period of cultural unrest in the late sixties. *The Wild Boys: A Book of the Dead* (1969–71) inaugurates this period, which continues through *The Job* (1969–70), *Exterminator!* (1966–73), *The Last Words of Dutch Schultz* (1970; revised 1975), and *Port of Saints* (1973; revised 1980). These middle-period texts, self-consciously written in the shadow of the Paris student riots of May 1968, the occupation of Columbia University (the alma mater of Burroughs's friends Ginsberg and Jack Kerouac), and what Norman Mailer called "the siege of Chicago,"[8] still present excessive fantasies of Control—as Burroughs calls the centralized authority that rules his paranoid system. But they also introduce completely new kinds of fantasmatic figures: revolutionary (instead of capitalist) double agents, such as the narrators of the novels, and the Wild Boys themselves, bands of young homosexuals who reproduce by a kind of fantasmatic parthenogenesis and whose purpose is to destroy the bourgeois world order. In *Naked Lunch* and the *Nova* trilogy, figures of resistance tended to be marginalized drug users and "queers," as if Burroughs could only find spaces of resistance in the confined interstices of a successful dominant (American/capitalist) order. These spaces of resistance were highly unstable and likely at any time to reverse into their opposites according to the dialectic of treason: "all Agents defect and all Resisters sell out." In these middle texts, however, resistance is almost ubiquitous—as it seemed to be in the new cultural order of the sixties—and springs not from the traditional subject of revolutionary activity, the working class, but from a new vanguard: boys and young men similar to the leaders and members of student movements like Students for a Democratic Society (SDS), the 22 March Movement, and the Yippies. According to Burroughs, speaking in 1969, "Authority in the West has never been more threatened than it is right now" (Burroughs and Odier 128), precisely because this new body of radicals supplanted the accommodated and quiescent working class. A *positive* or *affirmative* alternative to capitalist society, and not just a negative critique of it, seemed conceivable: a utopian fantasy not bounded by the mythological terms of modernism or foreclosed by the linguistic terms of postmodernism. The Wild Boys are Burroughs's intensified fantasy version of countercultural revolt, both the object and the audience of his writing: "The wild boys have no sense of time and date the beginning from 1969 when the first wild boy groups were formed" (Burroughs, *Port of Saints* 73).[9] These figures, for all their hyperbolic cruelty and willful ignorance, are Burroughs's phantom doubles or surrogate selves, even down to their initials, "W. B."

The gender specificity of Burroughs's fantasmatic revolutionaries should surprise no one familiar with his work prior to this point, or with his writings of the following decade. It may be useful for us to recall, however, that Burroughs's infamous misogyny, unlike that of heterosexual chauvinists like Norman Mailer or Ishmael Reed, is premised on a conception of the fundamental irreducibility of sexual difference as radical as that of a feminist like Luce Irigaray. Burroughs has never demanded the subordination of the feminine to the masculine, as many heterosexual male chauvinists have; he has argued, rather, for the total separation of the masculine from the feminine, as befits his theory that men and women are actually separate species that cannot be united under the rubric of an expanded, and therefore abstracted, definition of "humanity." In light of this, it seems more fruitful to view the project of *The Wild Boys* not simply as "the occlusion of women"[10] but as an attempt to take sexual difference as a point of departure for political transformation, rather than seeing it as a problem to be overcome. Though his own viewpoint is unrepentantly androcentric, Burroughs said at that time that "I certainly have no objections if lesbians would like to do the same" from a gynocentric point of view (Burroughs, "*Rolling Stone* Interview" 52). On the basis of this reading, Burroughs's novel might be seen as the anticipatory counterpart of feminist political fantasies like Monique Wittig's *Les Guérillères* and Joanna Russ's *The Female Man,* both of which share Burroughs's disregard for narrative continuity and his fascination with explicit, politicized violence. In addition to the formal experiments in which they engage, these books also offer new kinds of characters for their audiences' libidinal investment: Wittig's women warriors and the surgically altered female assassins of Jael's world in Russ's novel resemble Burroughs's Wild Boys in many (though by no means all) ways.

In addition to new character types, these texts also introduce new forms of composition, of which the most significant is the "book of the dead." *The Wild Boys: A Book of the Dead,* as its subtitle indicates, must be read as an example of a genre that has no equivalent in Western culture, and that therefore has received little attention from literary scholars. The most famous examples of this genre—the Tibetan *Bardo Thödol,* the Egyptian Books of the Dead, and the Maya codices—come out of non-Christian traditions. (Scholars disagree, but Burroughs insists that the Maya codices, which he studied in Mexico in the late forties and early fifties, "are undoubtedly books of the dead; that is to say, directions for time travel"; Burroughs, *Ah Pook* 15).[11] Burroughs had made reference to and use of these texts earlier, for example in "The Mayan Caper" section of *The Soft Machine* (85–97) but this use was always subordinated to the controlling metaphors of the *Nova* trilogy, criminal metaphors that Burroughs came to distrust because of their reliance on exclusionary Law: organized crime provided the image of control, and the police provided the image of objective resistance. In the middle-period texts we will consider, the "book of the dead" takes over as controlling structure. The function of these books of the dead is practical as well as spiritual; they provide guidance, in narrative and ritual form, to souls seeking paths through the dangerous and uncertain lands of the dead to the promised land.

Of course, the very idea of a book intended to guide the dead through the afterlife is either absurd or blasphemous to Christians, for whom the status and eternal fate of the individual dead soul has been determined at the moment of death, if not well before. The idea of purgatory in Roman Catholicism is no more than a baroque variation on the theme of salvation and damnation, by which souls can atone in predetermined ways for their transgressions; no real uncertainty exists. Because of this, no narrative can exist in the afterlife, at least not for the individual soul; the only narrative movement in the Judeo-Christian afterlife is the mass Hegelianism of the Apocalypse. The nearest correlative in European literature would perhaps be Dante's *Divine Comedy,* but it cannot be considered a "guide" to the afterlife except perhaps in topographical or political terms: none of its characters find themselves in the position of seeking a passage through the perils of the land of the dead, so the *Divine Comedy* can only be an allegorical map of virtue. Dante experiences narrative movement as an observer, but he himself is not subject to any of the punishments or rewards he sees bestowed around him in his journey, and the souls he meets are in no uncertainty concerning their fates; for a book of the dead to have any meaning as such, its readers, like its characters, must (be prepared to) fall into both categories, observer and observed.

Books of the dead suggest, again contrary to Judeo-Christian belief, that the afterlife resembles mortal existence, and therefore that the soul needs guidance there as much as it does here. This situation is clearest in Egyptian culture, which developed elaborate rituals and preservative practices to maintain the bodies of the dead, both by embalming (mummification) and by filling tombs with supplies for the use of the dead. The Egyptologist E. A. Wallis Budge (to whom Burroughs occasionally refers) reports that many early texts "seem to imply that the Egyptians believed in a corporeal existence, or at least in the capacity for corporeal enjoyment, in the future state. This belief may have rested upon the view that the life in the next world was but a continuation of life upon earth, which it resembled closely" (Budge, *Egyptian Book* lxxviii).[12] Consider, for example, this prayer from chapter 110 of the Book: "May I become a *khu* therein, may I eat therein, may I drink therein, may I plough therein, may I reap therein, may I fight therein, may I make love therein . . . " (Budge, *Book* 327).[13] They believed not only in the possibility of corporeal enjoyment, but also in the threat of corporeal danger, which is why the Egyptian Book is filled with prayers for the intercession of the gods in the progress of the soul through the lands of the dead.

That a book of the dead must be fantasmatic is clear: it is the desire-invested projection of a cultural group's identity into a world beyond, or at least other than, our own. But what specific kind of fantasy does it represent? To put the question bluntly and somewhat reductively, is it ideological in a bad sense, utopian in a good sense, or something else entirely? And how will Burroughs be able to put this fantasmatic genre to radical use? To determine the answers, we must articulate a method for distinguishing forms of fantasmatic desire that does not operate as a simple textual hermeneutic—that does not, in other words, fall back into the interminable dialectic of truth and mystification. If the hermeneutical search for meaning can only produce reproductions of the textual modes upon which it works, we should find another model for thought than the text if we wish to understand (and perhaps undertake) the transformation of practice that Burroughs's use of the book of the dead proposes. Deleuze, in his collaborations with Félix Guattari, suggests a radical, nonhierarchical and nonhermeneutic method for distinguishing the political ramifications of forms of mass fantasy like the book of the dead. The radical function of mass fantasy in their model is to allow and even promote investments of desire that are incompatible with the established social and economic order. This nonhierarchical, or rhizomatic, account of fantasy underpins the theory of social groups in *Anti-Oedipus,* which was itself inspired by the same student movements of the sixties that Burroughs engaged and supported, and which developed out of Deleuze's and Guattari's readings of Jean-Paul Sartre's last major work of philosophy, the *Critique of Dialectical Reason.*

As we saw in chapter 1, Sartre posits a fundamental distinction between two kinds of human social structures, the *series* and the *group* (or *fused group*). Most common of these types is the series, which is, roughly speaking, passive and dependent upon an outside force for the determination of its internal structure; relevant examples of series would be the sets of people lined up in a grocery store check-out line or at a polling booth, their seriality (in these cases their identities as consumers or citizens) "produced *in advance* as the structure of some unknown group" (Sartre 265) by the cash register or the voting machine. This means that an individual person forms part of a series when s/he participates in "a reality shared by several people . . . *which already exists,* and *awaits him,* by means of an inert practice, denoted by instrumentality, whose meaning is that it integrates him into an ordered multiplicity by assigning him a place in a prefabricated seriality" (Sartre 265). In other words, he or she belatedly joins an already existing social complex embodied in mechanical sorting, counting, and management devices (aspects of what Marx called "dead labor" and Sartre calls "inert practice" or "instrumentality"). These machines give him or her "a place in a prefabricated seriality" by reducing the subject's choices to the array of preestablished alternatives they offer. The place of such a complex in the overall social organization, or "socius," is stable and wholly determined by the constraints of that organization's formal structure and requirements. This passive and preordained seriality is obviously "the basic type of sociality" (Sartre 348) under capitalism and state socialism, and many more examples could no doubt be found. Deleuze and Guattari theorize a form of ensemble explicitly modeled on the series: the *subjugated group,* which is also entirely determined by the preexistent categories, choices, and structures that the social order provides. This kind of group invests "all of an existing social field, including the latter's most repressive forms," with desire (Deleuze and Guattari, *Anti-Oedipus* 30). Because of this, a subjugated group remains subjugated even when seizing political/social power if

> this power itself refers to a form of force that continues to enslave and crush desiring-production . . . : the subordination to a socius as a fixed support that attributes to itself the productive forces, extracting and absorbing the surplus value therefrom; the effusion of anti-production and death-carrying elements within the system, which feels and pretends to be all the more im-

> mortal; the phenomenon of group "superegoization," narcissism, and hierarchy—the mechanisms for the repression of desire. (Deleuze and Guattari, *Anti-Oedipus* 348)

These "investments" or "mechanisms" constitute constructions or articulations of simple desires into complex networks of libidinal connection and feedback that ultimately form one type of mass fantasy. Ideology is certainly one of the most powerful forms of fantasy produced by the social system for the purposes of its own reproduction, as is modernist myth, inasmuch as each is presented in its respective context as being simultaneously the permanent ("immortal") base of value and the legislating superego of the subjugated group.

Sartre's radical alternative to seriality is the *group in fusion,* or *fused group.* A fused group is a novel and unstable social structure, "constituted by the liquidation of an inert seriality under the pressure of definite material circumstances, in so far as particular practico-inert structures of the environment were synthetically united to designate it, that is to say, in so far as its practice was inscribed in things as an inert idea" (Sartre 361). The fused group negates the series by the force of its collision with material circumstances (including, in some cases, machines, legal penalties, sanctioned violence, and other forces) that are the products of other series of individuals who treat the proto–fused group as their object and thus threaten it. We might say that the threat wakes the subjugated group up to its dilemma, at which point it becomes a fused group. Like the existential subject in *Being and Nothingness,* the group is produced through the look of the Other, but as Fredric Jameson demonstrates, the Other in this case is no longer simply the abstract category of objective exteriority, but is in fact embodied in the other individual members of the group: "the group no longer has to depend on the look of the outsider or enemy" because "a structure has been evolved such that the group carries its source of being within itself" (Jameson, *Marxism and Form* 253). The stable and external determination of the series—its dependence upon an inert and instrumental element of the socius—is displaced into the group and simultaneously projected outward toward a material locus that is taken to measure both the threat to the group and its opportunity to protect and preserve itself. For example, the Parisians' storming of the Bastille during the French Revolution enacted the process of becoming-fused that allowed them to transform the existing social structure (Sartre 351–63).

The radical position of the fused group is extended in *Anti-Oedipus* by the *subject-group,* which is distinct from the subjugated group. When confronted by the repressive fantasies provided by the socius or by subjugated groups, the subject-group responds by "launch[ing] a counterinvestment whereby revolutionary desire is plugged into the existing social field as a source of energy" (Deleuze and Guattari, *Anti-Oedipus* 30).[14] This does not mean that the subject-group invests the existing forms of sociality or fantasy; rather, it is driven by the libidinal poverty of existing forms to find alternatives to them.

> [It] is a group whose libidinal investments are themselves revolutionary; it causes desire to penetrate into the social field, and subordinates the socius or the form of power to desiring-production; productive of desire and a desire that produces, the subject-group invents always mortal formations that exorcise the effusion in it of a death instinct; it opposes real coefficients of transversality to the symbolic determinations of subjugation, coefficients without hierarchy or a group superego. (Deleuze and Guattari, *Anti-Oedipus* 348–49)

In defiance of the stable subjugated order, the subject-group produces or invests "formations," or new group fantasies, that are actively hostile to the structures of the socius; but unlike myths, subject-group fantasies are in constant flux and are incapable of instituting a permanent and restrictive Law. Among these fantasies Deleuze and Guattari number certain popular utopian schemes (such as Charles Fourier's utopia of "passionate attraction" and "attractive work": Fourier 216–19, 274–83), to which I would add the apparently more "nihilistic" or "disgusting" images of revolutionary change that fill Burroughs's novels. Such effective fantasies, which draw out desires that have no established place within the existing society, embody what Deleuze will later call "the powers of the false" (Deleuze, *Cinema-2* 131).

The key element of this analysis, which is largely only implicit in Sartre's account but is foregrounded in Deleuze and Guattari's, is the fact that the process of displacement and projection that grants the subject-group its power is not conscious and rational but fantasmatic. As discussed earlier, the Bastille served the terrified people of revolutionary Paris as a focus for innovative social reorganization, but as an imaginary mirror for desire rather than as a fixed, rational object of calculation. This process of imaginary mirroring is fantasy itself, which serves as the catalyst for subject-group fusion. The voters and shoppers also see themselves in an imaginary mirror, but the relations and identities they see there are planned and preestablished, not by their novel desires, but by the structure of the institutions in which they seek satisfaction. Their seriality, in relation to the market or the polls, is permanent and indifferent. They willingly insert themselves into the given categories, willingly accept the desires that are offered to them along with the means of fulfilling them (for a short time). This is the method that Deleuze and Guattari practice in *Anti-Oedipus* and their other works, the method whereby they distinguish radical from reactionary desire: the investment of desire in and through fantasy can remain enmeshed in institutionalized, serialized ideology, but it can also itself produce group formations that are hostile (though not necessarily opposed, in the strict dialectical sense)[15] to the given relations of production, class, and subjectivity, without necessarily presenting themselves as permanent replacements for those relations. This method offers us a way to distinguish between forms of fantasy, and it is fantasy that attracts serialized or subjugated subjects, in order either to keep them subjugated or on the contrary to dissolve, or "deterritorialize," the subjects' conformity. The construction of viable subject-group fantasies, and the consequent fantasmatic production of revolutionary groups, is the burden of Burroughs's writing in *The Wild Boys* and later works.

From the perspective of Deleuze and Guattari's analysis of mass fantasy, the book of the dead is clearly an ambiguous genre: it generally serves its culture as a (direct or indirect) religious legitimation of social power structures, and thus serves conservative ideology, but it also treats the afterlife much like mortal life, as a fundamentally open process of contestation for which the book serves as a guide. The historical books of the dead, particularly the Egyptian and Maya texts on which Burroughs has focused, fall into the category of subjugated-group fantasy because of their positions within the institutionalized belief systems that characterized those cultures. Budge points out that all surviving copies of the Egyptian Book were owned by members of the dominant class, including "priestly officials [who] were still relatives of the royal family"; and "the tombs of feudal lords, scribes, and others, record a number of their official titles" (*Egyptian Book* xviii), which are also written into their books of the dead. Even during the most socially egalitarian periods, only a very small number of citizens could afford the expense of following the Book's rituals and suggestions. Of the Maya, Burroughs himself claims that "The workers could not read the books and undoubtedly they were prevented from learning" by "the absolute power of the priests, who formed about two percent of the population" (Burroughs, *Ah Pook* 16 and *SM* 87). They controlled the workers, Burroughs claims, by controlling the elaborate system of calendars that make up the Maya "book of the dead."[16] These claims suggest that the historical books of the dead served as markers of social status, and thus abetted the status quo as subjugated-group fantasies. The actual terms of the Egyptian burial ceremonies lend credence to this interpretation. The dead patrician is offered to the gods as an equal, who takes his (or her) place in an already constituted system: "Thou art purified with natron [soda], and Horus is purified with natron; thou art purified with natron, and Set is purified with natron; thou art purified with natron, and Thoth is purified with natron . . . ; Thou art stablished among the gods thy brethren, thy head is purified for thee with natron, thy bones are washed clean with water, and thou thyself art made perfect with all that belongeth unto thee" (Budge, *Egyptian Book* cxl). Note as well that property follows the deceased into the afterlife, in contrast to Christian doctrine.

Once the books of the dead move into contexts that do not correspond to their "proper" cultures, however, their status as subjugated-group fantasy changes, though not necessarily into subject-group fantasy; they no longer represent the imaginary of the existing socius, but this does not mean that they are hostile to it. Their difference from the established social order gives them the potential for revolutionary influence, as many members of the Anglo-European counterculture have realized, but the specific form and content of that difference may fail to realize that potential; this is the case with many varieties of so-called Eastern mysticism, including Buddhism, whose anticapitalist tenets are subsumed within a larger project of completely antimaterialist spirituality that, at least among many of its Anglo-European adherents, tips over into absolute idealism. Such idealism treats all material manifestations of the spirit as, at best, steps necessary for scaling the ladder of spiritual evolution; in very few cases can this idealism provide a rationale or strategy for the practice of social transformation. This may partly explain Burroughs's selectivity regarding historical books of the dead: his lack of interest in the Tibetan Book may be attributable to its popularity among those members of the Anglo-European counterculture who adopted versions of Zen Buddhist philosophy and therefore tended to refrain from active dissent. We may judge Burroughs's response to passive resistance by recalling the admission he made during the riots at the Chicago Democratic Convention: "nonviolence is not exactly my program" (Burroughs, *Exterminator!* 96).[17]

Even if the historical books of the dead remain subjugated-group fantasies when recontextualized into the late twentieth-century American social order, the possibility of a book of the dead that would act as a subject-group fantasy remains open. But it can only be realized by means of a careful analysis of the social order. The question must be asked, then:

in what precise way is Burroughs's novel *The Wild Boys* a book of the dead? A great deal rides on this question, because the radical book of the dead remains Burroughs's ultimate goal throughout his subsequent writing—his latest novel, *The Western Lands,* takes its terms directly from the Egyptian Book of the Dead. Jennie Skerl suggests that *The Wild Boys* is a book of the dead because all of its characters are in fact dead, apparently in several different ways: "The characters who die and who retain consciousness after death—the wild boys, the dead child, Audrey Carsons, and his friend John Hamlin—are part of the immortality theme. Other characters are 'dead' because they have never lived; that is, they are fictions . . . [like] the Mexican characters . . . created by Burroughs from cultural stereotypes. Still others are dead because they exist only in the past and are controlled by the writer's consciousness" (Skerl 84). Leaving aside the difficult task of making the subtle distinctions Skerl claims to find, I would agree that she is correct in reading the entire book as a posthumous narration, a book of the dead, not simply because its characters are "dead" (what is the difference between a dead character and a "dead" character, or even between a dead character and a living character?), but because it projects a world whose realization would entail the death of our world. In fact, Burroughs's book enacts the death of the old world in the fictional birth of the new. This new world, after death, is his subject-group fantasy, offered for investment to an audience that seemed, in the late sixties, already on the verge of such an imaginary fusion.

Burroughs recognizes the tension inherent in the historical book of the dead: if the Egyptians and the Maya, as he claims, offset the threat of social contestation contained in their books of the dead by limiting literacy (and therefore the means to salvation) to the dominant classes, he attempts to shift the balance in the other direction, by constructing a series of guidebooks that give lessons in intensifying rather than resolving or avoiding social antagonisms. If the historical books of the dead are "how-to" books for the reproduction of the socius, his books of the dead intend to show how to undo the socius and produce a different one. Of course, all utopian fantasies aspire to be such how-to books, directly or indirectly: they try to make good on the promise articulated by the narrator of Ellison's *Invisible Man,* of a "plan of living . . . [which gives] pattern to the chaos which lives within the pattern of your certainties" (Ellison 567). Most utopias do this by offering idealistic visions that offer no purchase for direct investments of desire, no suggestions for strategies or tactics of change. What makes Burroughs's effort singular is its insistence on "death," on the violent undoing of the status quo as it is incarnated both in the materiality of institutional practices *and* in the structure of the subjugated subject. Burroughs's fulfillment of Ellison's promise takes the form of a plan of dying, or better, a plan of afterliving.

Burroughs's overriding task is to make his book of the dead accessible. The historical books succeeded as subjugated-group fantasies because they were kept from the masses; their form of control was secret manipulation, for example through the Maya calendar of rituals managed by the priestly caste. In contemporary society, "The mass media of newspapers, radio, television, magazines form a ceremonial calendar to which all citizens are subjected" (Burroughs and Odier 44) and which serves the interests of the state. Exposure of its methods and instruction in how to evade its dictates are necessary, as is mass organization that must avoid the ossified forms of the nation and the party:

> He who opposes force with counterforce alone forms that which he opposes and is formed by it. History shows that when a system of government is overthrown by force a system in many respects similar will take place. On the other hand he who does not resist force that enslaves and exterminates will be enslaved and exterminated. For revolution to effect basic changes in existing conditions three tactics are required: 1. Disrupt. 2. Attack. 3. Disappear. Look away. Ignore. Forget. These three tactics to be employed *alternatively.* (Burroughs and Odier 101)

This almost Nietzschean imperative to forget power, rather than to overcome and reinscribe it dialectically, accounts for the anarchic structure of the revolution represented in the novel, which is to serve as a reference manual (though not strictly as a "blueprint," as Burroughs sometimes claimed) for revolution outside the novel. The Wild Boys are "utopian as a *force,* not as literal images of the ideal community" (Skerl 83). Revolution, like fantasy, is fundamentally polymorphous and impermanent. Resistance must be coordinated, relayed along a rhizome, but not controlled; the path through danger to the promised lands of the afterlife can be negotiated in many mutually irreducible ways. Burroughs must thus shift the status of his book of the dead (with respect to its historical forebears) by making it self-reflexive, as is evidenced both by the reference to the novel itself within the novel (*WB* 149) and by his choice of the indefinite article in "*A* Book of the Dead"; one embodiment of a genre, it cannot claim the privilege of being the only guide to the contemporary lands of the dead.[18] Its value will be determined solely by its utility.

In structure *The Wild Boys* is self-consciously kaleidoscopic, as are all of Burroughs's extended works, narrative or expository. The cut-up method is generally (though not exclusively, as we will see) applied to narration, as it was in *Naked Lunch,* rather than to syntax, as it was in the *Nova* trilogy. This approach might appear to be inappropriate in a book of the dead, but Budge insists that even the Egyptians were in fact rather "writerly" (to use Roland Barthes's term) in their textuality: "The Book of the Dead was, even in those early times, so extensive that even a king was fain to make from it a selection only of the passages which suited his individual taste or were considered sufficient to secure his welfare in the next world. . . . The 'Pyramid Texts' prove that each section of the religious books of the Egyptians was originally a separate and independent composition, that it was written with a definite object, and that it might be arranged in any order in a series of similar texts" (Budge, *Egyptian Book* xxiv). Thus in *The Wild Boys,* a series of routines (Burroughs's preferred compositional units) are organized around an apparently aleatory device called "The Penny Arcade Peep Show," which controls the arrangement and interpenetration of the routines. The standard peep show itself is a fantasmatic device, presenting a set of prefabricated images for erotic investment, but Burroughs's machine is far less predictable even as it maintains the erotic intent of the standard peep show. The character Audrey Carsons, who comes upon the device at a carnival and whose experience of its shows fills the bulk of the novel, describes its formal structure thus:

> 1. Objects and scenes move away and come in with a slow hydraulic movement always at the same speed. The screens are three-dimensional visual sections punctuated by flashing lights[. . . .] Sequences are linked by the presence of some arbitrary object [. . .]
>
> 2. Scenes that have the same enigmatic structure presented on one screen where the perspective remains constant[. . . .]
>
> 3. Fragmentary glimpses linked by immediate visual impact[. . . .]
>
> 4. Narrative sections in which the screens disappear. I experience a series of quite understandable and coherent events as one of the actors. The narrative sequences are preceded by the title on screen then I am in the film[. . . .] The structuralized peep show may intersperse the narrative and then I am back in front of the screen and moving in and out of it. (*WB* 40–42)

The novel as a whole thus presents itself as a film, or rather an anthology of films, unrolling from the peep show before the eyes of Audrey, an author-surrogate who is labeled, significantly, a "walking corpse . . .

[who] didn't know whose corpse he was" (*WB* 32, 40). Filmic structure and point-of-view identification abets this confusion of subjectivity, as the fourth point above makes clear.

Film has long been a powerful metaphor for Burroughs, going back at least as far as "Doctor Berger's Mental Health Hour" from *Naked Lunch*, and reaching its full development in the *Nova* trilogy: "Postulate a biologic film running from the beginning of time to the end, from zero to zero as all biologic film run in any time universe—Call this film X1 and postulate further that there can only be one film with the quality X1 in any given time universe. X1 is the film and performers—X2 is the audience who are all trying to get into the film" (*NE* 15n). The linear predetermination of film and its apparently objective referentiality make it the perfect figure for the ideology and false consciousness of hierarchical control situations. This is not a question of simple audience manipulation, to be complicated by reception or consumption theory. As an experimental filmmaker himself, Burroughs understands perfectly well the differences between the manipulative ideology of classical Hollywood narrative cinema and the defamiliarizing effects of avant-garde film, as well as the different uses to which viewers can put both kinds of film. When he uses film as a structural metaphor in his books, however, he insists on the *physical identity* of the two forms: each is, ultimately, a single physical strip of film stock, the material contents of which do not change from one viewing to the next. In the *Nova* trilogy, the primary task of the revolutionary partisans is to "storm the reality studio" in order to destroy the "reality film." This is not a film that is *shown* to audiences to control them; the film *is* reality itself, and there is no audience outside it. We do not watch the reality film; we are part of it. The same holds true for *The Wild Boys,* from its opening direction: "The camera is the eye of a cruising vulture flying over an area of scrub, rubble and unfinished buildings on the outskirts of Mexico City" (*WB* 3). Thus, although the Penny Arcade Peep Show fractures and multiplies the representational space of classical cinema, it shares with that cinema its identically repetitive, mechanically reproduced form. This is confirmed in the final image of the film "exploding in moon craters and boiling silver spots" (*WB* 184)—burning up, that is, under the heat of the projection lamp, an image that recurs throughout *The Wild Boys* and signals the escape from inert seriality into group activity, from atomized subjugation into the fusion of group subjectivity, and from the repetitive structure of representation into the anarchism of desire. After the burnout, "*the wild boys smile*" (*WB* 184).

The Penny Arcade Peep Show shows films of several sorts: nostalgic reveries presented in elegiac style ("The Silver Smile," "The Dead Child"); frenetic parodies of popular fictional genres ("The Frisco Kid"); pointed political satires ("Le Gran Luxe"); flights of science-fictional fancy ("The Miracle of the Rose," "The Wild Boys Smile"); and *hommages* to other writers (for example, to Jean Genet in "The Miracle of the Rose"). Almost all of these films contain explicit scenes of impersonal homosexual intercourse, which should alert us to the fact that, for Burroughs, homosexuality is not an inherently revolutionary form of desire but an ambiguous one that can fit into both radical and reactionary political groups. (For Burroughs, homosexuality is only revolutionary when it escapes the model of normative heterosexual love, which constructs the self as a subject by reducing the loved Other to an object.) There are at least four conflicting rationales for these explicit scenes. In the first place, for Burroughs's more ambiguous control figures, in the "space age . . . sex movies must express the longing to escape from flesh through sex. The way out is the way through" (*WB* 82). In the second place, for the radical figures in the novel, they demonstrate Burroughs's fundamental agreement with Wilhelm Reich's insistence that "Psychic health depends upon orgastic potency, i.e., upon the degree to which one can surrender to and experience the climax of excitation in the natural sex act" (Reich 6). Burroughs refers to Reich approvingly in many places, most often to Reich's work on the orgone; in a letter from 1949, he asserts that "My own experiments with [Reich's orgone] accumulator have convinced me that many of his conclusions are correct" (Burroughs, *Letters 1945–1959* 58). The radical power of orgasm is marked throughout the novel by the abrupt break in syntax that follows every climax; orgasm "cuts up" dogmatic verbal systems. Third, the explicit scenes emphasize "the erect phallus which means in wild-boy script as it does in Egyptian to stand before or in the presence of, to confront to regard attentively" (*WB* 151).[19] This interest in the actual glyphs of the books of the dead would later lead Burroughs to compose texts incorporating narrative illustrations of glyphs from the Maya (in *Ah Pook is Here,* 1979) and Egyptian books (in *The Book of Breeething,* 1974).[20] Lastly, and most importantly, "the point of sexual relations between men is nothing that we could call love, but rather what we might call *recognition*" (Burroughs and Odier 118). It is this recognition, this look of the Other displaced into the group, that marks the Wild Boys as a subject-group.

A schematic passage from "The Miracle of the Rose" demonstrates this multiplicity of significance. It begins in a fantasy North African setting (like those in some of Genet's works) where the narrator and his two guides, a Berber named Ali and an Arab named Farja, stop to make camp. The two guides engage in intercourse, an event which the narrator transforms into an "old book with gilt edges. THE MIRACLE OF THE ROSE written in gilt letters" (*WB* 73). The book consists of pictures, or glyphs, illustrating the stages of intercourse: "*The Proposition*" ("Ali points to the bed. Farja stands there sullen eyes downcast long lashes," *WB* 74), "*The Agreement*" ("Farja looks at the bed blushing to his bare feet"), and "*The Consummation*" ("Roses and thorns through translucent flesh squirming a slow scream of roses," *WB* 75). This set of images is interrupted by glyphs of Mayan priests harvesting human flesh and creating slave-boys who repeat the actions of Ali and Farja: "*The Recognition.* The other has dropped the sheet from his naked body. . . . *The Proposition.* Two boys in the room. 'That's kid stuff. I wanta.' One boy with eyes downcast sullen" (*WB* 76). The juxtaposition of homosexual intercourse produced by Mayan tyranny to the intercourse of the first scene implies that such intercourse is not necessarily an attribute of the Wild Boys and their revolutionary allies, but can also be used as material for control. Indeed, immediately after the conclusion of "The Miracle of the Rose," we are offered the "Great Slastobitch's" theories on the aesthetics and metaphysics of pornography, which I have already cited (*WB* 82).

The films contained in the novel can be divided, for the purposes of this political analysis of fantasy, into two categories whose boundaries are fluid and which can and do turn abruptly into one another: Control films, which correspond to subjugated-group fantasies, and Wild Boy films (including antiauthoritarian films that don't actually contain Wild Boys), which correspond to subject-group fantasies. The Control films, which embody the Great Slastobitch's aesthetics, take up a smaller total proportion of the book than the Wild Boy films do, but they predominate in its opening sections and contain some of its most memorable routines. Let us consider a few of them in some detail.

The Wild Boys of the title do not make a formally announced entrance until well into the text, but they are present in spirit from the very beginning, when Tío Mate, the masterless *pistolero,* kills González the Agente. This is the first in a long string of routines concerning the destruction of the hypocritical and monstrous representatives of the law, the state, and the family by characters who offer us none of the typical traits of the humane/humanist hero. In the same routine, the mother, Tía Dolores is described as a "war machine" whose "evil eyes rotate in a complex calendar, and these calculations occupy her for many hours each night" (*WB* 5). This description alludes to the interlocking wheels of the elaborate Maya calendar, the interpretation of which, Burroughs claims, forms the Mayan book of the dead. On the Egyptian side, Tío Mate has an apprentice, El Mono, who is described as his "Ka"; in Egyptian, *Ka* refers to the spiritual "double" of the dead soul, and in fact El Mono is a mimic. Tío Mate, the Chief, and Old Sarge—the antiauthoritarian figures of the first three routines—share with the Wild Boys a peculiarly beatific way of smiling; indeed, the chapter's titles and closing lines draw attention to it. Skerl sees in these smiles "that invite comparison with the smile of Dante's Beatrice and of the Mona Lisa—two hallowed female icons that embody traditional Western values" evidence that the Wild Boys and their allies "exist in a state of ecstasy" (Skerl 83). Perhaps, like Beatrice, the Wild Boys are to be our guides to/through the lands of the dead; perhaps as well, like Dante, we will not be subject to any of the perils and delights to be found there—but perhaps we will. At any rate, the smiles of the Wild Boys and of the characters who anticipate them do not bode well for those "traditional Western values."

Among the most important Control films is "A. J.'s Annual Party," narrated in the chapter "Le Gran Luxe." This routine, a sequel to one of the same title in *Naked Lunch,* resembles in structure and ambition Burroughs's earlier piece "Roosevelt after Inauguration" (1961), an elaborate send-up of the imperial presidency in which Franklin D. Roosevelt appoints criminals and degenerates to the highest offices of the land in order to run the state into the ground:

> Roosevelt was convulsed with such hate for the [human] species as it is, that he wished to degrade it beyond recognition. He could endure only the extremes of human behavior. The average, the middle-aged (he viewed middle age as a condition with no relation to chronological age), the middle-class, the bureaucrat filled him with loathing. . . .
>
> "I'll make the cocksuckers glad to mutate," he would say, looking off into space as if seeking new frontiers of depravity. (Burroughs, *Roosevelt* 21)

Like Roosevelt, A. J. represents the most extreme form of concentrated power: "His annual party collapses currencies and bankrupts nations," and he thinks nothing of suspending a section of Missouri countryside between two zeppelins in order to get a perfect meal of hog's liver (*WB* 53–54). The gratuitous waste of his annual party—attended only by his close patrician friends while the poor huddle in absolute scarcity outside, shredding each other for a chance to eat the refuse that A. J. sends them through a "huge phallus" and a "rubber asshole" (*WB* 59)—takes its model from Poe's "Masque of the Red Death," and eventually A. J., like Prince Prospero, finds the outside he tried so hard to keep out has gotten inside.

Like "Roosevelt after Inauguration," "A. J.'s Annual Party" serves as a demonic vision of the capitalist world order run amok, but in both routines the status of the leader is ironic: even in exercising power over people, Roosevelt is convulsed with hatred for them and in fact exercises his power to force them to mutate into some new and more extreme form, while the very extremity of A. J.'s conspicuous consumption is meant to be emblematic of capitalism at the same time as it provides the materials for its own destruction. The way out is the way through. A dead soul, according to the Egyptian Book, "eats with his mouth, and exercises other natural functions of the body, and gratifies his passions" (Budge, *Egyptian Book* lxxviii). As a good host to such dead souls, A. J. provides his guests with every conceivable amenity, from five-star restaurant service and a fully stocked arsenal to tailor-made "blue movies," one of which leads the routine away from A. J.'s excesses and toward the Wild Boys. This movie begins abruptly as one of Burroughs's elegiac evocations of young men engaging in sex, but it is intercut with dialogue suggesting that A. J. is directing and editing even this tableau of desire (*WB* 63–67). After another rapid spin through the Penny Arcade Peep Show, we are presented with the final product of this effort, "The Miracle of the Rose," which as we saw continues the elegiac daydream of casual sex with Genet-style props and language and without A. J.'s interruption, until the "silver light" (*WB* 81) of the projector reveals to us that it has all been just a flat representation without real "presence," despite the ejaculations that shatter syntactic continuity. Several other "blue movies" follow, each less stable than the last, until the film is stretched to the breaking point and, with a final Controlled scene of orgasm, snaps.

The break throws us back to the Penny Arcade Peep Show, which now introduces the relation between violence and order more explicitly in its shattered narration of the deaths of Jesse James, Dutch Schultz, and most importantly, Billy the Kid (himself a proto–Wild Boy whose last words, "*Quién es?*" ask the central question of Burroughs's late trilogy), alongside science-fiction evocations of decaying future cities, arbitrary schemes of order (the standard calendar, New Year's Eve, a referee's whistles), and the interchangeability of "Tissue, minerals, wood seen through electron microscope" and "Stars and space seen through telescope" (*WB* 100–101). The effect is surprisingly similar to the famous moment in Ingmar Bergman's *Persona* when Liv Ullman's petty violence precipitates a break in the film itself, revealing the psychic horrors held in check by the linear narration. Bergman's film reconstitutes itself slowly and incompletely after its break, but Burroughs's "Peep Show" empties out directly into "The Dead Child," which begins as another nostalgic tale of adolescent intercourse—a Control film—but mutates in the middle into a Wild Boy film, a narrative of revolution, in this case of enslaved planters against their Maya masters. Two boys escape into the Central American jungles and live there until one boy, unable to escape the masters' control, turns into a jaguar and dies (*WB* 114–15).[21] The other boy's soul, unable to escape the material world, haunts the locale until visiting tourists provide him with a new, young male body. This split fantasy, this hybrid of "blue movie" and revolution, serves as an introduction to the Wild Boys themselves, who are similarly hybrids of ourselves and a world beyond the death of our own.

From this point in the novel to the end, revolutionary Wild Boy films follow each other without a break. The term "Wild Boys" appears for the first time in the thirteenth chapter, "Just Call Me Joe," which narrates the raising of an American army to combat the Wild Boys and its subsequent defeat at their hands. This chapter is set up as a parody of a Hollywood propaganda film of the fifties, complete with soundtrack music and opening credits; most of its characters are played by named actors, except for the General in charge of the army, "played by himself," and the Wild Boys themselves, who are "played by native boys on locations" (*WB* 121). The plot of the film is the exposure of a conspiracy, which the General blames on Moscow, to undermine America's purity by drawing American boys into anarchist packs of Wild Boys; in the middle of the General's denunciation, the camera cuts to a suburban home where a couple reads the following note: "Dear Mom and Dad: I am going to join the wild boys. When you read this I will be far away. Johnny."[22] Once overseas, the Americans are greeted by the natives of the area that has been overrun by packs of Wild Boys; the natives appear glad to be rescued, but in fact they simply welcome whatever force passes through their country as an opportunity for profit (hence the chapter title). A few Wild Boys surrender and promise to lead the Americans to their "Chinese advisers," but this is a ploy to divide the army, which is cut down by linguistic and viral weapons as well as by standard guns. The surviving officer even settles down at the native location to set up a restaurant at which the "Wild Boys [are] welcome" (*WB* 137).

The diverse disruptive elements in the novel, whether transitional figures like Tío Mate or full-fledged Wild Boys, are united by the goal of total revolution:

> Despite disparate aims and personnel of its constituent members the underground is agreed on basic objectives. We intend to march on the police machine everywhere. We intend to destroy the police machine and all its records. We intend to destroy all dogmatic verbal systems. The family unit and its cancerous expansion into tribes, countries, nations we will eradicate at its vegetable roots. We don't want to hear any more family talk, mother talk, father talk, cop talk, priest talk, country talk *or* party talk. To put it country simple we have heard enough bullshit. (*WB* 139–40)

What unifies their agenda is the refusal of *talk,* of representation in the form of religious belief ("priest talk") and social or political ideology ("mother talk, father talk, . . . country talk *or* party talk"). In fact, it is this emphasis on "talk," on representation, that underlies Burroughs's explicit criticisms of the historical books of the dead as well: "Death is . . . a protean organism that never repeats itself word for word. . . . For this reason I consider the Egyptian and Tibetan books of the dead, with their emphasis on ritual and knowing the right words, totally inadequate. There are no right words" (Burroughs, *Ah Pook* 15).

This kind of statement, for all its value in articulating the explicit theme of the various revolutionary routines, never seems to come directly from the Wild Boys themselves, but comes instead from their recruits among the older generation, like the Chief, Old Sarge, and Colonel Bradly—a version of Burroughs's friend Brion Gysin who "was with one of the first expeditionary forces sent out against the wild boys" and who "Later . . . joined them" (*WB* 145). This seems to be Burroughs's own unambiguous desire, inasmuch as the Wild Boys are versions of his own "Ka," or spirit double, based in his identification with the student movements (whom he urged to use "more riots and more violence": Burroughs and Odier 81). The Wild Boys themselves do not speak much, and when they do, they speak in performatives, like the lies they tell to lead the American forces sent against them into a trap in the desert and the pleas they make to one another for sexual gratification (like Burroughs's original fantasy letters to Ginsberg). The Wild Boys do not demonstrate or denounce; they simply seduce and destroy, leaving others to explain their work. This is consistent with the imperative to forget rather than to consolidate power. Even their methods are parodies of representation, based as they are on Burroughs's viral theories of language: they kill by spreading "trained killer viruses" (*WB* 133), literally contagious forms of laughter, sneezing, hiccuping, and coughing that render their victims helpless and defenseless before the Wild Boys' killer legions. They use the representational structure of the socius against itself by sending out false calls for help to police units and by impersonating the police themselves to undermine their authority; moreover, "fifty boys with portable tape recorders record riots from TV . . . and hit the rush hour in a flying wedge riot recordings on full blast" to produce more riots through playback (*WB* 139).

The Wild Boys manifest what Deleuze and Guattari would call "becomings-animal" in their escape from the constituted social order. They do not become animals, as if "boys" and "animals" were two states that could be occupied essentially; rather, they deterritorialize, or dismantle their bodies' social representations, by adopting or "reterritorializing" on effective, nonrepresentational animal functions.[23] They do not *imitate* animals, but rather they adopt the animals' defense mechanisms. "Each group developed special skills and knowledge until it evolved into humanoid subspecies" (*WB* 147), like the Warrior Ants, handless boys who screw steel implements into their stumps; cat boys who wear poison-clawed gloves; Snake boys, who handle (and even become) venomous reptiles; and lycanthropic wolf boys. Other boys deterritorialize themselves through technology, attaching themselves to gliders, roller-skates, and other weapons systems in order to battle the state apparatus (*WB* 147–48, 150–54). In this way, the Wild Boys actively assume the hybrid forms of the gods of the Egyptian book of the dead—hawk-headed Horus, jackal-headed Anubis—and of the glyph-creatures of Maya writing, like Ah Pook the Destroyer, the subject of later Burroughs texts. Burroughs calls these Wild Boys "biologic adaptives" (Burroughs, *Port of Saints* 101).[24]

Perhaps the most significant scene in *The Wild Boys*, from the point of view of subject-group fantasy, comes near the end of the novel, in the "Wild Boys" chapter. This is the description of their reproductive technique, by means of which they increase their numbers and also reincarnate any members who have been killed or maimed in combat with counterrevolutionary forces (prefigured in the spirit-film at the end of the "Dead Child" chapter). These offspring are known as Zimbus, and they are created through masturbatory fantasy. This method allows the Wild Boys to escape both the binarism of gendered reproduction (which had previously trapped them in specular opposition to the women they artificially inseminated: *WB* 154) and the ideology of the nuclear family that constantly reinscribes it. One of these descriptions is worth quoting in its entirety:

> A boy with Mongoloid features steps onto the rug playing a flute to the four directions. As he plays phantom figures swirl around him taking shape out of moonlight, campfires and shadows. He kneels in the center of the rug playing his flute faster and faster. The shape of a boy on hands and knees is forming in front of him. He puts down his flute. His hands mold and knead the body in front of him pulling it against him with stroking movements that penetrate the pearly grey shape caressing it inside. The body shudders and quivers against him as he forms the buttocks around his penis stroking silver genitals out of the moonlight grey then pink and finally red the mouth parted in a gasp shuddering genitals out of the moon's haze a pale blond boy spurting thighs and buttocks and young skin. The flute player kneels there arms wrapped tightly around the Zimbu's chest breathing deeply until the Zimbu breathes with his own breathing quivering to the blue tattoo. The attendants step forward and carry the pale blond Zimbu to the blue tent. (*WB* 160)

This boy's masturbatory fantasy actually creates its own object: another Wild Boy. The Wild Boys as a group, then, are merely revolutionary (that is to say, subject-group) desire made flesh; they appear and exist because they desire and are desired in an affirmative manner that has nothing to do with lack, and the flow of this desire is self-generating (though assembled out of the materials at hand: other Zimbus are constructed by drawing "blue mist from the rug" and pulling "blue down from the sky," *WB* 158).[25]

The novel concludes with a chapter entitled "The Wild Boys Smile," which is also the last line of the text. In it, an unidentified narrator (perhaps Audrey, who is pronounced dead in the penultimate Penny Arcade Peep Show, or Rogers from "The Chief Smiles") joins the Wild Boys in their struggle for the streets and in their frequent copulations, which serve them also as means of teleportation. The sexual contact between the narrator and the Wild Boy called the Dib forges a link between the radical coalition, which still uses referential language, and the Wild Boys who do not. The Wild Boys' couplings, which also transmit information, are spontaneous and multivalent, carried out with the same level of interest and intensity as their battles. At the conclusion of the chapter, the narrator and his companion, confronted by policemen and photographers at the "time barrier" (*WB* 181) that separates the Wild Boys' "dead" world from our "live" historical world, escape by throwing a film grenade at them; this grenade, like the novel itself, is meant to blow a hole in the ideological "reality film" that controls social reproduction (as well as the producers) under the existent socius. After it goes off, we are left with the final fading images in the Penny Arcade Peep Show—naked boys fucking, laughing, and gaming—as the Peep Show (and the novel itself) burns out:

> The silver screen is exploding in moon craters and boiling silver spots.
> "Wild boys very close now."
> Darkness falls on the ruined suburbs. A dog barks in the distance.
> Dim jerky stars are blowing away across a gleaming empty sky, *the wild boys smile.* (*WB* 184)[26]

Since they must forget power if they are to avoid duplicating it, the Wild Boys cannot smile in triumph over their enemies. Instead they smile in invitation to the reader; such an invitation is precisely what the book of the dead must offer if it is to be a viable subject-group fantasy.

The Wild Boys' threat to capitalist society is immanent within that society in the form of desire that exceeds the available forms of fantasy and so constructs its own forms, its own enabling objects of investment. These forms may resemble myth, but they are, at most, joke myths that mock the very structure of myth, or throwaway myths to be used like condoms as protection against the infection of power, binarism, and hierarchy (apotropaic prophylaxis, if you like):

> According to the legend an evil old doctor, who called himself God and us dogs, created the first boy in his adolescent image. The boy peopled the garden with male phantoms that rose from his ejaculations. This angered God, who was getting on in years. He decided it endangered his position as CREATOR. So he crept upon the boy and anesthetized him and made Eve from his rib. Henceforth all creation of beings would process through female channels. But some of Adam's phantoms refused to let God near them under any pretext. After millenia [*sic*] these cool remote spirits breathe in the wild boys. (Burroughs, *Port of Saints* 97)

It is desire that must be policed, controlled, limited to the sterile pornographic simulacra of A. J. and the ruling classes, for when it erupts in fertile ground, as it appears to have done among the young and the dispossessed of the late sixties, it threatens to amplify the antagonisms that already fissure the socius into irreparable cracks. In 1969, Burroughs wrote, "Young people pose the only effective challenge to established authority. . . . The student rebellion is now a worldwide movement. Never before in recorded history has established authority been so basically challenged on a worldwide scale" (Burroughs and Odier 81). The Wild Boys are one form, Burroughs's form, of this desire, and it is either reactionary or foolish to claim, as Kazin does, that "The 'wild boys' who come into the book of that name are not important except as a culmination of the continual fantasy of boys in rainbow-colored jockstraps coldly doffing them and turning their totally impersonal couplings into a piece of American science fiction" (Kazin 268). They are not important if fantasy itself is unimportant, and if "American science fiction" is incapable of being something other than escapism; but if, as I have argued, fantasy is the catalyst in the constitution of subject-groups, and if science fiction is capable of providing such a fantasy, then the Wild Boys are an important incarnation of Burroughs's Lawrencean "pure present." They are an act of creation through which Burroughs intends to "renew the world," as Kazin would have it. In an interview given shortly after this period, Burroughs said, "Would I consider events similar to the *Wild Boys* scenario desirable? Yes, desirable to me" (Burroughs, "*Rolling Stone* Interview" 52).

The Wild Boys, then, is what it claims to be: a book of the dead and hence a powerful fantasy. But because of its relation to the late capitalist socius and the subjectivities in its charge, *The Wild Boys* was for a moment more than that: it was a subject-group fantasy, a revolutionary fantasy, a "plan for afterliving." As such it employed the "powers of the false" to become, in Ginsberg's words, "an exemplification of the world."[27] But for Burroughs, as for the radical student movements of the sixties, this "exemplification" was not sufficient; the fantasy he provided did not fuse people into subject-groups that could defeat the groups subjugated to capital. Burroughs's "detailed illustrated blueprints for operations against enemy personnel" (Burroughs, *Ah Pook* 115) were not carried out. The seventies saw not the total dismantling of worldwide state capitalism, but rather the retreat of the revolutionary forces of the sixties. Burroughs had to spend much of the seventies amplifying his futile Wild-Boy fantasies, expanding his "powers of the false," before he could create more precisely detailed, more profusely illustrated manuals in the form of a subtler, more complete book of the dead: the trilogy composed of *Cities of the Red Night, The Place of Dead Roads,* and *The Western Lands,* in which the moments of destruction that fill *The Wild Boys* are balanced by affirmative suggestions for the reorganization of society. The starting point of these books of the dead is the theoretical endpoint of *The Wild Boys:* "Nothing is true. Everything is permitted" (*WB* 170). But *The Wild Boys* remains unique in the purity of its destructive force.

Chapter Six

Quién es?

Reconstitution of the Revolutionary Subject in Burroughs's Late Trilogy

However successful it is as a novel, *The Wild Boys: A Book of the Dead* failed as a "blueprint for operations" against the capitalist world order. If the proto–Wild Boys to whom it was addressed—the student revolutionaries of the late sixties—seemed to be on the verge of triumph when the book was composed, they no longer seemed so by its publication date. The retreat of the counterculture into forms of accommodation revealed the gaps in its own project, and in Burroughs's radical architecture of desire as well. In *Port of Saints,* he admits at least temporary defeat:

> Camera pans the scattered forces and broken morale of the militants . . . teenage alcoholics, underground press closing down, black panthers finished, censorship coming back, pollution, over-population, atomic tests . . . [. . .] Flashback shows the wild boys mowed down by cold eyed narcs and Southern lawmen backed by religious women and big money. (Burroughs, *Port of Saints* 24, 26)

Though later in the novel Burroughs's narrator claims that "We won't be needing the knives and bolos, laser guns, slingshots, crossbows, blowguns, disease and virus cultures much longer" because "The final strategy [of] stopping the world, to ignore and forget the enemy out of existence" (Burroughs, *Port of Saints* 171) has been successful, the writer knows that this claim is only fantasy, in the narcissistic sense of which Kazin accused him. In fact, the task of Burroughs's fiction through the late seventies and eighties is to find some way to fill in the holes, to reconstitute the revolutionary allies, the fantastically active and actively fantasizing *audience,* that he lost at the end of the sixties. "*Quién es?*" "Who is it?" is the question that constantly recurs, and that Burroughs tries in several different ways to answer, in *Cities of the Red Night, The Place of Dead Roads,* and *The Western Lands.*

On the second page of *The Place of Dead Roads,* we are informed that *Quién es?* is the title of one of the "western stories" written by William Seward Hall under the pen name Kim Carsons, which is also the name of the subversive protagonist(s) of Burroughs's novel. Near the beginning of the novel's third "book," itself entitled "Quién es?" that story (which doubles the novel itself) is described as "a luridly fictionalized account of [Kim's] exploits as a bank robber, outlaw, and shootist" (*P* 201). The title page of the story leads into an extended meditation on the Spanish phrase:

> *Quién es?*
>
> Who is it?
>
> Kim Carsons does he exist? His existence, like any existence, is inferential . . . the traces he leaves behind him . . . [. . .]
>
> He exists in these pages as Lord Jim, the Great Gatsby, Comus Bassington, live and breathe in a writer's prose, in the care, love and dedication that evoke them: the flawed, doomed but undefeated, radiant heroes who attempted the impossible, stormed the citadels of heaven, took the last chance on the last and greatest of human dreams, the punch-drunk fighter who comes up off the floor to win by a knockout, the horse that comes from last to win in the stretch, assassins of Hassan i Sabbah,[. . .]of the Black Hole, where no physical laws apply, agents of a singularity[. . .]
>
> Ghostwritten by William Hall. (*P* 201–2)

This passage, moving from cliché through Burroughs's own earlier formulation "Hassan i Sabbah" to new metaphor, spells out the role of the writer in this reconstitution of the revolutionary subject: his "job," to use Burroughs's own preferred term, is to use what Deleuze calls the "powers of the false" to produce incompossible presents and not-necessarily-true pasts through which revolutionary subjectivity, incarnated in the "flawed, doomed but undefeated" gamblers on the "last and greatest of human dreams," again becomes possible. "Art . . . must take part in this task: not that of addressing a people, which is presupposed already there, but of contributing to the invention of a people. The moment the master, or the colonizer, proclaims 'There have never been people here', the missing people are a becoming, they invent themselves, in shanty towns and camps, or in ghettos, in new conditions of struggle to which a necessarily political art must contribute" (Deleuze, *Cinema-2* 217). We will investigate Burroughs's contribution to this invention of a people, this reconstitution of a revolutionary subject, after we examine his self-criticism and specify the powers and tasks he assigns to the writer.

Such a reconstitution of revolution in the eighties will entail two related projects that are briefly foreshadowed in *The Wild Boys* and *Port of Saints:* a more fully developed account of history and a model of revolutionary community. This affirmative double project, this filling of the gaps, necessitates the abandonment of two key assumptions of Burroughs's writing up to and including *The Wild Boys.* The first of these assumptions is the idea that the history of Western representational thought and politics is the only possible form of history; this assumption leads to Burroughs's rejection of all history as an inherently repressive force, as a kind of static or serial repetition.[1] For Burroughs during his early and middle periods, history is a form of what Sartre calls the "practico-inert." This is why Burroughs's fiction from *Naked Lunch* through *The Wild Boys* and *Port of Saints* is content to draw parallels between historical "totalitarian" situations like the ancient Egyptian and Maya civilizations, contemporary repressive situations like Eisenhower-era America, and syntactic/narrative control. Historical situations are invariably presented as film sets, within whose confines is played out "the old army game from here to eternity" (Burroughs, *Exterminator!* 115); history is merely another artifact, a stylized and linear set of semiotic markers always already mediated by its own simulation, which lends inertia to power relations. The basic revolutionary gesture implied by this view of history is the simple rupture, which in Burroughs's work of this middle period manifests itself in several ways: at the formal level, as the syntactic cut-up; at the thematic level, as the interweaving of digressive routines and the breaking of the ideological "reality film"; and at the hortatory level of material application, as the tape-recorder "drop-in/playback" technique advocated in many of Burroughs's "programmatic" revolutionary texts.

The second assumption is complementary to the first, and may even be reducible to it. If history is the totality of rigid and enslaving determinisms that can be broken by certain kinds of action, then it follows that this rupture of history will be sufficient in itself to generate a different, fundamentally open and free world. The revolutionary's only real task is a negative one, the destruction of historical authority, and his only real characteristic is also negative since he is merely an inversion of the good citizen. The logic is beautifully dialectical: history is the negation of freedom, so a revolution that simply negates history produces the affirmation of freedom, but only as a pure effect of the double negation. Burroughs recognizes this, as we saw above: "He who opposes force with counterforce alone forms that which he opposes and is formed by it. History shows that when a system of government is overthrown by force a system in many respects similar will take place" (Burroughs and Odier 101). To combat this specularity, he suggests the active forgetting of power rather than its consolidation, but this tactic too is insufficient. Not only do the Wild Boys neither talk nor legislate; they also do not plan, or build, or negotiate an alternative socius, and such total negation is their undoing. They are produced as a subject-group in the *logical* (and not temporal) moment when their fantasmatic negation of repressive history coincides with their fantasmatic affirmation of freedom *without giving that affirmation any distinct or positive content.* Their desire creates a homosexual group fantasy that is hostile to the status quo, but *symmetrically* hostile, specular, and thus ultimately unproductive of truly new relations. The Wild Boys' conditions of emergence are the point-for-point negation of the conditions of existence of the capitalist state; the Wild Boys actually invest their desire in the "existing social field, including the latter's most repressive forms" (Deleuze and Guattari, *Anti-Oedipus* 30), such as the armed forces (recall Old Sarge), organized crime (Tío Mate), and misogyny. Thus the one can only destroy the other, as antimatter destroys matter, without necessarily constituting a world that is liberated in any distinct affirmative way. Rupture is a necessary condition, but by itself it is an insufficient condition for change; break the reality film, and all that will confront you is the blinding glare of undifferentiated white light.

The Wild Boys' impasse forces us to confront the limitations of the middle-period Burroughs's Sartrean group dialectics, but it also reveals the important difference between the middle-period Burroughs and the late one, a difference which, I would claim, embodies the distinction between Sartre's theory of groups and that of Deleuze and Guattari. While they agree on the fantasmatic nature of group production, they disagree on the specific form of the subject-group fantasy. In Sartre's example, the Bastille serves as the object of investment for two distinct logical moments of revolutionary desire: the negative or destructive moment of defense and the affirmative or constructive moment of offense. The coincidence of these moments in the same fantasmatic object binds the moments together as specular images of each other, allowing them to resolve their differences into the synthesis of group identification (or vice versa; the relation is not causal but logically simultaneous and symmetrical). This structure accounts quite precisely for the Wild Boys' dialectical strategy of rupture, which should trouble us because it is, after all, the structure of the *bourgeois* subject-group at its historical moment of emergence (and before its ossification into inert seriality and subjugation) that is identified in Sartre's analysis of the French Revolution.

Recall Deleuze's and Guattari's displacement of Sartre: the revolutionary subject-group, they insist, "invents always mortal formations that exorcise the effusion in it of a death instinct; it opposes real coefficients of transversality to the symbolic determinations of subjugation, coefficients without hierarchy or a group superego" (Deleuze and Guattari, *Anti-Oedipus* 348–49). These coefficients of transversality, or of "deterritorialization," measure the group's resistance to hierarchy and seriality. The dialectical closure of Sartre's group identification falls immediately into the hierarchical, legislative role of group superego,[2] and in so doing lapses into an immortal but inert seriality; in a word, it quickly "reterritorializes" on a structurally similar role. This is not to say that Sartre's analysis of the storming of the Bastille is incorrect, but rather that Sartre errs in seeing the *historical* conditions of the emergence of the then-revolutionary bourgeoisie as the *ontological* conditions of emergence of all revolutionary groups. Measured against this standard, the incipient seriality or subjugation of the Sartrean Wild Boys also manifests itself plainly, not so much in their overt quest for immortality as in their paradoxical conservatism, their preservation of the opposing world order in the specular structure of their own negation of it. Since they do not separate destruction (of repressive history) from construction (of an alternative), they fall into the fallacy of equating the two moments and surreptitiously conserve the order they apparently fight. The key to Deleuze and Guattari's formulation and, I will argue, to Burroughs's late work, is the noncoincidence, or irreducibility, of these negative and affirmative moments of fantasmatic group formation: the "destructive task" proceeds by "successively undoing the representative territorialities and reterritorializations through which a subject passes in his/her individual history," while the "positive task consists of discovering in a subject the formation, or the functioning of *his/her* desiring-machines,"[3] that is, the connections that undo the subject's fixed identity by expanding into the world. This separation of negative and affirmative moments is also measured by a coefficient of deterritorialization, which is larger than that of Sartre's group and hence makes its reterritorialization more difficult and less stable. Following Deleuze, I have called this noncoincidence *paradox:* an antithesis or contradiction, bearing on the same object, that cannot be resolved dialectically. Burroughs calls it "a Manichean conflict [whose] outcome is in doubt" (Burroughs, *Adding Machine* 83) and, more suggestively, "art."

Burroughs's double project in the late trilogy is to forge such a noncoincident, paradoxical group fantasy, and his formal point of departure remains the book of the dead, the how-to guide to the afterlife. "Writing, if it is anything, is a word of warning" to the reader (*WL* 213). The trilogy is peppered with references to the Egyptian and Maya systems. The main text of the first volume of the trilogy, *Cities of the Red Night,* opens with an invocation to the gods (beginning "Nothing is true; everything is permitted") like that which opens the Egyptian Book of the Dead, though in *Cities* what is invoked is not the hierarchical pantheon of Egyptian deities but rather a multicultural band of "evil" spirits. The final volume of the trilogy is even named for the Egyptian "promised land," *The Western Lands;* but it differs markedly from the other two volumes in its approach to the problem of revolutionary subjectivity, as we will see. The trilogy as a whole rewrites *The Wild Boys,* from the reappearance of characters—including Audrey Carsons, Tío Mate, Colonel Greenfield, and Lola la Chata—to the repetition of scenes, such as the climactic assassination of the Muslim General by an agent of Hassan i Sabbah, which precedes the conclusions of both *The Wild Boys* and *The Western Lands.*

In *The Wild Boys,* the activity of writing is explicitly thematized in only a few places, such as in the appearance of a book entitled *The Wild Boys* in a late chapter. This thematization functions implicitly throughout the novel, however, in the "scripts" that the Penny Arcade Peep Show's "films" require, which are cut up with increasing frequency as the structures of corporate and state power weaken and as the Wild Boys themselves begin to appear in ever greater numbers and to act with ever increasing efficacy. In Burroughs's works preceding *The Wild Boys,* the term "script" refers both to a film scenario and to a prescription, forged or legitimate, used by an addict to obtain illicit drugs; "To 'make a Croaker for a Script' means to persuade a doctor to write a prescription for junk" (*J* 158). Thus, a pun-equation develops between them, an equation that continues into the late works: to write a script is to make magic, to prescribe or prewrite the performance of actions—specifically, actions the writer wants or needs to have performed. All of the characters in the late trilogy either compose scripts or perform according to them; moreover, each volume contains at least two distinct kinds of writer figures. *Cities of the Red Night* sets up the paradigm the rest of the trilogy will follow. It contains two writer figures: Noah Blake, the pirate volunteer whose diary constitutes the historical strand of the novel, and Clem Williamson Snide (note the middle name), who starts out not as a private dick but as a "private asshole" (*C* 35) searching for a missing person and ends up forging the master reality scripts that include Blake and everyone else in the novel.[4] In *The Place of Dead Roads,* gunfighter Kim Carsons and photographer Tom Dark are the Blake figures, while William Seward Hall (who shares two out of three names with his creator), the writer of western stories, takes the Snide part. In *The Western Lands,* it is revealed that another character from *Dead Roads* was also a reality scriptwriter: Joe the Dead, Kim Carsons' zombie technician. *The Western Lands* also reuses Hall as the "old writer" who opens and closes that book.

Noah Blake is first introduced as a regular character, a gunsmith, whose actions are narrated in third person, but soon he is represented solely through "Pages from [his] diary" (*C* 55) in first person; he plays the traditional role of the chronicler/participant, made familiar by the generations of epistolary and "journal" novels that have followed Defoe and Richardson. Blake does not reflect on the value or structure of his writing activity, but others, such as the pirate Captain Strobe, do: "Noah writes that I am interested in publishing his diaries 'for some reason.' Does he have any inkling what reason? He must be kept very busy as a gunsmith lest he realize his primary role" (*C* 91). Clearly writing is that "primary role," but why it is so important is only revealed later, by the self-reflexive Clem Snide. Snide begins as a first-person narrator, in the tradition of the hard-boiled detective novel, and does not become a writer until the second book of *Cities.* As his missing-person investigation leads him further into an international conspiracy, he meets the female Iguana Twin, who shows him a book entitled *Cities of the Red Night,* parts of which we have encountered in Book 1 (C 150). She tells him it is a copy and offers to pay him "one million dollars for recovery of the originals" because "'Changes[. . .]can only be effected by alterations in the *original.* The only thing [*sic*] not prerecorded in a prerecorded universe are the prerecordings themselves. The copies can only repeat themselves word for word. *A virus is a copy.* You can pretty it up, cut it up, scramble it—it will reassemble in the same form. Without being an idealist, I am reluctant to see the originals in the hands of [the novel's female villains]'" (C 166). This repudiation of the revolutionary valence of the cut-up method, the material of which will inevitably "reassemble in the same form," reminds us of Deleuze and Guattari's critique of the method's "supplementary dimension of folding" in which "unity continues its spiritual labor" (Deleuze and Guattari, *A Thousand Plateaus* 6). The job the Iguana Twin has in mind is clearly Platonic, however, with its emphasis on the "original"; despite her disavowal and her apparently revolutionary intentions, she is still apparently an idealist.

Snide accepts the commission, but transforms the plot into a Deleuzean exercise in simulation: "I had already decided to fabricate the complete books if I could find the right paper. In fact, I felt sure that this was exactly what I was being paid to do" (*C* 170). After buying supplies from an art forger, Snide and his assistant Jim "start making books. I write the continuity. Jim does the drawings" (*C* 173). They are literally rewriting and restaging the past, forging alternative histories: "The books seem to age two hundred years overnight. I am working mostly on my pirate story line. But since I am sure of the quality of the goods, I will invest some more money in Mayan and Egyptian paper and colors, and do two snuff films" (*C* 173). Snide is thus revealed as the author of the Blake plot. This simulated history draws its efficacy from its weakness. If, as the Iguana Twin says, the only things not prerecorded in a prerecorded universe are the prerecordings themselves, then those things lie outside the reality film, out of the reach of the prerecorded characters, in some Platonic transcendent realm. But those prerecordings can only emerge within the flat, linear reality film as "eternal" laws of distinction, truths that separate, exclude, and devalue like the myths used by Plato, Kant, and the ideologues of modernism. The power of such transcendent laws remains precarious, since they can only enter into the flat film in immanent form, in which form they become subject to the immanent desire that they seek to master. Any script, like any fantasy, is just such an immanent structure of desire, so the "transcendent" script of the law can only dominate by claiming to represent the outside of the film while remaining an immanent script, susceptible to editing and rewriting.

Hence the writer functions most importantly as a forger of film scripts throughout Burroughs's late trilogy: he constructs alternative scripts that undermine and even replace the transcendent script of the law. As Deleuze writes,

> the forger becomes *the* character of the cinema: not the criminal, the cowboy, the psycho-social man, the historical hero, the holder of power, etc., as in the action-image, but the forger pure and simple, to the detriment of all action. The forger could previously exist in a determinate form, liar or traitor, but he now assumes an unlimited figure which permeates the whole film. He is si-

> multaneously the man of pure descriptions and the maker of the crystal-image, the indiscernibility of the real and the imaginary; he passes into the crystal, and makes the direct time-image visible; he provokes undecidable alternatives and inexplicable differences between the true and the false, and thereby imposes a power of the false as adequate to time, in contrast to any form of the true which would control time. (Deleuze, *Cinema-2* 132)

Burroughs's forgers, who play the parts of criminals, cowboys, and the rest, are like Deleuze's forger in that they all work to produce this indiscernibility of imaginary and real in order to break the control of truth and law over time, to break the determinism of repressive history. In Burroughs's late work, too, the forger replaces the traitor, who predominated in the middle period. As Deleuze defines it,

> Truthful narration is developed organically, according to legal connections in space and chronological connections in time. . . . [N]arration implies an inquiry or testimonies which connect it to the true . . . [and it] always refers to a *system of judgement*. . . . Falsifying narration, by contrast, frees itself from this system; it shatters the system of judgements because the power of the false (not error or doubt) affects the investigator and witness as much as the person presumed guilty. . . . Narration is constantly being completely modified, in each of its episodes, not according to subjective variations, but as a consequence of disconnected places and de-chronologized moments. (Deleuze, *Cinema-2* 133)

Thus, from the point of view of the false, it is perfectly logical for Snide to begin as a private investigator, a servant of the law and seeker after truth, and then to become a forger of the false. Deleuze's analysis also justifies the rapid, montage-like shifts that pervade *Cities* following Snide's transformation, and the bulk of its two sequels as well. Burroughs's narrative is disconnected and de-chronologized, cutting across the lines that constitute the power network of the transcendent script. Deleuze quotes another of Burroughs's favorite references, proto–Wild Boy Arthur Rimbaud, to demonstrate the crucial difference between the two forms of narration represented by Blake and Snide: in truthful narration, the protagonist has a stable, preestablished identity (ego = ego) so that action always has a subject, while in forged, falsifying narration, action is impersonal and event-ual because "I is another" (Rimbaud, cited in Deleuze, *Cinema-2* 133).

Accordingly, for Deleuze, "There is no unique forger, and, if the forger reveals something, it is the existence behind him of another forger. . . . And the only content of narration will be the presentation of these forgers, their sliding from one to the other, their metamorphoses into each other" (Deleuze, *Cinema-2* 134). Thus, Blake is revealed as a character manipulated by Snide, who is himself manipulated by the Iguana Twins and by the conspiratorial businessmen Blum and Krup before he reveals himself to be an avatar (or delirious vision) of Audrey Carsons, the protagonist of *The Wild Boys*—who reprises that role in the plague cities passages, which alternate with the pirate story and the detective story (*C* 271, 274). Finally we are left only with Audrey, sitting "at a typewriter in his attic room, his back to the audience" as the theater in which the novel takes place collapses on him and on the audience (*C* 329–30). This series of forger-writers continues with Kim Carsons, Tom Dark, and William Seward Hall in *The Place of Dead Roads,* and with Hall, the Egyptian Neferti, and Joe the Dead in *The Western Lands.*

In the second novel, gunslinger Carsons and daguerreotypist Dark work together to forge historically effective scripts in the nineteenth-century United States, using both words and pictures:

> "They hanged a Mexican kid from that branch[. . . .]You may have read about it . . . made quite a stir . . . federal antilynching bill in Congress and the Abolitionists took some northern states. . . . All the papers wanted a picture of the hanging and I gave them one . . . fake of course[. . . .]I ran into this old lady[. . .]who is a very rich Abolitionist[. . .]and the idea comes to me[:] what is needed to put some teeth into the Abolition movement is an *incident* and she puts up some front money[.]" (*P* 84–85)

Not only is the photograph a fake, but the lynching itself is a fake, designed to forward a political agenda. "'How did I get away with it? Well there isn't any limit to what you can get away with in this business. Faked pictures are more convincing than real pictures because you can set them up to look real. Understand this: *All pictures are faked.* As soon as you have the concept of a picture there is no limit to falsification'" (*P* 84). Carsons and Dark each incarnate the warrior as writer-forger, fighting with false images against the image as such. They "attempt the impossible: to photograph the present moment which contains the past the future" (*P* 89) in order to transform all of them. Burroughs's novel is populated with simulations of this sort, which are subversive of the very concept of an original.

Hall—like Snide an even more self-reflexive writer figure than Carsons or Dark—is described as "a corridor, a hall leading to many doors[. . .]the man of many faces and many pen names, of many times and places" (*P* 115). As a writer of popular western fiction, he is in a position to forge effective knowledge on a huge scale, and with a huge impact; he is "a guardian of the knowledge and of those who could use it. . . . So he concealed and revealed the knowledge in fictional form" (*P* 115). Hall incarnates the writer-forger as warrior, who "will not hesitate to use the sword he is forging, an antimagnetic artifact that cuts word and image to fragments" and that allows him to "unplot and unwrite. Oh, it may take a few hundred years before some people find out they have been unwritten and unplotted into random chaos" (*P* 116). Hall is constantly on the run both from human enemies and from abstract conceptual ones, who see his knowledge and his manipulation of fiction as a threat to the hegemony they administer through the Law and truth. His contribution to revolutionary change, or the fantasmatic representation of change, is a bit more modest than Snide's magical scriptwriting, but "Even to envisage success on this scale is a victory. A victory from which others may envision further" (*P* 116), in an immense relay.

The last novel in the trilogy is different in general strategy than the first two. The old writer whose situation begins and ends *The Western Lands* is finally (at the end of the novel) revealed to be Hall, who is of course a surrogate for Burroughs himself, but this new Hall—the forger who controls the writer-warrior Joe the Dead and, through Joe, all the recurring characters from the earlier novels—has developed "a disgust for his words [that] choked him, and he could no longer bear to look at his words on a piece of paper" (*WL* 1). Occasionally he sees words "which were not his own" and which he thinks perhaps could be copied down and made into a book, "and then . . . yes, and then what?" (*WL* 2). His writing has lost whatever efficacy Snide's and even his own earlier work (in *The Place of Dead Roads*) had, and can lead to no result, no change in the world. Joe the Dead is blunter about it: he "didn't have ideas about rewriting history like Kim did. More of Kim's irresponsible faggotry, he's going to rewrite history while we wait" (*WL* 59). Kim himself, now "dead," learns that his writing did not create the situations he sought, but that he too merely transcribed someone else's writing. Throughout the novel, Hall battles this political and ontological "writer's block," this inefficacy of writing, by changing narratives every few pages, from Joe to Kim to other temporary characters and back, until he finally reaches "the end of words, the end of what can be done with words" (*WL* 258). The transition from the initial "rewriting of history" to this "end of words" parallels the development of Burroughs's project for the reconstitution of revolutionary allies, which moves from recognizably communitarian fantasies through an apotheosis of the disjointed, schizophrenic self to a concluding silence that, at first glance, looks like defeat. In order to demonstrate that this silence means more than simply defeat, we must follow in detail the development that leads up to it.

The two aspects of Burroughs's affirmative reconstitution project, history and community, cannot be strictly separated, but they can be distinguished tendentially and schematically for the purposes of exposition. The Wild Boys' reductive sense of history made them merely "utopian as a *force,* not as literal images of the ideal community" (Skerl 83). Summarily, we could say that in this trilogy, Burroughs recognizes, for the first time, the real indeterminism or contingency of Western history, and begins to hatch a plot that will interfere with its linear development. He recognizes that the smooth totality of repressive history, which he so long took for granted, has been produced from untotalizable fragments that can, in principle, be reclaimed, if only through fantasy. "The chance was there," he realizes, but "The chance was missed" (*C* xiv). These chance fragments will be the accretion points for his new virtual communities. The negative moment in his work—the violent undoing of the power structures of late capitalism—retains both the undiluted virulence and the narrative form it had in *The Wild Boys,* but this affirmative moment—the production of fantasmatic communities from the lost fragments of history—transforms the dynamics of his compositional practice.

Burroughs's new historical consciousness is evident from the introductory pages of *Cities of the Red Night,* which describe the establishment of anarchist communes in the Americas during the seventeenth and early eighteenth centuries. Like the other novels in the trilogy, this one results from a textual encounter: Burroughs's narrator cites Don C. Seitz's *Under the Black Flag* as the source of his ideas on historical communes.[5] Such communes, the narrator claims, were based on the then-revolutionary ideas of universal suffrage, freedom of religion, the abolition of slavery, and the elimination of capital punishment. The historical communes were wiped out by native attacks and disease, but "had they been able to [survive], the history of the world could have been altered" (*C* xiii). This historical reflection gives rise immediately to the issue of community (and fantasy):

> Imagine a number of such fortified positions all through South America and the West Indies, stretching from Africa to Madagascar and Malaya and the East Indies, all offering refuge to fugitives from slavery and oppression: "Come to us and live under the Articles."

> At once we have allies in all those who are enslaved and oppressed throughout the world, from the cotton plantations of the American South to the sugar plantations of the West Indies, the whole Indian population of the American continent peonized and degraded by the Spanish into subhuman poverty and ignorance, exterminated by the Americans, infected with their vices and diseases, the natives of Africa and Asia—all these are potential allies. (*C* xiii)

Burroughs's experiential and fictional milieus were always multiethnic (though sometimes merely ahistorically exotic or Orientalist), but this historical and political vision is something new that will be pursued doggedly throughout the trilogy.

What would be the outcome of the victory of such a communal movement? Here Burroughs applies his trademark causal hyperbole to utopian rather than dystopian ends, and the result is a Rousseauistic paradise, a "plan of living" that later books will complicate:

> Faced by the actual practice of freedom, the French and American revolutions would be forced to stand by their words. The disastrous results of uncontrolled industrialization would also be curtailed, since factory workers and slum dwellers from the cities would seek refuge in Articulated areas. Any man would have the right to settle in any area of his choosing. The land would belong to those who used it. No white-man boss, no Pukka Sahib, no Patróns, no colonists. The escalation of mass production and concentration of population in urban areas would be halted, for who would work in their factories and buy their products when he could live from the fields and the sea and the lakes and the rivers in areas of unbelievable plenty? And living from the land, he would be motivated to preserve its resources. (*C* xiv)

This "retroactive utopia [which] actually could have happened in terms of the techniques and human resources available at that time" would have solved every conceivable problem: colonialism, industrialization, urban blight, Fordism, pollution, and resource depletion. "[M]ankind might have stepped free from the deadly impasse of insoluble problems in which we now find ourselves" (*C* xiv).

This fantasy, this chance which was there and was missed and which, in diverse forms, will be one of the main subjects of the trilogy, does not blind Burroughs's narrator to the disheartening historical facts:

> The principles of the French and American revolutions became windy lies in the mouths of politicians. The liberal revolutions of 1848 created the so-called republics of Central and South America, with a dreary history of dictatorship, oppression, graft and bureaucracy, thus closing this vast, underpopulated continent to any possibility of communes[. . . .]In any case South Amer-

> ica will soon be crisscrossed by highways and motels. In England, Western Europe and America, the overpopulation made possible by the Industrial Revolution leaves scant room for communes, which are commonly subject to state and federal law and frequently harassed by the local inhabitants. (C xiv–xv)

Communal living was also a facet of the sixties counterculture, one to which Burroughs paid little attention at the time but which now offers him an escape from his impasse. Only a miracle or a disaster, the narrator insists, can restore this missed chance, so *Cities of the Red Night* offers a script for both.

The novel interweaves at least three separate narrative strands: the miraculous establishment and progress of pirate communes in the Americas during the early eighteenth century, told by Noah Blake, who participates in them; a perverse contemporary murder mystery that deepens into a conspiracy thriller, told by the detective involved, Clem Snide; and, for disaster, a fragmentary series of *Wild Boys*-style routines set in and around the ancient plague cities of the novel's title, many of which center on Audrey Carsons, the protagonist of *The Wild Boys.* Since this last strand resurrects the narrative techniques and content of *The Wild Boys* and *Port of Saints* more or less unchanged, we will not address it in any detail. The second and third narrative strands are linked initially by the plague that gives the cities their group name and Clem Snide his murder case, a disease that turns the patient red and kills him through sexual frenzy. Later in the novel, these two strands collapse into one another. The first strand, concerning the utopian pirate communes, is linked to the Snide plot through the Iguana Twins, who appear in both. This strand surfaces with decreasing frequency as the novel progresses, and ultimately collapses into the plague cities plot in Book 3. The first strand alone, however, contains Burroughs's first fully articulated *affirmative* model of revolutionary subjectivity.

Noah Blake, the narrator of this strand, is a young gunsmith and diarist from the Great Lakes who signs aboard a disreputable merchant ship in 1702, only to discover that the ship is secretly in the employ of a communal group of pirates, nominally led by Captains Strobe and Nordenholz (though manipulated by the mysterious Iguana Twins) and based in Panama. Blake's education in the pirates' communal social order provides the reader with an expository (and later narrative) account of that order. The pirates espouse the same "Articles" that Burroughs discusses in the introductory passage quoted above (with one notable addition that will be discussed below), and they accept all fugitives from the European colonial powers. They live together in communal dwellings, eat in communal kitchens, and train in various martial arts at Port Roger (*C* 125). This narrative strand is driven primarily by the (negative) conflict between the communes and the colonial powers, so it is no surprise that Blake puts his weapons-design skills at the service of the communes, soon supplying them with breech-loading firearms, grenades (based on a child's firecracker), and a number of other minor technical advantages that will give them an edge over the Spanish who control the region. He also passes the techniques on to the "natives," since "decentralization is a keynote of our strategy" and "Arming the native population is another essential step" (*C* 135). The passages that follow, which narrate the defeat of the Spanish and the occupation of Panama City by the pirates, are similar to the battle sequences in *The Wild Boys,* but the anachronistic science-fiction settings of that novel give way in *Cities* to tropical jungles and historically accurate technical descriptions.

The real novelty, in terms of Burroughs's compositional practice, appears in the expository passages concerned with representing daily life under the Articles. Here, for the first time, Burroughs offers a detailed glimpse of an affirmative society liberated from coercive power, or of what such a liberated society could have looked like in 1702. To be sure, the members of this society still spend a lot of time engaged in homosexual intercourse; Article 5, which does not appear in the historical list of rights in the introduction, states that "No man may interfere with the sexual practices of another or force any sexual act on another against his or her will" (*C* 187). But this intercourse is no longer privileged as a potentially revolutionary act, as it often was for the Wild Boys; it is merely a means to personal enlightenment, according to Wilhelm Reich's psychology. One of the chapters concerned with this communal daily life, "Mother is the best bet," contains two of the most significant scenes in Burroughs's entire body of work. The first is a lengthy and theatrical sequence describing, for the first time in affirmative terms, heterosexual intercourse. The women of the commune, both straight and lesbian, who want to bear children pair up first with the heterosexual men, or "husbands"; this leaves a number of women unattached, so the homosexual or "rabbit" men (who "fuck[. . .]and run"), including the narrator Blake, must perform elaborate theatrical scenes, complete with costumes and props, during which they impregnate the "rabbit" women (*C* 106, 108). Blake's own routine is, typically, a parodic Maya fertility ritual (*C* 110).

The second key scene presents the only affirmative female point of view in Burroughs's entire body of work, and so is worth citing at some length. This sequence quotes the "diary of Hirondelle de Mer," another writer figure:

> I am a sorceress and a warrior. I do not relish being treated as a breeding animal. Would this occur to Skipper Nordenholz? No force, he says, has been applied—but I am forced by my circumstances, cast up here without a peso, and by my Indian blood which compels me to side with all enemies of Spain. The child will be brought up a sorcerer or sorceress[. . . .]
>
> Suppose the Spanish have been driven out or brought under the Articles? Suppose, too, similar uprisings in North America and Canada have shattered the English and French. What now? Can this vast territory be held without the usual machinery of government, ambassadors, standing army and navy? They can only plan to hold the area by sorcery. This is a sorcerers' revolution. I must find my part as a sorceress. (*C* 111–12)

Women have been portrayed as breeding stock and as warriors in other Burroughs texts, but this woman is different. She recognizes the shortcomings and pretensions of the men and resents the necessity that dictates her actions, but willingly allies herself with them anyway. She also, unfortunately, foreshadows the pirates' ultimate self-defeat. Later, more typically Burroughsian scenes of open and violent warfare between the sexes in the plague cities should not obscure the breakthrough marked by this chapter. These two scenes demonstrate, for the first time in Burroughs's writing, that the sexes are not destined to be at war with each other, but can form alliances against a common enemy: irresponsible and coercive state and corporate power.

In the third book of the novel, the boundaries between the three narrative strands collapse, although a few discernible continuities remain. The commune strand, in particular, almost vanishes. Two chapters narrated by Noah Blake appear, however, immediately before the apocalyptic "plague cities" strand takes over the entire narration, and these chapters extend the pirates' world into later eras. In the first of these, Blake is traveling with Waring, the commune's resident painter (distantly based on Burroughs's friend and sometime collaborator Brion Gysin), on a North American train in the late twentieth century. They show their U.S. passports to the agent at the French Canadian border. The agent seizes and destroys the documents, denouncing them as "lies[. . .]purportedly issued by a government which ceased to exist two hundred years ago" (*C* 253). As the other passengers clamor for food and lodging, which they cannot buy with their now-worthless money, Blake escapes with another boy. In the next chapter, he rents a shack in an Old West landscape that foreshadows the generic markers of *The Place of Dead Roads;* at the end of the chapter Blake is approached by an alien boy from Venus, which makes him wonder "what tyranny had led him to leave his native planet and take refuge under the Articles" (*C* 265). Thereafter, the pirate characters appear only in the catastrophic "plague cities" strand.

Like *Cities of the Red Night,* its first sequel, *The Place of Dead Roads,* opens with an enabling historical reference, this time to the nineteenth rather than the eighteenth century. The original title of the novel, the note tells us, was *The Johnson Family.* (The final title of the novel is explained, rather laconically, late in the text: "The Place of Dead Roads[. . .]does not mean roads that are no longer used, roads that are overgrown, it means roads that are *dead*" [*P* 283], that is, reserved for the use of the dead, and thus inaccessible to the living.) The original title was "a turn-of-the-century expression to designate good bums and thieves. It was elaborated into a code of conduct" among the dispossessed: mind your own business, acknowledge your responsibilities, and give help when it is needed. That title comes from Jack Black's autobiography *You Can't Win,* an account of life outside the law in the late nineteenth century, long passages of which Burroughs incorporated into his early books and which he could still quote verbatim a half-century after he read them.[6] The note also allows the reader no doubt about the intent of the code or the theme of the novel itself: "*Happiness is a by-product of function.*" This phrase recurs throughout *The Place of Dead Roads* as the refrain to Burroughs's (anti-)utopian blues: "Nietzsche said, 'Men need play and danger. Civilization gives them work and safety'[. . . .]Some cultures cultivated danger for itself, not realizing that danger derives from conflicting purposes[. . . .]Happiness is a by-product of function. Those who seek happiness for itself seek victory without war. This is the flaw in all utopias" (*P* 237). Thus, Burroughs attempts to navigate between the Scylla of violent, specular rupture à la *The Wild Boys* and the Charybdis of idealistic utopianism, which constantly defers conflict and thus abets the status quo.

If *Cities of the Red Night* uses the conventions of historical and detective fiction to present its historical-fictional alternative, *The Place of Dead Roads*—which comprises only two distinct narrative strands rather than three—does something similar with the western. Burroughs first mentioned that he intended to write a western in 1965,[7] but gave no indication at that time that his western would form part of such an ambitious political project. Needless to say, Burroughs's version of the genre bears little resemblance to the works of Zane Grey or Louis L'Amour, beyond the ubiquitous Colt revolvers and stereotypical nicknames. It is concerned less with the "Zen gunfight" that Burroughs discussed in 1965 than with the possibilities for a subversive social order along the "lawless" American frontier. The book's protagonist is Kim Carsons, who, like Audrey (from *The Wild Boys*) and Blake (from *Cities*), is an outcast homosexual from the American middle west, who refuses the prospect of "Running away and living on sufferance in a ghetto" of urban homosexuals where there's "always somebody to spit in his face and call him what the boys called him at school" (*P* 45–46). His name, differing by two letters from that of a famous frontiersman, marks his difference from the generic gunfighter.

In the first and second books of the novel, Kim works to realize his "dream of a takeover by the Johnson Family, by those who actually do the work, the creative thinkers and artists and technicians" (*P* 104). Like the pirate commune fantasy of *Cities,* Kim's fantasmatic plan of living has both negative and positive moments. The negative moment contains all of the goals we have come to expect in Burroughs's manifestos since *The Wild Boys:*

> We will take every opportunity to weaken the power of the church[. . . .]We will fight any extension of federal authority and support States' Rights. We will resist any attempt to penalize or legislate against the so-called victimless crimes . . . [. . . .]We will endeavor to halt the Industrial Revolution before it is too late, to regulate populations at a reasonable point, to eventually replace quantitative money with qualitative money, to decentralize, to conserve resources. The Industrial Revolution is primarily a virus revolution, dedicated to controlled proliferation of identical objects and persons. (*P* 97–98)

This passage essentially repeats the introductory note to *Cities,* within the historical context of the nineteenth-century United States (hence the reference to the proliferation of "States' Rights" against the hierarchical hegemony of the federal government).

The gunslingers' communal organization practices different tactics than the pirate groups did, however; instead of frontal assault, "The Johnson Family must go underground" (*P* 130). "As soon as Kim started organizing the Johnson Family, he realized how basically subversive such an organization would appear to the people who run America. So the Johnson Family must not appear to these people as an organized unit[. . . .]He planned towns, areas, communities, owned and occupied by Johnsons, that would appear to outsiders as boringly ordinary or disagreeable, that would leave no questions unanswered" (*P* 130–31). Like Ralph Ellison's invisible narrator, however, the Johnsons do not intend to remain underground. The "takeover" Kim plans will proceed incrementally, avoiding open hostilities except in cases of self-defense. "He will organize the Johnsons in Civilian Defense Units[. . . .]He will buy a newspaper to push Johnson policy, to oppose any further encroachment of Washington bureaucrats. He intends to strangle the FDA in its cradle, to defeat any legislation aimed at outlawing liquor, drugs, gambling, private sexual behavior or the possession of firearms. He will buy a chemical company[. . . and] start a small-arms factory" (*P* 104–5). The Johnsons will play by the rules of American society until they amass sufficient force to change those rules; this is a dangerous course, constantly threatening to fall into either accommodation with the status quo or reductive neofascist libertarianism, like that of contemporary militia movements. The Johnsons neither rely upon nor abjure violent conflict, and their middle way must also evade the dialectic of treason that constantly lays siege to all of Burroughs's characters.

The subversive Johnsons "represent Potential America" (*P* 154) and therefore must, like the pirate communes, have a second, positive moment to their revolutionary strategy. In places, this moment reverts to the parthenogenetic fantasy of *The Wild Boys:* "We will give all our attention to experiments designed to produce asexual offspring, to cloning, use of artificial wombs, and transfer operations" (*P* 98). In general, women occupy an ambivalent position in *The Place of Dead Roads,* as both allies (such as Salt Chunk Mary, "mother of the Johnson Family," [*P* 122) and enemies ("Women must be regarded as the principal reservoir of the alien virus parasite," *P* 96). Burroughs's constructive social vision of an alternative Old West is much more fanciful than was his vision of eighteenth-century pirates. The basic principle of social organization, in fact, is cribbed from Borges's "Babylon Lottery" and from Hollywood: instead of a fixed and deadening social division of labor that leads either to mindless conformity or to class struggle, "the roles rotate. You can be *fils de famille* today and busboy tomorrow—*son cosas de la vida.* Besides it's more interesting that way[. . . .]This system of rotating parts operates on the basis of a complex lottery. . . . Some people achieved a lottery-exempt status for a time but for most it was maybe a month, often less, before they got the dread call. Turn in your tycoon suit and report to casting" (*P* 114). The purpose of this rather cinematic lottery is quite different from the one in Borges's story, however. The Babylon lottery's "silent functioning" is "comparable to that of God," even a nonexistent God (Borges 71), and therefore transcendent, while Burroughs's social lottery is intended to show "that an organization and a very effective organization can run without boss-man dog-eat-dog fear" (*P* 115), on the basis of purely immanent, even rhizomatic, relations of production.

This antihierarchical theme goes even further, to the very structure of the characters. The original Kim Carsons commits suicide, but he lives on in the "ten clones derived from Kim Carsons the Founder." The clone Kim is "under no pressure to maintain the perimeters of a defensive ego, and this left him free to *think*[. . . .]The clones exist in a communal mind in which the bodies are at the disposal of all the others, like rotating quarters" (*P* 113). The third book of the novel, "Quién es?" follows various cloned versions of Kim through subversive Old West adventures as well as ludicrous Mafia confrontations. By means of this immanent thematic device, Burroughs attempts to recast his narrative in communal terms; he thus constructs a direct *formal* alternative (like the Penny Arcade Peep Show of *The Wild Boys*) to the individualistic focus of the generic western, as Sergei Eisenstein did with respect to bourgeois narrative film and as Nanni Balestrini did with respect to the Italian proletarian novel.[8] The multiplication of intersecting routines concerning the divergent Kims creates this indirect formal alternative, and embodies Burroughs's principle of nonexclusivity: there is no original or true Kim; therefore, his clones are permitted to do everything.

This formal displacement of the narrative demands of genre fiction marks *Cities of the Red Night* as much as it does *The Place of Dead Roads,* though in a different way. The final chapter of *Cities,* an enigmatic "Return to Port Roger" by a narrator who appears to be Noah Blake, closes off the radical potentialities of the pirate commune along with the specular violence of its method. The commune is long deserted: "Nothing here but the smell of empty years" (*C* 331). He reads in the diary of the Spanish defeat at Panama City, and of the deaths of friends. More victories over the Spanish follow, yet he insists that "The easiest victories are the most costly in the end" (*C* 332). This implies that the victories eventually result in defeat, but how? "I have blown a hole in time with a firecracker. Let others step through. Into what bigger and better firecrackers? Better weapons lead to better and better weapons, until the earth is a grenade with the fuse burning" (*C* 332). This is Blake's defeat, a defeat similar to the one the Wild Boys suffered: the defeat of specularity, of achieving victory over one's enemies by merely negating them point for point, fighting on their terms and thus conserving their social order. The coincident point that defeats the pirates is the strategy of violent domination they share with the Spanish. It is a dialectical defeat in victory, one that cannot fail to produce new conflicts, new weapons for the next round of "the old army game from here to eternity." "Like Spain," the narrator laments, "I am bound to the past" (*C* 332). This lament applies as much to Blake's truthful form of narration as it does to the specular form of antagonism and destruction he undertakes.

Burroughs's own bond to the past, his preservation of narrative individuality according to character,[9] emerges most completely at the end of *The Place of Dead Roads,* when (one of the) Kim Carsons and his nemesis, bounty hunter Mike Chase, meet for an abortive gunfight. This scene reprises the "newspaper story" that opens the novel: Kim pretends to draw, points his index finger at Chase and says, "BANG! YOU'RE *DEAD,*" at which point Chase collapses; Kim feels a slap on the back and turns to remonstrate with his attacker, only to collapse, shot himself (*P* 306). Their killer is not identified (and will not be identified until the third volume of the trilogy), but his presence breaks the dramatic and ethical symmetry of the two-man gunfight that grounds the western as a genre; in this, the scene resembles the three-way gunfight that concludes Sergio Leone's 1967 film *The Good, the Bad and the Ugly.* The unidentified killer, the asymmetrical third party, reveals the dialectical complicity between Kim's apparently radical cowboy fantasy and Chase's conformist power lust, even as he destroys them. The mystery left unresolved by this scene grants a Joycean kind of circular closure to the novel, and also reinscribes *The Place of Dead Roads* alongside *Cities of the Red Night* in the detective genre. In putting an end to Kim, his enemies, and the novel itself, this scene finally closes off Burroughs's attempt to constitute a revolutionary subject in recognizably communitarian terms—in *The Western Lands,* community arises only from the schizophrenic splitting of the subject, as it did in *Queer.*

The Western Lands does contain the beginnings of another communitarian fantasy, set this time in the contemporary period and in the generic form of a spy novel concerning "Margaras Unlimited, a secret service without a country," which pursues "a series of modest goals leading to a series of modest achievements which become at some point quite considerable" (*WL* 24). The "dead" Kim Carsons sometimes reappears in this strand. But whereas the fantasmatic pirates of *Cities* and gunfighters of *Dead Roads* occupied and granted narrative continuity to large sections of each respective novel, the agents of Margaras Unlimited appear if anything *less* frequently than characters from other routines, and are consequently unable to supply any continuity to the disjointed narrative structure of *The Western Lands.* The other routines include those concerning Joe the Dead and his "natural outlaws," who are determined to break the "so-called natural laws of the universe foisted upon us by physicists, chemists [etc.], and, above all, the monumental fraud of cause and effect." These sections reprise much of the "Biologic Courts" material from the *Nova* trilogy. For "Uranian Willy," betrayal was a way to end the interminable dialectic of cops and criminals that was mediated by the form of the Law, while for these "natural outlaws," "the breaking of a natural law is an end in itself: the end of that law" (*WL* 30). Both of these sets of routines carry on Burroughs's earlier project of reconstituting the revolutionary subject, but the communitarian method on which these fantasies depend is constantly undercut by the "writer's block" that forces the narrator, Hall, to shift from dead-end routine to dead-end routine, from dream journal to entomological treatise (most of them obsessed with Maya-inspired centipedes), as "he writes about desperately for an escape route" (*WL* 13) out of the philosophical and political impasse that blocked both of the earlier novels.

The schizophrenic alternative to this communitarian method, which augments the multiplication of more or less similar subjective routines already used in *The Place of Dead Roads,* is explicated in *The Western Lands* as early as page 4, again in terms of the Egyptian Book of the Dead, from which the title is taken:

> The ancient Egyptians postulated seven souls.
>
> Top soul, and first to leave at the moment of death, is Ren, the Secret Name. This corresponds to my Director. He directs the film of your life from conception to death. The Secret Name is the title of *your* film. When you die, that's where Ren came in.
>
> Second soul, and second one off the sinking ship, is Sekem: Energy, Power, Light. The Director gives the orders, Sekem pushes the right buttons.
>
> Number three is Khu, the Guardian Angel. He, she or it is third man out . . . depicted as flying away across a full moon, a bird with luminous wings and a head of light[. . . .]The Khu is responsible for the subject and can be injured in his defense—but not permanently, since the first three souls are eternal. They go back to heaven for another vessel. The four remaining souls must take their chances with the subject in the Land of the Dead.
>
> Number four is Ba, the Heart, often treacherous. This is a hawk's body with your face on it, shrunk down to the size of a fist. Many a hero has been brought down, like Samson, by a perfidious Ba.

> Number five is Ka, the Double, most closely associated with the subject. The Ka, which usually reaches adolescence at the time of bodily death, is the only reliable guide through the Land of the Dead to the Western Lands.
>
> Number six is Khaibit, the Shadow, Memory, your whole past conditioning from this and other lives.
>
> Number seven is Sekhu, the Remains. (*WL* 4–5)[10]

Burroughs first "encountered this concept" in Norman Mailer's novel *Ancient Evenings* (*WL* 5), which rounds out the trio of textual encounters that granted impetus to Burroughs's trilogy.

The "subject" so conceived is clearly not a unified ego, nor is it simply split into the speaking subject and the grammatical subject of its own statements; Burroughs's ultimate vision of subjectivity presents it as an aggregate of irreconcilable fragments "with different and incompatible interests" (*WL* 27), whose ends (in both the narrative and intentional senses) are in conflict. The individual personality, the superficial "I," is the supernumerary "Mr. Eight-Ball, who has these souls" (*WL* 7), but is unable to totalize or unify them. The subject is not a totality or a whole, but is produced, rather, as another part alongside its seven component parts. Deleuze and Guattari present this formulation as a marker of their (and, by extension, Burroughs') distance from modernity:

> We no longer believe in the myth of the existence of fragments that, like pieces of an antique statue, are merely waiting for the last one to be turned up, so that they may all be glued back together to create a unity that is precisely the same as the original unity. We no longer believe in a primordial totality that once existed, or in a final totality that awaits us at some future date . . . We believe only in totalities that are peripheral. And if we discover such a totality alongside various separate parts, it is a whole *of* these particular parts but does not totalize them; it is a unity *of* all of these particular parts but does not unify them; rather, it is added to them as a new part fabricated separately. (Deleuze and Guattari, *Anti-Oedipus* 42)

The relation of the constituent "souls" to the subject, then, is immanent rather than hierarchical, and "Mr. Eight-Ball" cannot exert any control over the souls. Thus, when Burroughs invokes the *Communist Manifesto* again, he no longer directs his slogan at discrete social subjects as he did in *Naked Lunch* and *The Ticket That Exploded,* but at the untotalizable part-subject: "Eights of the world unite! You have nothing to lose but your dirty rotten vampires" (*WL* 7).

The seven souls are divided into two larger groups: those that are transcendent, or "eternal," and that therefore readily abandon the subject after "death," and those that must accompany the subject on its precarious and immanent quest for "immortality" in the Western Lands. In Deleuze and Guattari's terms, these are the two relations of social desire that characterize, respectively, the subjugated group and the subject-group, but they are now transposed from the molar social world into the very structure of the individual "subject." There is no contradiction here, of course, either for Burroughs or for Deleuze and Guattari, because for all of them, the unified, thinking/speaking subject is always multiple, its apparent unity an optical illusion produced by molecular multiplication or aggregation, while what is individuated is never a person but always a specific connection of desires, drives, or "desiring-machines." Each "person" is ontologically, rather than clinically, schizophrenic, and thus is a community unto him- or herself. What Burroughs reveals in the "deaths" of his subjects or characters is neither the end of their existences nor the failure of their efforts, but the liberation of their component "souls" from the servitude of despotic subjectivity, and the extension of their revolutionary efforts onto new terrains of struggle. If the impasse that blocked both the pirates of *Cities* and the gunfighters of *Dead Roads* was specularity, the dialectical opposition that caused them to preserve and reinscribe the aggregate social and subjective structures of their opponents, then the way out of that impasse will require the abandonment of those structures. Burroughs's refrains throughout *The Western Lands, "every man for himself"* and *"sauve qui peut"* (*WL* 5, 9, 10, etc.), might appear to mark the end of his revolutionary reconstitutional project, but since "every man" is already a conglomeration of conflicting souls, they merely mark that project's metamorphosis.

As Burroughs writes, "There is intrigue among the souls, and treachery. No worse fate can befall a man than to be surrounded by traitor souls" (*WL* 6). Within the "subject" there is a fundamental conflict between the mortal and eternal souls, but also between the various mortal souls that must struggle through the Land of the Dead to reach the Western Lands. The first struggle, between the mortal and eternal souls, is between the immanence of material existence and the transcendence of despotic divinity,[11] and determines the subject's radical potential: the subject can only enter the Land of the Dead, can only begin the real struggle, if his mortal souls are strong enough to survive the seductions of despotic and transcendent divinity. These seductions take many forms: "The Christian Heaven of pearly gates and singing angels, the Moslem paradise of eternal whores and plenty of water, the Communists' heaven of the workers' state" (*WL* 241). To accept any of these seductions is to lose the first struggle, to be abandoned at bodily death to "Soul Death[. . .]what the Egyptians called the Second and Final Death" (*WL* 9), figured throughout *The Western Lands* in the threat of nuclear annihilation.

The second struggle is no less important, however, even though it cannot begin until the subject has already achieved a victory of sorts over the eternal souls that would leave it just an animated corpse, a "walking Sekhu" (*WL* 6), like those who have given themselves to the powers of transcendence. The struggle between the mortal souls determines which soul(s) will guide the subject's "individual" progress toward the Western Lands and immortality, and this second struggle accounts for most of the narrative routines contained in the novel. Many parodic sequences, reminiscent of the excesses of *Naked Lunch* and the *Nova* trilogy, describe the multifarious ways in which souls can destroy themselves on their journeys through the dangerous Land of the Dead: the aristocratic Egyptians' dependence on mummies makes them vulnerable to the "mummy bashers," who destroy their Sekhus (*WL* 159–60), while naïve or foolish subjects are either betrayed by their own treacherous and wayward souls or set upon by the "demons" who guard the various roads through the Land of the Dead.

If the pilgrim succeeds in carving a trail through the dangerous Land of the Dead, if he can "meet and overcome his own death" (*WL* 115), he (or she) reaches the Western Lands of Egyptian myth, the promised abode of the immortal souls of the dead. To have come this far, the pilgrim has managed to escape the clichéd paradises of transcendence (the Christian Heaven, the dictatorship of the proletariat), but he or she is now faced with another potential trap: immortality as self-indulgence. "Look at their Western Lands. What do they look like? The houses and gardens of a rich man. Is this all the Gods can offer? Well, I say then it is time for new Gods who do not offer such paltry bribes" (*WL* 164). Burroughs's image of immortality is not one of bourgeois leisure, which he explicitly lampoons as a "sop [given] to the middle classes, to ensure their loyalty" (*WL* 161) to the hierarchical structure of the state. "Cut-rate embalmers offer pay-as-you-go plans, so much a month for mummy insurance. If you live fifty years or die tomorrow, your future in the Western Lands is assured. (An old couple with their arms around each other's shoulders stand in front of their modest little villa.)"(*WL* 160) Such a vision requires an intact self to be indulged, a self which is unlikely to survive the brutal exigencies of the Land of the Dead.

As he wrote in the prefatory note to *The Place of Dead Roads,* Burroughs believes instead that "Immortality is purpose and function" (*WL* 70), relations that precede the constitution of the subject and survive that subject's demise. To conceive immortality in terms of function instead of subjectivity is to evade the vicious circle of human history. Instead of investing the reactionary, subjugated-group fantasy offered by the Gods, "We can make our own Western Lands" (*WL* 164) by creating a radical subject-group fantasy that will enable desire to transform the structure of the capitalist socius.

> We know that the Western Lands are made solid by *fellaheen* blood and energy, siphoned off by vampire mummies, just as water is siphoned off to create an oasis. Such an oasis lasts only so long as the water lasts, and the technology for its diversion. However, an oasis that is self-sustaining, recreated by the inhabitants, does not need such an inglorious vampiric lifeline.
>
> We can create a land of dreams. (*WL* 164–65)

Just as the linguistically parasitic Nova Mob lived off the energy of its "marks," so the Western Lands offered by the Gods require the stolen life-energy and labor-power of the great mass of *fellaheen,* or workers. The productive masses already know how to create a realized dreamland in which to live, a fantasy that will end the repressive history of the capitalist world, because, "Well, that's what art is all about, isn't it? All creative thought, actually. A bid for immortality" (*WL* 165) in functional form.

The terms of Burroughs's intervention here—"death," "soul" and "immortality"—are ancient, and, as he recognizes, they are solidly embedded in the histories and traditions that he is fighting, though they are by no means uncontested even within those traditions. Perhaps a strategic change of terms will clarify Burroughs's project, provided that those terms do not alter the relations that he identifies. If the struggles between eternal and mortal souls are struggles between transcendence and immanence, between the subjugated group's fantasmatic desire and the subject-group's fantasmatic desire, then a more precise anatomy of their differences may clarify the stakes of the second, purely immanent struggle in Burroughs's metamorphosed project. Recall, from our discussion of Sartre, that the series or subjugated group produces or invests fantasies that are offered by and supportive of the status quo, while the subject-group's fantasies are hostile to that status quo, even though they may thereafter produce a structurally similar seriality. The measure of any group's revolutionary efficacy is what Deleuze and Guattari call its "coefficient of deterritorialization," the logical and structural distance separating its enabling fantasies from those of the already constituted socius and therefore separating the group's destructive tasks, which are determined by that socius, from its constructive ones, which are logically independent of the socius.

Deleuze and Guattari further specify that there are two levels of this fantasmatic desiring-production or investment that complicate the determination of the coefficients; they label these two levels the "preconscious investment of class or interest" and the "unconscious investment of desire or group." At the preconscious level, the "break" between reactionary and revolutionary investments of class or interest is merely "between two forms of socius, the second of which is measured according to its capacity to introduce the flows of desire into a new code . . . of interest" that may yet preserve the aggregate form of the subject or the subjugated form of the group, as Noah Blake's and Kim Carsons' communal utopias do. At the unconscious level, the reactionary-revolutionary break is "within the socius itself, in that it has the capacity for causing the flows of desire to circulate following their positive lines of escape" (Deleuze and Guattari, *Anti-Oedipus* 348) from the structure of that subject- or subjugated group, in the manner of Burroughs's multiple souls. This split means that the fantasmatic formation of the group, whether subjugated or subject-group, is constantly being negotiated within each "individual" subject as well as in the aggregate social world. In a very singular way, the "personal" is directly "political" in Burroughs's novel.

Coefficients of deterritorialization, unlike the utopian myths of totality they replace, are ephemeral, or rather variable in the mathematical sense: capable of taking on any value in a given domain. The two levels of investment can combine in four different ways, resulting in four virtual domains into which the coefficients can fall and among which the coefficients can move: a group can be marked (1) by revolutionary preconscious *and* unconscious desire, or (2) by reactionary preconscious *and* unconscious desire, or (3) by revolutionary preconscious desire and reactionary unconscious desire, or (4) by reactionary preconscious desire and revolutionary unconscious desire. Only the first combination is thoroughly fused in its revolutionary commitments, and this fusion remains precarious. The topography of desire is unstable: "Quarters and streets, squares, markets and bridges change form, shift location from day to day like traveling carnivals. Comfortable, expensive houses arranged around a neat square[. . .] can change, even as you find your way there, into a murderous ghetto. Oh, there are maps enough. But they are outmoded as soon as they can be printed" (*WL* 152). Concepts like inside and outside, public and private, self and other have little or no sense there. "A word about conditions in the Land of the Dead: quarters are precarious and difficult to find one's way back to, and privacy is fleeting. Doors are flimsy, often absent, leaving your quarters open to corridors, passageways, streets, and there are always other means of access, so one is subject to find anybody or anything in one's digs, if one is lucky enough to have digs" (*WL* 213). Burroughs's routines concerning the different relations between eternal and mortal souls in *The Western Lands* are not intended as systematic embodiments of Deleuze and Guattari's variable domains, but the resonances between the two formulations can shed light on the structures and stakes involved in both.

Those stakes are quite high, because everyone participates in the struggle, voluntarily or not.

> The road to the Western Lands is by definition the most dangerous road in the world, for it is a journey beyond death, beyond the basic God standard of Fear and Danger. It is the most heavily guarded road in the world, for it gives access to the gift that supersedes all other gifts: Immortality.
>
> Every man starts the course. One is a million finishes. However, biologically speaking, one in a million is very good odds. The Egyptians and the Tibetans made this journey after Death, and their Books of the Dead set forth very precise instructions—as precise as they are arbitrary. (*WL* 124–25)

The Egyptian and Tibetan instructions, like the ideologies that define the modern capitalist world, are arbitrary because they were imposed in order to limit immortality to a few individuals chosen because of their class positions. "From death they built the Western Lands, and from pain, fear and sickness and excrement they built the Duad as a moat around the Western Lands, lest this exclusive country club be overrun by the peasantry" (*WL* 196). In fact, "Since the dangers are manifold and different for each pilgrim, what equipment and provisions he will need is conjectural" (*WL* 128). There is no certain, repeatable route because every pilgrim is a different mixture of incompatible souls, which drag him or her in many different directions.

I have already mentioned the "demons" that lie in wait for the unwary, like the "Thuggees" or "Deceivers," who are based on the Indian cult of Kali (*WL* 122–23, 129–30). These Deceivers play noble roles and gain the pilgrims' trust before betraying the travelers, like the "aging ingénue" who rescues his "liberal Vassar" girlfriend from a mamba before murdering her (*WL* 130). These routines point up the danger of blind trust in comforting and familiar stereotypes—that is, in reactionary or subjugated-group investments of personal interest at the preconscious, imaginary level. "The Road to the Western Lands is devious, unpredictable. Today's easy passage may be tomorrow's death trap. The obvious road is almost always a fool's road, and beware the Middle Roads, the roads of moderation, common sense and careful planning" (*WL* 151). This ideological "common sense" is the same blind trust in stable identity that invalidates the monolithic Leninist conception of class interest that can be represented in a centralized party structure. The demons of identity, who "must possess human hosts to operate" (*WL* 193), are in fact identical to the Gods who seek to restrict access to the Western Lands, who are in turn versions of the Nova Mobsters who control their "marks" by means of language. Pilgrims who bring this kind of trust into the Lands of the Dead are carrying their own final deaths with them unknowingly.

Other perils derive not from blind faith in comforting appearances but from misguided commitment to reductive forms of opposition, in particular to the reductive forms of opposition that Burroughs recognizes in his own earlier works. For example, "Any pilgrim who has in life solved problems with violence must go through Last Chance or back to square one" (*WL* 141). Last Chance is a parodic Wild West boomtown, populated by itinerant souls who engage in constant dueling with handguns, rapiers, and even atomic weapons. The most frightening challenge in Last Chance is not the sheer amount of violence, but the possibility that the violence will emerge symmetrically: "A contestant with no special skills may insist on the deadly 50–50: one gun loaded, one with blanks, the choice by lots[. . . .]The 50–50 is the most dreaded of all duels, since the factor of skill in combat is ruled out" (*WL* 146). The symmetry of this situation reveals the fundamental identity of the antagonists, whose superficially distinct personal attributes disappear in the relentless movement of the abstract, specular dialectic of violence. The 50–50 duel cuts through the imaginary, preconscious commitment to violent contradiction and bares the unconscious collaboration between the terms of the opposition, the reactionary form of their shared, subjugated desire.

As he interrogates the preconscious and unconscious desires of other exemplary pilgrims, Burroughs also comes to recognize, through the narrator Hall, the instability of his own coefficient of deterritorialization, his own unconscious structure of desire. Throughout this book and those that preceded it, he has invoked Hassan i Sabbah as the embodiment of total aggression, total commitment, and absolute difference that escapes from the specularity of dialectics, but he has often done so in a dangerously reductive way. "I realize that my whole approach to HIS [Hassan i Sabbah] has been faulty. I have put him on a remote pedestal; then, with a carry-over of Christian reflexes, have invoked HIS aid, like some Catholic feeling his saint medal. And when I was defeated I felt betrayed. I did not stop to think that he was also defeated, that he is taking his chances with *me*[. . . .]I am HIS and HIS is me. I am not an agent or representative"(*WL* 203–4).[12] As far back as the *Nova* trilogy, Burroughs had already imagined his own voice to be that of Hassan i Sabbah (HIS), who could *"rub out the word forever,"* but he imagined that this was a form of telepathy like any other he had experienced as a writer, and thus that he was merely a "coordinate point" for HIS. This meant that his relation to HIS was representational, so he could not rigorously distinguish revolutionary, subject-group desire (HIS) from the reactionary, subjugated-group desire (the Nova Mob, capitalism) that worked through language and representation. But if and when Burroughs is fully HIS, then he can distinguish between conflicting forms of desire and glimpse the Western Lands.

These hard-won visions of escape from history, from language, and from specular symmetry and identity confirm the prophecy that HIS, through and as William S. Burroughs, first articulated a quarter-century earlier: nothing is true, so everything is permitted. "Sure, I know I'm breaking every range law and flight regulation you got. So what?" (*WL* 201) In the writer's paradoxical visions of the Western Lands,

> There are no rules, no series of steps by which one can be in a position to see. Consequently such visions are the enemy of any dogmatic system. Any dogma must postulate a way, certain steps which will lead to the salvation which the dogma promises[. . . .]Otherwise there is no place for a hierarchical structure that mediates between dogma and man, that dictates *the* way.
>
> To endure in time, any structure must present predictable recurrences. The visions, the glimpses of the Western Lands, exist in space, not time, a different medium and a different light, with no temporal coordinates or recurrences. (*WL* 241–42)

If there are no rules to the visions, there are no rules for the creation of the Western Lands. These dreamlands, composed of desire, conform to no dogmatic Law, social or physical, that would impose hierarchy and static repetition as conditions of existence. The only order there emerges from the spontaneous improvisations of collective desire, from work and art.

Burroughs's conception of the conflicting seven souls and their vicissitudes intensifies and completes his contemporary book of the dead by again "exemplifying" the world, not by offering representative samples of revolutionary desire to be copied, but by revealing the unconscious conflicts within the very form of the subject that can undo whatever revolutionary potential that subject may hold in its preconscious libidinal investments. In Burroughs's novel, as in Deleuze's and Guattari's theory, "something essential is taking place, something of extreme seriousness: the tracking down of all varieties of fascism, from the enormous ones that surround and crush us to the petty ones that constitute the tyrannical bitterness of our everyday lives."[13] Both works produce topographies of deterritorialization, anatomies of desire, taxonomies of fragmented part-subjects that can serve as touchstones for an affirmative reconstitution of desiring-production. The current outlook for such an ambitious project is necessarily rather bleak, but not utterly hopeless, as Burroughs's narrator recognizes. During the communal experiments of the fifties and sixties, "We were promised transport out of the area, out of Time and into Space. We were getting messages, making contacts. Everything had meaning" (*WL* 252). Now, it seems clear that "there is no transport out. There isn't any important assignment. It's every man for himself. Like the old bum in the dream said: Maybe we lost. And this is what happens when you lose" (*WL* 252). Still, "there were moments of catastrophic defeat, and moments of triumph. The pure killing purpose. You find out what it means to lose. Abject fear and ignominy. Still fighting, without the means to fight. Deserted. Cut off. Still, we wore the dandy uniform, like the dress uniform of a distant planet long gone out. Message from headquarters? *What* headquarters? Every man for himself—if he's got a self left. Not many do" (*WL* 253). Those who do, the ones who share the "dandy uniform" of collective revolutionary purpose, are those who have resisted the blandishments of transcendence and are prepared to fight their way through to Western Lands of their own devising. "Battles are fought to be won, and this is what happens when you lose. However, to be alive at all is a victory" (*WL* 254). Allies and contacts may evaporate or ossify into a new status quo, as many of the student radicals of the sixties did. Even in the contemporary period, in the absence of such radical contacts, subject-groups or revolutionary communities are still accessible, among the multiple souls that make up the disjointed self. Though their victory is not assured, loss is not permanent as long as there is life; subjugation can be deterritorialized again, if it makes or finds the right constitutive fantasy with the right coefficient, because "to be alive at all is a victory" for the flows of desire, the only victory they need.

Burroughs concludes his last book of the dead where all such books must end, at the threshold of the Western Lands:

> I want to reach the Western Lands—right in front of you, across the bubbling brook. It's a frozen sewer. It's known as the Duad, remember? All the filth and horror, fear, hate, disease and death of human history flows between you and the Western Lands. Let it flow![. . .]How long does it take a man to learn that he does not, cannot want what he "wants"?
>
> You have to be in Hell to see Heaven. Glimpses from the Land of the Dead, flashes of serene timeless joy, a joy as old as suffering and despair. (*WL* 257–58)

The Christians were right about a few things, even though they got everything else wrong: there is no historical time in the promised land, only space, and so there is no narrative beyond the "filth[. . .]of human history," only disjunct flashes. If "You have to be in Hell to see Heaven" and to speak of Heaven, then the last narrative before the border crossing must tell the story of the end of storytelling, a nice dialectical flourish at the Duad, the double edge of dialectical history. This is the tale Burroughs has tried to tell, in various forms, for his entire career. The promised Western Lands cannot be represented, only made. In reaching the Duad, the old writer Hall, like Burroughs himself, has reached the "end of words, of what can be done with words. And then?" (*WL* 258) The open question that rings like a refrain through the novel suggests that we should not assume that, words having reached their limit in this fantasmatic journey toward liberation, nothing else can be done. *The Western Lands* closes with Burroughs's final quotation—and displacement—of his philosophical antithesis and fellow St. Louis native, one of the literary models for the cut-ups, T. S. Eliot: "Hurry up please. It's time." Part 2 of Eliot's *The Waste Land,* "A Game of Chess," cites these same words, the English pub-keeper's last call before closing, but to a different end: "HURRY UP PLEASE ITS TIME," all in uppercase letters and without punctuation, interrupts and draws attention away from the impotent banality of the women's conversation. They speak of desire, its causes, vagaries, and consequences, but the voice of the pub-keeper overrules them with the demand that they "HURRY UP" and lay these concerns aside in order to better attend the coming revelation, the "TIME" of "Shantih" from the Upanishads that concludes the poem as a whole (Eliot, *Poems* 58–59, 69, 75, 76). But Burroughs's last words[14] do not simply eject us from the desperate, last-minute conviviality of the lively but ultimately sterile public house into some tidy Christian metaphor of death, Last Judgment, and redemption, as Eliot's do; instead they put us back out on the street, the contested, underdetermined, liminal space of amodernity, where material revolutions, and not just poetic ones, often start: "*Sous les pavés la plage*"; "We are here to go!"[15]

Conclusion

Burroughs's Fin de siècle

Listen to My Last Words Everywhere

Generally, the writing we call "literary" is an activity carried on in private, in offices, libraries, apartments, and homes. The "literary" writer works, for the most part, in social, if not imaginary, solitude. The few chances the writer gets to perform in public, before a mass of people, are limited to polite readings at colleges, bookstores, and "cultural centers," or critical discussions at more or less academic conferences. If a contemporary literary writer is particularly renowned or influential, she may be the subject of a documentary film shot on a shoestring budget for screening at a few "art" cinemas in the major cities, or perhaps broadcast on public television. Rarely, a literary writer may sell one or more of her books to movie producers and allow them to create film versions of her writing, but this usually happens only after the writer's death and is negotiated by her estate. In the U.S., the writer and the other mass media intersect fleetingly, tangentially, because the media have their own privileged aesthetic creators; in smaller cultural "markets" like France,[1] it has been easier for literary writers to gain wide access to the media, but the audience they reach is also commensurately smaller. This chasm between the writer and the media is both the cause and the result of the mutual hostility with which they often regard one another: the technological media strive to efface the traces of text—scripts or lyrics—that provide them with narrative motion and closure, while "Most serious writers refuse to make themselves available to the things that technology is doing."[2]

In light of this near-total separation, what are we to make of William S. Burroughs's ubiquity in the mass media? For if his imperative, in the overture to *Nova Express,* to "Listen to my last words anywhere" (*NE* 11) once partook of the black irony of a lost revolutionary slogan buried under centuries of ideology, it now appears to be a quite adequate description of a very real cultural conjunction. Burroughs may still be an interloper in the academy, but he has become a crucial figure on the popular scene. Readers familiar with Burroughs's "media presence" may wish to skip ahead a few pages; the list that follows is intended merely to document the extent of that "presence." I have already discussed David Cronenberg's film version of *Naked Lunch,* released by Twentieth-Century Fox in 1991. Burroughs has been the subject of at least two documentary films, Howard Brookner's 1980 *Burroughs* and Klaus Maeck's 1991 *Commissioner of Sewers.* He has also acted in narrative films, both successful (Gus Van Sant's 1989 *Drugstore Cowboy*) and unsuccessful (Conrad Rooks's 1966 *Chappaqua*), as well as several cult films and videos (Michael Almereyda's 1989 *Twister,* David Blair's 1993 *Wax, or the Discovery of Television Among the Bees*). Burroughs has also made films himself, in collaboration with the late British director Antony Balch; they produced five important short experimental films in the mid-sixties, *Towers Open Fire, The Cut-Ups, Ghosts at No. 9, Bill and Tony,* and *William Buys a Parrot,* as well as a strange "reconstruction" of an old Swedish film on witchcraft, *Witchcraft through the Ages (Häxan).* During the same period, Burroughs was also experimenting with the cut-up potential of tape recording, and he subsequently released albums of such experiments (*Nothing Here Now But the Recordings, Break Through in Grey Room*).[3] *Break Through in Grey Room* also contains Burroughs's tapes of renowned free jazz saxophonist Ornette Coleman improvising with the Master Musicians of Jajouka in Morocco during a visit there; Coleman would later provide some of the music for the *Naked Lunch* film.[4]

Like many writers in this century, Burroughs has released sound recordings of his readings (*Call Me Burroughs, Ali's Smile,* and *The Doctor is on the Market,* as well as tracks on many of John Giorno's "Giorno Poetry Systems" records through the eighties),[5] but he has also collaborated with contemporary musicians from a variety of idioms on what we might call "text settings," musical compositions built around Burroughs's readings or conversations. His collaborators in these settings constitute a virtual Who's Who of the contemporary popular avant-garde: Laurie Anderson (songs and videos from *Mister Heartbreak* and

Home of the Brave); Gus Van Sant (*The Elvis of Letters*); Bill Laswell and Material (*Seven Souls* and *Hallucination Engine*); Hal Willner, Donald Fagen, John Cale, and Sonic Youth (*Dead City Radio*); Ministry (the single and video *Just One Fix*); Willner and the Disposable Heroes of Hiphoprisy (*Spare Ass Annie and Other Tales*); the late Kurt Cobain of Nirvana (*The "Priest" They Called Him*); and R.E.M. (a version of the band's "Star Me Kitten" on the compilation *Songs in the Key of X*). Burroughs also provided "texts" for director Robert Wilson (of *Einstein on the Beach* fame) and singer Tom Waits to use in their a stage version of *Der Freischütz* (the folktale rather than the Carl Maria von Weber opera).[6] We should also recall Burroughs's contribution of texts and images to a collaboration with the late Keith Haring, as well as his own successful exhibitions of abstract painting, starting with a 1987 show at the Tony Shafrazi Gallery in New York and culminating in a major retrospective show at the Los Angeles County Museum of Art in 1996.[7]

If we expand our horizon to include popular works directly influenced by Burroughs's ideas or techniques, we can survey an even broader range of artifacts. Gus Van Sant's follow-up to *Drugstore Cowboy,* the film *My Own Private Idaho* (1991), was scripted by using the cut-up technique to incorporate scenes from Shakespeare's *Henry IV* into a Burroughsian drama of young male hustlers. Mick Jagger used similar techniques to write the words to "Memo from Turner."[8] Laurie Anderson has appropriated Burroughs's claim that "Language is a virus from outer space" and turned it into a song (in her performance piece *United States,* 1979–1983). Three important rock bands of the late sixties and seventies, linked otherwise only by their common reliance on improvisation, are named in homage to Burroughs: Donald Fagen's urbane jazz-rock assemblage Steely Dan, named after a memorable series of dildoes in *Naked Lunch* (*NL* 91), and Robert Wyatt's two art-rock ensembles, Soft Machine and Matching Mole (a pun on the French for "Soft Machine," *machine molle*), named after the first volume of the *Nova* trilogy. The almost-forgotten Insect Trust and Grant Hart's not-yet-successful band Nova Mob are also named for villains in that trilogy. Some critics even trace the origin of the term "heavy metal," originally a chemical term for radioactive elements but now most often used to describe heavily amplified blues-based rock that generally relies on fantastic or surrealistic imagery, to Burroughs's metaphorical usage of the phrase in the *Nova* trilogy.[9]

Then there are the homages, the testimonials both direct and indirect to Burroughs's influence. The late British filmmaker Derek Jarman made

Pirate Tape (1982), a slight, gentle film documenting one of Burroughs's reading trips to England, and *The Dream Machine* (1984), a strikingly graphic realization of the ideas and techniques of Burroughs and Brion Gysin; both films feature Burroughs voice-overs. The Velvet Underground's Lou Reed, who said that he "had gone out and bought *Naked Lunch* as soon as it was published" and that he "felt that *Junky* was [Burroughs'] most important book because of the way it says something that hadn't been said before so straightforwardly," composed the tongue-in-cheek "Lonesome Cowboy Bill" in Burroughs's honor,[10] while 10,000 Maniacs presented a bittersweet (and rather pretentious) homage to Burroughs and Ginsberg as well as Kerouac in their song "Hey Jack Kerouac" (on *In My Tribe*). Bob Dylan has also paid tribute to Burroughs and Ginsberg as two of his own literary antecedents. Clearly, the range of Burroughs's influence is vast, even if we confine ourselves, as we have here, to nontextual media.

Is this ubiquity really, as Burroughs ironically suggests, just one of "the things that can happen if you live long enough"?[11] If he's right, why haven't other "old writers," like Saul Bellow, Norman Mailer, or Doris Lessing (to pick names more or less at random), benefited from this perk of longevity? On the other hand, could this ubiquity be completely anomalous, something that has accrued to Burroughs by virtue of some singular aspect of his work or public persona? This explanation doesn't appear to be adequate, either, because other writers, like Allen Ginsberg, Ishmael Reed, and Alice Walker, have achieved some degree of presence in the popular media,[12] though not as broad-based a presence as Burroughs has. The schism would appear to be generational if we left Burroughs out of it: in direct opposition to his ironic suggestion, we might guess that older writers, with the exception of Burroughs, have not forged relations to other media, while slightly younger ones have. Stylistic maturity is a better measure, though: writers who came to prominence from the late fifties through the early seventies have built connections to other media, while writers who matured earlier have remained for the most part tied to the more traditional forms of media intervention (journal and newspaper articles, printed interviews).

To suggest that Burroughs's career presents a new paradigm for the writer's active, shaping involvement with other mass media (as opposed to the passive, constrained involvement characteristic of older writers) would be premature, but to offer a detailed analysis of his own involvement is, if anything, long overdue. A discussion of Burroughs's *influence* on other artists with whom he has not actually worked is beyond the scope of the present study, as is a comprehensive analysis of the cameo *appearances* he has made in others' works (though I will address perhaps his strangest appearance at the end of this conclusion), but I can consider in detail the media projects that represent active *collaborations* between Burroughs and his admirers in the two extratextual domains on which he has focused: film and sound (comprising both music and speech). Collaboration has long served Burroughs as a method of escaping from the tyranny of the individual subject, a way to create a "third mind" superior to the minds of the collaborators.[13] The considerations that follow will demonstrate that Burroughs's collaborative work in extratextual forms is not peripheral or tangential to his long-standing literary concerns, but is rather both the necessary condition and the consequence of those concerns. Burroughs's filmic and musical works articulate a radical theory of deixis that remains implicit in his literary works, and in so doing they reveal the nontextual ground of his critiques of language and society at the same time as they carry out the imperatives of those critiques.

•

As I have noted at intervals throughout this study, film has been a controlling concept and metaphor in Burroughs's writing from the very beginning. From the equivocal morphine "scripts" of *Junky* through the Reality Studio of *The Soft Machine* to the Ren Film Director of *The Western Lands,* Burroughs has relied upon the immense figurative potential of film; indeed, he wrote two books labeled explicitly (perhaps ironically) as screenplays: *The Last Words of Dutch Schultz: A Fiction in the Form of a Film Script* and *Blade Runner, a Movie.*[14] Nevertheless, Burroughs's literal ventures into filmmaking have never been given serious consideration by film critics or theorists, even though these films were often shown at the very same festivals that brought the works of other contemporary experimental filmmakers—including lyrical autobiographer Stan Brakhage and hermetic animator Harry Smith—to a relatively wide audience. For example, P. Adams Sitney's classic study *Visionary Film* contains no reference to or analysis of Burroughs's films, though it does quote Smith, who credits Burroughs with the realization that chance composition, like the cut-up and Smith's own permutational technique, "wasn't just chance . . . something was directing it."[15] Because it was so directed, Burroughs's use of chance in the making of these films was, in his own words, "experimental in the sense of being *something to do*. . . . Not something to talk and argue about."[16]

The composition of the films was not only "directed" by this "something," but also directed in a different sense: the late English director Antony Balch directed and photographed all of Burroughs's film collaborations. In the discussions that follow, we will analyze these collaborations in terms of Burroughs's contemporaneous theoretical concerns, rather than in terms of Balch's contributions to the enterprise, for two reasons. First, these films fit quite neatly into the categories and concepts that Burroughs was articulating in his other work (unlike Cronenberg's film of *Naked Lunch,* whose distortions of Burroughs's ideas can only be attributed to the director's dubious interpretive moves); therefore, the Balch films represent a closely convergent or sympathetic collaboration. Second, Balch does not seem to have produced any significant films on his own, beyond the *Witchcraft* reconstruction, which might have allowed us to judge the precise extent of his contribution to the Burroughs films (at least, none that are readily available for comparison). In short, the following discussion of Burroughs's collaborations with Balch will be necessarily reductive in that it will not be able to account in detail for Balch's contributions beyond the purely technical ones of shooting and editing. Burroughs's precise contributions to the collaborative film projects are therefore somewhat uncertain as well, though some points can be documented with precision.

Sitney's omission of Burroughs's and Balch's films from his survey may indicate simply his ignorance of them, but it is more probably the result of the structure of Sitney's argument: drawing on the phenomenological criticism of Paul de Man, Harold Bloom, and Annette Michelson, Sitney explicates the contours of a Romantic, "mythopoeic" American experimental cinema obsessed with self (and) perception, a cinematic tradition which is quite alien to Burroughs's enterprise, whether in literature or film. Burroughs and Balch are much closer to the "objective," nonphenomenological experimental cinema of the dadaists than to the lyrical subjectivity of Maya Deren or Brakhage. Indeed, Burroughs credits Zurich dadaist Tristan Tzara, among others, with the original invention of the cut-up technique.[17] The absurdist juxtapositions and montage effects used by Burroughs and Balch to "cut word lines" in *Towers Open Fire* (1963) can be traced directly to Hans Richter's acausal flying derbies and self-serving tea sets in *Vormittagsspuk* (1927)—and perhaps ultimately to Georges Méliès's original discontinuity effects. Moreover, the permutation- and pattern-generating techniques that they employ in *The Cut-Ups* and *Bill and Tony* extend arguments on the relation of image to word first explored by Marcel Duchamp—one of Burroughs's acknowledged aesthetic ancestors—in his Rousselian *Anémic-Cinéma* (1926).[18]

Paradoxically, Burroughs's two last and shortest films with Balch, *Bill and Tony* and *William Buys a Parrot* (both 1963), are actually his simplest exercises in word-image manipulation, and each one constitutes a tidy little experiment with a single aspect of filmic material. The last and shortest, at ninety seconds, is *William Buys a Parrot,* which is simply a silent encounter between Burroughs and a young man who shows him a caged parrot (actually a cockatoo, I believe). The bird becomes agitated because of Burroughs's attention and the intrusion of the camera, at which point the film abruptly ends. There are no titles or credits. The film consists entirely of medium-length fixed camera shots (of Burroughs approaching a door and knocking on it, then chatting briefly with the young man who answers) and short, mobile hand-held camera shots (of Burroughs entering the garden where the bird is, for a drink, and of the bird becoming agitated). The film is in color, which, along with the unobtrusive editing, gives the same impression of "natural" narrative motion that commercial film and television montage do. The only aspect missing is the sound, which is precisely the point; this is Burroughs's and Balch's only soundless film. Sound, and more specifically speech, is thematized, not only in the silent conversations that advance the "action" but in the bird's soundless agitation: the parrot is the bird that can speak like a human being. In this way, the film is drained of its expected content: we do not hear Burroughs converse with the parrot. In purely structural terms, the minimal narrative moves along quite well without words, however—as it would, Burroughs claims, with completely unrelated words dubbed in. The greetings and small talk that would move the film along are generic and can easily be provided by the viewer. This silent narrative's success depends, however, on the last unspoken words left in the film: the title. Though the title seems descriptive, it is not: Burroughs merely observes the parrot during the brief film; he does not purchase it. No money changes hands, and the parrot's cage remains on the garden table throughout. Its purchase, the purpose and implied narrative resolution of the film, must be inferred from or perhaps projected onto the film, but cannot be observed in it.

William Buys a Parrot demonstrates that even when silence eliminates the specific word—the external word of mundane narrative interaction that is susceptible to technical reproduction and animal mimicry—it leaves intact the general, generic, internal Word—the structural Word of addictive subjectivity that allows the viewer to provide her own narration for this film. *Bill and Tony* demonstrates that *deixis* offers an even more useful weapon than silence against this tyranny of language.

Deixis is a "major site of subjectivity in language. . . . [D]eictic signs are created in and by an act of *énonciation* [utterance], as they exist only in relation to the 'here' and 'now' of the speaker/writer. . . . [D]eictics are double referential, indicating simultaneously the act of *énonciation* in which they were produced and the designated object(s), the nature of which can solely be determined within the context of the particular instance of discourse containing the deictic expression" (entry on "Énonciation/énoncé" in Makaryk, 541). Deictic signs include personal pronouns ("I," "you"), demonstratives ("here," "this"), adverbs of time ("now"), present-tense verbs, and even the definite article "the."[19] *Bill and Tony* examines deixis just as simply and just as effectively as *William Buys a Parrot* examines silence: by reducing to a minimum the other aspects of film construction in order to isolate and exhaust the issue under consideration. *Bill and Tony* is shot in color, but there isn't much of it: Balch, in black turtleneck, and Burroughs, in brown suit alternating with black shirt, stand side by side against a flat black background. Only their heads and shoulders are visible. Neither man moves. Both stare fixedly at the camera while crisply enunciating their lines. After each recital, the film cuts immediately. This extreme restriction of visual images throws speech into high relief, and indeed it is speech that is the object of investigation here, as it was in *William Buys a Parrot*. The film is the only one by Burroughs and Balch shot in synchronous sound, though the synchronization is inconsistent. The opening shot finds Burroughs and Balch speaking in their own voices but swapping proper names: Bill says "I'm Tony," who is in London, while Tony says "I'm Bill," who is "in a 1920 movie," thereby thematizing the temporal disjunction implicit in representation. The second shot is a close-up on Burroughs's face as he recites, in his own voice, a section of a Church of Scientology training exercise about extricating one's "self" from one's head. The third shot returns to the two men side by side, who repeat their original greetings but reclaim their own names: Bill claims to be Bill, and Tony claims to be Tony. Shot four is a close-up on Balch's face as he recites, in his own voice, a carnival barker's routine about circus freaks. Shot five returns to the two men, who this time swap voices *and* names: Bill claims to be Tony using Tony's dubbed voice, while Tony claims to be Bill using Bill's. The sixth shot returns to the close-up on Burroughs, reciting the same Scientology text, but this time in Balch's dubbed voice. Shot seven finds the two men again greeting one another, using their own names, but each other's dubbed voices. The final shot returns to the close-up on Balch reciting the same carnival routine, but this time in Burroughs's dubbed voice. The entire film lasts five minutes and twenty seconds, and has no titles or credits.

Clearly, the film is a combinatory apparatus for permuting its three variable elements to exhaustion: faces, voices, and names. It shares this permutational method, as well as its basic concern with image-word relations, with Duchamp's *Anémic-Cinéma.* In Duchamp's silent film, shots of rotating disks emblazoned with decentered patterns of nested circles (which give false impressions of depth) are intercut with shots of other disks on which are printed, in spiraling sentences of raised letters, sequences of French puns. These puns themselves are self-similar permutations, decentered linguistic circles doubling the visual ones; for example, the seventh sequence, "*Avez vous déjà mis la moëlle de l'épée dans la poële de l'aimée?*" ("Have you already put the sword's marrow in the lover's oven?"), shifts the consonants within the object noun phrases from "*moëlle/épée*" to "*poële/aimée.*" Another sequence, "*Esquivons les ecchymoses des esquimaux aux mots exquis*" ("Let us avoid the Eskimos' welts with exquisite words"), contains four permutations of its basic phonetic elements "*es,*" "*qui,*" and "*mo.*" The sounds, which cannot enter the film's silent world, can only be given different physical shapes (spellings) and changes in word order to produce statements that defy reference; one can treat them as sexual metaphors, as Sitney does, and then read them psychoanalytically, of course, but not all of the permuted phrases are as clearly symbolic as our first example. In any case, the unifying or centering element of each sentence, its sound, is excluded from the film just as the apparent visual depth of the other disks is necessarily excluded by the flatness of the screen.

The structure of Burroughs's and Balch's film is also double, though in a different way. First, with regard to the formal arrangement of shots, it falls into two parallel halves, each of which is composed of four shots: A1 B1 A1′ C1 and A2 B2 A2′ C2. A1 and A1′ represent the two versions of the two-man shots in the first half, and A2 and A2′ the two versions in the second half. Each shot is precisely the same length as its counterpart in the other half of the film (i.e., A1=A2, B1=B2, etc.), so the two halves are exactly the same length, two minutes and forty seconds. The break into halves is marked by the only singular, unrepeated event in the film: Balch's exaggerated pronunciation of the word "Cut!" at the end of shot C1, which is not repeated when Balch recites the same speech using Burroughs's dubbed voice in C2. This statement starts the procession of shots over again. The second, superimposed structure arises from the differences between the content of the two halves rather than from their formal similarities. In the first half of the film, all of the voices are attached to the right faces, even though the names are swapped in the opening scene; in the second half, all of the voices are swapped and are never associated with the right faces, though again in the final two-man scene (shot seven), the names are correctly attributed. This second structure is symmetrical, specular rather than parallel like the first. The first structure is the structure of the face, the visual image of physical identity that remains the same, while the second is the structure of the word, as both voice and proper name, which is subject to displacement through quotation, alias, impersonation, and the editor's "cut." Recording technology makes the voice and the proper name as shifting—as deictic—as the personal pronoun "I"; in so doing, technology also sets the identity of the face adrift among conflicting names and voices. This is, of course, one of the central themes of Burroughs's writing as well. If Duchamp's film set meaning adrift by positing sound and depth of field as the unrepresentable meanings, the absent grounds of the silent film, then Burroughs and Balch have extended this drift by demonstrating that sound and depth—in this case, the voice and the subjective identity guaranteed by the proper name—are themselves as shifting and uncertain as words on a page or optical illusions.

Now that we understand that the basic issues involved in Burroughs's film collaborations are the same issues involved in his writing, but transposed into a different medium which extends his means of treating those issues, we can turn back to his earlier, more complex, and more ambitious films. *Towers Open Fire* (1963) is Burroughs's and Balch's earliest and best-known film, probably because of all his films it's the closest to a recognizably straightforward narrative. Burroughs composed the script for *Towers Open Fire* alone (and published it shortly after the film was completed), and his circle of friends constituted the entire cast and crew. Balch not only shot the film but appears briefly in it, as do Burroughs's sometime lover Ian Sommerville, the writer Alex Trocchi, and Burroughs's first "groupie," Michael Portman, who portrays the young man at the conclusion of the film. Though the narrative is obscured in a number of ways, it is an overstatement to claim, as Anne Friedberg does, that "There is no discernible structure—the shots are spliced together to follow the 'cut-up' strategy of disjunction."[20] In broad outline, *Towers Open Fire* is actually a fairly simple story of a commando raid carried out by resistance fighters against the syndicates of verbal and image control. Truly disjunctive cut-ups are used more sparingly than relatively standard montage techniques. After the opening titles and credits (the only ones attached to any of these films), Burroughs's immobile face appears in close-up, as his voice recites a vicious and insinuating proposition: "Kid, what are you doing over there with the niggers and the apes? Why don't you straighten out and act like a white man? After all, they're only human cattle."[21] Burroughs's face does not speak the words, but it is not until the next shot, of Burroughs dressed differently and standing at a conference table surrounded by blank-faced bureaucrats and hieroglyphic books and paintings, that we realize that the first Burroughs, the immobile face, was being addressed by the second, bureaucratic Burroughs.[22] The first Burroughs is the resistance leader, like Hassan i Sabbah from the *Nova* trilogy, while the second is the syndicate chief, a version of Uranian Willy or Mr Bradly Mr Martin; this distinction is unclear during the first part of the film, but emerges at the climax.

Syndicate chief Burroughs describes resistance leader Burroughs as a telepathic "medium"—in other words, a writer, someone who can escape the prison of his addictive self through telepathic identification with others, as we discovered in *Queer.* This power allows him to descend into the material substratum of *Towers Open Fire:* the next shot shows Burroughs's hands conjuring over film canisters as his voice intones a spell to lock out the syndicates and send their curse back doubled. More footage of this conjuring is then intercut with shots of Gysin's projection of images onto human faces, shots of Balch masturbating, interference and noise bands on TV screens, and finally print pages being cut up as the out-of-sync soundtrack itself begins to break up: "Shift—cut—tangle—word lines." Newspaper headlines announcing the 1929 stock market crash appear, intercut with shots of milling crowds over which Burroughs, briefly seen talking on the phone, orders his minions to "sell fifty thousand units at arbitrary intervals." This is probably Burroughs the syndicate chief rather than the medium/resistance leader. Shots of Burroughs walking the streets, standing by a river, and visiting a zoo follow, including one shot which fakes a sound sync to the words "Dramatic relief from anxiety." As Burroughs's voice claims that "Anything that can be done chemically can be done in other ways," shots of Gysin's "dream machines," whirling columns that give off hypnotically shifting patterns of light, appear on screen. The dream machines recur at irregular intervals for the next several minutes, intercut with Burroughs's face and ruined buildings, as resistance leader Burroughs's voice-over insists that "I wrote your fading movie—feed in all the words you think developed, pouring in the resistance message, handcutting dirty films here. . . . " As Burroughs injects himself with heroin on screen, his voice promises to "shatter the theatre—the ovens—your two-bit narrative line from Wallgreens."

The climax of the narrative nears as resistance leader Burroughs appears in camouflaged combat fatigues with a radio transmitter to his mouth. Another camouflaged commando (also Burroughs) who is carrying a toy rifle enters a room in the next shot, where he finds an alcove full of family photos arranged on shelves. The commando fires Ping-Pong balls from his rifle at the photos, scattering them. A very brief scene of people disappearing out of their clothes, which collapse to the ground (this episode is reminiscent of Richter's animated hats), leads back to Burroughs with the transmitter ordering "TOWERS OPEN FIRE!" Quick shots of microwave relay towers accompanied by "laser" sound effects follow; the towers' fire shatters the image continuities underlying the film, resulting in a six-second sequence of high-speed visual cut-ups. After another brief shot of Burroughs with his transmitter and another of TV interference, the conference table surrounded by bureaucrats reappears. One by one, syndicate chief Burroughs and his staff members are erased from the scene by interference and noise, leaving their hieroglyphic books and paintings to be blown off the table, out into the street, and into the mud and water by a whistling wind. After a brief moment of blank screen, a street scene appears: a young man dances a quick, goofy Charleston to some old jazz, then sits on the curb to smoke. He looks up and notices that the sky is filled with jagged blotches, hand-painted on the film. Middle Eastern music plays as we get a slow-motion mirror-image glimpse of the gun-toting commando. END appears; the total elapsed time is nine minutes, forty-eight seconds.

Clearly, *Towers Open Fire* is a libertarian science-fiction movie, a fairly simple morality play complicated by imaginary weapons, terroristic linguistic theories, and the doubling (or tripling) of the protagonist in the villain. *Towers Open Fire* is a condensed retelling of the *Nova* trilogy, in which cut-ups appear only at precise moments, such as the instant when the towers actually open fire. The resistance fighters, "breaking bounds by flicker" of dream machines rather than by chemical means, appear to prevail, destroying the "two-bit narrative line from Wallgreens" that creates despotic subjectivity and control, and in the process eliminating the syndicate controllers themselves. The young man dances in the streets in joy after the conflict, but the jagged blotches he sees in the sky imply that the victory may be short-lived. Indeed, the doubling of Burroughs the resistance leader and Burroughs the syndicate chief implied as much from the very beginning: oppositional forces defined by binary conflict are liable to turn into each other, according to the dialectic of treason. As *Bill and Tony* demonstrates, the self is a manipulable surface effect of deeper conflicts and control structures, and has no more essential meaning than a deictic pronoun does. The mirrored doubling of the commando at the very end confirms this reversibility. Similarly, the shots of Burroughs conjuring the film canisters and "handcutting dirty films" reflexively reveal the film's central paradox: *Towers Open Fire* narrates the destruction of narrative as a form of control, but in so doing at least partially restores that defeated and dismembered narrative, as so many of Burroughs's earlier and later fictions do.

Burroughs's other two collaborations with Balch attempt to escape from that metanarrative impasse. Both *The Cut-Ups* and *Ghosts at No. 9* (both made in 1963) extend the disjunctive cut-up technique, used sparingly in *Towers Open Fire,* to the entire film. Anne Friedberg succinctly describes the principles of *The Cut-Ups'* construction:

> *Cut-Ups* has a more precisely planned structure [than *Towers Open Fire*] for the cinematic transposition of the "cut-up" technique. Balch cut the original film into four pieces and hired an editor to perform the mechanical task of taking one foot of film from each roll (1—2—3—4). The one-foot segments were joined in consecutive and repeated 1—2—3—4 fashion. The only variation in shot length occurs when there is a shot change within the foot-long section.
>
> The soundtrack, made by [Ian] Sommerville, Gysin, and Burroughs to the twenty-minute and four-second length, consists of four phrase units, read at different speeds, but always in the same order:
>
> Yes. Hello.
> Look at this picture.
> Does it seem to be persisting?
> Good. Thank you.[23]

This strict avoidance of planned juxtaposition is very different from standard film montage techniques, which are generally guided at all times by the narrative in which they appear, or at least by recognizable principles of similarity or metonymy. Because of this strict structural approach, *The Cut-Ups* (and the quite similar *Ghosts at No. 9*, constructed out of the same body of material but according to somewhat different constraints) has no definable narrative structure. Many micronarrative strands—such as the recurring scenes of Burroughs packing his bags to leave his apartment, Burroughs as doctor examining a young man, or Gysin producing a hieroglyphic painting—can be followed for a time, but ultimately fail to connect in any simple way either with the shots that are "cut up" into them or with the shots that follow them.

The soundtrack offers us the only direct clue to an understanding of the film's specific details. Like the image track, the soundtrack is quadripartite and arranged in a fixed, repetitive order; two voices, Burroughs's and Gysin's, alternate in reciting the short phrases, sometimes so quickly that the recitations almost overlap. This soundtrack is a continuous cyclic address to the viewer. The first phrase of any cycle is the greeting "Yes. Hello," which signifies a new beginning that is simultaneously a repetition. Likewise, the fourth phrase concludes the four-phrase structure with an implicit farewell: "Good. Thank you." As Friedberg notes, these two verbal markers, along with the four-shot cycle of images, define the basic structural unit of the film, although sound and image are in no way synchronized. Each such unit is distinct in the particular content of its visual images and in the precise intonation of its voice-over, even as it is identical to the others in montage (i.e., order of numbered film sections) and in scripted words. The two middle phrases, however, provide us with a single interpretive clue, which, though small, can open up the specific meaning of *The Cut-Ups*. The second phrase is the imperative to "Look at this picture," in which the demonstrative (and deictic) adjective "this" draws the viewer's attention to the coincident visual image, whatever its specific content, as an image or "picture" *in general.* The imperative is followed by the interrogative statement "Does it seem to be persisting?" in which the pronoun "it" appears to refer back to the deictic "this picture" in the previous command. If the imperative has not sufficiently distanced the viewer from the flow of images, the question—with its veiled allusion to the "persistence of vision" that makes cinema possible—pushes reflexivity even further in an attempt to make the viewer recognize her own perceptive and associative processes.

Any specific answer to a specific instance of this question is more or less irrelevant because the purpose of the question is both diagnostic and didactic. This is why it is a yes/no question, and why it is invariably followed by the phrase "Good. Thank you" so often used by doctors, teachers, and other people who administer diagnostic (rather than evaluative) tests: every answer, regardless of its specific content, is a good answer because it reveals something about the test-taker, who is in this case the viewer. The question is didactic because it is intended to make the viewer ask, in turn, why a particular "picture" persists (an answer of "yes") while a different one fails to persist ("no"). What causes a particular picture to stay in the mind and influence later perceptions, while other pictures are almost immediately forgotten? In other words, what kinds of connection (if any) can be established between randomly juxtaposed images? The whole labor of the cut-up method—the key to its success or failure both in writing and in film—is contained in this question. Meaning does not reside in the images and words themselves, as the infinitely repeatable deictic imperative shows; the viewer must actively participate in the construction of meaning using the raw materials of the indexical signs provided by Burroughs and Balch. The associations that occur to the viewers (or readers), including the cutter himself, will create the meaning of the cut-up artifact spontaneously and idiosyncratically, but most definitely not subjectively: "Cutups [sic] *establish* new connections between images, and one's range of vision consequently *expands*."[24] In this the film differs from the conventional Rorschach ink blot test of subjective associations, to which cut-ups are often compared. It is not a question of revealing a preestablished identification of images, even an unconscious one, but of extending the internal difference revealed by the deixis of voice and word: connecting established associations with other, novel points of view to form a new and disjunct set of perspectives. Cut-ups are objective art. The cut-up is an objective form of what Burroughs called "telepathy" in *Queer,* and *The Cut-Ups* is a lesson in such telepathy that would be learned by many filmmakers later. Indeed, the entire MTV video aesthetic of rapid, narratively discontinuous cuts synchronized to an apparently unrelated soundtrack is prefigured in Burroughs's and Balch's film, though very few performers (with the exception of Sonic Youth and perhaps Ministry's Alain Jourgensen) seem to recognize this relation.

In *The Third Mind* (1978), the belated manifesto and theorization of the cut-up named for the idea that "when you put two minds together . . . there is always a third mind . . . as an unseen collaborator," Burroughs claims that "Cutting and rearranging a page of written words introduces a new dimension into writing enabling the writer to turn images in cinematic variation."[25] Cinema, conceived in Burroughs's idiosyncratic way, is thus the theoretical foundation of textual cut-ups, rather than the reverse, and as such offers Burroughs an immediately accessible form through which to lead his audience to an understanding of his textual innovations. In 1965, when Conrad Knickerbocker asked Burroughs if he believed "that an audience can be eventually trained to respond to cutups," Burroughs replied, "Of course, because cutups make explicit a psychological process that is going on all the time anyway."[26] *The Cut-Ups,* like *The Job* and the *Mayfair* "Academy" essay series of the early seventies, acts as an overtly didactic exercise for such training in the cut-up method, and as such provides a good introduction to Burroughs's literary experiments. Barry Miles claims that "Ideally one would read the cut-up trilogy with Burroughs's cut-up tapes playing in the background, taking time off occasionally to examine a photo-collage or play *Towers Open Fire* or *The Cut-Ups* on the VCR" (Miles 157).

•

A brief look at Burroughs's tape-recorder experiments, on which he collaborated with Brion Gysin and Ian Sommerville at the same time as he was making films with Balch, can serve as a transition from his work in film to his musical collaborations. These experiments have been released on albums entitled *Nothing Here Now But the Recordings* and *Break Through in Grey Room,* the latter a cut-up phrase that recurs throughout *Nova Express*. Burroughs offers his own gloss on this phrase in his *Paris Review* interview:

> I see that as very much like the photographic darkroom where the reality photographs are actually produced. Implicit in *Nova Express* is a theory that what we call reality is actually a movie. It's a film—what I call a biologic film. What has happened is that the underground and also the nova police have made a break-through past the guards and gotten into the darkroom where the films are processed, where they're in a position to expose negatives and prevent events from occurring.[27]

This "break-through" takes several forms, including the cut-up method of literary and filmic composition that I have just discussed. Burroughs's tape recorder experiments are given this group title to emphasize their importance in his own "break-through past the guards" to the apparatus of control, the "word-and-image banks" of the mass media that preprogram the future according to the past. The experimental tapes are the results of several different techniques: the drop-in method, in which new sounds are recorded—"dropped in"—over sections of an already existing recording, creating new juxtapositions; permutation, in which a phrase composed of discrete words is rearranged to exhaust all the possible orders of terms; "inching," in which the tape is moved manually, and thus irregularly, across the head of the recorder while an audible signal is being recorded; and the simultaneous recording of several sources, generally broadcast media. Some of these techniques, like permutation and "inching," parallel the contemporary work of electronic music pioneers such as Karlheinz Stockhausen (in "Gesang der Junglinge," a manipulation of synthetic sounds and children's voices reciting passages from Daniel 3:21–27), Luciano Berio (in "Thema," a permutation of the overture to "Sirens" from Joyce's *Ulysses*), or Milton Babbitt (in "Philomel," the transformation of a female voice into a synthetic sound and vice versa), and of musique concrète composers such as Pierre Schaeffer and Pierre Henry (in "Variations pour une Porte et un Soupir," the orchestration and manipulation of two nonmusical sounds).[28] The first technique, the "drop-in," and the last one, overlapping sources, like the cut-up writing method from which they derive, provide an important precursor to the kind of sampling that would become ubiquitous in the eighties and nineties.

"Silver Smoke of Dreams" on *Break Through in Grey Room* shows how the drop-in method can produce quite lyrical effects, similar to that of the children's voices in Stockhausen's "Gesang," even though it does not always produce intelligible phrases. Burroughs's and Ian Sommerville's voices, reciting imagistic passages from the last pages of *The Ticket That Exploded,* interrupt each other at short and irregular intervals, often in the middle of words. The interruption usually results in a rapid modulation of timbre as Burroughs's sharp tenor gives way to Sommerville's more diffuse one; when the drop-in occurs in the middle of a word, it often creates an unarticulable phonetic sound reminiscent of dadaist Kurt Schwitter's phonetic symphony, the *Ursonate,* and of Berio's technically demanding "Sequenza" for solo voice. "Sound Piece," constructed by Sommerville with Burroughs's theoretical guidance, makes use of the inching technique to produce a sonic assemblage that also sounds, in places at least, very much like some of the electronic work of Stockhausen and Babbitt. Sommerville's manual movement of the tape over the recording head shortens, elongates, and distorts the vocal sounds that are being recorded, at some points shortening or lengthening them beyond recognition. The human voices are transformed into rapid electronic vibratos, quavering up and down in pitch much like Babbitt's Philomel as she turns into an electronic nightingale. Brion Gysin's piece "Recalling All Active Agents," produced in the BBC's London studios, runs through all the intelligible permutations of the order of its five component words ("Recalling" is divided in two, "re" and "calling"): "Calling all reactive agents," "Calling all active reagents," "Calling re: all active agents," and so on. Though it does not attempt to blur the distinction between speech, song, and electronic tone as Berio's "Thema" does, Gysin's piece does work from the same principles of permuted repetition.

Burroughs's objectives in his collaborative sound experiments are quite different from the objectives of the post-serial composers, however, and closer to those of at least some of the guerrilla samplers brought to prominence in the wake of rap music's accession to the mainstream. Both Stockhausen and Babbitt found in the use of electronically generated and manipulated sounds a way for the composer to exert total control over his sonic material, to achieve a level of precision in the generation of tonal intervals and rhythmic patterns that would have been impossible to reach (or at least to maintain) with human players. From this point of view, electronic composition was an extension of the experiments in "total serialism" undertaken by Olivier Messiaen, Pierre Boulez, Babbitt, and others in the forties that sought to bring all the aspects of music under the direct (i.e., unmediated by the rules of tonal harmony or classical motivic development) control of the composer. Likewise, Henry and other advocates of musique concrète sought to reconstitute, on the basis of recorded natural sounds that could be manipulated electronically, the timbral variety and tonal harmony of the traditional human ensemble.[29] Even Berio's work, which relies much more on the resources of traditional tonal constraints, calls for great virtuosity and technical control on the part of the performer. Burroughs, on the other hand, was working with the potential of tape recording to minimize or even eliminate conscious control over his material, as well as to prove that "Cut-ups are for everyone."[30] His work is thus much closer to John Cage's Zen-inspired attempts to eliminate personality and intention from music by reducing the "composition" to a set of parameters that could be permuted in a large number of ways according to the whim of the performer. Indeed, Burroughs claims that "John Cage and Earle Brown have carried the cut-up method much further in music than I have in writing" (Burroughs and Odier 33). He differs from Cage primarily in his belief that the elimination of *conscious* intention gives access to *unconscious* knowledge and intent, the things "that we don't consciously know that we know," rather than the total elimination of the "I" or "we."[31] The "I" is a deictic term, without essential meaning but given momentary meaning by its context; thus, it floats on a vast multiplicity of meanings contained within the words. These momentary meanings are freed by cut-ups and drop-ins. Burroughs's method is a fragmentation, extension, or multiplication, rather than a suppression, of the self.

This fragmentation/extension is quite clear in the extended tape cut-up "K-9 Was in Combat with the Alien Mind Screens" (1965), the first track on *Break Through in Grey Room*. With Sommerville's help, Burroughs recorded himself reading and also taped several radio and television news broadcasts (in those days, before inexpensive video recording technology, media broadcasts were not specifically copyrighted, as they are now) and cut them into each other at random, producing in the process juxtapositions that have the continuous rhythm of actual sentences but which "refer" to events that never took place. An example that Burroughs often "quotes" elsewhere is the following, spoken in the generic voice of a television announcer: "Johnson, addressing a meeting of editorial cartoonists at the White House, held three maids at gunpoint, and proceeded to ransack the apartment." This sentence is the result of the chance juxtaposition of two separate source sentences, one of which provided the "Johnson . . . White House" phrase and the other of which provided the "held . . . apartment" phrase, yet thanks to the intentionally generic quality of the announcers' voices, the parts flow together perfectly to form a new sentence that was never actually spoken. Moreover, the new sentence is not simply a neutral description but, as Burroughs insists, a prediction or prophecy: "If you cut into the present, the future leaks out."[32] Since the future lies in the present control over time and events maintained by the mass media, cutting the present media word-line will reveal the future. In this case, Lyndon Johnson's responsibility for the imperialist violence of the Vietnam War appears figured in his acts of robbery and the taking of working-class hostages. Similar effects dominate most of the other pieces on *Break Through in Grey Room,* especially "Present Time Exercises" and "Working with the Popular Forces."

According to Deleuze and Guattari (and other critics), this preprogrammed, *mediatic* future is in the subject but more than the subject—in other words, constitutive of the subject but beyond that subject's control. In trying to reveal this future, Burroughs's work becomes relevant to discussions of the metaphysics of sampling in dub, rap, and other forms of urban dance music of the late twentieth century. Burroughs's and Sommerville's "Sound Piece" not only hearkens back to the electronic works of Stockhausen and Babbitt, but also looks forward to the "scratch" techniques popularized by hip-hop deejays and rap technicians in the eighties. These techniques called for the deejay to spin records manually on turntables to repeat or "scratch" the sound, often so quickly that the original recorded sound became unrecognizable; this produces almost exactly the same effect that inching does, though the latter lacks the noise of record grooves that gives the former its name. Likewise, the drop-in technique used in "K-9" and elsewhere anticipates the practice of digital sampling and permutation that has become ubiquitous in rap production. When Burroughs advises artists to "steal freely" because "Words, colors, light, sounds, stone, wood, bronze . . . belong to anyone who can use them" (Burroughs, *Adding Machine* 20–21), he denounces not only private property but the Romantic ideal of the artist as a creator of something "original," whose genius (unlike the labor power of the worker) cannot be alienated. The artist has always been a thief, a *bricoleur,* and never a creator ex nihilo. Burroughs practices such theft himself, in his writing and especially in his tape experiments, just as contemporary musicians practice sampling. Sampling dramatizes the highly unstable nature of cultural production in the present period: the system of copyrights and royalty payments that both supports and constrains the composer/musician is fundamentally threatened by the advent of sampling technology that allows others to "cite" and use the composer/musician's performance directly from any recording of that performance. This system is caught in a double bind, in that it depends on the mass reproduction of performances to extract profit, but it must restrict this constitutive reproducibility in order to protect that profit. This is the same situation Deleuze denounced in Platonism, the judgment in favor of the pious copy and against the simulacrum—such as the sample (Deleuze, *Logic of Sense* 253–66). Reproduction must be legitimated; copies must clearly pay their respects (and their royalties) to the original.

Perhaps the clearest statement of this central issue has been made by the rap group Public Enemy in their piece entitled "Caught, Can We Get a Witness?"[33] The conceit, inspired by the group's run-ins with producers and performers whose works the group sampled, is that Public Enemy's leader Chuck D. has been "Caught, now in court 'cause I stole a beat." Accused of violating copyright, D.'s partner Flavor Flav insists that "beats"—that is, sampled sounds—are natural resources, not subject to private ownership, just as Burroughs claimed that artistic materials belong to anyone who can use them: "I found this mineral that I call a beat/I paid zero." The rappers recognize that this conflict, between their sampling and the fundamental property rights of other performers, calls into question the very existence of the court that claims to judge them:

> Now, what in the heaven does a jury know about hell
> If I took it, but they just look at me
> Like, Hey I'm on a mission
> I'm talkin' 'bout conditions
> Ain't right sittin' like dynamite
> Gonna blow you up and it just might
> Blow up the bench and
> Judge, the courtroom plus I gotta mention
> This court is dismissed when I grab the mike[34]

Of course, the very concept of private property, over which the court claims jurisdiction, is one of the court's own "conditions" of existence, as Chuck D says; thus the court can do nothing but uphold that concept against the rappers' challenge. The situation is what Deleuze would call a paradox, or what Jean-François Lyotard would call a "differend," and thus the court is biased, not by virtue of any individual corruption but because of its founding premises.[35] The court's decision is necessarily premised, not on rational argument, but on the violence of private appropriation. Public Enemy's practice of sampling demands a total rejection of this conception, and thus of the legal system premised upon it, as the group realizes. The issue here is not the dialectical transgression of theft, which would simply reinscribe the conception of property underlying American copyright law; rather, Public Enemy suggests that theft exists as such only within that dialectical horizon, so if the concept of property could be abolished, so would its transgression. They could actually "blow up the bench and judge the courtroom." One "steals" food in order to eat, not to reinforce the concept of private property; likewise, one "steals" words or beats in order to write or sing, not to replace another's ownership by one's own. Burroughs foresaw this development and its political ramifications thirty years ago, and would certainly endorse Public Enemy's perspective.

•

Conversely, Public Enemy would probably endorse the threat implicit in Burroughs's claim that "Sound can act as a painkiller. To date we do not have music sufficiently powerful to act as a practical weapon" (*WL* 136).[36] This deficiency is not for want of trying, at least on Burroughs's part. Like film, music has often been a controlling figure in Burroughs's most powerful and aggressive writing; *Port of Saints,* in particular, is "structured like a musical composition, in fact, there are musical leads for every chapter" (Burroughs, "Interview with Allen Ginsberg"). As befits an avant-gardist at the tail end of this most eclectic of centuries, Burroughs uses all types of music as figures in his writing, from the American national anthem through Jelly Roll Morton's "Dead Man Blues" to the Sex Pistols' "God Save the Queen." Moreover, he has also performed and collaborated with musicians from every progressive idiom. Without hoping to do full justice to all these collaborations, I will now outline the most significant features of Burroughs's forays into musical creation, as they relate to his overriding concerns.

Like most writers of his generation, Burroughs was exposed simultaneously to the established tradition of European concert music (already a marker of class distinction), the centrist popular songs of the early days of radio, and the culturally marginal improvisations of jazz during his years at Harvard in the early thirties; indeed, jazz figures in many of Burroughs's works as the accompaniment to his attacks on authority, while snatches of popular song—as well as parodies thereof—occupy the much less stable, ironic position of mediators between reversible social roles (like junky and narcotics agent). Nevertheless, Burroughs does not seem to have had a profound experience of or relation to music until the late fifties, when Brion Gysin introduced him to the music of the Master Musicians of Jajouka (a farming village in the Rif Mountains of northern Morocco), who would become the musical counterparts to the Wild Boys of Burroughs's literary mythology.

> I first heard the music of the Master Musicians of Jajouka in Tangier in Brion Gysin's restaurant, "The 1001 Nights," in late 1957. . . . Just as I did not at first appreciate Brion's extraordinary personality, the music of Jajouka was lost on me at first hearing, in 1957. But in Paris a year later, Brion played me his tapes of the music and explained [Edward] Westermar[c]k's theory that the annual festival at Jajouka coinciding with the Moslem lunar calendar feast of Aid el Kebir was in fact a reenactment of the ancient Roman Rites of Pan, the Lupercalia, ensuring fertility and maintaining the age-old balance of power between men and women. And then at last I could hear the music, and understand. (Burroughs, Liner notes)

The Master Musicians are members of a "special caste exempt from farm work" who trace their lineage back thousands of years.[37] Their music unrolls like an irregularly knotted rope of overlapping harmonies, dissonances, and rhythms, improvised on native wind, string, and percussion instruments. It conforms to no structure given in advance, but only to the momentary impulses of the performers. This freely structured music sounds utterly unlike most music of European descent, and its immediate use-value in the fertility rituals of Bou Jeloud marks its difference from generic, commodified Western musical forms. For Burroughs, it was a confirmation of his belief that order and form could arise spontaneously from the articulation of aesthetic material rather than being imposed on the material preemptively—in other words, that cut-ups could be a way of living for common people rather than just another class marker for a hermetic group of aesthetes. Thus, he often invokes the Master Musicians in contexts of revolutionary change, as he does in "Apocalypse," for example.

Not only did the Master Musicians provide Burroughs with an image of music freed from the binarism of European art music and African American folk music (and the hybrid popular songs that mediated this opposition)—and therefore with a conception of a culture freed from the parallel binarisms of control and "dogmatic verbal systems"—but they also provided him with the opportunity to make contact with some of the most influential musicians of his day. In 1970 Brion Gysin took Brian Jones of the Rolling Stones to hear the Master Musicians; Jones returned to record them shortly before his death, and Burroughs provided the liner notes to the resulting record. Later, in 1973, free jazz saxophonist Ornette Coleman traveled to Morocco to study with the Master Musicians during the festival of Bou Jeloud, in the same year that Burroughs accepted a magazine assignment to cover the festival (Morgan 457, Litweiler 150–53). Burroughs taped many of the performances and used them, as he had used Gysin's earlier recordings, in his own tape experiments. Fragments of these original recordings included on Coleman's album *Dancing in Your Head*[38] and on Burroughs's album *Break Through in Grey Room* demonstrate that Coleman's music, "harmolodic" free jazz, is one of the few Western musical forms that bears a close resemblance to the Master Musicians' work. As John Litweiler notes, "Ornette's sound fits the context [of the Master Musicians' playing] perfectly, and his lines appear to be a broken commentary on the raitas' [Moroccan oboes'] melodies. The effect is of constant movement, and, on Ornette's part, continual response to the Master Musicians" (Litweiler 161). Coleman's performance with the Master Musicians seemed to Burroughs like "a 2000-year-old rock 'n' roll band. When the two forms met, this music from Punic times and modern jazz, it created a new frontier of sound" (Morgan 457–58), if not quite a practical weapon.

Coleman's innovations in jazz are analogous to Burroughs's innovations in writing, and occurred during the same period, the Cold War fifties. While Burroughs was challenging the parallel control structures of the State and syntax as well as the essentialist logic of the verb "to be" with discontinuous routines and cut-ups, Coleman was quietly but openly dismantling the rules of tonal harmony and chord changes that had dictated the entire prior development of jazz, from Scott Joplin's ragtime to Charlie Parker's bebop. In this, Coleman was playing the same role as Arnold Schönberg played in the history of European concert music, though without retreating from his own insight, as Schönberg had, to the ossified forms of that tradition.[39] Echoing Burroughs's claim that "Nothing is true, everything is permitted," Coleman claims that "There is a law in what I'm playing, but that law is a law that when you get tired of it you can change it."[40] Coleman's work in free jazz corresponds to Schönberg's period of free atonality (or "pantonality," as Schönberg preferred to call it) preceding his discovery of twelve-tone composition. Out of this radical dismantling arose Coleman's own compositional principle, "harmolodics," succinctly described by Coleman's longtime colleague Don Cherry as "a profound system based on developing your ear along with your technical proficiency on your instrument. . . . We have to know the chord structure perfectly, all the possible intervals, and *then* play around it. . . . If I play a C and have it in my mind as the tonic, that's what it will become. If I want it to be a minor third or a major seventh that had a tendency to resolve upward, then the quality of the note will change" (Cherry quoted in Litweiler, 148). Each musician plays his own unconstrained, constantly mutating line, but in relation to the lines of the other players. Free jazz is not formless; rather, it generates many instantaneous forms, but "none of these forms existed before their relation to each other" (Coleman, Liner notes). Harmolodics, then, is a way for musicians and listeners to escape the restrictive demands of musical orthodoxy while remaining part of a performing and listening community, just as Burroughs's cut-ups are a way for readers and writers to escape from linguistic control into a shared radical fantasy. And just as Burroughs considered cut-ups "a psychological process that is going on all the time anyway," Coleman insists that harmolodics is "not supposed to be a secret; it's supposed to be something that anyone should be able to do" (Coleman quoted in Litweiler, 150).

The Master Musicians of Jajouka and Ornette Coleman are relevant to this study for other reasons than just because they provide suggestive analogies to Burroughs's literary work, however. The "new frontier of sound" evident in their music also forms the basis, at least indirectly, of the music on Burroughs's first (and still his most successful) collaborative musical recording. Before his work with Bill Laswell and Laswell's group Material, all of Burroughs's recordings were either unaccompanied readings of written texts or private tape recorder experiments; *Seven Souls* (1989), his first album with Material, represents his first full performance collaboration with musicians of any sort.[41] The album's music is a particularly aggressive example of an increasingly popular style called, rather imprecisely, "world music." World music is the "frontier of sound," the bridge between European and non-European—especially Middle Eastern, African, and Latin American—musical forms, prefigured in Ornette Coleman's performances with the Master Musicians of

Jajouka, among others. Indeed, Laswell returned to Jajouka in 1991 to rerecord the Master Musicians for a sequel to the Brian Jones project. Combining European song structures and ensemble dynamics with Middle Eastern modal harmonies and instrumentation, Material's music provides an appropriate multicultural context for Burroughs's words.

The album consists of seven tracks, of which five contain vocals by Burroughs drawn from his 1987 novel *The Western Lands.* Admittedly, Burroughs does not sing, attempt *Sprechgesang,* or even chant the words; nevertheless, his inimitable voice, reminiscent of both Jack Webb's affectless drone and George Bush's strained whinny, gives the songs a good part of their power, and he is given songwriting credit on the five tracks. The album's overture, "Ineffect," begins with a wailing vocal in the Middle Eastern style and scales of the Master Musicians, followed by Burroughs's lament that "we do not have music sufficiently powerful to act as a practical weapon"; both vocal parts are supported by a heavy bass beat that is interrupted by sitars and electric guitars. Burroughs speaks of a revolutionary "musical intelligence" operating in secret around the world as the song fades into the title track (which is built around Burroughs's text on the seven component souls in Egyptian mythology), a series of minimalist bass and percussion lines alternating with synthesized fortissimo polyrhythms. "Soul Killers," the third track, is composed of string, keyboard, and wind discords sounding in irregular rhythms behind Burroughs's ominous warnings against nuclear weapons and the state: "only those who can leave behind everything they have ever believed in can hope to escape" this impasse. Against this image of despair, the mid-tempo track "The Western Lands" offers an image of hope, of the "gift that supersedes all other gifts, immortality," tempered with the warning that "the road to the Western Lands is by definition the most dangerous road in the world." This song unites passages from all parts of Burroughs's novel, from this early warning to the penultimate "flashes of serene timeless joy, a joy as old as suffering and despair," and is followed by the aggressive African chant "Deliver," sung by Foday Musa Suso of Gambia. The hypermetallic "Equation," juxtaposing cut-up news reports on the Palestinian *Intifada* with American fundamentalist broadcasts and rap, leads into "The End of Words," the album's (and the novel's) conclusion. "The End of Words" combines Middle Eastern scales and overdubbed chants, which gradually fade as Burroughs recites the closing words of *The Western Lands,* which cite and displace T. S. Eliot: "The old writer couldn't write anymore because he had reached the end of words, of what can be done with words. And then? . . . Hurry up please, it's time" (*WL* 258).

Since this initial musical effort, recordings of Burroughs in collaboration with contemporary musicians have flooded the market; there have been so many that Burroughs has launched his own music publishing company, Nova Lark Music (administered by the American Society of Composers, Authors and Publishers [ASCAP]), to handle the copyrights. Unfortunately, most of these collaborations are less effective than *Seven Souls,* primarily because the musical structures they contain are conceived simply as text settings and thus efface themselves as music rather than engaging with Burroughs's vocal performances on more equal terms. This is true of both of Burroughs's "solo albums," *Dead City Radio* (1990) and *Spare Ass Annie* (1993); nonetheless, they contain some wonderful performances by Burroughs, including his reading of "Thanksgiving Prayer," which Gus Van Sant has made into a short film. Burroughs does actually sing a rather hammy and off-key version of "Ich bin von Kopf bis Fuss auf Liebe eingestellt," the German translation of "Falling in Love Again," at the conclusion of *Dead City Radio.* The two albums do demonstrate the wide variety of musicians who have been attracted to Burroughs's work recently, from Hollywood producer/arranger Hal Willner, who sets Burroughs's performances to orchestral music from the NBC Symphony archives, to Michael Franti and Rono Tse of the Disposable Heroes of Hiphoprisy, who set Burroughs against rumbling "scratch" beats.

The industrial rock band Ministry, whose leader, Alain Jourgensen, has clearly taken Burroughs as a role model in a number of questionable ways, provides a much more aggressive and interactive musical setting for Burroughs's words than Willner or the Disposable Heroes do. But Jourgensen, like many of the performers in all media who refer to Burroughs, ultimately values the writer primarily as an agent provocateur. On the *Just One Fix* CD single, Burroughs's demand to "Smash the control structures, smash the control machine" leads into an extended remix of the song that includes other Burroughs voice-overs; in the "Just One Fix" video, which resurrects many of the images used in Burroughs's films with Balch, Burroughs appears as a withdrawal vision, an apocalyptic figure surrounded by tornadoes, who blasts signs that read "Control," "History," "Language" and "Reality" with a double-barrel shotgun. These elements, no doubt, explain why this video was featured prominently in the "Tornado" episode of the obnoxious but amusing MTV animated program *Beavis and Butthead* in 1993. Impressed by the metallic, industrial sound of the band and convinced that "tornadoes are cool," the spectacularly inarticulate protagonists predictably decide that "even the old dude is cool." "Quick Fix," the second track on the single, however, appears to be an original though typically apocalyptic Burroughs text, and its musical arrangement compares favorably with those on the Material album, although it is by no means a world music setting. The minimalist approach of the single-track CD *The "Priest" They Called Him,* recorded in collaboration with Nirvana's late guitarist Kurt Cobain, is also more successful in its spare and lyrical presentation of an otherwise quite ironic narrative variation on a well-known short story by O. Henry: a junky priest, having scored for heroin on Christmas Eve, gives the drug instead to a young man with kidney stones and is rewarded with the "immaculate fix" of death. Cobain improvises freely on the chords to "Silent Night," providing an eerie, distortion-laced backdrop to Burroughs's deadpan narration.

The penultimate piece of evidence in the case for Burroughs's "media presence" does not fit precisely into any of the categories we have investigated so far: his collaboration with director Robert Wilson (who staged *The Civil Wars* and Philip Glass's *Einstein on the Beach*) and singer/songwriter Tom Waits on a stage piece entitled *The Black Rider: The Casting of the Magic Bullets,* which is based on the German "folk tale" "Der Freischütz." (actually written by August Apel and Friedrich Laun, after a story by Thomas de Quincey, Burroughs's acknowledged forebear in the literature of addiction). *The Black Rider* premiered at the Thalia Theater in Hamburg in 1990 and has been staged in several other cities; an album of Tom Waits' songs from the production, three of them cowritten with Burroughs—along with a classic vaudeville song from the thirties, "T'ain't No Sin," sung by Burroughs—was released in 1993. Burroughs's exact contribution to this project is unclear, at least on the basis of the album. He is credited with "texts," and Waits writes that Burroughs's "cut up text and open process of finding a language for this story became a river of words for me to draw from in the lyrics for the songs. He brought a wisdom and a voice to the piece that is [sic] woven throughout."[42] If Waits' description is accurate, then Burroughs has simply put his cut-up procedures in another writer's service and we should be leery of making any detailed claims of continuity with his other, more personally involved works. Some points seem clear enough, however: the show's theme, a version of the "devil's bargain," has clear affinities with Burroughs's constant preoccupation, the reversibility of oppositional social relations—like the junky–narcotics agent, criminal-cop, or revolutionary-capitalist binarisms—and the metaphor of the devil's bullets must surely appeal to Burroughs's long-standing mania for firearms.

While harder to insert into my critical narrative of the elaboration of his theory of deixis, Burroughs's musical collaborations do illuminate that aspect of his work in a number of indirect ways. The settings have the potential to extend the range of meanings available to his texts, just as the cut-ups revealed new dimensions within his very writing. The active collaborations—the Wilson/Waits stage show and the Material records—go further in desubjectifying Burroughs's work through collaboration and the concomitant production of ever more "third minds" between subjects. Most importantly, in entering the media of "mechanical reproduction" (as Walter Benjamin would have it), Burroughs's work becomes available for citation, for sampling, read in his "own" voice and accompanied by his "own" face. As he and Balch showed in *Bill and Tony,* the voice and face themselves, in their reproducibility, are deictic signs that can move from context to context without ever exhausting their potential for new meaning; likewise, Burroughs's recordings give the new generations of samplers an inexhaustible resource for the creation of indirectly collaborative works—that is, collaborations between the present and the future.

•

In July of 1994 Nike, the Seattle-based manufacturer of sports shoes, began to run a series of television, billboard, and print advertisements around the entire U.S. to promote its new "Air Max²" shoe line. The television ads contain much of the standard imagery that has come to be associated with sports-related advertising: muscular athletes—mostly African American males (including NBA stars Charles Barkley and Michael Jordan)—dressed in form-fitting workout gear; funky rhythm and blues musical accompaniment; rapid, MTV-style editing; and semi-reflexive images of television screens within television screens. But they also contain something quite alien to the clichés of sports ads: the face and voice of William S. Burroughs. Burroughs speaks the advertising slogans written by Jean Rhode, the copywriter for the campaign: "The purpose of technology is not to *confuse* the mind but to *serve* the body"; "The basic unit of technology is not the bit but the body"; and "What is technology but mind pushing the limits of muscle?" This is one of the first television ads to use a literary figure for purposes of promotion (a Gap poster series featuring Burroughs and Allen Ginsberg ran a few years earlier), and as such is worth investigating. Generally, of course, such ads use media or sports figures, who do not normally have antagonistic perspectives on the media and on corporate control, as Burroughs does. So why Burroughs?

The ads were designed and constructed by the Wieden and Kennedy Agency of Portland in order to exploit precisely those factors of defamiliarization that Burroughs would embody. For one thing, as an elderly white man, he is symbolically antithetical to the young black and Latino athletes who otherwise populate the ads, and thus he would catch the attention of viewers tired of advertising clichés—even viewers who do not recognize Burroughs (who is not identified in the ads). This antithesis is reinforced by the contrasting presentations of Burroughs, who appears as an artificial pixelated image on video screens in the manner of Max Headroom, and of the athletes, who appear "realistically" in both grainy pseudodocumentary footage and "artistic" picture-postcard landscape shots. In addition, Burroughs's growing presence in other media as an icon of "authentic" rebellion and subversion (for example, his collaboration with Cobain and his appearances in Ministry's "Just One Fix" video, in Van Sant's film *Drugstore Cowboy.* and elsewhere) grants a hip legitimacy to the commercial "art" of television advertising design and to the company for whom he agrees to work; these ads represent the apotheosis of Burroughs's iconic cameo appearances. Burroughs has come to symbolize a certain popular avant-garde—if such a concept can be thought without self-contradiction—to the hip audience that can recognize him.

These are probably Nike's intended meanings for this series of ads. But are these the only meanings they can have? Let's consider the erotics of sports advertising, to which Nike has contributed many tropes over the last decade. The television ads present Burroughs both as a source of privileged information about Nike's commodities and as a spectator of the young athletes in the ads. Several shots show Burroughs on his own screen reacting to movements the athletes make on other screens. What would William S. Burroughs, queer revolutionary and literary innovator, see in the montage of sweating, seminude, mostly male bodies that fill each ad? It seems unlikely that he would see the athletes as successful role models or "heroes," as perhaps many "innocent" middle-class urban/suburban boys (a clearly privileged sector of Nike's audience) and even some adults would; rather, Burroughs would probably see the bodies of these athletes as objects of erotic fantasy, and see their exertions and perspiration as emblems of the physicality simultaneously offered and foreclosed by the medium of television. He would see it as a kind of elaborately choreographed soft-core pornography. This is not a new development, as Horkheimer and Adorno already knew in the forties; all sports ads, like virtually all ads *tout court,* rely on such scarcely concealed, perpetually unconsummated eroticism. What is novel here is the fact that this is an overtly *homosexual* eroticism, a male gaze unabashedly objectifying (mostly) male bodies. Through this parallel voyeurism, Burroughs becomes a stand-in or metonymy for the audience, a situation which retrospectively reveals the homosocial desire underpinning even the supposedly "innocent"—that is, acceptably competitive and heterosexual—adoration middle-class boys have for sports stars. Burroughs's perspective on and in the ads brings to the surface the disavowed desire from which sports industries profit even as they and many of their customers deny it.

Burroughs, as a spectator of and commentator on the athletes within the ads, is offered thus as a new trope, a reflexive figure for the viewing audience itself. He begins several of the ads, however, with a direct address to the viewer: "Hey! I'm talking to you!" This specification of roles (speaker and addressee) serves to establish his authority, to give notice of his privileged knowledge of both the products and the consumer desires they are intended to fulfill. "What we have done," Burroughs later says, referring to the corporate first person plural made up of himself as speaker and Nike as institutional agent, "is square the air." The process of pluralization or schizophrenization appears even more clearly in the print/billboard ads, which juxtapose the left half of Burroughs's face with the right halves of several African American athletes' faces (including Barkley and baseball player Ken Griffey Jr.), all within larger images of the Air Max^2 shoes. The structure of this schizoid verbal and visual incorporation brings to mind Burroughs's description of the controlling Nova Mobsters and their modus operandi—controlling the human coordinate points (*TE* 57–58)—as well as the benign form of pluralization Burroughs calls "the third mind," but it is also a dramatization of the issue of deixis around which Burroughs's other media interventions cluster. The commercial situation of endorsement replicates the shifting subjectivities of the film *Bill and Tony.* In a single statement with multiple implications, Burroughs, the subject or speaker of the enunciation, says "we" but actually refers to the faceless corporation, the subject of the statement, and, by extension, to its otherwise unmentioned workers, the ones who have actually "squared the air" if anybody has. In parallel fashion, Burroughs both embodies his own subjective viewpoint as spectator and also offers the mass audience an explicitly queer perspective to adopt or admit as its own. By permutation he occupies and renders ambiguous all subject positions.

We might be tempted to ask, as a follow-up to this analysis of the ads, if Nike would endorse such an extended reading. If I am right that they chose Burroughs in part because of his iconic status, then perhaps they did so under the impression that in order to become an icon one must be neutralized, separated from the specifics of one's own history and works, as Michael Jackson has allowed himself, in large measure, to be neutralized through choice of material (which serves to distance him from the aggressively gendered and politicized urban rhythm and blues scene out of which he first appeared), cosmetic surgery (which distances him from his African American physical heritage), and personal secrecy (which minimizes possible scandal from his ambiguous sexuality). Spokespeople for large corporations must generally avoid even the appearance of impropriety; they must appear neutral, without desires or drives that deviate from the popular norm, in order to remain iconic. Jackson has recently failed to maintain such an appearance, but he may be able to reneutralize himself as he has in the past. Burroughs, on the other hand, has never attempted to neutralize himself or his work; he has been so open for so long about his addictions, his shooting of his wife, his political radicalism, and his homosexuality that no "unauthorized" biography or media exposé could possibly reveal anything "negative" about him that hasn't been known for decades already. Indeed, most members of Burroughs's audience, whether casual or committed, know far more about the extraordinary events of his life than they do about its "normal" side. Since he hides nothing, he has no secrets which can be revealed, no confidences which can be betrayed; he knows those dialectics too well. It may be, however, that Nike executives had hoped that Burroughs's unneutralized position would generate controversy and publicity when its significance was perceived by the watchdogs of media morality. If that had happened, what appeared at first to be Burroughs's accession to the American cultural mainstream (or what some might call his "sell-out") might have turned out to be his most influential subversive act. Surprisingly or not, the only controversy the Nike ads generated concerned Burroughs's apparent opportunism, his willingness to take money from the very corporations and media he had spent so many years satirizing, which troubled readers who failed to appreciate the paradoxical nature of his celebrity. Burroughs himself has acknowledged the irony of his situation, in which "There's no contradiction to subverting something and profiting from it at the same time," since the subversion has not been compromised in order to get at the profits.[43]

•

At the conclusion of *The Western Lands,* Burroughs offered an apparently elegiac farewell to writing: "The old writer couldn't write anymore because he had reached the end of words, of what can be done with words. And then?" (*WL* 258). It should be clear that, in reaching the end of words—that is, the end of writing—himself, Burroughs has not necessarily reached the end of art, of the world, or of living, as critics who overemphasize his ironic allusions to T. S. Eliot might be tempted to think (in fact he still writes, and has recently published a new book of dream fragments, *My Education*). The matter of this chapter has, I hope, gone some way toward proving that point by showing how, exactly, Burroughs has managed to go beyond that ambiguous open question in the collaborative media works that both precede and succeed his last novel to date. If one were to object, justly, that this "beyond" still seems to contain a surprisingly large number of words, and thus appears to consign itself to interminable deconstruction, I can only reply that if it still contains words, it also contains far more than that: mobile visual images, asignifying sounds, musical tones and rhythms, and even (if I am allowed to refer to the paintings I have not discussed) abstract patterns of color. Moreover, this "beyond" exists outside William S. Burroughs the subject, outside Burroughs the author or agent provocateur or éminence grise, and even outside "Burroughs" the text and commodity, in a space and a time that have imperceptibly become coterminous with our media culture. This is the final implication of Burroughs's radical extension of deixis: not merely an intertextuality that escapes covertly from the constraints of fully self-present meaning, but an explosive *intermediation* or scrambling of all the codes faster than capital, subjectivity, or language can resituate them. In this way Burroughs's work is nomadological, or schizoanalytic. Deleuze and Guattari would say that "Burroughs" is no longer just the name of an author, a celebrity, or an artist; it is the name, rather, of a set of potentials, an effect that propagates itself from medium to medium by the force of its difference, bringing into contact incompatible functions, incommensurable concepts, and unrelated materials.[44] Even when Burroughs is no longer able to serve as the focus for this force, it will continue to reverberate, indefatigably sounding its critical imperative: listen to my last words everywhere.

Notes

Introduction: "Nothing is True, Everything is Permitted"

1. See Latour, chapter 5.

2. See especially Negri, "Spinoza's Anti-Modernity." See also Negri, *The Politics of Subversion: A Manifesto for the Twenty-First Century,* and Negri's book with Michael Hardt, *Labor of Dionysus: A Critique of the State-Form.*

3. See Saussure 65–70. By "negative definition" I mean the principle that linguistic signs acquire meaning only through their difference from other equally arbitrary signs. The tendency to homogenize all differences into this single form is most evident in Jean Baudrillard's work, especially *For a Critique of the Political Economy of the Sign,* chapters 6–8.

4. See Bérubé's *Marginal Forces/Cultural Centers.*

5. This is especially true in light of the fact that Ellison himself apparently gave up the attempt (he was unable to complete the "sequel" to *Invisible Man*) or perhaps even reneged on its most basic terms: see the narrative of Ellison's behavior during the awarding of the American Academy's Gold Medal for Fiction to Bernard Malamud, which took place on the day Burroughs was inducted into the Academy, in Morgan 10–13.

6. On the development of Deleuze's systematic anti-Hegelianism and evasion of the dialectic, see Hardt's *Gilles Deleuze: An Apprenticeship in Philosophy.*

7. Deleuze, *Foucault* 131, my emphasis. Deleuze is generally uninterested in the problematics of modernism and postmodernism; given its context, his usage of the term "modern" here is less an intervention in the struggle to define (post)modernism than a marker to distinguish this literature from "classical" (i.e., pre-Cartesian) writing in Foucault's sense.

8. Deleuze has written essays on Herman Melville, Walt Whitman ("Bartleby, ou la formule" and "Whitman," both in *Critique et clinique*), Henry James, and F. Scott Fitzgerald ("Three Novellas" in Deleuze and Guattari, *A Thousand*

Plateaus); he also refers often to Stephen Crane, Edgar Allan Poe, Henry Miller, Jack Kerouac, and Burroughs. In addition to these canonical and semicanonical figures, Deleuze is familiar with a wide range of American popular writers, including H. P. Lovecraft, Raymond Chandler, and Chester Himes; see his essay "Philosophie de la Série noire" on the very popular series of French pulp novels and translations from American pulp literature, in which he also articulates his theory of the "powers of the false" (45).

9. Deleuze, letter to the author, 26 Mar. 1991. My translation.

10. The term *fantasmatic* is my adjectival derivation from Deleuze's substantive *phantasm,* which he defines as follows: "The phantasm has three main characteristics. (1) It represents neither an action nor a passion, but a result of action and passion, that is, a pure event. The question of whether particular events are real or imaginary is poorly posed. The distinction is not between the imaginary and the real, but between the event as such and the corporeal state of affairs which incites it about [*sic*] or in which it is actualized" (Deleuze, *Logic of Sense* 210). The pure event is the thing, occurrence, or encounter prior to its recognition and categorization as an object by subjective representational thought. He continues: "(2) The second characteristic of the phantasm is its position in relation to the ego, or rather the situation of the ego in the phantasm itself. . . . What appears in the phantasm is the movement by which the ego opens itself to the surface and liberates the a-cosmic, impersonal, and pre-individual singularities which it had imprisoned" (212–13). The phantasm is thus not a narcissistic fantasy of individual satisfaction but a flight beyond the fixed boundaries of the self or ego, a dissolution of the self into its repressed libidinal components. "(3) It is not an accident that the development inherent in the phantasm is expressed in a play of grammatical transformations. . . . The phantasm is inseparable from the infinitive mode of the verb and bears witness thereby to the pure event. . . . From this pure and undetermined infinitive, voices, moods, tenses and persons will be engendered" (214–15). Therefore the phantasm is a virtuality, a generator of new relationships within language, within the individual subject, and in the broader social world. By changing the spelling to *fantasmatic,* I intend to establish a relation between Deleuze's term and the "fantasies" that Burroughs provides through his writing. I argue in chapters 5 and 6 that Burroughs's goal as a writer is to produce such phantasms or fantasies as a way of rewriting the oppressive structure of contemporary capitalism.

11. The original subtitle of Burroughs's first novel, *Junky,* is *Confessions of an Unredeemed Drug Addict.*

12. For Mailer and Ginsberg, see "*Naked Lunch* on Trial" in *NL;* for Lodge, see his "Objections to Burroughs" in Skerl and Lydenberg; for Fiedler, see his essay "The New Mutants." Robin Lydenberg discusses many of these "moral" accounts of Burroughs in *Word Cultures: Radical Theory and Practice in William S. Burroughs' Fiction* 3–8.

13. See Lydenberg, *Word Cultures,* and Skerl, *William S. Burroughs.*

14. On the shooting of Joan Vollmer Burroughs, see Miles 53 and Morgan 193–96. Morgan in particular offers three different eyewitness narratives of the shooting, none of which suggests murderous intent.

15. Finley's work consists of a selection of art books and magazines, arranged on a wooden table under plate glass, on which Finley has recorded her reactions to the texts and artworks in red grease pencil. The original work was assembled in 1994 and recreated in 1996 for the show "Sexual Politics: Judy Chicago's *Dinner Party* in Feminist Art History" at the UCLA/Armand Hammer Museum of Art in Los Angeles.

16. Pound's relationship to Mussolini and Italian Fascism is well known, but Stein's interest in Marshal Pétain is not; on both writers' politics, see Luke Carson, *The Public Trust: Consumption and Depression in Gertrude Stein, Louis Zukofsky and Ezra Pound.*

17. Ginsberg, describing Burroughs's project of the sixties in Burroughs, "Interview with Allen Ginsberg," no pagination.

18. The most extensive and sophisticated discussion I know of Burroughs's theoretical relation to feminism is Lydenberg 167–73.

19. Unsurprisingly, Andrea Dworkin concurred in this linkage of Sade and Burroughs, though she denounced rather than celebrated what she saw as its pernicious effects on women: "Sade is precursor to Artaud's theater of cruelty, Nietzsche's will to power, and the rapist frenzy of William Burroughs" (Dworkin 71). She does not specify that the rape scenes so common in Burroughs's works rarely involve women, nor does she seem to realize that such scenes are included as examples of the dangers of control and repression and not as a transgressive metaphysics, as they are in Sade.

Chapter One. Invisibility and Amodernism

1. See Lyotard, *The Postmodern Condition* and, with Jean-Loup Thébaud, *Just Gaming.*

2. See Baudrillard, *The Mirror of Production* and *For a Critique of the Political Economy of the Sign.*

3. See Adams, especially chapter 25, "The Dynamo and the Virgin" (379–90).

4. Compare this statement of intent of Ellison's narrator with Stephen Dedalus's more ambitious claim in James Joyce's *Portrait of the Artist as a Young Man:* "I go to encounter for the millionth time the reality of experience and to forge in the smithy of my soul the uncreated conscience of my race" (*Portable Joyce* 526).

5. A similar critique of anthropology's asymmetrical treatment of cultures is articulated in Johannes Fabian's *Time and the Other: How Anthropology Makes Its Object,* but Fabian concentrates on the temporal disjunction between the "here and now" of our culture and the "there and then" of primitive cultures rather than on the "continuity"—or what we might call the "totalizability"—of these opposed cultures. Fabian is primarily concerned with the coexistence of advanced and primitive cultures at the same historical moment, which he calls "coevalness," and not with modernism and postmodernism, as is Latour (and this study).

6. Barth's *LETTERS* is the most extreme example of this rococo effect, though the works that follow it, such as *Sabbatical,* are only slightly less elaborate in their reflexive structuring.

7. Greil Marcus, "Anarchy in the U.K." in Jim Miller, ed., *The Rolling Stone Illustrated History of Rock & Roll* 456. I would argue that punk rock, Marcus' subject in this essay, represents an alternative to postmodernism that is similar in some ways to the amodernism I will sketch in this essay. Indeed, the final essay in William Burroughs's *The Adding Machine: Selected Essays,* titled "Bugger the Queen," begins as an *hommage* to the Sex Pistols.

8. See, for example, Habermas's essay "Modernity—An Incomplete Project" and Luhmann's *Essays on Self-Reference.* My gestures here are completely inadequate as criticism of Habermas and Luhmann, but I hope to extend my remarks in the future. For now, I would direct the interested reader to the more detailed analysis undertaken by Michael Hardt and Antonio Negri in *Labor of Dionysus: A Critique of the State-Form,* especially chapter 6, "Postmodern Law and the Withering of Civil Society."

9. This, it seems to me, is the fundamental difference between my argument and that advanced by Hal Foster in his preface to *The Anti-Aesthetic.* Foster argues for a distinction between a "postmodernism of resistance," which "seeks to deconstruct modernism and resist the status quo," and a "postmodernism of reaction," which "repudiates the former [modernism] to celebrate the latter [the status quo]" (Foster xii). Let's take him literally: if "resistance" means first and foremost the "deconstruction of modernism," does this not imply that, like deconstruction, this resistance will remain suspended within the modernist determinations it reverses and reinscribes, since deconstruction (at least in its most rigorous forms, like Derrida's work) perpetually defers any specification of alternatives to the metaphysics it interrogates? To "question rather than exploit cultural codes, to explore rather than conceal social and political affiliations" (Foster xii) is not to offer alternatives to those codes and affiliations. The offering of such alternatives, both Marx and Jean-Paul Sartre would agree, is the *specific* precondition of social change—which the predominantly negative critique of the status quo cannot provide. This invention of alternatives is the project of amodernism.

10. See also Martin Jay's important comparative study of the category of totality, *Marxism and Totality: The Adventures of a Concept from Lukács to Habermas.*

11. See Jameson xvii.

12. See Popper's *The Open Society* and Martin Jay's chapter on Habermas in *Marxism and Totality* 462–509.

13. See the final selection in Baudrillard's *Selected Writings,* as well as his *In the Shadow of the Silent Majorities, or The End of the Social.*

14. On Islamic fundamentalist revolutions, see Michel Foucault, "Iran: The Spirit of a World Without Spirit" in *Politics, Philosophy, Culture: Interviews and Other Writings* 1977–1984, 211–24. On the social potentialities of gang organization, see Mike Davis, *City of Quartz: Excavating the Future in Los Angeles,* especially chapter 5, "The Hammer and the Rock"; see also Michael Hardt's analysis of Davis in "Los Angeles Novos" 22–26.

15. On Autonomia, see the documentary anthology *Working-Class Autonomy and the Crisis* and the special issue of *Semiotext(e)* devoted to *Italy: Autonomia—Post-Political Politics* (1980), edited by Sylvère Lotringer. On the

Makhnovshchina, see Arshinov, *History of the Makhnovist Movement* 1918–1921.

16. Paul Feyerabend articulated a position very similar to Latour's for nearly twenty years, from the publication of his influential polemic *Against Method* (1975) to his death. In later editions of the text he makes a compelling argument for the subordination of science, and of the dominant influence of rigid disciplinary competence, to democracy. Feyerabend makes this argument from the perspective of analytical philosophy, however, rather than from the theory of modernity, as Latour does, so his version is less useful to my argument here.

17. See Negri, *Politics* 203, and his "On Gilles Deleuze & Félix Guattari, *A Thousand Plateaus.*" See also Ronald Bogue's essay "Gilles Deleuze: Postmodern Philosopher?" for a cautious and interesting but ultimately inconclusive argument, which claims merely that "Deleuze is postmodern in that he is a post-Enlightenment, post-Hegelian philosopher" (404). Deleuze's frequent collaborator, the late Félix Guattari, addresses the question of postmodernism quite polemically in "The Postmodern Dead End."

18. See Deleuze and Guattari, *Anti-Oedipus,* chapter 3, section 9, "The Civilized Capitalist Machine" (222–40). Marx's analysis of this tendency appears in *Capital,* volume 3, section 1, part 3, "The Law of the Tendency of the Rate of Profit to Fall" 211–66.

19. Perhaps the context of this quotation can clarify the point: "the two sexes imply a multiplicity of molecular combinations bringing into play not only the man in the woman and the woman in the man, but the relation of each to the animal, the plant, etc.: a thousand tiny sexes" (Deleuze and Guattari, *A Thousand Plateaus: Capitalism and Schizophrenia* 213). For considerations of this suggestion from a feminist perspective, see Rosi Braidotti, *Patterns of Dissonance,* and Elizabeth Grosz, "A Thousand Tiny Sexes: Feminism and Rhizomatics" in Constantin V. Boundas and Dorothea Olkowski, eds., *Gilles Deleuze and the Theater of Philosophy* 187–210.

20. See Bataille, *The Accursed Share: An Essay on General Economy,* volume 1. Deleuze and Guattari reject, however, the dialectical notion, which Bataille borrows from Hegel, of a transgression that reinscribes the law it breaks.

21. The text continues with an example: "The great socialist utopias of the nineteenth century function, for example, not as ideal models but as group fantasies—that is, as agents of the real productivity of desire, making it possible to disinvest the current social field, to 'deinstitutionalize' it, to further the revolutionary institution of desire itself" (Deleuze and Guattari, *Anti-Oedipus* 30–31n).

22. This theory of fantasy allows me to hazard an answer to those who would dismiss *Anti-Oedipus* as naïvely antitextualist, like Vincent B. Leitch, who insists that "representation remains for schizoanalysis the essential means to its ends. Yet the problematics of (mis)reading through representations elicit little response from Deleuze and Guattari. The rhetoricity and materiality of representational language, its stickiness and liquefaction, receive hardly any attention. In renouncing the signifier for the schiz-flow, schizoanalysis circumvents textuality and its enigmas, but they return, doglike, to pester and threaten the enterprise" (Leitch 222). In fact, Deleuze and Guattari are perfectly aware of the materiality of their own discourse, as well as its

potential for what Leitch calls "(mis)readings," but this objection functions only under the aegis of referentiality. Rhetoricity and materiality can only undermine a discourse which makes claims to truth content, that is, to "adequacy to the facts"; within a discourse whose mark is usefulness, these may be amusing questions but they can hardly be called criticisms. This text, like all of Deleuze's texts, is not a set of signifiers looking for signifieds but a "box of tools," as he put it in a discussion with Foucault. *Anti-Oedipus,* like any good subject-group fantasy, strives to be useful for the creation of desire rather than true in some hermeneutical way.

23. See Derrida's "Plato's Pharmacy" in *Dissemination* 137–39. See also Paul Patton's analysis of the difference between Deleuze's and Derrida's accounts of simulation in "Anti-Platonism and Art" in Boundas and Olkowski, eds., *Gilles Deleuze and the Theater of Philosophy* 148–53.

24. Deleuze calls this function "fiction" in *Empiricism and Subjectivity: An Essay on Hume's Theory of Human Nature* 131–33 and "*la fonction fabulatrice*"—which I would render "fabulation" rather than "story-telling function," as the translators do—in *Bergsonism* 108–111.

25. Don Cherry, quoted in John Litweiler, *Ornette Coleman: A Harmolodic Life* 148.

Chapter Two. No Final Glossary

1. This introductory text, "Deposition: Testimony concerning a Sickness," was originally published in *Evergreen Review* 4.11 (Jan./Feb. 1960) and was included with the Grove Press edition (1962 and later) of the novel; the original Olympia Press edition of the novel did not contain an introduction.

2. See Deleuze and Guattari, *Kafka: Toward a Minor Literature,* chapter 3.

3. On the modernization of urban space, particularly New York City, see Marshall Berman's *All That Is Solid Melts Into Air: The Experience of Modernity,* chapter 5.

4. On Burroughs's use of his mother's maiden name, see Lydenberg, *Word Cultures* 167–72.

5. As Burroughs notes in the glossary, "M.S." is morphine sulphate, a "croaker" is a doctor, and a "script" is a prescription for regulated drugs. "Script" in particular enters Burroughs's textual economy; we will trace some of its vicissitudes in the chapters that follow.

6. Even Foucault's Benthamesque panoptic disciplinary society is discontinuous in this sense: the "guards" cannot watch all of the "prisoners" all of the time, though the "prisoners" cannot know exactly when they are under direct observation. See *Discipline and Punish: The Birth of the Prison,* part 3, chapter 3. If one were to imagine a form of police control that was not rhythmic, not pulsed, but continuous, one would have to pattern it along the lines laid down by George Orwell in 1984.

7. Burroughs comments extensively on these laws in Burroughs and Odier, *The Job* 147–49, as well as in Burroughs and Bockris, *With William Burroughs: A Report from the Bunker,* and returns to the subject in light of the "War on

Drugs" in "Afterthoughts on a Deposition," the new (1992) introduction to *Naked Lunch*, 15.

8. For examples of the characterization of drug addicts in the contemporary mass media, see Harry J. Anslinger and William F. Tompkins, *The Traffic in Narcotics*. The title of one of Anslinger's later books gives a good indication of his perspective on addiction: *The Protectors: The Heroic Story of the Narcotics Agents, Citizens, and Officials in Their Unending, Unsung Battles against Organized Crime in America and Abroad.* Most historians and police officials believe now that traditional organized crime (i.e., the Mafia) did not become involved in drug trafficking until the late sixties or early seventies. Anslinger, the U.S. Commissioner of Narcotics in the fifties and sixties, came to represent the inhuman face of control to Burroughs, who often quotes Anslinger's dictum that "the laws must reflect society's disapproval of the addict" (in *The Ticket That Exploded* 216 and elsewhere).

9. In this, Burroughs marks a temporary disagreement with Samuel Beckett, for whom the relation is exactly the opposite: the long-sought sequel to speech, for Beckett, is silence, though it is a silence that, in pure form, may be impossible to achieve. Later in his career, Burroughs will reverse himself on this issue and claim that the silence that comes after words is "The *most* desirable state" (Burroughs, "Interview" in *Writers at Work: The Paris Review Interviews* 150). This is not to say that one of these perspectives on the relation of speech and silence is radical and the other conservative, but rather that this relation itself is crucial to the work of important contemporary writers other than Burroughs. Burroughs reflects on Beckett's work and declares himself closer to Proust than to Beckett in "Beckett and Proust," in *The Adding Machine: Selected Essays* 182–86.

10. Deleuze, preface to Guy Hocquenghem, *L'Après-mai des faunes: Volutions* 10. My translation.

11. Recall that "connection" is another term for "pusher," although it is not included in Burroughs's glossary at the end of *Junky*.

12. "Confessions" of this kind are scattered throughout contemporary texts on psychopathology, civil rights, and religious tolerance. A number of them are collected in the volume edited by A. M. Krich, *The Homosexuals As Seen by Themselves and Thirty Authorities;* see Part 1, "As Seen by Themselves," particularly the first-person narratives "Autobiography of a Homosexual Writer" (70–74) and "Crisis in the Life of a Homosexual" (80–84). This volume also reprints texts on homosexuality (understood throughout as referring to both male and female homosexuality) by Freud, Jung, Sandor Ferenczi, and others. Burroughs does not cite Krich's volume to my knowledge, but he does refer, quite disparagingly, to Donald W. Cory's *The Homosexual in America* in a letter to Ginsberg: the book is "Enough to turn a man's gut. This citizen says a queer learns humility, learns to turn the other cheek, and returns love for hate. Let him learn that sort of thing if he wants to. I never swallowed the other cheek routine, and I hate the stupid bastards who won't mind their own business. They can die in agony for all I care. . . . I could never be a liberal except in a situation where the majority was made up of people I like" (Burroughs, *Letters 1945–1959* 105–6).

13. No less an authority than Norman Mailer has said, apropos of Burroughs's aggressively uneffeminate homosexuality, that "Burroughs is a real

man. . . . I remember when we read the first sections of *Naked Lunch* we felt so relieved. We knew a great man had spoken" (quoted in Burroughs and Bockris, *With William Burroughs,* xix).

14. When Burroughs recycles this routine in his later works, he attributes very different words of wisdom to Bobo: "as a wise old black faggot said to me years ago: 'Some people are shits, darling.'" See "My Own Business," among other texts, in *The Adding Machine,* 15–18.

15. See Sedgwick, *Epistemology of the Closet,* especially her comparative analysis of Racine's *Esther* in chapter 1. George Chauncey claims that "Originally, the concept of gay *coming out* spoofed the debutante's; *coming out* didn't mean disclosing one's homosexuality to straights, but rather, it meant initiation into gay networks" (Wayne Koestenbaum's paraphrase from his review of Chauncey's *Gay New York: Gender, Urban Culture and the Making of the Gay Male World 1890–1940* in the *Los Angeles Time Book Review* 7 Aug. 1994: 2). This would be closer to Burroughs's experience as it appears in *Queer.* Chauncey also examines the liminal spaces of the prewar gay world: the bathhouses, parks, and bars that paralleled the underdetermined spaces of the junky that I examined above.

16. Burroughs, "Letter from a Master Addict to Dangerous Drugs," originally published in the *British Journal of Addiction* 53 (1957): 2 and reprinted as an appendix to the Grove Press edition of *Naked Lunch,* 253.

17. Burroughs has often said of his writing, "Every word is autobiographical, and every word is fiction." See, for example, Burroughs and Bockris, *With William Burroughs* 28.

18. Burroughs, statement included in the catalogue of his painting exhibition at Cleto Polcina (Rome, 1989), quoted in Barry Miles, *William Burroughs, El Hombre Invisible: A Portrait* 241. "Nagual" is Carlos Castaneda's term for the unpredictable, magical universe that coexists with the "tonal," or causal and predictable, universe of science.

Chapter Three. "All Agents defect and all Resisters sell out"

1. These trials took place in 1965 and 1966 respectively. See the prefatory material included in the Black Cat edition of *Naked Lunch* (New York: Grove Press, 1966). Earlier, in 1959, when sections of *Naked Lunch* were to be published in the University of Chicago's literary magazine, *Chicago Review,* the faculty advisors suppressed the forthcoming issue; the student editors resigned and founded the independent magazine *Big Table,* which was prosecuted on and cleared of obscenity charges for publishing excerpts from *Naked Lunch.* See Michael B. Goodman, *Contemporary Literary Censorship: The Case History of Burroughs' Naked Lunch,* and Ted Morgan, *Literary Outlaw* 295–98.

2. See the prefatory material included in the 1961 edition of *Ulysses* (New York: Vintage, 1961), in which Joyce's lawyer Morris L. Ernst claims that the *Ulysses* case "marks a turning point. It is a body blow for the censors. . . . Writers . . . may now describe basic human functions without fear of the law . . . [and] it should henceforth be impossible for the censors legally to sustain an attack

against any book of artistic integrity, no matter how frank and forthright it may be" (v–vi). The difficulty, of course, lies in the phrase "artistic integrity." Ernst also draws a parallel between the *Ulysses* decision and the repeal of Prohibition: "Perhaps the intolerance which closed our distilleries was the intolerance which decreed that basic human functions had to be treated in books in a furtive, leering, roundabout manner" (vi). If he's right, then the legal opposition Burroughs faced in the late fifties and the sixties constituted the literary incarnation of the legislative anti-drug hysteria Burroughs chronicled in *Junky.*

3. See Elaine Dutka's article on Chernin, "The Lunches Won't Be Naked."

4. Cronenberg quoted in Ira Silverberg, ed., *Everything is Permitted: The Making of Naked Lunch* (London: Grafton, 1992), 61; see also 13 and 57.

5. The script has been published in France: David Cronenberg, *Le Scénario du "Festin Nu."* It gives no writing credit to Burroughs, and therefore the Cronenberg film cannot be treated as a collaboration. Brion Gysin wrote a different screenplay for a *Naked Lunch* film, with Burroughs's help, in the early seventies; a small section of it is published in Burroughs and Gysin, *The Third Mind* 150–58, and another section in Gysin and Terry Wilson's *Here to Go: Planet R-101* 131–57.

6. See also Cronenberg, *Scénario du "Festin Nu"* 102–3.

7. The quotation is taken from the novel (*NL* 216), but it is taken completely out of context.

8. Cronenberg, *Scénario du "Festin Nu"* 114, my translation.

9. Cronenberg, *Scénario du "Festin Nu"* 11, my translation.

10. *Naked Lunch* was not composed using the strict cut-up method, which functions at the level of syntax; instead, it was composed by juxtaposing separate, self-contained routines, according to a kind of narrative-level cut-up.

11. A similar formalist neutralization has allowed Robert Mapplethorpe's photographs to be defended within the very academy that they were, at least in part, meant to mock and disturb. A "formal" portrait of Burroughs in black tie and tails, taken by Mapplethorpe, faces the title page of Burroughs and Bockris's *With William Burroughs,* a collection of interviews.

12. See, for example, Julia Kristeva, *Revolution in Poetic Language* 17: "The text is a practice that could be compared to political revolution: the one brings about in the subject what the other introduces into society."

13. Burroughs, Introduction to Silverberg, ed., *Everything is Permitted: The Making of Naked Lunch* 15.

14. The first quote is from Burroughs and Odier, 69; the second from Burroughs, "My Purpose is to Write for the Space Age" in Skerl and Lydenberg, eds., *William S. Burroughs at the Front,* 268.

15. This citation is actually a free rendering of proposition 3.328 of Wittgenstein's *Logisch-Philosophische Abhandlung [Tractatus Logico-Philosophicus]* 56–57: "Wird ein Zeichen nicht gebraucht, so ist es bedeutungslos. Das ist der Sinn der Devise Occams" ("If a sign is not necessary then it is meaningless. That is the meaning of Occam's razor").

16. Burroughs uses ellipses quite often in *Naked Lunch* and later works, as Pynchon does in *Gravity's Rainbow.* Burroughs's ellipses consist of three or four periods separated by spaces. To avoid confusion, I will keep ellipses added to

quotations to a minimum. When added ellipses are unavoidable, they will appear in brackets to distinguish them from Burroughs's own ellipses. Burroughs also imitates various dialects in print, often through conscious misspelling or distortion of syntax that anticipates his cut-up work of the sixties; all of the quotations in this book have been carefully checked against their sources in Burroughs's novel and the spelling and syntactic "errors" that remain are in the original text.

17. This point on Burroughs's trajectory can be fruitfully compared to Joyce's strategy of "silence, exile and cunning." Joyce went into continental exile in protest against the parochial philistinism of Irish culture that threatened to constrain his literary experiments (and, to a lesser extent, against the legal sanctions that threatened to constrain his unorthodox living arrangements with his "wife," Nora); see Richard Ellmann's *James Joyce,* revised edition 109–10. He was never explicitly threatened with violence or incarceration, as Burroughs often was.

18. Actually, there is a third alternative: to remain within the superficially fragmentary aesthetic of modernity, which is the course Adorno himself took.

19. On this organization of the subject and its vicissitudes through recorded history, see the three volumes of Foucault's *History of Sexuality,* as well as *The Order of Things: An Archaeology of the Human Sciences* and *Discipline and Punish.* Louis Althusser's "Ideology and Ideological State Apparatuses" in *Lenin and Philosophy* also discusses the interpellation of the subject as the image of the capitalist social structure.

20. Horkheimer and Adorno have a significantly different idea of addiction than Burroughs does, however, as their discussion of the "Lotus Eaters" episode of the *Odyssey* demonstrates: "This kind of idyll, which recalls the happiness of narcotic drug addicts reduced to the lowest level in obdurate social orders, who use their drugs to help them endure the unendurable, is impermissible for the adherents of the rationale of self-preservation. . . . [T]he tempting power ascribed to [the drug] is none other than that of regression to the phase of collecting the fruits of the earth and of the sea—a stage more ancient . . . than all production . . . a state in which the reproduction of life is independent of conscious self-preservation, and the bliss of the fully contented is detached from the advantages of rationally planned nutrition" (*DE* 62–64). Burroughs would perhaps accept the idea of addiction as regression, even to a vegetative, precapitalist state, but hardly to a primitive state of "bliss." On the contrary, in his experience the addict's life is much closer to the mechanization Horkheimer and Adorno discern in the reproduction of labor: the addict, particularly the heroin or morphine addict, has no affective existence whatsoever and is virtually indistinguishable from a corpse: "Morphine have depressed my hypothalamus, seat of libido and emotion, and since the front brain acts only at second hand with back-brain titillation, being a vicarious type citizen can only get his kicks from behind, I must report virtual absence of cerebral event. I am aware of your presence, but since it has for me no affective connotation, my affect having been disconnect by the junk man for nonpayment, I am not innarested in your doings. Go or come . . . but the Dead and the Junky don't care" (*NL* 231).

21. See Lukács, "Reification and the Consciousness of the Proletariat" in *History and Class Consciousness,* especially section 3, "The Standpoint of the Proletariat."

22. See Foucault, *Discipline and Punish,* especially parts 2 and 3.

23. Burroughs dabbled in anthropology while a student at Harvard and knew enough about the field to make inside jokes about it. For example, in the midst of a passage on the fatalism of South American *Brujos,* a parenthesis demands a "straightjacket for Herr [Franz] Boas [one of the founding fathers of modern anthropology]—trade joke—-nothing so maddens an anthropologist as Primitive Man" (*NL* 110). *Naked Lunch* also contains many parenthetical asides that purport to explain, objectively, obscure social practices; for example, "smother parties"are "a rural English custom designed to eliminate aged and bedfast dependents," and "leading out" is "an African practice[. . .]of taking old characters out into the jungle and leaving them there" (*NL* 10). These asides take the place of the futile glossary with which *Junky* concluded.

24. The resemblances between the critiques of Reason by Sade and Burroughs extend beyond their approaches to criminality; a common point of interest, which I cannot address here, is their shared belief that "We have just as good grounds for denying woman a title to be part of our race as we have for refusing to acknowledge the ape as our brother" (Sade, cited in *DE* 110). If Burroughs is less inclined to deny humanity's kinship with apes (see for example *NL* 86–87 and elsewhere), he is no less inclined to view women as a separate species.

25. Coleridge's Mariner is a figure recurring throughout *Naked Lunch* who seems to exemplify what Burroughs sees as the relation between writer and reader; consider this passage, from the "Campus of Interzone University" routine:

> consider the Ancient Mariner without curare, lasso, bulbocapnine or straightjacket, albeit able to capture and hold a live audience. . . . What is his hurmp gimmick?[. . .]He does not, like so-called artists at this time, stop just *anybody* thereby inflicting unsent for boredom and working random hardship. . . . He stops those who cannot choose but hear owing to already existing relation between the Mariner (however ancient) and the uh Wedding Guest. . . .
>
> "What the Mariner actually says is not important. . . . He may be rambling, irrelevant, even crude and rampant senile. But something happens to the Wedding Guest like happens in psychoanalysis when it happens if it happens[. . . .]an analyst of my acquaintance does all the talking—patients listen patiently or not[. . .]He is illustrating at some length that nothing can ever be accomplished on the verbal level[. . . .]*You can find out more about someone by talking than by listening.*" (*NL* 87–88)

This passage implies that *Naked Lunch,* itself apparently rambling and crude, may be intended to reveal more about its readers in their various reactions to it than about its writer in his construction of it. See Anthony Channell Hilfer, "Mariner and Wedding Guest in William Burroughs' *Naked Lunch.*"

26. Horkheimer and Adorno's (implicit) attitude toward homosexuality diverges rather sharply from Burroughs's. Whereas for Burroughs, at this point in his career, homosexuality is capable of being both radical (in its challenge to the sexual division of labor on which capitalism is founded) and reactionary (in its continued resemblance to heterosexual norms of subjectivity and interpersonal control), in Horkheimer and Adorno's view homosexuality remains within a horizon of pure reactionary psychopathology, as a characteristic of Fascism. Consider this remark, from the "Notes and Drafts" section of *Dialectic of Enlightenment:*

> This hostility—which was once carefully fostered by the worldly and spiritual rulers—felt by the lowly against the life which held out nothing for them and with which they

> could establish a homosexual and paranoiac relationship by murdering, was always an essential instrument of the art of government. (234)

And this description:

> Man surrenders to man, cold, bleak and unyielding, as woman did before him. Man turns into woman gazing up at her master. In the Fascist collective with its teams and labor camps, everyone spends his days from the tenderest years in solitary confinement. The seed of homosexuality is sown. (252)

Further study is necessary to determine to what extent this attitude problematizes Horkheimer and Adorno's analysis of the sexual division of labor articulated elsewhere in *Dialectic of Enlightenment.*

27. U.S. Supreme Court, *A Book Named "John Cleland's Memoirs of a Woman of Pleasure" v. Attorney Gen. of Mass.*, cited in the decision by the Massachusetts Supreme Court in its decision deeming *Naked Lunch* not obscene (*NL* viii).

28. See Lydenberg, chapter 2, "Notes from the Orifice: Language and the Body in *Naked Lunch.*"

29. Deleuze, *Francis Bacon: Logique de la sensation* 34–35. Translation by Daniel W. Smith forthcoming. These two passages also appear, in a very similar context, in *A Thousand Plateaus* 150, 153.

30. This "point of intersection" is narrated in Burroughs's short autobiographical text "Exterminator!" (1966), included in the 1973 collection of the same title.

Chapter Four. "*I Hassan i Sabbah* rub out the word forever"

1. See Gysin, "Cut Me Up * Brion Gysin . . . " in Burroughs, Gysin, Beiles, and Corso, *Minutes to Go* 42–43, and Burroughs, "The Cut-Up Method of Brion Gysin" 29. See also Hans Richter, *Dada: Art and Anti-Art* 54.

2. Burroughs, "Origin and Theory of the Tape Cut-Ups" on the compact disk *Break Through in Grey Room.*

3. Here again we see Burroughs's dissent from Beckett's position on language. As noted in chapter 2, for Burroughs the silence of solitary addiction comes before the speech of community, while for Beckett the speech of community comes before the silence of solitude. Likewise, for Burroughs the words contain not only past and present time, in which we are controlled, but also the future, in which we can be free; Beckett, on the other hand, admits that "All I know is what the words know," which is only "a handsome little sum, with a beginning, a middle and an end as in the well-built phrase and the long sonata of the dead" (*Molloy* 31); this seems to rule out any novelty or freedom that the words might contain.

4. This source text by Monroe is, unfortunately, too long to quote; Burroughs's published cut-up utilizes only short random sections of it.

5. Burroughs, "Interview with Allen Ginsberg," no pagination. This interview contains what appears at first to be a contradiction: although *The Ticket That Exploded* is only the second book of the trilogy, both Ginsberg and Burroughs agree that it actually "brought it all to a climax" through "the action of the Nova

or of the explosion itself, by dissolving everything into a vibrating, soundless hum." We will return to this apparent contradiction later.

6. Burroughs, "Appendix to The Soft Machine," quoted in Barry Miles, *William Burroughs, El Hombre Invisible* 120–21. This text was included in the third British edition of *The Soft Machine* (1968), but not in any other editions. We should also recall that the concept of "right" is intimately related to that of the Law, both in Burroughs's writing and in the German philosophical tradition that forms the basis of most modern discussion of Law. In the latter, the term *Recht* refers to "right," "state," and "law." See Hegel's *Philosophy of Right* and Marx's "Critique of Hegel's Doctrine of the State [*Recht*]" in *Early Writings.*

7. Burroughs, "Interview with Allen Ginsberg."

8. The cited passage on "Willy the Rat" recurs in identical form in *Nova Express* 56, and in cut-up form in many places throughout the trilogy.

9. On Burroughs's album of tape recorder experiments from the mid-sixties, *Break Through in Grey Room.*

10. See also Jameson, *Marxism and Form* 255–57.

11. See the documents assembled by Robert V. Daniels in *A Documentary History of Communism,*2: 54–67.

12. On McCarthy, see David M. Oshinsky, *A Conspiracy So Immense: The World of Joe McCarthy.* On the general development of American anticommunist movements, see David Caute, *The Great Fear: The Anti-Communist Purge under Truman and Eisenhower.*

13. Burroughs subjects this opposition to a reductio ad absurdam in his most concentrated work on gangsters, *The Last Words of Dutch Schultz.* Schultz's last delirious monologue, recorded by a police stenographer after Schultz has been shot, provides Burroughs with a natural cut-up, which he uses to construct a hallucinatory "film" of Schultz's criminal career.

14. On Valachi's testimony and its ramifications, see Peter Maas, *The Valachi Papers.*

15. See Burroughs, *Naked Scientology* 83. This volume consists of texts reprinted from the *LA Free Press, The East Village Other,* and *Rolling Stone.*

16. The passage as a whole is a striking prophecy of the Watergate cover-up, particularly in its appeal to executive privilege and its reference to secret tape recordings.

17. Here Burroughs is citing Wittgenstein's *Tractatus Logico-Philosophicus* 56–57.

18. The Latin goes like this: "Frustra fit per plura quod potest fieri per pauciora."

19. Gysin, "Cut-Ups: A Project for Disastrous Success" in Burroughs and Gysin, *The Third Mind* 43–44.

20. Eric Mottram claims, and Gysin seems to confirm, that Burroughs's "immediate source of information [on Hassan i Sabbah] was Betty Bouttel's *Le Vieux de la Montagne,* 1924" (Mottram, *William Burroughs: The Algebra of Need* 61). Mottram probably got this information from Burroughs in conversation or correspondence; he does not seem to have inspected the novel himself. Marshall Hodgson, in his history of the Ismâ'îlîs, Hassan i Sabbah's Islamic sect, refers to a "historical novel" entitled *Grand Maître des Assassins* by B. Bouthoul, pub-

lished in 1936, which "held the field alone" (Hodgson 27n). I have not been able to locate a copy of the novel, whatever its title, for analysis, but it seems fair to assume that Burroughs would have learned more about Hassan i Sabbah from his friend Gysin than from an obscure French novel.

21. Gysin was also familiar with the most important Ismâ'îlî publications, including the thirteenth-century Persian historian Juwayni's hostile contemporary account of their doctrines and the translations of Henry Corbin; see Gysin and Wilson xiii–xiv, 64–65. Hodgson reports virtually the same story of Hassan i Sabbah and Nizâm al-Mulk, with less emphasis on the method by which the manuscripts were "jumbled"; see Hodgson 137–38.

22. This recurrent phrase, like the "Razor" discussed above, may derive from the novel that Mottram claims was Burroughs's source for information on Hassan i Sabbah, or it may simply be Burroughs's combination of Gysin's Ismâ'îlî anecdotes, Dostoyevsky's assertion that "If God is dead, everything is permitted" (from *The Brothers Karamazov*), and his own antiauthoritarianism.

23. In the transliteration of Arabic and Persian spelling, I will follow the source of the moment. Please note that some authors add a terminal "t" to words ending in vowels; thus *sharî'a* and *sharî'at* refer to the same object, as do *haqîqa* and *haqiqat.*

24. More recent works on Ismailism, including Henry Corbin's *History of Islamic Philosophy* and Farhad Daftary's *The Ismâ'îlîs: Their History and Doctrines,* do not in general contradict Hodgson's claims, so I have used his volume as my primary source because it could well have been known to Gysin or Burroughs, as the more recent works could not.

25. This emphasis on the external nature of the law, and its ultimate transitoriness, shows that the *sharî'a* was a pre-Kantian form of law. Deleuze defines this generally *heteronomous* pre-Kantian law as follows: "If men knew what good was, and knew how to conform to it, they would not need laws. Laws, or the law, are only a 'second resort,' a representative of the Good in a world deserted by the gods. When the true politics is absent, it leaves general directives according to which men must conduct themselves. Laws are therefore, as it were, the imitation of the Good which serves as their highest principle. They derive from the Good under certain conditions." This is clearly the function of the *sharî'a.* Kantian law, on the other hand, is defined by its internal characteristics, its formal *autonomy,* rather than its content or its relation to human behavior in the material world: "Kant reverses the relationship of the law and the Good. . . . It is the Good which depends on the law, and not vice-versa. . . . The law can have no content other than itself, since all content of the law would lead it back to a Good whose imitation it would be. In other words, the law is pure form and has no object: neither sensible nor intelligible. It does not tell us *what* we must do, but to what (subjective) rule we must conform, whatever our action. Any action is moral if its maxim can be thought without contradiction as universal, and if its motive has no other object than this maxim. . . . The moral law is thus defined as the pure form of universality" (Deleuze, "On Four Poetic Formulas Which Might Summarize the Kantian Philosophy," preface to *Kant's Critical Philosophy,* x). This distinction is theoretically important, but it has little direct relevance to Burroughs's project; indeed, Burroughs seldom if ever refers to Kant, and never to his formal definition of the law.

26. Brion Gysin visited Alamout in 1973 and wrote an unpublished report on it; see Gysin and Wilson xii–xiv, 64, 96–100.

27. Gysin in fact refers to all of the leaders of Alamout, including Hassan i Sabbah and his successors, as "Old Men of the Mountain"; see Gysin and Wilson xiii. This may be the source of Burroughs's fusion of the historically distinct figures.

28. This abolition of the law that entails the resurrection of the dead will provide the rationale for Burroughs's next major work, *The Wild Boys: A Book of the Dead.*

29. This proclamation implied that, given the necessary order of appearance of prophets and *hujjas* dictated by the Ismâ'îlî faith, if Hasan II was *Qâ'im,* then Hassan i Sabbah, as Hasan II's *hujja,* occupied a role parallel to Christ; indeed, Hassan i Sabbah would be the Second Coming of Christ before the final Judgment. See Hodgson 154 and *WL* 195.

30. For example, there are laws on food in the sura (chapter of the Koran) on "The Table"; on familial and sexual relations in the sura "Women"; on the obligation to make the pilgrimage to Mecca in the sura "Pilgrimage," and many others. See *The Koran* 386–400, 366–84 and 401–7.

31. Burroughs, "Apocalypse" on the compact disk *Dead City Radio.* Text published as introduction to Keith Haring, *Apocalypse* (New York: George Mulder Fine Arts, 1989).

32. *Kalâm-i Pir,* cited in Buckley 146.

33. *TE* 49–50. In this statement, Burroughs's attitude toward the speech/silence relation appears to be shifting to one of agreement with Samuel Beckett, for whom the compulsion to speak is the most tenacious element in the structure of the self.

34. See Plato, the *Republic* 5: 474–80, in *Collected Dialogues.*

35. In *The Western Lands,* where he takes up the implications of Hassan i Sabbah's work again in detail, Burroughs suggests that this is the reason "the Ismailians were singled out for special persecution, since they commit the blackest heresy in Islamic books, assuming the prerogatives of the Creator" (*WL* 198).

36. Burroughs, "Interview" in *Writers at Work* 159–60. Burroughs adds, provocatively, that the reader may, "For 'nova police,' read 'technology,' if you wish" (160); despite its undeniable interest, this point is beyond the scope of the present study.

37. Nietzsche warned his readers to "beware of speaking of chemical 'laws': that savors of morality." Consider, for example, his insistence that in the physical sciences,

> "Regularity" in succession is only a metaphorical expression, *as if* a rule were being followed here; not a fact. In the same way "conformity with a law." We discover a formula by which to express an ever-recurring kind of result: we have therewith discovered no "law," even less a force that is the cause of the recurrence of a succession of results. That something always happens thus and thus is here interpreted as if a creature always acted thus and thus as a result of obedience to a law or a lawgiver, while it would be free to act otherwise were it not for the "law." But precisely this thus-and-not-otherwise might be inherent in the creature, which might behave thus and thus, not in response to a law, but because it is constituted thus and thus. All it would mean is: something cannot also be something else, cannot do now this and now something

> else, is neither free nor unfree but simply thus and thus. *The mistake lies in the fictitious insertion of a subject.*
>
> And also the next fragment:
>
> Two successive states, the "cause," the other "effect": this is false. The first has nothing to effect, the second has been effected by nothing. It is a question of a struggle between two elements of unequal power: a new arrangement of forces is achieved according to the measure of power of each of them. The second condition is something fundamentally different from the first (not its effect): the essential thing is that the factions in struggle emerge with different quanta of power. (Nietzsche, *The Will to Power,* fragments 630, 632, and 633, pp. 336–37)

Compare Nietzsche's critique to Burroughs's fullest formulation of the problematic of biologic law, from *The Western Lands:*

> NOs, natural outlaws [are] dedicated to breaking the so-called natural laws of the universe foisted upon us by physicists, chemists, mathematicians, biologists and, above all, the monumental fraud of cause and effect, to be replaced by the more pregnant concept of synchronicity[. . . .] To an ordinary criminal, breaking a law is a means to an end: obtaining money, removing a source of danger or annoyance. To the NO, breaking a natural law is an end in itself: the end of that law. (*WL* 30)

The Law, whether social or natural, is nothing other than a power structure used to impose predictable uniformity—generally in the form of an intentional, speaking human subject—on the multiplicity of relations that constitute the chaotic universe. For Burroughs as for Nietzsche, unpredictable and unprecedented hybrids are the substance of the world.

38. Compare Marx's similar perspective on historical repetition and novelty: "Hegel remarks somewhere that all facts and personages of great importance in world history occur, as it were, twice. He forgot to add: the first time as tragedy, the second as farce" (*The Eighteenth Brumaire of Louis Bonaparte* in Marx and Engels 1: 247).

39. Burroughs, "Interview" in *Writers at Work* 159.

40. In "Cut-Ups: A Project for Disastrous Success," Gysin writes that "The Divine Tautology came up at me off a page one day: I AM THAT I AM, and I saw that it was lopsided. I switched the last two words to get better architectural balance around the big THAT. There was a little click as I read from right to left and then permutated the other end. AM I THAT AM I? 'It' asked a question. My ear ran away down the first one hundred and twenty simple permutations and I heard, I think, what Newton said he heard: a sort of wild pealing inside my head, like an ether experience, and I fell down. Burroughs looked grave. 'Unfortunately, the means are at hand for disastrous success.' . . . You can't call me the author of those poems, now, can you? I merely undid the word combination, like the letter lock on a piece of good luggage, and the poem made itself" (Burroughs and Gysin 45).

41. For a more detailed explication of these syntheses, see Murphy, "The Theater of (the Philosophy of) Cruelty in Gilles Deleuze's *Difference and Repetition.*"

42. Burroughs, "Origin and Theory of the Tape Cut-Ups" on the compact disk *Break Through in Grey Room.*

43. Tom Phillips, "Notes on *A Humument,*" included as an appendix to *A Humument,* revised edition, unpaginated.

44. See "The Mayan Caper" in *The Soft Machine.*

45. See chapter 1, above, on the relation of the law of value to postmodernism.

46. See "The Coming of the Purple Better One" in *Exterminator!*

47. On such total, nonconserving aggression, see Hardt, *Gilles Deleuze* 52–53.

Chapter Five. The Wild Boys

1. Alfred Kazin, *Bright Book of Life: American Novelists and Storytellers from Hemingway to Mailer* 269. Much of Kazin's discussion of Burroughs in this volume is a revision of his review of *The Wild Boys* (from *The New York Times Book Review* 12 Dec. 1971: 4, 22).

2. Consider, for example, Louis Althusser's "Ideology and Ideological State Apparatuses" in *Lenin and Philosophy* and Slavoj Žižek's *The Sublime Object of Ideology,* among others.

3. See Marcuse, *One-Dimensional Man* and Adorno, *Minima Moralia,* and *Negative Dialectics.*

4. See Derrida, "Structure, Sign and Play in the Discourse of the Human Sciences" in *Writing and Difference,* 278–93.

5. This does not mean that hermeneutic studies have no use, but the status of their inquiry must be conceived differently; in the model I am articulating, hermeneutics must be approached as a form of fantasmatic invention rather than as the revelation of obscured truth.

6. Allen Ginsberg, in his introduction to Burroughs, *Letters to Allen Ginsberg 1953–1957* 6. Ginsberg notes that "schlupp" means "to devour a soul parasitically."

7. Marshall McLuhan, "Notes on Burroughs" from *The Nation* 28 Dec. 1964: 519, reprinted in Skerl and Lydenberg 73.

8. This refers to the 1968 Democratic National Convention; see Mailer's *Miami and the Siege of Chicago.* For a good general overview of the events to which Burroughs responded, often directly, see David Caute, *The Year of the Barricades: A Journey through 1968;* Caute mentions Burroughs's presence in Chicago on 315.

9. I will occasionally cite *Port of Saints* without additional comment because, as Burroughs admits, it is not strictly distinct from *The Wild Boys:* "There isn't very much difference [between *The Wild Boys, Exterminator!* and *Port of Saints*]. I found the material for *Wild Boys* when I had to make, at some point, a more or less arbitrary choice . . . sometimes you realize that the things you left out are better than what you've put in. So three books came from that block of material" (Burroughs, "Interview with Allen Ginsberg").

10. Ginsberg in Burroughs, "An Interview with Allen Ginsberg." On the question of Burroughs's misogyny, see Lydenberg 167–74.

11. On Burroughs's anthropological studies in Mexico, see *Letters 1945–1959* 69 and Morgan 173. He refers frequently to the Egyptian Book of the Dead and to the Maya codices, but rarely to the Tibetan Book.

12. Jewish and Christian doctrines of resurrection also contain elements of this posthumous corporeality in the theme of the "resurrection of the flesh," but such doctrines do not generally share the Egyptian concern with the danger and uncertainty of the afterlife.

13. Budge defines the *khu* as the "spiritual soul . . . which under no circumstances could die" (*Book of the Dead* lxviii).

14. The text continues with an example: "The great socialist utopias of the nineteenth century function, for example, not as ideal models but as group fantasies—that is, as agents of the real productivity of desire, making it possible to disinvest the current social field, to 'deinstitutionalize' it, to further the revolutionary institution of desire itself" (Deleuze and Guattari, *Anti-Oedipus* 30–31n).

15. For Sartre, subject-group fantasy is dialectical in that it affirms an alternative social relation only by negating the negation of that alternative. In the Bastille example, it is only because the negative (defensive) and affirmative (offensive) moments of the fantasy coincide in the same object that the group can form. For Deleuze and Guattari, these moments are separate and bear on distinct objects; therefore they cannot be reduced to a synthesis.

16. Burroughs's interpretation of the Maya hieroglyphs is consistent with the dominant interpretation of the forties, when he studied the hieroglyphs in Mexico, but this account is no longer accepted among archaeologists. Peter Mathews reports that "there was a rather serious mind set switch that went on. You start to see coming into the literature in the 1940's that [sic] the Maya were worshipping time" (*Proceedings of the Maya Hieroglyphic Weekend* 118).

17. Burroughs is also skeptical of countercultural claims about the liberational potential of drugs: "It seems to me that drugs are one of the ideal power devices. The so-called drug problem is a pretext—thin, and getting thinner—to extend police power over areas of actual or potential opposition. In Western countries, opposition is concentrated in the 18-to-25 age group. So, make more drug laws, publicize all drug news, and a good percentage of the opposition is criminal by legal definition . . . [the police] can keep young people under continual threat of police search or action, at the same time divert rebellion into the dead-end channels of addiction and criminality" (Burroughs and Odier 127–28).

18. In fact, the two other famous books of the dead, the Tibetan and the Egyptian, are not actually entitled "Book of the Dead"; the Tibetan *Bardo Thödol* translates literally as "Liberation by Hearing on the After-Death Plane," and the Egyptian *Pert em hru* means "Coming forth from (or by) day." See W. Y. Evans-Wentz, ed., *The Tibetan Book of the Dead* xvi, and Budge, *Egyptian Book* xxx.

19. Such phallic glyphs are common throughout the Book of the Dead, appearing as early as the twenty-third line of the very first plate in the papyrus of Ani (Budge, *Egyptian Book* 4). The phallus-glyph, as Burroughs acknowledges, is also part of the Egyptian pictograph for "absence."

20. Both texts are published in Burroughs, *Ah Pook Is Here and Other Texts*. They both suggest a hieroglyphic method of reading Burroughs's works: "Models can pose the glyphs and act them out in charades. It's the great work of making words into pictures into so called real people and places. . . . Transposing these stylized glyphs into photos and drawings we find that there can be any number of representations of any glyph" (68–69). Of course, the glyphs can also be

transposed into narrative descriptions of the sort I have just mentioned; this would mean that the scenes could be read as glyphs, and their arrangement as sentences. I regret that I am unable to undertake such a novel and difficult reading of Burroughs's novels at present.

21. In *The Job,* written contemporaneously with *The Wild Boys,* Burroughs explains this form of Control: "The goal to submit was implanted by a threat so horrible that he could not confront it, and the Mayan secret books obviously consisted of such horrific pictures. The few that have survived bear witness to this. Men are depicted turning into centipedes, crabs, plants" (42). This explanation also accounts for the "Garden of Flesh" sequence in *The Wild Boys* 44–46.

22. This escapist aspect of the book has led Burroughs to claim, disingenuously, that "*The Wild Boys* could be considered a kind of homosexual *Peter Pan*" (Burroughs, "My Purpose Is to Write for the Space Age" in Skerl and Lydenberg 266).

23. See Deleuze and Guattari, "Plateau 10. 1730: Becoming-Intense, Becoming-Animal, Becoming-Imperceptible," 232–309 in *A Thousand Plateaus: Capitalism and Schizophrenia.*

24. Pages 80–89 of *Port of Saints* specify even more "adaptive" types.

25. The Wild Boys are all made of blue material because, as creatures constructed of desire, they must be the color of desire: "Doctor Wilhelm Reich has isolated and concentrated a unit that he calls 'the orgone'—Orgones, according to W. Reich, are the units of life—They have been photographed and the color is blue" (*NE* 16n). The reference is to Reich 384.

26. The "silver spots" that mark the burnout of the reality film are prefigured in the "silver spots" of orgasm, *WB* 107.

27. Ginsberg in Burroughs, "Interview with Allen Ginsberg."

Chapter Six. Quién es?

1. *Queer* also escapes from this assumption to some extent through its gestures toward revolutionary community, but it remained unfinished and unpublished until after the publication of *Cities of the Red Night* and *The Place of Dead Roads.*

2. On Sartre's privileged preservation of the categories of right and Law, see Foucault's implicit response in "On Popular Justice" in *Power/Knowledge: Selected Interviews and Other Writings 1972–1977* 1–36.

3. Deleuze and Guattari, *Anti-Oedipus* 318, 322. Translation slightly modified.

4. Snide is first introduced in the routine entitled "The Market" in *NL* 119–21. Recall also that *Queer* ends with a first-person narrative by Lee's "Skip Tracer" persona, another seeker of missing persons.

5. I have not been able to examine Seitz's *Under the Black Flag.*

6. See Burroughs's foreword to the reissue of Black's work, *You Can't Win,* v–viii.

7. Burroughs, "Interview" in *Writers at Work* 163–65.

8. See Eisenstein's *Battleship Potemkin* (1925) and Balestrini's *Vogliamo tutto,* as well as Michael Hardt's discussion of the latter in *Gilles Deleuze,* 45–47.

9. Burroughs has always said that he is "very much concerned with the creation of character. In fact I can say that it is my principal preoccupation. If I am remembered for anything, it will be for my characters" (Burroughs, "Beckett and Proust" in *The Adding Machine* 183).

10. On this division of souls, see also Budge's chapter on "The Doctrine of Eternal Life" in his introduction to *The Egyptian Book of the Dead,* lv–lxxxi. Burroughs's reading of this passage has been set to music by Bill Laswell and his compatriots in the group Material, and it forms the title track of their album *Seven Souls.* Five of the album's seven tracks are constructed around Burroughs's readings from *The Western Lands.*

11. This is reflected in Burroughs's opposition between the Manichean "Magical Universe[. . .]of many gods[. . .]in conflict," where even Osiris must hustle for a living, and the "One God Universe," whose all-powerful deity can "do nothing, since the act of doing demands opposition" and who "can't go anywhere, since He is already fucking everywhere" (*WL* 113). The opposition is grounded finally in Burroughs's despotic theory of language: "The One God is *Time.* And in Time, any being that is spontaneous and alive will wither and die like an old joke. And what makes an old joke old and dead? Verbal repetition" (*WL* 111).

12. Obviously, the fact that "Hassan i Sabbah" can be abbreviated "HIS," the masculine possessive pronoun, is not irrelevant to Burroughs's enterprise. Throughout *The Western Lands* he couches the struggle for immortality in terms of a struggle of men and masculine principles, figured in HIS and disembodied immortality, against women and feminine principles, which literally *embody* mortality; see particularly *WL* 74–75 and 200–201.

13. Michel Foucault, Preface to Deleuze and Guattari, *Anti-Oedipus* xiv.

14. Remember the other last words:

> Listen to my last word anywhere. Listen to my last words any world. Listen all you boards syndicates and governments of the earth. And you powers behind what filth deals consummated in what lavatory to take what is not yours. To sell the ground from unborn feet forever . . .
> Listen: I call you all. Show your cards all players. Pay it all pay it all pay it *all* back. Play it all play it all play it *all* back. For all to see[. . . .] (*NE* 11).

15. The first quotation is a famous graffito from the May 1968 student riots in the Latin Quarter in Paris: "Beneath the paving stones, the beach." The second is Brion Gysin's answer, enthusiastically endorsed and quoted by Burroughs, to the question that constitutes the "great metaphysical nut": "What are we here for?" (Gysin, jacket note to Gysin and Wilson, and Burroughs, "William's Welcome" on *Dead City Radio*).

Conclusion: Burroughs's Fin de siècle

1. I am thinking of the late, lamented French literary talk show *Apostrophes,* hosted by Bernard Pivot. Even it, however, became accessible to writers only on the basis of their proven or anticipated market "muscle"; see the analyses in Debray.

2. Burroughs, "Interview" in *Writers at Work* 153.

3. *Nothing Here Now But the Recordings* was released by Industrial Records, Throbbing Gristle's label, and is no longer available.

4. See Howard Shore and Ornette Coleman, *Naked Lunch: Music from the Original Soundtrack.*

5. Both *Call Me Burroughs* (English Bookshop, 1965) and *Ali's Smile* (Unicorn Press, 1971) have been reissued on a single compact disc, under the title *Vaudeville Voices.* A more complete list of Burroughs's recorded readings is included in Christian Vilà's unsympathetic *William S. Burroughs: Le génie empoisonné.*

6. Burroughs's texts for Wilson's production have not yet been published, but he did write lyrics and sing on Tom Waits's recording of the score for *The Black Rider.*

7. See Robert Sobieszek's *Ports of Entry: William S. Burroughs and the Arts* and James Grauerholz's essay "On Burroughs' Art," as well as the other specific gallery catalogs.

8. Jagger, "Memo from Turner,"on the soundtrack to the film *Performance.*

9. For example, Geoffrey Stokes, on page 399 of Ward, Stokes, and Tucker's *Rock of Ages: The Rolling Stone History of Rock and Roll,* claims that the radical American band Steppenwolf took the line "heavy metal thunder" in their 1967 hit "Born to be Wild" (the first usage of the term "heavy metal" in popular music) from *Naked Lunch.* Unfortunately, that phrase does not appear as such in any of Burroughs's texts, though "heavy metal" appears as an adjective throughout the *Nova* trilogy.

10. Reed's statement is reported in Burroughs and Bockris, *With William Burroughs* 18–19; the song is on the Velvet Underground, *Loaded.*

11. Burroughs, Introduction to Silverberg, ed., *Everything is Permitted* 13.

12. Ginsberg has released many recordings, including his performance of Blake's *Songs of Innocence and Experience* and an album of performances and text "settings," similar to Burroughs's, called *The Lion for Real.* Recently, Rhino Records released a four-CD set of Ginsberg readings and performances entitled *Holy Soul Jelly Roll.* He has also provided the libretto to Philip Glass's recent mini-opera *Hydrogen Jukebox.* Ishmael Reed has long run his own communications consulting firm (Reed, Cannon and Johnson) and has also collaborated with noted jazz musicians like Taj Mahal, Carla Bley, and Allen Toussaint (*Conjure: Music for the Texts of Ishmael Reed,* American Clavé 1006). Since the success of *The Color Purple* as novel and film, Alice Walker has become a public spokesperson for a certain kind of African-American feminism; this has brought her into conflict in the media with, among others, Ishmael Reed. Most recently, Walker has used her visibility to galvanize opposition to the practice of female genital mutilation in Africa.

13. Hence the title of Burroughs's collaborative manifesto of the cut-up method and its variants, *The Third Mind,* written with Brion Gysin.

14. Burroughs's *Blade Runner* is based on Alan Nourse's novel of the same name, which is also the source of the title only of Ridley Scott's 1984 film *Blade Runner,* itself based on Philip K. Dick's *Do Androids Dream of Electric Sheep?* Burroughs's book has no other relation to Scott's film.

15. Smith quoted in Sitney, *Visionary Film: The American Avant-Garde 1943–1978* 256.

16. Burroughs in Burroughs and Gysin, *The Third Mind* 31.

17. Burroughs, "Interview" in *Writers at Work* 153. He also gives credit to T. S. Eliot and John Dos Passos.

18. Sitney discusses these dadaist films briefly in *Visionary Film,* presenting them in his first version of the book as the precursors of structural filmmaking, the sixties' reaction against the dominant subjective aesthetic of avant-garde cinema that is nevertheless "dialectically related" to subjective cinema (369); see Sitney 228–29. In the revised edition of *Visionary Film,* Sitney grants more significance, especially to Duchamp's film, but still treats it within a dialectical horizon that returns to the primacy of subjective experience; see 399–401. For an interpretation of Duchamp and Richter (apparently) more in line with Burroughs's own cinematic intentions, see Richter's *Dada: Art and Anti-Art,* especially 94, 221–22.

19. The standard references on deixis are Roman Jakobson, "Shifters, Verbal Categories and the Russian Verb" in *Selected Writings* vol. 2, and Émile Benveniste, *Problems in General Linguistics.*

20. Friedberg, "'Cut-Ups': *A Synema of the text*" in Skerl and Lydenberg, 172. Originally published in *Downtown Review* 1.1 (1979). Barry Miles makes the same claim in *William Burroughs, El Hombre Invisible: A Portrait,* 154.

21. Script for *Towers Open Fire,* from *IT: International Times* 31 Oct.–13 Nov. 1966: 8. Unattributed citations in the next three paragraphs come from this text.

22. Friedberg points out the irony of this scene: it was shot in "the boardroom of the British Film Institute, the major organ of censorship and control of film in Britain" (Skerl and Lydenberg 173).

23. Friedberg in Skerl and Lydenberg 173. Miles confirms this procedure on 155.

24. Burroughs, "Interview" in *Writers at Work* 154. My emphasis.

25. Burroughs in Burroughs and Gysin, 19, 32. The second citation is from the essay "The Cut-Up Method of Brion Gysin," originally published in T. Parkinson, ed., *A Casebook on the Beat* (1961).

26. Burroughs, "Interview" in *Writers at Work* 154–56.

27. Burroughs, "Interview" in *Writers at Work* 159.

28. On these trends in music, see Griffiths, chapter 11.

29. See Griffiths 142–50, 158–63.

30. Burroughs in Burroughs and Gysin, 31.

31. Burroughs, "Origin and Theory of the Tape Cut-Ups" on *Break Through in Grey Room.* I should make the comparison between Burroughs and Cage a bit more specific. Burroughs's cut-ups are similar in formal structure to Cage's early aleatory compositions such as "Music of Changes," which, like a cut-up text, is a piece that was composed using chance operations (in Cage's case, consultation of the I Ching), but which, once composed, gives no further place to chance. "Music of Changes" must be performed according to its written score, just like any Beethoven piano sonata, and Burroughs's cut-up texts must be read in linear order, like any Dickens novel, though of course the experiences of the respective audiences will differ. In intent, however, Burroughs's cut-ups share with Cage's later "parametric" works an imperative di-

rected at the performer and the audience to take active part in the production of music and writing.

32. Burroughs, "Origin and Theory of the Tape Cut-Ups" on *Break Through in Grey Room.*

33. Public Enemy, on their album *It Takes a Nation of Millions to Hold Us Back.*

34. Lyrics contained in liner notes to Public Enemy, *It Takes a Nation of Millions.*

35. For a full theoretical explanation of this kind of antagonism, see Jean-François Lyotard's *The Differend: Phrases in Dispute,* 10, 12–13.

36. This line opens "Ineffect," the overture to Material's album *Seven Souls.*

37. Burroughs, "Face to Face with the Goat God" from *Oui* 2.8 (August 1973), quoted in Burroughs, liner notes to *Apocalypse Across the Sky.*

38. The track "Midnight Sunrise" on *Dancing in Your Head* is the only piece Coleman's record companies have seen fit to release of his three-day session with the Master Musicians.

39. On Schönberg's retreat, see Pierre Boulez, "Schönberg is Dead" in *Stocktakings from an Apprenticeship,* 209–14.

40. Ornette Coleman quoted in Robert Palmer et al., liner notes to *Beauty is a Rare Thing: Ornette Coleman—The Complete Atlantic Recordings,* 49.

41. The recording and release of *The Elvis of Letters,* Gus Van Sant's EP of songs constructed around looped samples of Burroughs's readings, predates *Seven Souls,* but *Elvis* is less than a direct collaboration because Van Sant used previously recorded readings as the source of his samples, while Laswell recorded Burroughs specifically for the Material album. *Seven Souls,* released internationally by Virgin Records, also reached a much wider audience than *Elvis,* on Portland-based T.K. Records, did.

42. Tom Waits, liner notes to *The Black Rider.*

43. Burroughs, "Grandpa from Hell" interview in the *LA Weekly* 19–25 July 1996: 24.

44. See Deleuze and Guattari, *Anti-Oedipus* 244–47, 251–55.

Works Cited

Adams, Henry. *The Education of Henry Adams*. 1918. Ed. Ernest Samuels. Boston: Houghton Mifflin, 1973.

Adorno, Theodor W. *Aesthetic Theory*. 1970. Trans. C. Lenhardt. New York: Routledge & Kegan Paul, 1984.

———. *Minima Moralia*. 1951. Trans. E F. N. Jephcott. New York: Verso, 1974.

———. *Negative Dialectics*. 1966. Trans. E. B. Ashton. New York: Continuum, 1973.

Almereyda, Michael, dir. *Twister*. Videocassette. Vestron Pictures Video, 1989.

Althusser, Louis. *Lenin and Philosophy*. Trans. Ben Brewster. New York: Monthly Review, 1971.

Anderson, Laurie. *Home of the Brave*. CD. Warner Bros., 1987.

———. *Mister Heartbreak*. CD. Warner Bros., 1985.

———. *United States Live*. 4 LPs. Warner Bros., 1984.

Anslinger, Harry J. *The Protectors: The Heroic Story of the Narcotics Agents, Citizens, and Officials in Their Unending, Unsung Battles against Organized Crime in America and Abroad*. New York: Farrar, Strauss, 1964.

Anslinger, Harry J., and William F. Tompkins. *The Traffic in Narcotics*. New York: Funk & Wagnalls, 1953.

Arshinov, Peter. *History of the Makhnovist Movement 1918–1921*. 1923. Trans. Lorraine and Fredy Perlman. Detroit: Black & Red, 1974.

Babbitt, Milton. "Philomel." Perf. Judith Bettina. *Electro Acoustic Music: Classics*. CD. Neuma, 1990.

Balestrini, Nanni. *Vogliamo tutto*. Milan: Feltrinelli, 1971.

Barth, John. *LETTERS*. New York: Putnam, 1978.

———. *Sabbatical*. New York: Putnam, 1981.

Bataille, Georges. *The Accursed Share: An Essay on General Economy*. 1967. Trans. Robert Hurley. Vol. 1. New York: Zone, 1988.

Baudrillard, Jean. *For a Critique of the Political Economy of the Sign.* 1972. Trans. Charles Levin. St. Louis: Telos Press, 1981.
———. *In the Shadow of the Silent Majorities, or the End of the Social.* Trans. Paul Foss, John Johnston, and Paul Patton. New York: Semiotext(e), 1983.
———. *The Mirror of Production.* 1973. Trans. Mark Poster. St. Louis: Telos Press, 1975.
———. *Selected Writings.* Ed. Mark Poster. Stanford: Stanford University Press, 1988.
Beckett, Samuel. *Molloy.* 1951. *Three Novels.* Trans. Samuel Beckett and Patrick Bowles. New York: Grove Press, 1959.
Benjamin, Walter. *Illuminations.* Ed. Hannah Arendt. Trans. Harry Zohn. New York: Schocken, 1968.
Benveniste, Emile. *Problems in General Linguistics.* 1966. Trans. Mary Elizabeth Meek. Coral Gables: University of Miami Press, 1971.
Berio, Luciano. "Sequenza III" for Voice. 1967. Perf. Cathy Berberian. *Luciano Berio.* CD. Wergo Schallplatten, 1991.
———. "Thema." 1958. *Electronic Music III.* LP. Turnabout Vox, n.d.
Berman, Marshall. *All That Is Solid Melts into Air: The Experience of Modernity.* 1982. New York: Penguin, 1988.
Bérubé, Michael. *Marginal Forces/Cultural Centers.* Ithaca: Cornell University Press, 1992.
Black, Jack. *You Can't Win: The Autobiography of Jack Black.* 1926. Foreword by William S. Burroughs. New York: Amok Press, 1988.
Blair, David, dir. *Wax, or the Discovery of Television Among the Bees.* Videocassette. First Run Features, 1993.
Bogue, Ronald. "Gilles Deleuze: Postmodern Philosopher?" *Criticism: A Quarterly for Literature and the Arts* 32.4 (Fall 1990): 401–18.
Borges, Jorge Luis. *Ficciones.* 1956. Ed. Anthony Kerrigan. New York: Grove, 1962.
Boulez, Pierre. *Stocktakings from an Apprenticeship.* Comp. Paule Thévenin. 1966. Trans. Stephen Walsh. Oxford: Clarendon Press, 1991.
Boundas, Constantin V., and Dorothea Olkowski, eds. *Gilles Deleuze and the Theater of Philosophy.* New York: Routledge, 1994.
Braidotti, Rosi. *Patterns of Dissonance: A Study of Women in Contemporary Philosophy.* Translated by Elizabeth Guild. New York: Routledge, 1991.
Brookner, Howard, dir. *Burroughs.* 1980. Videocassette. Giorno Video, 1985.
Buckley, Jorunn J. "The Nizârî Ismâ'îlîtes' Abolishment of the Sharî'a During the 'Great Resurrection' of 1164 A.D./559 A.H." *Studia Islamica* 60 (1984): 137–65.
Budge, E. A. Wallis. *The Book of the Dead.* 1899. New York: Penguin, 1989.
———. *The Egyptian Book of the Dead: The Papyrus of Ani—Egyptian Text, Transliteration and Translation.* 1895. New York: Dover, 1967.
Burroughs, William S. *The Adding Machine: Selected Essays.* 1985. New York: Seaver, 1986.
———. "Afterthoughts on a Deposition," new introduction to *Naked Lunch.* London: Paladin, 1992. 15.

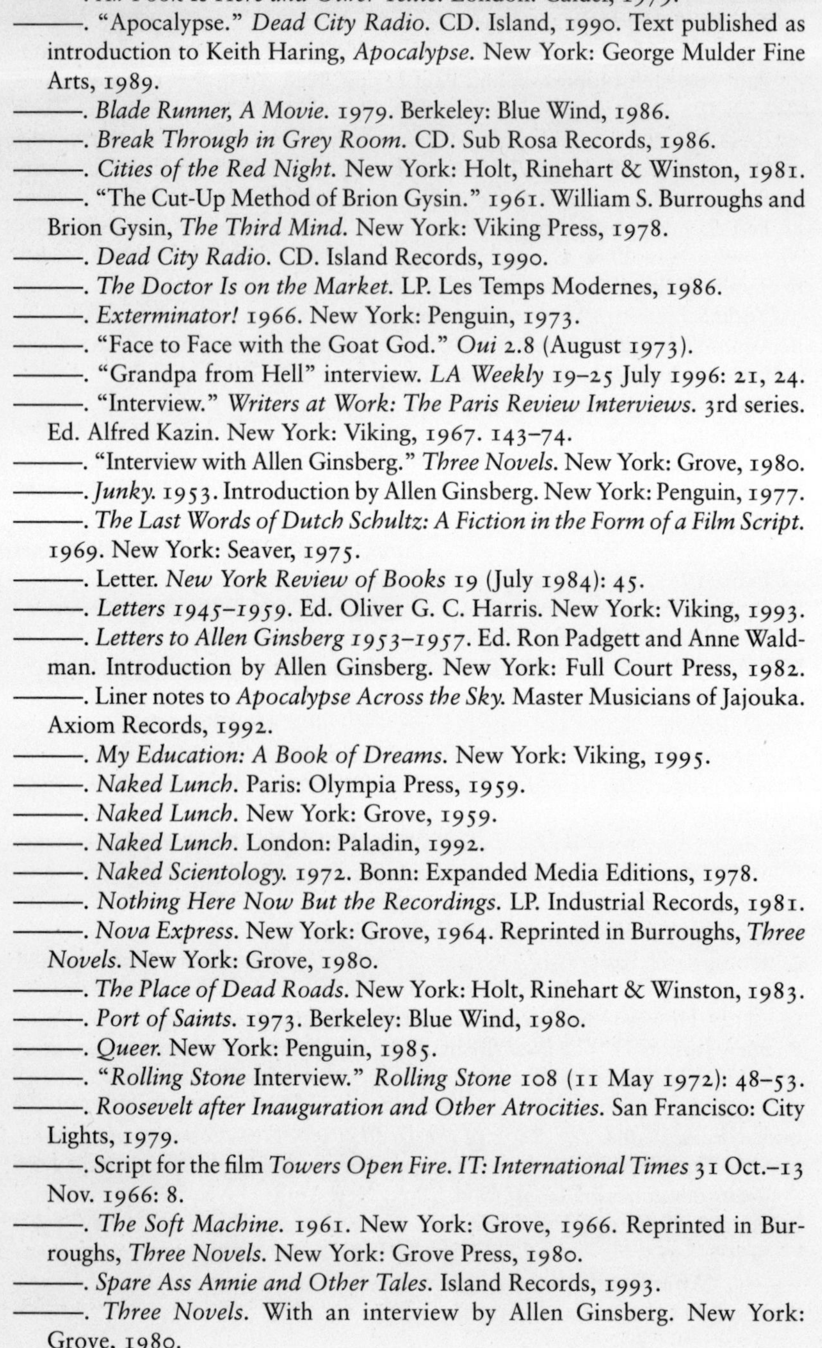

———. *Ah Pook Is Here and Other Texts.* London: Calder, 1979.

———. "Apocalypse." *Dead City Radio.* CD. Island, 1990. Text published as introduction to Keith Haring, *Apocalypse.* New York: George Mulder Fine Arts, 1989.

———. *Blade Runner, A Movie.* 1979. Berkeley: Blue Wind, 1986.

———. *Break Through in Grey Room.* CD. Sub Rosa Records, 1986.

———. *Cities of the Red Night.* New York: Holt, Rinehart & Winston, 1981.

———. "The Cut-Up Method of Brion Gysin." 1961. William S. Burroughs and Brion Gysin, *The Third Mind.* New York: Viking Press, 1978.

———. *Dead City Radio.* CD. Island Records, 1990.

———. *The Doctor Is on the Market.* LP. Les Temps Modernes, 1986.

———. *Exterminator!* 1966. New York: Penguin, 1973.

———. "Face to Face with the Goat God." *Oui* 2.8 (August 1973).

———. "Grandpa from Hell" interview. *LA Weekly* 19–25 July 1996: 21, 24.

———. "Interview." *Writers at Work: The Paris Review Interviews.* 3rd series. Ed. Alfred Kazin. New York: Viking, 1967. 143–74.

———. "Interview with Allen Ginsberg." *Three Novels.* New York: Grove, 1980.

———. *Junky.* 1953. Introduction by Allen Ginsberg. New York: Penguin, 1977.

———. *The Last Words of Dutch Schultz: A Fiction in the Form of a Film Script.* 1969. New York: Seaver, 1975.

———. Letter. *New York Review of Books* 19 (July 1984): 45.

———. *Letters 1945–1959.* Ed. Oliver G. C. Harris. New York: Viking, 1993.

———. *Letters to Allen Ginsberg 1953–1957.* Ed. Ron Padgett and Anne Waldman. Introduction by Allen Ginsberg. New York: Full Court Press, 1982.

———. Liner notes to *Apocalypse Across the Sky.* Master Musicians of Jajouka. Axiom Records, 1992.

———. *My Education: A Book of Dreams.* New York: Viking, 1995.

———. *Naked Lunch.* Paris: Olympia Press, 1959.

———. *Naked Lunch.* New York: Grove, 1959.

———. *Naked Lunch.* London: Paladin, 1992.

———. *Naked Scientology.* 1972. Bonn: Expanded Media Editions, 1978.

———. *Nothing Here Now But the Recordings.* LP. Industrial Records, 1981.

———. *Nova Express.* New York: Grove, 1964. Reprinted in Burroughs, *Three Novels.* New York: Grove, 1980.

———. *The Place of Dead Roads.* New York: Holt, Rinehart & Winston, 1983.

———. *Port of Saints.* 1973. Berkeley: Blue Wind, 1980.

———. *Queer.* New York: Penguin, 1985.

———. "*Rolling Stone* Interview." *Rolling Stone* 108 (11 May 1972): 48–53.

———. *Roosevelt after Inauguration and Other Atrocities.* San Francisco: City Lights, 1979.

———. Script for the film *Towers Open Fire. IT: International Times* 31 Oct.–13 Nov. 1966: 8.

———. *The Soft Machine.* 1961. New York: Grove, 1966. Reprinted in Burroughs, *Three Novels.* New York: Grove Press, 1980.

———. *Spare Ass Annie and Other Tales.* Island Records, 1993.

———. *Three Novels.* With an interview by Allen Ginsberg. New York: Grove, 1980.

———. *The Ticket That Exploded.* 1962. New York: Grove Press, 1967.
———. *Vaudeville Voices.* CD. Grey Matter, 1993.
———. *The Western Lands.* New York: Viking, 1987.
———. *The Wild Boys: A Book of the Dead.* 1969. New York: Grove, 1971. Reprinted in Burroughs, *Three Novels.* New York: Grove, 1980.
Burroughs, William S., and Antony Balch. *Towers Open Fire and Other Short Films.* 1963–69. Videocassette. Mystic Fire Video, 1990.
———. , adapt. *Witchcraft Through the Ages (Häxan).* Videocassette. MPI Video, 1992.
Burroughs, William S., and Victor Bockris. *With William Burroughs: A Report from the Bunker.* New York: Seaver Books, 1980.
Burroughs, William S., and Kurt Cobain. *The "Priest" They Called Him.* CD. Tim/Kerr Records, 1993.
Burroughs, William S., and Brion Gysin. *The Third Mind.* New York: Viking Press, 1978.
Burroughs, William S., Brion Gysin, Sinclair Beiles, and Gregory Corso. *Minutes To Go.* Paris: Two Cities Editions, 1960.
Burroughs, William S., and Eric Mottram. *Snack . . . Two Tape Transcripts.* London: Aloes Books, 1975.
Burroughs, William S., and Daniel Odier. *The Job: Interviews.* 1969. Rev. ed. New York: Grove, 1974.
Burroughs, William S., and R.E.M. "Star Me Kitten." *Songs in the Key of X.* CD. Warner Bros., 1996.
Burroughs, William S., and Gus Van Sant. *The Elvis of Letters.* CD. T. K. Records, 1985.
———. *Thanksgiving Prayer.* 1990. Videocassette. Island Video, 1991.
Carson, Luke. *The Public Trust: Consumption and Depression in Gertrude Stein, Louis Zukofsky and Ezra Pound.* London: Macmillan, forthcoming.
Carter, Angela. *The Sadeian Woman and the Ideology of Pornography.* New York: Pantheon, 1978.
Caute, David. *The Great Fear: The Anti-Communist Purge under Truman and Eisenhower.* New York: Simon & Schuster, 1978.
———. *The Year of the Barricades: A Journey through 1968.* New York: Harper & Row, 1988.
Chauncey, George. *Gay New York: Gender, Urban Culture, and the Making of the Gay Male World 1890–1940.* New York: Basic Books, 1994.
Coleman, Ornette. *Dancing in Your Head..* CD. A&M Records, 1977.
———. Liner notes. *Naked Lunch: Music from the Original Soundtrack.* By Howard Shore and Ornette Coleman. Milan America, 1992.
Corbin, Henry. *History of Islamic Philosophy.* Trans. Liadain Sherrard and Philip Sherrard. London: Kegan Paul, 1993.
Cory, Donald W. *The Homosexual in America.* New York: Greenburg, 1951.
Cronenberg, David, dir. *Naked Lunch.* Perf. Peter Weller, Judy Davis, et al. Twentieth Century Fox, 1991.
———. *Le Scénario du "Festin nu."* Trans. Brice Matthieussent. Paris: Christian Bourgois, 1992.

Daftary, Farhad. *The Ismâ'îlîs: Their History and Doctrines.* Cambridge: Cambridge University Press, 1990.

Daniels, Robert V., ed. *A Documentary History of Communism.* 2 vols. in 1. New York: Random House, 1960.

Davis, Mike. *City of Quartz: Excavating the Future in Los Angeles.* New York: Verso, 1990.

Debray, Régis. *Teachers, Writers, Celebrities: The Intellectuals of Modern France.* 1979. Trans. David Macey. New York: Verso, 1981.

Deleuze, Gilles. *Bergsonism.* 1966. Trans. Hugh Tomlinson and Barbara Habberjam. New York: Zone, 1988.

———. *Cinema-2: The Time-Image.* 1985. Trans. Hugh Tomlinson and Robert Galeta. Minneapolis: University of Minnesota Press, 1989.

———. *Critique et clinique.* Paris: Editions de Minuit, 1993.

———. *Difference and Repetition.* 1968. Trans. Paul Patton. New York: Columbia University Press, 1994.

———. *Empiricism and Subjectivity: An Essay on Hume's Theory of Human Nature.* 1953. Trans. Constantin V. Boundas. New York: Columbia University Press, 1991.

———. *Foucault.* 1986. Trans. Seán Hand. Minneapolis: University of Minnesota Press, 1988. Foreword by Paul Bové.

———. *Francis Bacon: Logique de la sensation.* 2 vols. Paris: Editions de la Différence, 1981. Translation by Daniel W. Smith forthcoming.

———. "The Intellectual and Politics: Foucault and the Prison." *History of the Present* 2 (Spring 1986): 1–2, 20–21.

———. *Kant's Critical Philosophy: The Doctrine of the Faculties.* 1963. Trans. Hugh Tomlinson and Barbara Habberjam. Minneapolis: University of Minnesota Press, 1984.

———. Letter to the author. 26 March 1991.

———. *The Logic of Sense.* 1969. Trans. Mark Lester with Charles Stivale. Ed. Constantin V. Boundas. New York: Columbia University Press, 1990.

———. *Negotiations* 1972–1990. 1990. Trans. Martin Joughin. New York: Columbia University Press, 1995.

———. "Philosophie de la Série noire." *Arts & Loisirs* 18 (26 Jan.–1 Feb. 1966): 12–13. Reprinted in *Roman* 24 (Sept. 1988): 43–47.

———. "Préface" to Guy Hocquenghem, *L'Après-mai des faunes: Volutions.* Paris: Grasset, 1974. 7–17.

Deleuze, Gilles, and Michel Foucault. "Intellectuals and Power." 1972. Michel Foucault, *Language, Counter-Memory, Practice.* Ed. and trans. Donald F. Bouchard. Ithaca: Cornell University Press, 1977. 205–17.

Deleuze, Gilles, and Félix Guattari. *Anti-Oedipus.* Vol. 1 of *Capitalism and Schizophrenia.* 1972. Trans. Robert Hurley, Mark Seem, and Helen R. Lane. New York: Viking, 1977.

———. *Kafka: Toward a Minor Literature.* 1975. Trans. Dana Polan. Minneapolis: University of Minnesota Press, 1986.

———. *A Thousand Plateaus:* Vol. 2 of *Capitalism and Schizophrenia..* 1980. Trans. Brian Massumi. Minneapolis: University of Minnesota Press, 1987.

Deleuze, Gilles, and Claire Parnet. *Dialogues*. 1977. Trans. Hugh Tomlinson and Barbara Habberjam. New York: Columbia University Press, 1987.

Derrida, Jacques. *Dissemination*. 1972. Trans. Barbara Johnson. Chicago: University of Chicago Press, 1981.

———. *Writing and Difference*. 1967. Trans. Alan Bass. Chicago: University of Chicago Press, 1978.

Duchamp, Marcel, dir. *Anémic Cinéma*. 1926.

Dutka, Elaine. "The Lunches Won't Be Naked." *Los Angeles Times* Calendar Section, 7 Feb. 1993: 7, 28–30.

Dworkin, Andrea. *Pornography: Men Possessing Women*. 1979. New York: Plume, 1989.

Eisenstein, Sergei, dir. *Battleship Potemkin*. 1925.

Eliot, T. S. *Collected Poems 1909–1962*. New York: Harcourt Brace Jovanovich, 1970.

———. "*Ulysses*, Order, and Myth." *The Dial* 75 (Nov. 1923): 480–83.

Ellison, Ralph. *Invisible Man*. 1947. New York: Vintage, 1952.

Ellmann, Richard. *James Joyce*. 1959. Rev. ed. New York: Oxford University Press, 1982.

Evans-Wentz, W. Y., comp. and ed. *The Tibetan Book of the Dead*. Trans. Lama Kazi Dawa-Samdup. 3rd ed. Forewords by C. G. Jung, Lama Anagarika Govinda, and Sir John Woodroffe. New York: Oxford University Press, 1960.

Fabian, Johannes. *Time and the Other: How Anthropology Makes Its Object*. New York: Columbia University Press, 1983.

Feyerabend, Paul. *Against Method*. 1975. 3rd ed. New York: Verso, 1993.

Fiedler, Leslie. "The New Mutants." *Partisan Review* 32.4 (Fall 1965): 505–25.

Finley, Karen. *Moral History*. 1994; recreated 1996. Collection of the artist.

Foster, Hal, ed. *The Anti-Aesthetic: Essays on Postmodern Culture*. Port Townsend, WA: Bay Press, 1983.

Foucault, Michel. *Discipline and Punish: The Birth of the Prison*. 1975. Trans. Alan Sheridan. New York: Vintage, 1977.

———. *The History of Sexuality*. 3 vols. 1977–1984. Trans. Robert Hurley. New York: Vintage, 1978–86.

———. *The Order of Things: An Archaeology of the Human Sciences*. 1965. [No translator listed.] New York: Vintage, 1967.

———. *Politics, Philosophy, Culture: Interviews and Other Writings 1977–1984*. Ed. Lawrence D. Kritzman. New York: Routledge, 1988.

———. *Power/Knowledge: Selected Interviews and Other Writings 1972–1977*. Ed. and trans. Colin Gordon. New York: Pantheon, 1980.

Fourier, Charles. *The Utopian Vision of Charles Fourier*. Trans. and ed. Jonathan Beecher and Richard Bienvenu. Boston: Beacon, 1971.

Gilbert, Sandra, and Susan Gubar. *No Man's Land: The Place of the Woman Writer in the Twentieth Century*. Vol. 1. *War of the Words*. New Haven: Yale University Press, 1988.

———. *No Man's Land: The Place of the Woman Writer in the Twentieth Century*. Vol. 3. *Letters from the Front*. New Haven: Yale University Press, 1994.

Ginsberg, Allen. *Collected Poems 1947–1980*. New York: Harper & Row, 1984.

———. *Holy Soul Jelly Roll*. 4 CDs. Rhino Word Beat, 1994.

———. *The Lion for Real.* CD. Island Records, 1990.

———. "Recollections of Burroughs Letters" in Burroughs, *Letters to Allen Ginsberg* 1953–1957. New York: Full Court Press, 1982. 5–10.

Glass, Philip, with Allen Ginsberg. *Hydrogen Jukebox.* CD. Nonesuch Records, 1993.

Goodman, Michael B. *Contemporary Literary Censorship: The Case History of Burroughs' Naked Lunch.* Metuchen, NJ: Scarecrow Press, 1981.

Grauerholz, James. "On Burroughs' Art." William S. Burroughs, *Painting.* Amsterdam: Suzanne Biederberg Gallery, 1988.

Griffiths, Paul. *Modern Music: A Concise History from Debussy to Boulez.* New York: Thames & Hudson, 1978.

Guattari, Félix. "The Postmodern Dead End." Trans. Nancy Blake. *Flash Art* 128 (May/June 1986): 147–48.

Gysin, Brion, and Terry Wilson. *Here to Go: Planet R-101.* London: Quartet, 1982.

Habermas, Jürgen. "Modernity—An Incomplete Project." Trans. Seyla Ben-Habib. *The Anti-Aesthetic: Essays on Postmodern Culture.* Ed. Hal Foster. Port Townsend, WA: Bay Press, 1983. 3–15.

Hardt, Michael. *Gilles Deleuze: An Apprenticeship in Philosophy.* Minneapolis: University of Minnesota Press, 1993.

———. "Los Angeles Novos." *Futur antérieur* 12–13, no. 4–5 (1992): 12–26.

Hardt, Michael, and Antonio Negri. *Labor of Dionysus: A Critique of the State-Form.* Minneapolis: University of Minnesota Press, 1994.

Hegel, G. W. F. *Philosophy of Right.* 1821. Trans. T. M. Knox. Oxford: Oxford University Press, 1952.

Henry, Pierre. "Variations pour une Porte et un Soupir." 1963. *Variations pour une Porte et un Soupir/Voile d'Orphée.* CD. Harmonia Mundi France, 1987.

Hilfer, Anthony Channell. "Mariner and Wedding Guest in William Burroughs' *Naked Lunch.*" *Criticism* 22 (1980): 252–65.

Hodgson, Marshall G. S. *The Order of Assassins: The Struggle of the Early Nizârî Ismâ'îlîs against the Islamic World.* The Hague: Mouton, 1955.

Horkheimer, Max, and Theodor W. Adorno. *Dialectic of Enlightenment.* 1944. Trans. John Cumming. New York: Continuum, 1972.

Jagger, Mick. "Memo from Turner." *Performance: Original Motion Picture Soundtrack.* LP. Warner Bros., 1969.

Jakobson, Roman. *Selected Writings.* Vol. 2. *Word and Language.* The Hague: Mouton, 1971.

Jambet, Christian. *La grande résurrection d'Alamût: Les formes de la liberté dans le shî'isme ismaélien.* Lagrasse, France: Verdier, 1990.

Jameson, Fredric. *Marxism and Form: Twentieth Century Dialectical Theories of Literature.* Princeton: Princeton University Press, 1971.

———. *Postmodernism, or, The Cultural Logic of Late Capitalism.* Durham: Duke University Press, 1991.

Jardine, Alice A. *Gynesis: Configurations of Woman and Modernity.* Ithaca: Cornell University Press, 1985.

Jarman, Derek. *The Dream Machine.* Independent film, 1984.

———. *Pirate Tape.* Independent film, 1982.

Jay, Martin. *Marxism and Totality: The Adventures of a Concept from Lukács to Habermas*. Berkeley: University of California Press, 1984.
Joyce, James. *Portable Joyce*. 1974. Ed. Harry Levin. New York: Viking, 1975.
———. *Ulysses*. 1922. New York: Vintage, 1961. Prefatory materials by Morris L. Ernst, John Woolsey, and James Joyce.
Kazin, Alfred. *Bright Book of Life: American Novelists and Storytellers from Hemingway to Mailer.* New York: Dell, 1973.
Koestenbaum, Wayne. "Vagabond Blues." Review of George Chauncey's *Gay New York: Gender, Urban Culture and the Making of the Gay Male World 1890–1940*). *Los Angeles Times Book Review* 7 Aug. 1994: 2, 13.
The Koran. Trans. with notes by N. J. Dawood. New York: Penguin, 1974.
Krich, A.M., ed. *The Homosexuals As Seen by Themselves and Thirty Authorities*. New York: Citadel Press, 1954.
Kristeva, Julia. *Revolution in Poetic Language*. 1974. Trans. Margaret Waller. New York: Columbia University Press, 1984.
Latour, Bruno. *We Have Never Been Modern*. 1991. Trans. Catherine Porter. Cambridge: Harvard University Press, 1993.
Leitch, Vincent B. *Deconstructive Criticism: An Advanced Introduction*. New York: Columbia University Press, 1983.
Litweiler, John. *Ornette Coleman: A Harmolodic Life*. New York: William Morrow, 1992.
Lotringer, Sylvère, ed. *Italy: Autonomia—Post-Political Politics*. Special issue of *Semiotext(e)* (1980).
Luhmann, Niklas. *Essays on Self-Reference*. New York: Columbia University Press, 1990.
Lukács, Georg. *History and Class Consciousness*. 1967. Trans. Rodney Livingstone. Cambridge: MIT Press, 1971.
Lydenberg, Robin. *Word Cultures: Radical Theory and Practice in William S. Burroughs' Fiction*. Urbana: University of Illinois Press, 1987.
Lyotard, Jean-François. *The Differend: Phrases in Dispute*. 1983. Trans. Georges Van Den Abbeele. Minneapolis: University of Minnesota Press, 1988.
———. *The Postmodern Condition: A Report on Knowledge*. 1979. Trans. Geoff Bennington and Brian Massumi. Minneapolis: University of Minnesota Press, 1984.
———. *The Postmodern Explained*. 1988. Trans. Julian Pefanis, Morgan Thomas et al. Minneapolis: University of Minnesota Press, 1992.
Lyotard, Jean-François, and Jean-Loup Thébaud. *Just Gaming*. 1979. Trans. Wlad Godzich. Minneapolis: University of Minnesota Press, 1985.
Maas, Peter. *The Valachi Papers*. New York: Putnam, 1968.
Maeck, Klaus, dir. *Commissioner of Sewers*. 1984. Videocassette. Mystic Fire Video, 1991.
Mailer, Norman. *Ancient Evenings*. Boston: Little, Brown, 1983.
———. *Miami and the Siege of Chicago*. New York: Random House, 1969.
Makaryk, Irena, ed. *Encyclopedia of Contemporary Literary Theory.* Toronto: University of Toronto Press, 1993.
Marcuse, Herbert. *One-Dimensional Man*. Boston: Beacon, 1964.

Marx, Karl. *Capital: A Critique of Political Economy.* Vol. 1. 1867. Trans. Ben Fowkes. New York: Vintage, 1976.

———. *Capital: A Critique of Political Economy.* Vol. 3. Ed. Frederick Engels. 1894. [No translator listed.] New York: International Publishers, 1967.

———. *Early Writings.* Trans. Rodney Livingstone and Gregor Benton. New York: Penguin, 1974.

———. *The Eighteenth Brumaire of Louis Bonaparte.* 1869. Marx and Frederick Engels. Vol. 1 of *Selected Works.* [No translator listed.] New York: International Publishers, 1963. 243–344.

———. *Grundrisse: Foundations of the Critique of Political Economy (Rough Draft).* Trans. Martin Nicolaus. Harmondsworth: Penguin, 1973.

Marx, Karl, and Frederick Engels. *Manifesto of the Communist Party. Selected Works.* Vol. 1. [No translator listed.] New York: International Publishers, 1963. 21–65.

Master Musicians of Jajouka featuring Bachir Attar. *Apocalypse across the Sky.* Liner notes by William S. Burroughs and Brion Gysin. CD. Axiom Records, 1992.

Material. *Hallucination Engine.* CD. Axiom Records, 1993.

———. *Seven Souls.* CD. Virgin Records, 1989.

Mathews, Peter. *The Proceedings of the Maya Hieroglyphic Weekend: October 27–28, 1990, Cleveland State University.* Transcr. and ed. Phil Wanyerka. Photocopy.

Miles, Barry. *William Burroughs, El Hombre Invisible: A Portrait.* New York: Virgin Books, 1992.

Miller, Jim, ed. *The Rolling Stone Illustrated History of Rock & Roll.* 1976. New York: Random House, 1980.

Millett, Kate. *Sexual Politics.* 1969. Garden City: Doubleday, 1970.

Ministry. *Just One Fix.* CD. Sire, 1992.

———. *Just One Fix.* Videocassette. Sire Video, 1992.

Monroe, Malcolm. "Fighting Drug Addiction: The 'Clinic Plan'." *Western World* 2.10 (October 1959): 45–48.

Morgan, Ted. *Literary Outlaw: The Life and Times of William S. Burroughs.* New York: Henry Holt, 1988.

Mottram, Eric. *William Burroughs: The Algebra of Need.* London: Marion Boyars, 1977.

Murphy, Timothy S. "The Theater of (the Philosophy of) Cruelty in Gilles Deleuze's *Difference and Repetition.*" *PLI: Warwick Journal of Philosophy* 4.1–2 (1992): 105–35.

———. "William Burroughs between Indifference and Revalorization: Notes Toward a Political Reading." *Angelaki* 1.1 (1993): 113–24.

Nabokov, Vladimir. *Pale Fire.* New York: Vintage, 1962.

Negri, Antonio. "On Gilles Deleuze & Félix Guattari, *A Thousand Plateaus.*" 1992. Trans. Charles T. Wolfe. *Graduate Faculty Philosophy Journal* 18.1 (1995): 93–109.

———. *The Politics of Subversion: A Manifesto for the Twenty-First Century.* Trans. James Newell. Cambridge: Polity, 1989.

———. "Spinoza's Anti-Modernity." 1991. Trans. Charles T. Wolfe. *Graduate Faculty Philosophy Journal* 18.2 (1995): 1–15.

Nietzsche, Friedrich. *The Will to Power.* Trans. Walter Kaufmann and R. J. Hollingdale. New York: Vintage, 1967.

Nike Corporation. Print/billboard advertisements for Nike Air Max² (3). Slogans by Jean Rhode. Summer/fall 1994.

———. Television advertisements for Nike Air Max² (5). Scripts by Jean Rhode. Summer/fall 1994.

Ockham, William. *Philosophical Writings.* Ed. and trans. Philotheus Boehner. New York: Nelson, 1957.

Oshinsky, David M. *A Conspiracy So Immense: The World of Joe McCarthy.* New York: Free Press, 1983.

Palmer, Robert, et al. Liner notes to *Beauty Is a Rare Thing: Ornette Coleman—The Complete Atlantic Recordings.* Rhino/Atlantic Jazz Gallery, 1993.

Phillips, Tom. *A Humument.* Rev. ed. London: Thames & Hudson, 1987.

Plato. *Collected Dialogues.* Ed. Edith Hamilton and Huntington Cairns. Princeton: Bollingen, 1961.

Popper, Karl. *The Open Society and Its Enemies.* 2 vols. 1966. Princeton: Princeton University Press, 1971.

Public Enemy. *It Takes a Nation of Millions to Hold Us Back.* Def Jam, 1988.

Reed, Ishmael. *Conjure: Music for the Texts of Ishmael Reed.* Perf. Carla Bley, Lester Bowie, Taj Mahal, Allen Toussaint, et al. American Clavé, 1984.

Reich, Wilhelm. *The Function of the Orgasm.* 1947. Trans. Vincent R. Carfagno. New York: Farrar, Straus & Giroux, 1973.

Richter, Hans. *Dada: Art and Anti-Art.* Trans. David Britt. New York: Oxford University Press, 1965.

Rooks, Conrad, dir. *Chappaqua.* Independent film, 1966.

Russ, Joanna. *The Female Man.* Boston: Beacon, 1975.

Sartre, Jean-Paul. *Critique of Dialectical Reason.* Vol. 1. 1960. Trans. Alan Sheridan-Smith. Ed. Jonathan Rée. New York: New Left Books, 1976.

Saussure, Ferdinand de. *Course in General Linguistics.* Ed. Charles Bally et al. 1915. Trans. Wade Baskin. New York: McGraw-Hill, 1966.

Schwitters, Kurt. *Ursonate.* 1922–1932. CD. Wergo Schallplatten, 1993.

Sedgwick, Eve Kosofsky. *Epistemology of the Closet.* Berkeley: University of California Press, 1990.

Shore, Howard, and Ornette Coleman. *Naked Lunch: Music from the Original Soundtrack.* CD. Milan America, 1992.

Silverberg, Ira, ed. *Everything Is Permitted: The Making of "Naked Lunch."* London: Grafton, 1992.

Sitney, P. Adams. *Visionary Film: The American Avant-Garde* 1943–1978. 2nd ed. Oxford: Oxford University Press, 1974, 1979.

Skerl, Jennie. *William S. Burroughs.* Boston: Twayne, 1985.

Skerl, Jennie, and Robin Lydenberg, eds. *William S. Burroughs at the Front: Critical Reception 1959–1989.* Carbondale: Southern Illinois University Press, 1991.

Sobieszek, Robert. *Ports of Entry: William S. Burroughs and the Arts.* New York: Thames and Hudson/LACMA, 1996.

Stockhausen, Karlheinz. "Gesang der Jünglinge." 1955–1956. *Gesang der Jünglinge/Kontakte*. LP. Deutsche Grammophon Gesellschaft, n.d.
10,000 Maniacs. *In My Tribe*. CD. Elektra Records, 1987.
"Tornado." *Beavis and Butthead*. Created by Mike Judge. MTV. 10 Sept. 1993.
Tytell, John. *Naked Angels: The Lives and Literature of the Beat Generation*. New York: Grove, 1976.
Van Sant, Gus, dir. *Drugstore Cowboy*. Avenue Pictures/IVE Inc., 1989.
———. *My Own Private Idaho*. New Line Cinema, 1991.
Velvet Underground. *Loaded*. CD. Cotillion Records, 1970.
Vilà, Christian. *William S. Burroughs: Le génie empoisonné*. Monaco: Editions du Rocher, 1992.
Waits, Tom. *The Black Rider*. CD. Island Records, 1993.
Ward, Ed, Geoffrey Stokes and Ken Tucker. *Rock of Ages: The Rolling Stone History of Rock and Roll*. New York: Summit Books, 1986.
Wittgenstein, Ludwig. *Tractatus Logico-Philosophicus*. 1922. Trans. C. K. Ogden. Introduction by Bertrand Russell. New York: Routledge, 1933.
Wittig, Monique. *Les Guérillères*. 1969. Trans. David Le Vay. Boston: Beacon, 1971.
Working-Class Autonomy and the Crisis. London: Red Notes/CSE, 1979.
Žižek, Slavoj. *The Sublime Object of Ideology*. New York: Verso, 1989.

Index

Academic community, on Burroughs, 3–4, 8, 67, 72, 241n11
Acker, Kathy, 3, 15
Adams, Henry, 18–19
Addict-agents. *See* Informers
Addiction. *See* Drug addiction
Adorno, Theodor W., 4, 17, 82, 93–94, 96–97, 242n20, 243–44n26; Burroughs's ties to, 77–78, 87, 242n18; exile of, 76, 77; on mass media, 89, 90
African Americans, 93–94, 228
Afterlife beliefs. *See* Immortality
Against Method (Feyerabend), 237n16
Ah Pook Is Here and Other Texts (Burroughs), 140, 159, 250–51n20
Alamout (*Alamût*) legend, 121–23, 247n26
Alcoholism, 53
Ali's Smile (recorded reading), 202, 253n5
Almereyda, Michael, 202
Althusser, Louis, 74, 77
Amodernism, 23–25, 32–34, 236n7; as alternative to (post)modernism, 2–3, 25, 29, 236n9
Ancient Evenings (Mailer), 191
Anderson, Laurie, 202–3
Anémic-Cinéma (film), 207, 209
Anslinger, Harry J., 239n8
Anthropology, 20, 47, 235n5, 243n23
The Anti-Aesthetic (Foster), 236n9
Anti-Oedipus (Deleuze and Guattari): on "body without organs," 97–98; peripheral totalization models of, 36–38, 191; subject-group fantasy of, 40–42, 149–50, 152–53, 173, 237nn21,22, 250nn14,15; subject group of, 40, 151–52; subjugated group of, 39, 150–51. *See also* Deleuze, Gilles
Anti-Semitism, 54–55, 92–95
Apocalypse. *See* Qiyâma
"Apocalypse" (Burroughs), 6
Apomorphine, 131
Art, 6–7, 74, 88–89, 100–101, 220; fantasmatic function of, 6–7, 42–43, 44–45, 66, 170
Assassin (*hashîshiyyûn*): of Hassan i Sabbah, 122–23
Autonomia movement, 33

Babbitt, Milton, 217, 218
"Babylon Lottery" (Borges), 187–88
Balch, Antony: film collaborations with, 202, 206, 208–15
Balestrini, Nanni, 188
Bardo Thödol. *See* Tibetan book of the dead
Barth, John, 23, 235n6
Barthes, Roland, 72
Bastille, the: and group fantasy, 40–41, 151, 152, 172–73
Bataille, Georges, 38, 237n20
Bâtin. See *Zâhir/bâtin* doctrine
Baudrillard, Jean, 2, 17–18, 43, 68, 96
Beat Generation, 11–12, 141
Beavis and Butthead (MTV program), 226–27
Beckett, Samuel, 239n9, 244n3, 247n33
Beiles, Sinclair, 103

Being and Nothingness (Sartre), 39, 151
Bergman, Ingmar, 163
Berio, Luciano, 217, 218
Big Table, 240n1
Bill and Tony (film), 202, 206–7, 208–10, 230, 254n18
Black, Jack, 185
The Black Rider: The Casting of the Magic Bullets (Apel and Laun), 227–28
Blade Runner, A Movie (Burroughs), 205, 253n14
Blair, David, 202
Bloom, Harold, 206
"Body without organs," 97–98. *See also* Revolutionary resistance
Bogue, Ronald, 237n17
Books of the dead, 147–49, 153–56, 164, 174.. *See also* Egyptian Book of the Dead; *The Wild Boys: A Book of the Dead*
Borges, Jorge Luis, 44, 187–88
Boulez, Pierre, 218
Bouthoul, B., 245–46n20
Bouttel, Betty, 245–46n20
Bowles, Jane, 69
Brakhage, Stan, 205, 206
Brave New World (Huxley), 83
Break Through in Grey Room (album), 202, 216, 217, 218–19, 223
Bright Book of Life (Kazin), 142
Brookner, Howard, 202
Brown, Earle, 218
Buckley, Jorunn J., 127
Buddhism, 154
Budge, E. A. Wallis, 149, 157, 250n13
Bureaucracy. *See* Capitalist system
Burroughs (film), 202
Burroughs, William S.: on addiction, 8, 234n11, 242n20, 250n17; anthropology interest of, 47, 83, 243n23; on biologic law, 247–48n37; and Church of Scientology, 115–16; on creation of characters, 252n9; exile of, 76–77, 242n17; on genius, 65, 240n18; and Ginsberg, 144, 249n6; and Hasan-i Sabbâh, 119, 245–46n20; on homosexuality, 60, 61, 159, 239nn12,13, 243–44n26; Marxist ties of, 74–75, 76, 77; mass media presence of, 202–4, 232, 253nn3,5, 253nn6,9; on Maya codices, 153, 250n16; misogynist reputation of, 9, 14, 147; music influences on, 222–24; on *Naked Lunch's* title, 77–78; Nazism experience of, 54–55; in Nike advertisement, 228–32; on *Nova* trilogy's organization, 108, 244–45n5; protofeminist function of, 14–15; on speech-silence relation, 239n9; and student movements, 141, 146–47, 167, 168, 169; and wife's death, 12, 13, 234n14
Burroughs, William S., films of: Balch's collaborations on, 202, 206, 208–15; cut-ups in, 210–11, 213–16; dadaist approach of, 206–7, 254n18; double structure of, 209–10, 212–13; investigation of speech in, 207–9; Sitney's omission of, 205, 206
Burroughs, William S., works of: academic response to, 3–4, 8, 67, 72–73, 241n11; autobiographical novels, 46–47; disruption/reorganization strategies of, 4–5, 6–7; early vs. middle-period, 146–47; ellipses in, 241–42n16; experimental tapes, 216–20, 223; feminist views of, 10–12, 14–15; Kazin on, 142, 143–44; McLuhan on, 144–45; middle vs. late period, 172–74; moral denunciation of, 8–9, 75; musical collaborations, 224–28, 255n41; music as figures in, 221–22; queer theory's avoidance of, 60–62, 240n15; western narrative in, 185–86, 188, 189; women's role in, 9, 13–14, 147, 183–84. *See also* Burroughs, William S., films of; *individual works*
Butler, Samuel, 107

Cage, John, 218, 254–55n31
Cale, John, 203
Call Me Burroughs (recorded reading), 202, 253n5
Capital: A Critique of Political Economy (Marx), 29, 96
Capitalist system, 29–31, 48–50, 96–97, 100–101, 145–46, 161–62; addict's incorporation into, 75–76, 80, 84; criminality's symmetry with, 4, 55–56, 76, 112, 113; exclusionary logic of, 75, 92–95; groups as alternatives to, 32–34, 97–99, 146–47, 167–68; and law-of-value crisis, 30–32, 140; Marxist critique of, 74–75, 241n15; and peripheral totalization models, 37–38, 237n20; Reason's subordination to, 80–82, 84–86
Capital punishment, 78
Carter, Angela, 15
Castaneda, Carlos, 240n18
Catch-22 (Heller), 3
"Caught, Can We Get a Witness" (rap piece), 220–21
Censorship, 8, 67, 240nn1,2
Chandler, Raymond, 73

Chappaqua (film), 202
Chauncey, George, 240n15
Chernin, Peter, 67
Cherry, Don, 224
Chicago Review, 240n1
Chomsky, Noam, 32
Christianity. *See* Judeo-Christian doctrine
Cinema-2: The Time-Image (Deleuze), 40, 43
Cities of the Red Night (Burroughs), 5, 168, 174–75, 182–84; narrative strands of, 182, 184–85; pirate communes of, 180–82, 188–89. *See also* Late trilogy
Cloning, 87–88
Cobain, Kurt, 203, 227
Coefficients of deterritorialization, 194–96
Coleman, Ornette, 202, 223–24, 255n38
Coleridge, Samuel Taylor, 89, 243n25
Collectivities. *See* Social groups
Coming-out narrative, 60–61, 240n15
Commissioner of Sewers (film), 202
Communism, 54, 75, 92, 114, 239n8
Community: *Cities'* affirmative model of, 180–81, 182–84; *Junky's* negation of, 57–58, 239n9; of "the Market," 99; in *The Place of Dead Roads,* 186–88; *Queer's* elaboration of, 58, 65–66; schizophrenic alternative to, 190–92; undercut in *The Western Lands,* 189–90, 199. *See also* Revolutionary resistance; Social groups
Computers, 82–83
Confessions of deviance, 60, 239n12
Control, 4–5, 88, 218; Control films' routine of, 160, 161–63, 251n21; criminalization projects of, 52–54, 61–62, 63–64, 82–83, 105–6; instrumental Reason and, 80–82, 84–85; by mass-media, 89–91, 156; medical metaphor of, 81–83, 102; police's temporal patterns of, 50, 238n6; subjectivity and, 58–59. *See also* Capitalist system; Language; Law, the; Subjectivity
Cooper, David, 64
Coover, Robert, 3
Copyright law, 220–21
Corbin, Henry, 124–25, 129, 134
Corso, Gregory, 103–4
Cory, Donald W., 239n12
Criminality, 84–87; police's symmetry with, 56–57, 84, 105–6, 112
Cronenberg, David. See *Naked Lunch* (film)
Cultural asymmetry. *See* Double asymmetry
Culture Industry. *See* Mass media
Cut-up method, 5, 10–11, 103–4, 106–7, 135–36, 139–40, 206–7; to break determinist time, 138–39, 218–19; in Burroughs's films, 210–11, 213–16; in construction of meaning, 105, 215; Deleuze on, 71, 175–76; of Hassan i Sabbah's speech, 119, 246n21; musical application of, 218, 227, 254–55n31; Oxygen Impasse case and, 132–33; prophetic power of, 105–6, 218–19, 244n3. *See also* Deixis
The Cut-ups (film), 202, 206–7, 213–16, 254n18
"Cut-Ups: A Project for Disastrous Success" (Gysin), 248n40

D., Chuck, 220, 221
Dadaist films, 206–7, 254n18
Dancing in Your Head (album), 223, 255n38
Dante, 148
Darstellung: Forschung and, 79, 92. *See also* Reason
Davis, Judy, 68, 69
Dead City Radio (album), 6, 226
Deixis, 208, 214, 218, 228, 230–31
Deleuze, Gilles, 35, 56, 107, 176–78, 138–39, 194–96, 234n10, 237n17, 246n25; American-fiction interest of, 7, 233–34n8; on "body without organs," 97, 98; critical invisibility of, 2, 4, 36; on cut-up method, 71, 175–76; on "end of language," 5, 233n7; on fantasmatic function of art, 6–7, 42–45; on multiplicities, 33, 65, 79; on organic vs. crystalline narration, 43–44, 177; peripheral totalization models of, 36–38, 191, 237n19, 237n20; on simulacra, 41, 220; subject-group fantasy of, 40–42, 143, 149–50, 152–53, 173, 237nn21,22, 250nn14,15; subject-group of, 40, 151–52; subjugated group of, 39, 150–51
de Man, Paul, 206
Democratic National Convention (Chicago, 1968), 141, 154
Deren, Maya, 206
Derrida, Jacques, 35, 36, 72, 143
Detective novel, 107
Dialectic, 4–5, 60–61; of modernism and postmodernism, 1–3, 25, 26–27, 29, 236n9; negative, 28, 96–97, 100, 143; paradox vs., 56–57; of treason, 70, 113–14. *See also* Capitalist system; Control; Language; Law, the

Dialectic of Enlightenment (Horkheimer and Adorno), 4, 76, 78, 79, 96–97, 243–44n26. *See also* Adorno, Theodor W.
Difference and Repetition (Deleuze), 7
Digital sampling, 219–21
Discipline: punishment vs., 82–83. *See also* Control
Divine Comedy (Dante), 148
The Doctor is on the Market (recorded reading), 202
Doctor Sax (Kerouac), 11
Domination: reason's complicity with, 79–82, 84–86, 96–97. *See also* Capitalist system; Control
Dos Passos, John, 105
Dostoyevsky, Fyodor, 120, 246n22
Double asymmetry: as double bind, 26–27; Ellison's break with, 21–22, 25–26; modernist myth of, 19–20, 235n5
The Dream Machine (film), 204
Drop-in method, 216, 217, 219
Drug addiction: Burroughs on, 8, 234n11, 242n20, 250n17; capital's incorporation of, 75–76, 80, 84; criminalization of, 52–55, 64; Cronenberg's treatment of, 69; Horkheimer and Adorno on, 242n20; media's false generality of, 90; and negated sociability, 57–58, 239n9; and political subversion, 54, 75, 239n8
Drugstore Cowboy (film), 202
Duchamp, Marcel, 206–7, 209, 254n18
Dworkin, Andrea, 235n19
Dylan, Bob, 204

The Education of Henry Adams (Adams), 18
Egyptian Book of the Dead, 148, 153–54, 155, 157, 162, 164; and afterlife beliefs, 149, 154, 250nn12,13; on division of souls, 190–91, 252n10; phallic glyphs in, 159, 250n19. *See also* Books of the dead
Eisenstein, Sergei, 188
Electronic composition, 218
Eliot, T. S., 16–17, 18, 36, 200
Ellison, Ralph, 3–4, 18–19, 233n5. See also *Invisible Man*
Elvins, Kells, 132
The Elvis of Letters (album), 255n41
Erewhon (Butler), 107
Ernst, Morris L., 240–41n2
Esquire, 141
Everything is Permitted: The Making of "Naked Lunch" (Burroughs), 73
Exterminator! (Burroughs), 146

Fabian, Johannes, 235n5
Fagen, Donald, 203
The Fall of America (Ginsberg), 140
Fantasy, 145–47, 180–82; Kazin's narcissistic model of, 142, 143–44. *See also* Revolutionary resistance; Subject-group fantasy; Subjugated-group fantasy
Faust (Goethe), 71
The Female Man (Russ), 147
Feminist criticism, 10–12, 15
Feyerabend, Paul, 237n16
Fiction, Deleuze's theory of, 6–7, 43–45
Fiedler, Leslie, 8
Fifth Amendment, 113–14
"Fighting Drug Addiction: The 'Clinic Plan'" (Monroe), 104–5
Film, 91, 159, 215–16; biologic identity of, 136–37, 158; Control category of, 160, 161–63, 251n21; Dadaist, 206–7, 254n18; parody of Hollywood, 90–91, 163; Sitney's study of, 205, 206; Wild Boy category of, 160, 163–67, 251n22
Finley, Karen, 12, 235n15
Finnegans Wake (Joyce), 104
Flavor Flav, 220
Floating signifier, 21. *See also* Reflexive postmodernism
Forgers, 176–79
Forschung: and *Darstellung,* 79, 92. *See also* Domination
Foster, Hal, 236n9
Foucault, Michel, 32, 34, 35, 36, 42, 82, 238n6
Frankfurt School of Social Research, 76–77, 96
Franti, Michael, 226
Friedberg, Anne, 210, 213, 214
Fused group, 39–40, 151. *See also* Subject group; Subject-group fantasy

"Garden of Forking Paths" (Borges), 44
Gender dualism, 9, 14
Ghosts at No. 9 (film), 202, 213
Gilbert, Sandra, 11–12
Ginsberg, Allen, 8, 14, 87, 168, 244–45n5; on Burroughs's courtship, 144, 249n6; literary method of, 140; media presence of, 204, 253n12; on "naked lunch," 78
Giorno, John, 202
The Good, the Bad and the Ugly (Leone), 189
Gramsci, Antonio, 96
Grand Maître des Assassins (Bouthoul), 245–46n20
Great Resurrection. *See* Qiyâma

Grundrisse: Foundations of the Critique of Political Economy (Marx), 96
Guattari, Félix, 42–43, 65, 194–95, 237n17; peripheral totalization models of, 36–38, 191, 237n19, 237n20. See also *Anti-Oedipus*
Gubar, Susan, 11–12
Les Guérillères (Wittig), 147
Gynesis: Configurations of Woman and Modernity (Jardine), 10
Gysin, Brion, 9, 103, 164, 217, 241n5, 248n40, 252n15; cut-up method of, 104, 118–19; in films, 211, 213, 214; Hasan-i Sabbâh and, 117, 119, 245–46n20, 247n27; music interests of, 222, 223

Habermas, Jürgen, 25, 29
Hadîth (record of Prophet's actions), 120, 121, 124
Haqîqa (essential reality), 127, 128. See also *Zâhir/bâtin* doctrine
Haring, Keith, 6, 203
Harmolodics system, 224
Harrison Narcotics Act (1914), 52, 53
Hart, Grant, 203
Hasan II, 123–24, 125, 247nn28,29
Hasan III, 129
Hasan-i Sabbâh: Alamout legend of, 121–23; Burroughs's sources on, 119, 245–46n20, 246n21, 247n27
Hassan i Sabbah (term), 115, 116,118–20, 252n12; Burroughs's ties to, 197–98; "Last Words" of, 6, 116–18, 129–30, 138, 198
"Hauser and O'Brien" routine (*Naked Lunch*), 100–101
Hegel, G. W. F., 56
Heller, Joseph, 3
Henry, O., 227
Henry, Pierre, 217, 218
Here to Go: Planet R-101 (Gysin and Wilson), 119
Heterosexual intercourse, 183–84
"Hey Jack Kerouac" (song), 204
Historical time, 218–19, 138–39, 177–79; determinist vision of, 134–35, 171–72, 248n38, 251n1; indeterminism/contingency of, 180–81, 200
History and Class Consciousness (Lukács), 96
Hodgson, Marshall, 127, 128, 134, 245–46n20, 246n21
Hollywood film, 90–91, 163
The Homosexual in America (Cory), 239n12
Homosexuality, 8, 57–58, 61–62, 69, 183–84, 243–44n26; and dominant culture, 75–76, 90–93, 114, 229–30; and effeminacy, 60, 61, 239nn12,13; as radical and reactionary, 159–60, 166; routines' revelation of, 59–60, 239n12
The Homosexuals As Seen by Themselves and Thirty Authorities (Krich, ed.), 239n12
Horkheimer, Max, 4, 82, 93–94, 96–97, 242n20, 243n26; Burroughs's ties to, 77–78, 87; exile of, 76, 77; on mass media, 89, 90
House Un-American Activities Committee (HUAC), 52, 114
Hubbard, L. Ron, 115–16
A Humument (Phillips), 140

Ideology critique, 77–80, 143
Imâm (religious teacher), 120, 121, 123, 125–26, 129
Immortality, 193–94, 196–97, 252n12; as corporeal existence, 149, 250nn12,13; Judeo-Christian doctrine of, 148, 250n12; struggle of souls for, 190–93, 252n11. *See also* Books of the dead; Egyptian Book of the Dead
Incest, 20–21
Inching method, 216–17, 219
Informers, 114–15, 51, 56–57, 111-12, 112–13
Instrumental rationality. *See* Reason
Invisible Man (Ellison), 18–20, 21–23, 155; as alternative to (post)modernism, 1, 23–26
Invisible postmodernism. *See* Amodernism
Irigaray, Luce, 147
Islam, 124–25
Ismâʿîl, 120
Ismâʿîlîs (Ismailism), 120, 121, 134; abolition of *sharîʿa* by, 124, 129; tripartite ontology of, 127–29, 247n35. *See also* Hassan i Sabbah

Jackson, Michael, 231
Jagger, Mick, 203
Jambet, Christian, 127
James, Darius, 3
Jameson, Fredric, 27–28, 39–40, 112–13, 151
Jardine, Alice A., 10–11
Jarman, Derek, 203–4
Jazz innovations, 223–24
Jews, 54–55, 92–95
The Job (Burroughs and Odier), 9, 146, 251n21
Johnson, Lyndon, 219

Jones, Brian, 223
Jourgensen, Alain, 226
Joyce, James, 16–17, 19, 77, 104, 235n4, 242n17
Judeo-Christian doctrine: of afterlife, 124–25, 148, 250n12
Junky (Burroughs), 4, 46,47–48, 50–51, 56–59, 63, 234n11; addiction-radicalism connection of, 53–54, 239n8; antiproductive entities of, 49–50, 55
"Just One Fix" (video), 226–27
Juwayni, 246n21

Kafka, Franz, 133
Kalâm-i Pir, 127
Kant, Immanuel, 56, 85, 246n25
Kazin, Alfred, 61, 142, 143–44, 167
Kerouac, Jack, 11, 204
Khu (spiritual soul), 149, 190, 250n13
Klapper, Ilse, 55
Knickerbocker, Conrad, 215
Krich, A. M., 239n12
Kristeva, Julia, 72
"K-9 Was in Combat with the Alien Mind Screen" (recording), 218–19

Labor: capitalist subsumption of, 29–31
Lacan, Jacques, 40–41
Laing, R. D., 64
Language, 58–59, 78–79, 125–26, 129–30; abandoned dialectic of, 4–5, 200; and claims of prophecy, 105, 244n3; cut-ups' end to, 135–36, 138–39; weapons against, 207, 208; Image concept and, 136–37, 207; as process of control, 4, 110, 115–18. *See also* Silence
The Last Words of Dutch Schultz: A Fiction in the Form of a Film Script (Burroughs), 146, 205, 245n13
Laswell, Bill, 203, 224, 225, 252n10, 255n41
Late trilogy (Burroughs), 174–79, 180–82. See also *Cities of the Red Night; The Place of Dead Roads; The Western Lands*
Latour, Bruno, 1–2, 20, 34
Law, the, 106–7, 110–11, 132–33, 245n6; constitutive dialectic of, 105–6, 129–30; external vs. internal nature of, 121, 246n25; *Ismâ'îlîs* abolition of, 124, 129; problematic of biologic, 134, 247–48n37. See also *Sharî'a*
Law enforcement. *See* Police
Law of value: crisis of, 30–32, 140
Lawrence, D. H., 142
Leibniz, G. W., 44
Leitch, Vincent B., 237–38n22
Lenin, Vladimir, 96
Leone, Sergio, 189
LETTERS (Barth), 235n6
Lévi-Strauss, Claude, 143
Lexington Narcotics Farm (Kentucky), 49
"The Limits of Control" (Burroughs), 140
Linguistic self-referentiality, 21–23, 28
Linguistic signs, 17–18, 125–26, 47; as negatively defined, 2, 233n3. *See also* Language
Litweiler, John, 223
Lodge, David, 8
The Logic of Sense (Deleuze), 36
"Lonesome Cowboy Bill" (song), 204
Lubitsch, Ernst, 91
Luhmann, Niklas, 25
Lukács, Georg, 81, 96
Luxemburg, Rosa, 96
Lydenberg, Robin, 10, 72–73, 92, 142, 146, 235n18
Lyotard, Jean-François, 2, 16, 17, 18, 31–32, 36, 96

McCarthy, Joseph, 70, 114
McLuhan, Marshall, 18, 144–45
Maeck, Klaus, 202
Mailer, Norman, 8, 14, 65, 146, 147, 191, 239–40n13
Makhnovist movement, 33
Malamud, Bernard, 233n5
Manfred (Byron), 71
Manifesto of the Communist Party (Marx and Engels), 74, 106, 191
Mann, Thomas, 77
Mapplethorpe, Robert, 241n11
Marcus, Greil, 24, 236n7
Marcuse, Herbert, 28, 29, 77, 96, 143
Marx, Karl, 29–30, 248n38
Marxism, 95–96; Burroughs's relation to, 74–75, 76, 77
"Masque of the Red Death" (Poe), 162
Mass fantasy. *See* Fantasy
Mass media, 90–91, 92–93, 156; Burroughs's presence in, 202–4, 232, 253nn3,5, 253nn6,9; literary writer and, 201, 252n1; as one-way control, 89–90, 156
Master Musicians of Jajouka, 222–23, 224–25, 255n38
Material (band), 203, 224–25, 228
Mathews, Peter, 250n16
Maya codices, 148, 153, 155, 156, 250n16, 251n21. *See also* Books of the dead
Medical doctors, 102; junky's symmetry with, 48–49, 81

Méliès, Georges, 206
Messiaen, Olivier, 218
Michelson, Annette, 206
Mies van der Rohe, 19
Miles, Barry, 216
Miller, Henry, 14
Millett, Kate, 14–15
Ministry (band), 203, 226
Minutes to Go (Burroughs, Gysin, Beiles, and Corso), 103–4, 118–19
Misogyny, 9, 14, 147
Modernism, 2, 18–19, 25, 34–35; Deleuze's alternative to, 36–38, 40–45; Ellison's break with, 21–22, 25–26; fragmentation emphasis of, 34, 237n16; mythical method of, 16–17, 19–20, 235n5. *See also* Postmodernism; (Post)modernism; Reflexive postmodernism
Monroe, Malcolm, 105
Moral History (Finley), 12, 235n15
Morgan, Ted, 234n14
Morrison, Toni, 3
Mottram, Eric, 245–46n20, 246n22
Muhammad II, 124, 128, 129
Music, 219–21, 221–23, 224–25; Burroughs's collaborations in, 225–28, 255n41; of Ornette Coleman, 223–24, 255n38; cut-up method in, 218, 227, 254–55n31
My Education (Burroughs), 232
My Own Private Idaho (film), 203
Myth: of cultural asymmetry, 16–17, 19–22, 25–27,37–38, 235n5; postmodern rejection of, 17–18, 35; subject-group fantasies vs., 40, 167

Nabokov, Vladimir, 23
Naked Angels (Tytell), 11
Naked Lunch (Burroughs), 4, 13, 77–79, 81–83, 85–87, 89–91, 97–101, 108, 145–46, 243n23; censure of, 8, 67, 240n1; cut-up method and, 71, 241n10; film's aestheticization of, 68–72; Interzone Parties of, 87–89, 99; introductory text to, 46, 238n1; racism analysis in, 92–93, 94–95
Naked Lunch (film), 67–68, 69, 71–72; writing theme of, 68–70, 241n5
Narration: organic vs. crystalline, 43–44, 177
Negri, Antonio, 2, 29, 30, 32, 36, 140
New York (city), 47–48
New York Public Health Law 334, 52
Nietzsche, Friedrich, 85, 134, 247–48n37
Nike advertisement, 228–31
Nizâm al-Mulk, 119
No Man's Land (Gilbert and Gubar), 11
Nothing Here Now But the Recordings (album), 202, 216, 253n3
"Nothing is True, Everything is Permitted," 6, 119–20, 123, 198, 246n22
Nova Express (Burroughs), 103, 108, 122, 216; "Last Words" imperative of, 116–18, 119–20, 135–36, 245n16. See also *Nova* trilogy
Nova Lark Music, 226
Nova Mob (*Nova* trilogy), 126, 109–10, 112–13, 117, 131–34; betrayal of, 111–12, 114–15
Nova Police (*Nova* trilogy), 109–10, 111, 130–31, 247n36. *See also* Police
Nova trilogy (Burroughs), 4–5, 9, 107–8, 122–23, 130–34, 136–38, 140, 145–46; central dilemma of, 105–6, 114–15, 245n13; "heavy metal" term of, 203, 253n9. See also *Nova Express;* Nova Mob; Nova Police; *The Soft Machine; The Ticket That Exploded*

Oaths, 112–13, 114–15
Occam's Razor, 74, 118–19, 241n15
Ockham, William of, 118. *See also* Occam's Razor
Odier, Daniel, 9
Omar Khayyam, 119
Organized crime. *See* Nova Mob
Orgasm, 159, 251n26
Orgone, 159
Overlapping-sources method, 216, 217

Pale Fire (Nabokov), 23
Paris Review, 216
Paul, St., 130
Peep shows, 157, 158–59, 162–63, 174
Peirce, Charles Sanders, 127
Permutation method, 216–17
Persona (film), 163
Pétain, Marshal, 13, 235n16
Phallic glyphs, 159, 250nn19,20
Phantasm (term), 234n10
Phillips, Tom, 140
Physicians. *See* Medical doctors
Picasso, Pablo, 19
Pirate Tape (film), 204
Pivot, Bernard, 252n1
The Place of Dead Roads (Burroughs), 5, 168, 175, 178, 185–88. *See also* Late trilogy
"Plan of living" (*Invisible Man*), 155–56; approaches to, 3–4, 25, 33–34, 236n9
Plato, 41, 43

"Plato and the Simulacrum" (Deleuze), 41
Police: contradictory positions of, 50–51, 131; criminalization response by, 52, 53–54; criminal's symmetry with, 56–57, 84, 105–6, 112; temporal control pattern of, 50, 238n6. *See also* Nova Police
Popper, Karl, 29
Pornography, 91–92
Portman, Michael, 210
Port of Saints (Burroughs), 146, 147, 169, 221, 249n9
Portrait of the Artist as a Young Man (Joyce), 71, 235n4
Postmodernism, 16–18, 236n9. *See also* Reflexive postmodernism
(Post)modernism: alternatives to, 1–3, 25, 26–27, 29, 236n9. *See also* Modernism; Postmodernism; Reflexive postmodernism
Postmodernism, or, The Cultural Logic of Late Capitalism (Jameson), 27
Pound, Ezra, 13, 235n16
The "Priest" They Called Him (CD), 227
Property rights: sampling and, 220–21
Public Enemy (rap group), 220–21
Punishment: discipline vs., 82–83. *See also* Control
Pynchon, Thomas, 3

Qâ'im (divine Judge), 124, 129
Qiyâma (Great Resurrection), 125–26, 127–29; and abolition of *sharî'a*, 124, 129; proclamation of, 123, 247nn28,29
Queer (Burroughs), 58–59, 61–63; first person narration of, 65, 251n4; idea of community in, 57–58, 65–66
Queer theory, 60–62, 240n15

Racism, 92–95
Rap music, 219–21
Reason: instrumental subordination of, 79–82, 84–86, 96–97; Sade's critique of, 85, 243n24
"Recalling All Active Agents" (recording), 217
Reed, Ishmael, 3, 147, 204, 253n12
Reed, Lou, 204
Reflexive postmodernism: aestheticization process of, 27–28, 31, 32–33, 34–35, 68; amodernism vs., 2–3, 29, 233n3; Ellison's prophetic shift to, 18–19, 21–23
Reich, Wilhelm, 159, 251n25
Revolutionary resistance, 96–99, 147, 156, 194–96; Burroughs's reconstitution of, 169–71, 199–200; first affirmative model of, 180–81, 182–84; symmetrical vs. noncoincident form of, 172–74, 250n15. *See also* Community; Subject-group fantasy
Rhode, Jean, 228
Richter, Hans, 206
"Rime of the Ancient Mariner" (Coleridge), 89, 243n25
Rinehart Effect, 21–23, 24, 31
Romanticism, 30, 31
Rooks, Conrad, 202
Roosevelt, Franklin D., 161, 162
"Roosevelt after Inauguration" (Burroughs), 161, 162
Routines: as hallucinations, 63, 69, 157–58; narrative discontinuity of, 61, 108–9; otherness of, 59–60, 62; as projected love fantasies, 144, 249n6; as telepathic transmissions, 63–66, 240n17. *See also* Telepathic transmissions
Rushdie, Salman, 76
Russ, Joanna, 3, 147

Sabbatical (Barth), 235n6
Sade, Marquis de, 15, 85, 235n19, 243n24
Sampling, 219–21
Sartre, Jean-Paul, 27, 32, 112, 171; fused group of, 39–40, 151; the series of, 38–39, 150; on subject-group fantasy, 172, 250n15
Saussure, Ferdinand de, 2, 127, 233n3
Schaeffer, Pierre, 217
Schönberg, Arnold, 77, 223, 224
Schultz, Dutch, 245n13
Schwitters, Kurt, 217
Science fiction, 107, 168
Scientology, Church of, 115–16, 208
"Scratch" techniques, 219
Scripts: forgers of alternative, 176–79; meanings of term, 174–75, 238n5
Sedgwick, Eve, 60
Seitz, Don C., 180
Series, 38–39, 150. *See also* Subjugated group; Subjugated-group fantasy
Seven Souls (album), 224, 225–26, 255n41
Sex Pistols, 236n7
Sexuality: heterosexual model of, 183–84; schizophrenic totalization model of, 38, 237n19. *See also* Homosexuality
Shahâda (statement of witness), 120
Sharî'a (ritual canon law): acceptable versions of, 120, 129–30; behavior

constraints of, 124, 247n30; external nature of, 121, 125, 246n25; Qiyâma's abolition of, 124, 129. *See also* Law, the
Shî'a (Shiites), 120, 121, 124. *See also* Ismâ'îlîs; *Zâhir/bâtin* doctrine
Signs. *See* Linguistic signs
Silence: cut-ups and, 135–36, 138–39, 207–8; speech and, 58, 126, 239n9, 244n3, 247n33
"Silver Smoke of Dreams" (recording), 217
Simulacra: Platonic copy vs., 41, 220
Sitney, P. Adams, 205, 254n18
Skerl, Jennie, 10, 108, 155, 161
Slaughterhouse-Five (Vonnegut), 108
Smith, Harry, 205
Snyder, Gary, 12
Social groups, 32–34, 97–98, 192, 194–96; fused groups, 39–40, 151; series, 38–39, 150; subject-group, 40, 151–52; subjugated group, 39, 150–51. *See also* Community; Subject-group fantasy; Subjugated-group fantasy
The Soft Machine (Burroughs), 50, 103, 108–9, 113–14, 148
Sommerville, Ian, 132, 210, 217, 219
Souls: corporeal existence of, 149, 250nn12,13; division of, 190–91, 252n10; eternal vs. mortal, 191–93, 194, 196–97, 252n11
"Sound Piece" (recording), 217, 219
Soviet Union, 113
Spare Ass Annie (album), 226
Speech/silence relationship. *See* Silence
Sports advertising, 228–31
Stalin, Joseph, 70, 113
Stein, Gertrude, 13, 104, 235n16
Steppenwolf (band), 253n9
Stockhausen, Karlheinz, 216–17, 218
Stokes, Geoffrey, 253n9
Student movements, 141, 146–47, 167, 168, 169
Subject group, 40, 151–52, 194–95
Subject-group fantasy, 41, 154–56, 164–65, 194–95; art's role in, 42–43, 44–45; as investment of revolutionary desire, 40–41, 149–50, 152–53, 167–68, 237n21, 250n14; symmetrical vs. noncoincident form of, 172–74, 250n15; Wild Boy films as, 160, 163–67
Subjectivity: component souls of, 58–59, 190–92, 193–94, 230–31; otherness of, 59, 60; telepathic fragmentation of, 64–66, 240n17
Subjugated group, 39, 150–51
Subjugated-group fantasy, 153–54, 160, 161–63, 194–95, 251n21
Sunnìs, 120, 121, 124, 134
Swift, Jonathan, 9

Taqiyya (dissimulation practice), 121
Telepathic transmissions, 63–65, 88–89, 99, 215, 240n17
Tel Quel model, 73, 241n12
Tender Buttons (Stein), 104
Theory-practice relationship, 42
Thinking machines (computers), 82–83
The Third Mind (Burroughs and Gysin), 215–16
Thompson, Hunter S., 3
Tibetan book of the dead (*Bardo Thödol*), 148, 154, 164, 250n18. *See also* Books of the dead
The Ticket That Exploded (Burroughs), 103, 106–7, 108, 109–12, 122–23, 217; anti-narrative conclusion in, 136–38, 244–45n5
Time. *See* Historical time
Time and the Other: How Anthropology Makes Its Object (Fabian), 235n5
Totality, 27, 28, 36–37
Totalization, 26–27, 28, 29, 37–38, 41–42, 78–79; schizophrenic model of, 38, 237n19
Towers Open Fire (film), 202, 206, 210–13, 254n22
Treason, 111–15; manipulated dialectic of, 70
The Trial (Kafka), 133
Trocchi, Alex, 210
Tse, Rono, 226
Twister (film), 202
Tytell, John, 11
Tzara, Tristan, 104, 206

Ulysses (Joyce), 67, 240–41n2
"*Ulysses,* Order, and Myth" (Eliot), 16
Under the Black Flag (Seitz), 180
Urban spaces: displacement/control of, 47–50, 238n6
U.S.A. (Dos Passos), 105

Valachi, Joseph, 115
Van Sant, Gus, 202, 203, 226, 255n41
Le Vieux de la Montagne (Bouttel), 245–46n20
Visionary Film (Sitney), 205, 254n18
Vollmer, Joan (wife of Burroughs), 12, 13, 234n14
Vonnegut, Kurt, 3, 108
Vormittagsspuk (film), 206

Waits, Tom, 203, 227, 228, 253n6
Walker, Alice, 204, 253n12
The Waste Land (Eliot), 200
Watergate cover-up, 245n16
Wax, or the Discovery of Television Among the Bees (film), 202
Webern, Anton, 19
Weller, Peter, 68
Wells, H. G., 4
Western genre, 185–86, 188, 189
The Western Lands (Burroughs), 5, 168, 175, 189–92, 197–200, 225–26, 247nn35,37; "end of words" in, 179–80, 232. *See also* Late trilogy
Western World, 105
Wieden and Kennedy Agency (Portland), 229
The Wild Boys: A Book of the Dead (Burroughs), 9, 141, 147–48, 155, 156, 157, 164–65, 251n22; as fantasy of countercultural revolt, 5, 146, 167–68, 172–73, 249n9; filmic structure of, 157–59, 174. *See also* Books of the dead; Film
William Buys a Parrot (film), 202, 207–8
William S. Burroughs at the Front (Skerl and Lydenberg), 10
Willner, Hal, 203, 226
Wilson, Robert, 203, 227, 228, 253n6
Wilson, Terry, 119
Witchcraft through the Ages (*Häxan,* film), 202, 206
With William Burroughs (Burroughs and Bockris), 241n11
Wittgenstein, Ludwig, 74, 106, 118, 241n15
Wittig, Monique, 147
Women: affirmative model of, 183–84; Burroughs's views on, 9, 13–14, 147; dualistic culture and, 9, 14. *See also* Feminist criticism
Word, the. *See* Language
Word Cultures: Radical Theory and Practice in William S. Burroughs's Fiction (Lydenberg), 72
Writers: mass media and, 201, 252n1; readers and, 89–90, 243n25
Writing: of alternative scripts, 174–79; as imposed aesthetic, 68–69, 71; inefficacy of, 179–80, 232
Wyatt, Robert, 203

You Can't Win (Black), 185

Zâhir/bâtin doctrine, 121, 127–29; and signifier/signified dualism, 125–26, 127

Compositor: BookMasters, Inc.
Text: 10/13 Sabon
Display: Univers Condensed Light and Univers Condensed Bold
Printer and Binder: Haddon Craftsmen, Inc.